FRONTISPIECE

Tomb-chest and brass of William Dalison, formerly in Lincoln Cathedral.
From Sir William Dugdale's Book of Monuments, BL MS. Add. 71474, fo. 102.

THE PUBLICATIONS

OF THE

Selden Society

περὶ παντὸς τὴν ἐλευθερίαν

VOLUME CXXIV

FOR THE YEAR 2007

Selden Society

THE REPORTS OF WILLIAM DALISON

1552–1558

EDITED FOR
THE SELDEN SOCIETY
BY

SIR JOHN BAKER, Q.C., LL.D., F.B.A.

Downing Professor of the Laws of England, Cambridge;
Honorary Bencher of the Inner Temple

LONDON
SELDEN SOCIETY
2007

Printed on acid-free paper

ISBN 085423 210 9

Typeset by Paul Barrett Book Production, Cambridge
Printed in the United Kingdom at the University Press, Cambridge

CONTENTS

SIGLA

A = BL MS. Add. 24845

B = BL MS. Add. 35941

C = BL MS. Hargrave 3

D = *Les Reports des divers special Cases … colligees par Gulielme Dalison un des Justices del Bank le Roy* (1689)

E = BL MS. Hargrave 4

F = BL MS. Add. 25188

H = BL MS. Harley 5141

L = Lincoln's Inn, Hill MS. 123 (cited by case-number)

R = Bodleian Library, MS. Rawlinson C.112

PREFACE

The name of William Dalison, justice of the King's Bench under King Philip and Queen Mary, has always enjoyed a position among the reporters of the common law, although the printed text bearing his name has never been accounted canonical. The principal defect of the text published as *Dalison* in 1689 is the fundamental one that most of the cases in it were decided after Dalison's death in 1559. A number of manuscripts contain reports associated with the same name, and some of their contents are to be found in the printed text, but it seems that Dalison's reports have become confused with the work of other contemporary reporters, notably Richard Harpur. An Elizabethan text of what purports to be pure Dalison, authenticated by William Lambarde, is in the British Library (MS. Harley 5141). I transcribed that text with a manual typewriter about thirty years ago, but postponed the attempt to carry an edition further in the hope that further related material would come to light. It has not. But it seems on mature reflection that, even if what Lambarde copied is not the entire oeuvre, the text positively associated with Dalison is sufficiently discrete and interesting to merit publication as it stands. An injury which prevented me from making extensive use of the word-processor compelled me to complete this edition, including the translation, with the ancient tools of pen and ink. I am deeply grateful to Mrs Jane Stevens, the Master's Secretary of St Catharine's College, for deciphering and transcribing both my fading typescript and my manuscript with remarkable understanding and accuracy.

J.H.B.
March 2007

TABLE OF NAMED CASES REPORTED

TABLE OF YEAR BOOKS CITED

TABLE OF STATUTES

ABBREVIATIONS

See also the table of sigla on p. vi.

abr.	abridged.
Bendl.	*Les Reports de Gulielme Benloe Serjeant del Ley* (1689). Published together with Dalison's reports, these were derived from the reports of William Bendlowes (d. 1584), serjeant at law, which begin in the 1530s.
BL	British Library, London.
Bro. Abr.	R. Brooke, *La Graunde Abridgement* (1573). This was compiled by Sir Robert Brooke (d. 1558), Chief Justice of the Common Pleas, and contains some original reports from the 1540s and 1550s.
c.a.v.	curia advisari vult: indicating the continuation of a case for further advisement.
C.B.	Chief Baron of the Exchequer.
C.J.	Chief Justice.
CP 40	Public Record Office, plea rolls of the Court of Common Pleas.
Dyer	*Les Reports des Divers select Matters et Resolutions … Collect & Report per tres-Reverend Judge, Sr Jaques Dyer* (1688 ed.). First printed in 1585/6. These were compiled by Sir James Dyer (d. 1582), Chief Justice of the Common Pleas, beginning in the 1530s.
Fitz. Abr.	*La Graunde Abridgement, Collecte par le Judge tresreverend Anthony Fitzherbert* (1577 ed.). First printed in 1514–16. This was compiled by Sir Anthony Fitzherbert (d. 1538), Justice of the Common Pleas.
HPHC 1509–1558	*History of Parliament: the House of Commons 1509–1558*, ed. S. T. Bindoff (1982), 3 vols.
HPHC 1558–1603	*History of Parliament: the House of Commons 1558–1603*, ed. P. W. Hasler (1981), 3 vols.
Hil.	Hilary term.
J.	Justice (of the King's Bench or Common Pleas).
KB 27	Public Record Office, plea rolls of the Court of King's Bench.
Mich.	Michaelmas term.
NED	*A New English Dictionary on Historical Principles*, ed. J. A. H. Murray and others (1888–1928).
ODNB	*Oxford Dictionary of National Biography*, ed. H. C. G. Matthew and others (2004), 60 volumes.

OHLE, vi	J. Baker, *Oxford History of the Laws of England*, vol. vi, 1483–1558 (2003).
P.C.C.	Prerogative Court of Canterbury, registered wills, now in the Public Record Office (PROB 11).
Pas.	Easter term.
Plowd.	E. Plowden, *Les Comentaries* (1st part, 1571). These were written by Edmund Plowden (d. 1573), bencher of the Middle Temple, in the 1550s and 1560s.
Rast. Ent.	W. Rastell, *A Colleccion of Entrees* (1566).
SR	*Statutes of the Realm* (Record Commission, 1810–28).
Trin.	Trinity term.
YB	Year Books. References are to the old folio editions unless otherwise stated.

Superscript [f] after a reference on the text side indicates that the report in question follows in the text so marked immediately after the previous case as here printed. Superscript [i] after a reference on the text side indicates that the preceding word, or group of words in angle-brackets, has been interlined.

INTRODUCTION

William Dalison,[1] justice of the King's Bench, was born in the early sixteenth century, the second son of William Dalison of Laughton, Lincolnshire, and his wife Anne, daughter of George Wastneys. His father came from a long line of Dalisons at Laughton, mostly called William, many of whom attended the inns of chancery. One of his forebears was probably of Clifford's Inn in the 1470s,[2] and there was a principal of Barnard's Inn of the same name in the time of Henry VII (died *c.* 1493).[3] It may have been his father who was sued for dues by Strand Inn in 1517 as of Laughton.[4] The father went on to Gray's Inn in 1522 but does not seem to have practised law in London. He may well have been a country lawyer; at any rate, he was steward to a number of religious houses in Lincolnshire, a justice of the peace, and at the time of his death in 1546 was serving as sheriff.[5] His eldest son George was aged 34 in 1546, and we may guess that our William, his second son, was born around 1513–14. William is sometimes said to have attended Cambridge University, but this is probably mistaken; it must have been a different namesake who was at King's Hall from 1532 to 1543.[6] The first known reference to the lawyer is his admission to Gray's Inn in 1534, which would have been at the usual age of around 21. He is supposed to have been called to the Bar there in 1537, though the source is unreliable; he was elected an ancient in 1542 and gave his first reading in 1548. His residence was in the city of Lincoln, where he lived with his wife Elizabeth, sole daughter and heir of Robert Dighton

1 This spelling is here adopted as the most usual, though in his will he is 'Dalyson'. Our principal text (*H*) has 'Dallison', and his judicial patents were in the name of 'Dallyson'. Although *HPHC* says he was knighted in 1556, this is an error.

2 Action for dues in 1474: CP 40/850, m. 373d. A Chancery suit for lands in Hagworthingham, Lincs., *c.* 1500, mentions a William Dalison and Thomas, his son and heir: C1/132/38; C1/250/20.

3 H. Pugh, *Notes & Queries* (7th series), iii. 203 (citing lost records before 13 Hen. VII); will in P.C.C. 25 Doggett.

4 CP 40/1018, m. 387d. The judge's father was son of George Dalison of Laughton: C1/978/12; C1/1116/8 (William, son and executor of George, identified as the sheriff serving in 1546); C142/89/94. But there was a William Dalison of Laughton in 1513 (*Letters & Papers of Henry VIII*, i. 1803(2), p. 822); died c. 1530 (C142/51/70). This may have been George's father.

5 *Valor Ecclesiasticus*, iv. 72, 133, 139; v. 64; C142/84/117; P.C.C. 27 Alen; brass monumental inscription at Laughton. His wife Anne survived him: C142/84/117. For a Chancery suit against Anne Malary of Laughton, widow of William Dalison, concerning his goods, see C1/1214/24 (1547/51).

6 Unless otherwise stated, the biographical details which follow are from *ODNB* and *HPHC 1509–58*, ii. 5–6.

of Little Stourton,[7] who brought him also a small estate at Stourton.[8] Dalison served as a justice of the peace for the county of Lincoln from 1547, and in 1553 was elected a member of parliament for the county.

In 1552 Dalison was chosen to be a serjeant at law, and as serjeant-elect in the autumn delivered a second reading in Gray's Inn, probably on the statute 32 Hen. VIII, c. 33, concerning descents cast.[9] He was created serjeant on 17 October 1552, with six others, including three future chief justices (Brooke, Dyer and Catlyn).[10] Three years later, on 2 November 1555, he was appointed a justice of the Queen's Bench in the vacancy occasioned by William Portman's advancement to be chief justice.[11] Doubtless already armigerous, he was granted a crest in 1557.[12] He served as a judge throughout the remainder of Mary's reign, taking the Northern circuit as an assize judge,[13] and in the latter capacity sat also as secondary justice of the county palatine of Lancaster. His judicial patent was renewed by Elizabeth,[14] but he served only one term of the new reign, dying (while still in his mid-40s) on 18 January 1559.[15] He was buried under an altar tomb in the chanter's alley of Lincoln cathedral which bore upon the slab, in accordance with the directions of his last will, 'my pycture with my justices robeis and coyf even as I sytt in jugement'.[16] The brass was destroyed in the Civil War, but Dugdale's drawing of it survives and is reproduced as the frontispiece to this volume.[17]

By his will the judge left 20s. 'to the company and fellowshipp of Grays Inne towardes their commons', and £5 'towardes the reparations of their hall and other necessaries as by their discretions shalbe thought good'. He also left 40s.

[7] He is of the city of Lincoln, serjeant at law, in the 1553 coronation pardon: *Cal. Patent Rolls 1553–54*, p. 436. The pedigrees say his wife was Elizabeth Dighton, and the inquisition says that his widow was called Elizabeth. Cf. a post-nuptial marriage settlement between a William Dallison and an Anne Dighton dated 1557 (Staffs. Record Office, D861/T/4/78/1–2).

[8] Inquisition *post mortem* (C142/118/94), which mentions also Halton Grange, lands in Blyton and Laughton, a rectory and an advowson.

[9] *Readers and Readings in the Inns of Court and Chancery* (Selden Soc. Suppl. Ser. 13, 2000), pp. 38, 39; Dyer, fo. 219 (cited in 1562); Cambridge Univ. Lib. MS. Gg.6.18, ff. 56–59v (not certainly identified). His arms were formerly in the hall windows: W. Dugdale, *Origines Juridiciales* (1680 ed.), p. 302.

[10] *The Order of Serjeants at Law* (Selden Soc. Suppl. Ser. 5, 1984), p. 169; Dyer, fo. 72.

[11] Patent tested 2 Nov., enrolled 4 Nov. 1555: KB 27/1176, m. 63d; below, p. xxiv.

[12] BL MS. Harley 1359, fo. 69; W. H. Rylands ed., *Grantees of Arms*, i (1915), 66 Harleian Soc. 70. He is described here as J.C.P., and of 'Leighton' [Laughton], Lincs.

[13] In 1558, however, he seems to have been involved in a case at Lincoln (his home town), which was on the Midland circuit: *OHLE*, vi. 519 n. 83.

[14] Patent tested 18 Nov., enrolled on the Saturday after the octave of St Martin (19 Nov.) 1558: KB 27/1188, m. 114.

[15] Inquisition *post mortem*: C142/118/94 (described as esquire); lost inscription.

[16] P.C.C. 9 Chaynay.

[17] BL MS. Add. 71474, fo. 102; inscription noted in F. Peck, *Desiderata Curiosa* (1779), ii. 297, no. 6. There is a drawing of the tomb, made in 1826, in Lincs. Archives, Hill 46/4/1.

'to the maisters of Serjeantes Inne in Chauncery Lane towardes their commons and reparations of their howse'. To his eldest son William (admitted to Gray's Inn in 1552) he bequeathed 'all my bookes wyth my bookes of the lawes of this realme'. An inventory of the son's library survives from 1584, but his father's reports cannot be identified there.[18]

Dalison has been known to the legal profession since the time of his death as a reporter of cases.[19] In 1609 eleven cases attributed to 'Justice Dalison' were printed, with others from Bendlowes' reports, as an appendix to Thomas Ashe's *Επιείκεια*, and these were reprinted in the 1633 edition of 'Keilwey'. A more substantial selection appeared in 1689, again partnered with Bendlowes, as *Les Reports des divers special Cases ... colligees par Gulielme Dalison un des Justices del Bank le Roy*. The editor, John Rowe, noticed that most of the contents were Elizabethan and therefore dated from after the judge's death, but he nevertheless deemed them worthy of publication and did not choose to alter the name. The confusion in nomenclature no doubt arose from manuscripts, which had been in circulation since Elizabethan times, in which reports attributed to Dalison are combined with earlier and later material. The confusion is noted as early as 1601, when Coke cited a case of 1567 from what he called Dalison's notebook, and was properly corrected.[20] The present edition represents an attempt to isolate the real Dalison from the associated material.

The starting point is MS. Harley 5141 in the British Library, which we have designated *H*. It purports to contain reports entirely from Dalison's manuscript and is markedly different from all the other texts. It consists of 45 leaves, written in an Elizabethan law-hand, and is headed: 'De Annis Regis E: 6. ex libro manu Willelmi Dallison olim Justiciarii conscripto.' In fact it contains only the last year of Edward VI's reign, from Mich. 6 Edw. VI to Trin. 7 Edw. VI (1552–53).[21] That reign ends on fo. 14v of the manuscript with the explicit: 'Gulielmus Lamberdus transcripsit 1569.' On the next leaf the reign of Mary begins, in the same hand, with the caption: 'Termino Michaelis Anno regni Regine Marie primo 1553 a libro manu Willelmi Dallison conscripto.' The reports continue until the end of the reign in 1558, though with some cases and terms out of order, ending on fo. 45v: 'Hucusque ex libro manu Willelmi Dallison conscripto. Willelmus Lambert Examinavit 1569.' This explicit is followed by what appear to be the intials H. T. The Harleian manuscript cannot be the original transcript of 1569, because it contains (on fo. 9) an interpolation dated 14 & 15 Eliz. (1572) in the same

18 Kent Archives Office, Maidstone, MS. E1/1/2. William Dalison (d. 1581) had settled in Kent: below, p. xviii.

19 For an earlier discussion of the questions which follow see L. W. Abbott, *Law Reporting in England 1535–85* (1973), ch. IV.

20 Goulds. 153; see also Abbott, *Law Reporting*, p. 114. In *Wade's Case* (1622) Hob. 41, at pp. 42–43, Hobart C.J. questioned the authenticity of the printed reports attributed to Dalison.

21 There are headings only for Mich. 1552 and Hil. 1553, but MSS. *A* and *L* give further headings (within the same group of cases) for Pas. and Trin. 1553.

hand.[22] It is probably, therefore, a copy made from Lambarde's transcript by 'H. T.', whom we cannot certainly identify. There is nevertheless no reason to doubt that in 1569 Lambarde transcribed the whole volume from a manuscript – perhaps divided into two volumes – which he believed to be Dalison's autograph. As John Rowe pointed out in 1689, Lambarde himself cited Dalison's reports in his *Perambulation of Kent* (1576). It seems probable that Lambarde borrowed the autograph manuscript directly from the Dalison family. In 1583 he married, as his second wife, Sylvestria, widow of the judge's son William.[23] The marriage brought the younger William Dalison to Halling, in Kent, which was also Lambarde's county, and it may be conjectured that Lambarde knew Dalison as early as 1569, when he was a young barrister of two years' call. At any rate, our copy of Lambarde's transcript, for all its faults,[24] is better and more complete than any of the other texts and provides the basis for the present edition.

The next most complete text is also in the British Library, MS. Add. 24845 (our MS. *A*). It is in handwriting of similar date to the Harleian manuscript, and may be precisely dated, because after the explicit at the end of 1 Mar. the copyist has added: 'Le vint jour del moyis de December 1583.'[25] The name of the copyist does not appear; the signature 'Henry Bradshawe' on the first page seems to belong to the next century.[26] This text contains the greater part of the cases in Lambarde's transcript, many of them grouped in the same sequences, but the sequences are in a different order. It is difficult to explain the discrepancies of arrangement, and impossible to say that one is more faithful to the lost autograph than the other, since both have chronological errors. For the purposes of this edition, the Lambarde order has been retained, but with notes on the chronology where appropriate. *A* appears to derive from a different transcript, because it occasionally gives details not in the other manuscript,[27] and sometimes gives what appears to a more sensible rendering of the French. It has, however, been heavily abridged and paraphrased throughout, and therefore it has not been thought helpful – even had it been practicable – to collate it fully. The Edward VI portion, though differently arranged from *H*, ends with a similar

[22] There is also (on fo. 24) a reference to Plowden's reports (1571), incorporated into the text.

[23] *HPHC 1558–1603*, ii. 429; *The Vistation of Kent 1619–21*, ed. R. Hovenden (42 Harleian Soc., 1898), p. 167; W. Lambarde, *Perambulation of Kent* (1576), p. 398.

[24] It does contain errors not in the other texts: e.g. the plaintiff in *Brydges* v. *Warneford*, below, p. 40, is 'Burgh' in *H*, but 'Bridges' in the other texts.

[25] Cf. fo. 82v, where the end of 6 Eliz. is dated 21 Feb. 1583/4.

[26] He is probably the Henry Bradshawe, admitted to Gray's Inn in 1686, who also owned Harvard Law School MS. 2079 (reports 1558–84); and a manuscript sold at Sotheby's, 10 Feb. 1898, lot 119 ('Legal Digest'). The only other man of this name in the inns of court registers is the Chief Baron who died in 1553.

[27] E.g. the name of Brooke C.J. on p. 77, below, pl. 13; and the names of three judges on p. 2, below, pl. 5. In one instance, however, an alteration was evidently (though inexplicably) fictional: the substitution of the name Henry Vavasour for John Warnford in a case of 1552 (p. 40, below, pl. 45; the Wilts. place-name is also changed to Ripon). The same emendation is also found in *L* (Hill MS. 123, no. 191).

explicit (fo. 22): 'Finis secundum Dalison Justice del Banck le Roy.' This would seem to support the conjecture that the autograph was in two parts, divided by reign. There is an identical explicit at the end of Philip and Mary (fo. 35). The reports then continue from Hil. 1560 to Mich. 1573, evidently from some other source.

A closely similar text to MS. *A*, with the same Dalison explicits and all the same cases in the same order, is to be found in Lincoln's Inn, MS. Hill 123 (our MS. *L*). This copy, according to a note inside the cover, was begun on 7 December 1632 and finished on 20 September 1633, a date repeated at the top of the first page. It clearly shares a common source with *A*, but is not a copy of it; it sometimes contains small details not in *A*,[28] and is sometimes more correct.[29] There are 268 numbered cases from Mich. 1546 to 4 & 5 Phil. & Mar., and then a further series from 2 to 6 Eliz. Our other texts, including the printed edition of 1689 (*D*), seem generally to follow the order of *A* and *L* rather than *H*, but they are inferior in quality and have not been much used in the preparation of this edition.

These Elizabethan reports found in association with Dalison are not attributed, and obviously cannot have been written by Dalison, though many of them are found in the printed 'Dalison'. *A*, in particular, resembles the printed Dalison in having a gap from 7 to 13 Eliz. There is good reason to attribute the 1560–73 cases to Richard Harpur (died January 1577), justice of the Common Pleas; but that is another story.[30] It is enough for present purposes to eliminate them from the Dalison canon. More perplexingly, however, both *A* and *L* begin with the remainder of Edward VI's reign, preceded by the last term of the previous reign, Mich. 38 Hen. VIII. It is possible that the Dalison explicit in *A*, fo. 22, was intended to include these earlier cases as well, since there is no Dalison incipit anywhere. At least fifteen other manuscripts have collections of cases beginning with some or all of these reports of Mich. 38 Hen. VIII,[31] though most of them contain little or nothing of the Dalison material preserved in MS. Harley 5141. In one of them, MS. Hill 123 in Lincoln's Inn (our *L*), the copyist of 1633 has indeed inserted an attribution 'secundum Justice Dalison' in the heading of the 38 Hen. VIII reports. And in another (BL MS. Add. 35941), an earlier but very abridged collection of cases from 38 Hen. VIII to 1 Mar., bears the heading: 'Ascuns cases hors del Reportes del Dalison Justice del Bank le Roy'. It is not

[28] E.g. no. 191 has the names of three judges which are not in *A*, fo. 26: p. 79 below, pl. 19.

[29] E.g. Portman instead of Port, Baker instead of Barker.

[30] See Abbott, *Law Reporting*, pp. 122–141. Harpur's reports probably ran to 1576; but in many manuscripts containing material by Harpur the reports continue beyond his death, and in the absence of explicits it will be a considerable editorial challenge to isolate them.

[31] E.g. BL MS. Hargrave 4; MS. Hargrave 6 (abridged); MS. Hargrave 8 (abridged); Lansdowne 1121 (abridged); Add. 25188; Add. 25198 (abridged); Add. 35941, fo. 261v (abridged); Lincoln's Inn MS. Hill 123; MS. Misc. 791; Gray's Inn MS. 27 (abridged); Bodleian Library MS. Rawlinson C.112; Longleat House MS. 221; Folger Shakespeare Library MSS V.b.498 (17th-century collections); X.d.365 (abridged); Philadelphia Free Library MS. LC 14.41(5) (abridged).

inherently unlikely that Dalison could have written or collected them; they begin soon after his call to the Bar, and they end the very term before the Lambarde copy begins.[32] On the other hand, it would seem strange that Lambarde should have omitted almost half of Dalison's work, and it is difficult to account for the seemingly separate circulation of the reports from Mich. 1546 to Trin. 1552: for in at least six manuscripts the reports skip from 1551/52 to 1558/59, leaving out all the material (1552–58) found in *H*,[33] while four more include a series of Marian cases which differ entirely from those in *H* and likewise omit all the material in *H*.[34] Moreover, in at least one Elizabethan manuscript these earlier reports are attributed to 'Harper'; and there was perhaps a professional tradition to the same effect in the next century.[35] Since the reporter Richard Harpur was admitted to the Inner Temple in 1537, he was presumably by 1546 an utter-barrister and not an improbable candidate.

Although the question of authorship cannot at present be resolved with certainty, it is significant that the style of these earlier reports seems to be different. The reports are almost all in the Common Pleas, and are written more in the year-book manner, with a good deal of reported speech, including interchanges between judges and counsel, whereas the reports attributed to Dalison by Lambarde seldom put particular words in the mouths of individuals. A text and translation of the first term (Mich. 1546) is appended to this introduction for comparison; leaving aside the many abridged versions, the texts are all quite close to each other, although in the final case of the term a reference to Highgate is altered in some versions to Islington. If these reports are indeed by Dalison, the surviving manuscript texts may be presumed to be abridged and paraphrased, as the identifiable Dalison material in the same same manuscripts can be shown to be abridged and paraphrased by comparison with *H*. In view of all these doubts, it has been thought safest to omit the 1546–52 reports from this edition.

32 Note also a reference to his father-in-law in *Wastnes* v. *Earl of Shrewsbury* (Mich. 1 Edw. VI) in *A*, fo. 5v.

33 BL MS. Lansdowne 1121 (1–5 Edw. VI, then 1/2 Eliz.); MS. Add. 25188 (1–5 Edw. VI, then 2 Eliz.); MS. Add. 25198 (1–5 Edw. VI, then 6 Eliz., heavily abridged); Cambridge Univ. Lib. MS. Dd.5.50(II) (1–5 Edw. VI, then 3 Eliz.); Lincoln's Inn MS. Misc. 791 (1–4 Edw. VI, then 2 Eliz., heavily abridged); Harvard Law School MS. 5048 (4–5 Edw. VI, then 2 Eliz.).

34 Bodleian Library MS. Rawlinson C.112 jumps from Mich. 4 Edw. VI to Mich. 4 & 5 Phil. & Mar. (quite different from Dalison in *H*) and then to Mich. 2 Eliz. In BL MS. Hargrave 4 (ff. 97–152v), MS. Hargrave 6 and MS. Hargrave 8 the reports skip from Pas. 5 & 6 Edw. VI to 4 & 5 Phil. & Mar. (again different from those in *H*) and then to 1 or 2 Eliz. Note also MS. Hargrave 4, ff. 47v–51, which has cases of Pas. 6 Edw. VI followed by 2 Eliz.

35 BL MS. Hargrave 6, fo. 1 ('Harpers Reports Mich. 38 H. 8', a heavily abridged text in an Elizabethan hand; the reports extend to Mich. 1584, after Harpur's death, and there were originally more at the end). The same attribution is made in Lincoln's Inn MS. Misc. 791 by Richard Levinge (admitted to the Inner Temple in 1632). The similar attributions in MS. Hargrave 8 and MS. Lansdowne 1121 were made in the early eighteenth century by Edward Umfreville, no doubt on the strength of the other manuscripts in his possession. Other 'Harpur' texts begin in 2 Eliz.: e.g. BL MS. Hargrave 10; MS. Lansdowne 1060.

It will be noted that none of the explicits found in the manuscripts positively attribute authorship to Dalison, unless 'secundum' necessarily carries that meaning. Lambarde merely says that he was a copying from a manuscript in Dalison's hand. The case for authorship, however, is not difficult to make. There are several references to Lincoln and Lincolnshire.[36] Moreover, the start of the reports (as published here) in Michaelmas term 1552 coincides with Dalison's creation as a serjeant, and there is plenty of internal evidence demonstrating that the author was a serjeant or judge attending discussions in Serjeants' Inn. These constitute, in fact, the earliest substantial collection of Serjeants' Inn cases.[37] But there has been some understandable confusion as to which of the two serjeants' inns this might have been.[38] Dalison's will shows clearly enough that he was himself a member of the Chancery Lane society, and that inn is mentioned five times in the reports.[39] From these references,[40] and other unspecific allusions to Serjeants' Inn, we can establish that the other prominent members of the Chancery Lane inn during the 1550s were Sir Robert Brooke,[41] Sir Thomas Bromley,[42] Sir James Hales,[43] Sir William Portman and Sir William Staunford.[44] This discovery confirms the suspicion that the armorial windows of the Fleet Street inn, as noted by William Burton in 1599, are an unsafe guide to membership; for Burton's account shows the arms of Brooke, Dalison, Portman and Staunford displayed there.[45] It might be possible, of course, to account for this by migrations from one to the other; but the present reports, and other evidence, suggest a generally constant membership. That is not to say that the serjeants and judges of one inn could not visit the other to discuss cases. We find Sir Edward Mountague

36 E.g. three put cases: below, p. 45, pl. 1 (1553); p. 81, pl. 25; p. 98, pl. 8 (1556) (altered to Oxford in *A*). Cf. a recollection of Lincoln assizes in the 1540s: below, p. 66, pl. 21.

37 See *OHLE*, vi. 483.

38 E.g. Abbott, *Law Reporting*, p. 120, supposes that Hales, Portman and Dalison were members of the Fleet Street inn.

39 See below, p. 82, pl. 27, and p. 84, pl. 34 (Mich. 1554); p. 199, pl. 10, and p. 108, pl. 29 (Pas. 1556); p. 119, pl. 34 (Mich. 1556).

40 The report on p. 99, pl. 10, specifically states that Brooke, Portman and Staunford were members of the Chancery Lane inn. Dalison himself is only mentioned once in Serjeants' Inn (without specifying which): p. 62, pl. 16.

41 He recorded a deed there in 1555: CP 40/1164, m. 850.

42 He recorded a deed there in 1554: KB 27/1170, m. 140.

43 He recorded a deed there in 1552: CP 40/1152, m. 437.

44 Dyer and Mountague CJJ., however, were members of the Fleet street inn: see 94 Selden Soc. *137*; 109 Selden Soc. xxv; below, n. 46.

45 'Insignia in fenestris Refectorii infra Hospicium cognom: Serjeants Inne in Fleetestreete A°. D. 1599. uti tunc temporis reperta sunt per Guil: Burton interioris Templi socium, in rebusque Heraldicis non minime peritum': Dugdale, *Origines Juridiciales*, pp. 324–326. We have already made the same observation in relation to some of the Elizabethan judges: 109 Selden Soc. xxv, n. 37. A possible explanation is that Burton had listed windows in both inns but not made the division clear; most of the Chancery Lane members seem to be grouped together on p. 325. The earliest arms in the Chancery Lane windows engraved in Dugdale (p. 329) are those of Lord Keeper Puckering (*c.* 1592/96), which are still extant in the Law Society hall.

speaking at a Chancery Lane discussion, and he was certainly a member of the Fleet Street society.[46] And in another we encounter Sir John Baker, bencher of the Inner Temple and chancellor of the Exchequer, but not a serjeant.[47] Some of the serjeants' inn cases were presumably informal discussions at the dinner-table or 'board'.[48] But this was the period in which the judges were beginning to hold more formal meetings in one or other of the serjeants' inns to discuss matters of common concern, especially questions of criminal law arising on their circuits.[49] The inns must have been more convenient for this purpose than the Exchequer Chamber, since the judges and serjeants would be relieved from returning to Westminster Hall after dinner; and their increasing use may have been a result of improvements to the halls.[50] Dalison noted an 'assembly of justices' in his own inn, which attracted the notice of three other reporters,[51] and three assemblies in the Fleet Street inn,[52] one of which is also reported in Dyer's circuit notebook.[53] These assemblies were attended by the justices of both inns, which explains Dalison's occasional presence in Fleet Street, and sometimes by non-judicial serjeants, and even on occasion by non-serjeants such as Sir John Baker, Sir Nicholas Hare M.R., or the law officers. In criminal matters, which predominate in Dalison's reports after his appointment as a judge, such gatherings represent a half-way stage towards the system of 'crown cases reserved'.[54] It is doubtful whether they were public: at any rate, the proceedings do not seem to be mentioned by reporters not of the coif such as Plowden.[55] Dalison's accounts of them, in consequence, are an incomparable source for the history of the criminal law during the Tudor period. His reports of civil cases, though far less polished than those by Plowden, will be seen by comparison with the records to be very accurate in their summaries of the written pleadings, and are therefore probably reliable in capturing the essence of what passed in court.

[46] Below, p. 27, pl. 17. He recorded a deed the Fleet Street inn in 1545 (KB 27/1134, m. 60) and was a patentee of the freehold in 1549. See also Dyer, fo. 59.

[47] Below, p. 108, pl. 29. Dyer mentions him on other occasions at judicial gatherings.

[48] For this expression see Dyer, fo. 155 (1557); 109 Selden Soc. xlv, n. 96. An earlier example occurs in Spelman's reports, 93 Selden Soc. 208.

[49] *OHLE*, vi. 527–528; J. H. Baker, *The Law's Two Bodies* (2001), pp. 79–80.

[50] Little is known of them save that they were small – smaller than those of the inns of court, which the serjeants borrowed for some of their creation ceremonies. The accounts of the Chancery Lane inn show that in the early 17th century the old hall (demolished in 1678) was a small timbered building with a 'compass' window; but it is not known how old it was. The old hall of the Fleet Street inn contained the arms of all the serjeants who renewed the lease in 1523, suggesting that it may have been rebuilt or restored around that time, though there were some arms of 15th-century judges and serjeants as well; it was rebuilt *c.* 1615/20.

[51] Below, p. 119, pl. 34 (Mich. 1556); also in Dyer, fo. 132; Dyer's notebook, 109 Selden Soc. 16–18; Bro. Abr., *Corone*, pl. 219; Saunders' reports, 110 Selden Soc. 19.

[52] Below, p. 126, pl. 1 (Mich. 1557); pp. 125–127, pl. 1–3 (Trin. 1558); next note.

[53] Below, pp. 102–104, pl. 17–23; pp. 124–125, pl. 1–5 (Trin. 1557); 110 Selden Soc. 411–412.

[54] For the distinction between reserved cases, properly so called, and these general assemblies see *OHLE*, vi. 526–528.

[55] The much-noticed session of 1556, above, was reported by Brooke, Dalison, Dyer and Saunders, all members of the order of the coif.

APPENDIX ONE

DALISON'S PATENT AS A JUDGE

2 NOVEMBER 1555

APPENDIX ONE
THE ENROLMENT OF DALISON'S PATENT AS A JUDGE

KB 27/1176, m. 63d, Rooper and Heywood

Anglia. Memorandum quod quarto die Novembris isto eodem termino coram dominis rege et regina apud Westmonasterium venit Willelmus Dallyson serviens ad legem in propria persona sua. Et protulit hic in curia dominorum regis et regine quasdam litteras dominorum regis et regine patentes, et petiit illas irrotulari coram dominis rege et regina. Et irrotulantur, in hec verba:

> Philippus et Maria Dei gracia Rex et Regina Anglie, Francie, Neapolis, Jerusalem et Hibernie, fidei defensores, principes Hispaniarum et Cicilie, archiduces Austrie, Mediolani, Burgundie et Brabancie, comites Haspurgi, Flandrie et Tirolis, omnibus ad quos presentes littere pervenerint salutem. Sciatis quod constituimus dilectum et fidelem nostrum Willelmum Dallyson, servientem ad legem, unum justiciariorum nostrorum ad placita coram nobis tenenda assignatorum, habendum quamdiu nobis placuerit cum vadiis et feodis ab antiquo debitis et consuetis. In cujus rei testimonium has litteras nostras fieri fecimus patentes. Testibus nobis ipsis apud Westmonasterium secundo die Novembris annis regni nostri secundo et tercio.

APPENDIX ONE
THE ENROLMENT OF DALISON'S PATENT AS A JUDGE

Michaelmas term, 2 & 3 Phil. & Mar. (1555)

England. It is to be remembered that on the fourth day of November [1555] this same term, before the lord king and lady queen at Westminster, William Dallyson, serjeant at law, came in his own person and proffered here in the court of the lord king and lady queen certain letters patent of the lord king and lady queen, and prayed that they might be enrolled before the lord king and lady queen. And they are enrolled, in these words:

> Philip and Mary, by the grace of God King and Queen of England, France, Naples, Jerusalem and Ireland, Defenders of the Faith, princes of Spain and Sicily, archdukes of Austria, Milan, Burgundy and Brabant, counts of Hapsburg, Flanders and Tyrol, to all to whom these present letters shall come, greeting. Know ye that we have constituted our well beloved and faithful William Dallyson, serjeant at law, as one of our justices assigned to hold pleas before ourselves, to have for as long as it shall please us, with the wages and fees due and accustomed of old. In witness whereof we have caused these our letters to be made patent. Witness ourselves at Westminster on the second day of November [1555] in the second and third year of our reign.

APPENDIX TWO

REPORTS IN THE COMMON PLEAS
MICHAELMAS TERM 1546

APPENDIX TWO

[1]De termino Sancti Michaelis
Anno Regni Regis Henrici Octavi xxxviii^{o}

[1]

Nota que fuit agree per tout la courte en le Comen Banck que si capias soit direct al viscount de arrester un home lou nul originall est file, et le viscount arrest le defendant, et le defendant luy fait rescous, que cest rescous, pur ceo que le capias fuit un sufficient warrant al viscount nient obstant que le originall nest fyle.

[2]

Un obligation fuit prise per le viscount daver[2] home que fuit arrest per un capias de[3] garder son jour et le partye arrest apres obligation fait et devaunt le retorne del brefe est devenue languidus issint que il ne poet vener. Et cest matter fuit monstre per *Sanders*, que pur le defendant pria jour pur ceo que il fuit languidus.

Montague Cheif Justice. Est le brefe retorne languidus[4] envers luy, cepi corpus ou non est inventus?

Saunders. Le brefe nest retornable tanque al fine del terme.

Montague. Nous ne poimus doner jour sur nul recorde. Et si le brefe fuit retorne cepi corpus nous ne poimus doner jour oustre, nient obstant que il est languidus, pur ceo que le retorne del brefe serra prise veray.

[1] *Text from BL MS. Add. 24845 (A), collated with Lincoln's Inn, Hill MS. 123 (L); BL MS. Hargrave 4 (E); BL MS. Add. 25188 (F); Bodleian Library, MS. Rawlinson C.112 (R).*

[2] dun *F.*

[3] pur *F.*

[4] *Om. F, R.*

APPENDIX TWO

Michaelmas term [1546]
in the 38th year of the reign of King Henry VIII

1.

Common Pleas. Also reported by William Yelverton, 121 Selden Soc. 354, pl. 85; and Anthony Gell, Library of Congress MS., fo. 45.

Note that it was agreed by the whole court in the Common Bench that if a *capias* is directed to the sheriff to arrest someone, where no original is filed, and the sheriff arrests the defendant, and the defendant makes rescue, this is a rescue, because the *capias* is a sufficient warrant for the sheriff even though the original is not filed.

2.

Common Pleas.

A bond was taken by the sheriff in order to have someone who was arrested by *capias* keep his day; and after the bond was made, but before the return of the writ, the party arrested became ill so that he could not come. These facts were shown by *Saunders*, who prayed a day on behalf of the defendant because he was ill.

MOUNTAGUE C.J. Is the writ against him returned 'ill' (*languidus*), or *cepi corpus*, or *non est inventus*?

Saunders. The writ is not returnable until the end of the term.

MOUNTAGUE. We cannot give a day upon a non-existent record. If the writ had been returned *cepi corpus*, we would not have been able to give a day over, even if he is ill, because the return of the writ must be taken to be true.

[3]

Action sur lestatute de forcible entre de anno 5. R. 2. fuit port et le pl. counta que le defendant avoit entre ove force encounter le statute, et le defendant dit que il navoit entre encountre le forme de lestatute, et sur ceo a issue. Et le pl. don en evidence al jurie que un W. S. fuit seisi del mesme la terr en fee et avoit issue deux files, scilicet <Katerine et Alice>,[1] et Alice prist le defendant al baron, que luy tient eins come tenant per le curtesie en tout le terre, sur quel entre le pl. port <action sur lestatute del anno 5. R. 2. envers lauter. Ceo fuit le question.>[2]

Morgan, apprentice de Lincolnes Inne, pur le defendant, dit que levidence don nest bon matter a mainteyner son action: car jeo ay prise cest diversitie,[3] que tenauntes en comen ne poent aver ascun action personell envers son companion mes solement actions reals. Donques, cest action est personell et ne[my] reall, car en cest action il recovera forsque treble damages [et les profittes],[4] et les proffits sont forsque damages, et le damages sont forsque personells, donque quant le chose que serra recover en laction est personell ceo prove que laction est personall, et si laction soit personall, donques il ne gist enter tenauntes en comen. Auxi lentre de[l] action[5] prove que il est personall, quar lentre est [de placito][6] transgressionis et contempt[us], issint damages serra recover pur le trns.[7] a treble, et fyne al roy pur le contempt. Et cest un case 47 E. 3. que poet estre vouche peradventure al contrary, et ceo fuit que deux tenauntes en comen dun columbarye, [et lun destroy toutes les columbes],[8] et lauter port action de trns. envers lauter, et fuit adjudge pur le pl. Mes come jeo croy ceo judgment ne fuit accordant al ley. Mes en mesme le case fuit [dit et][9] agree que si deux tenauntes en comen sont, et semer[10] la terr, et quant les grains sont matures lun deux prist tout, et lauter prist action, et ne poet giser mes fuit abate: per que [etc.].

Foster al contrary. Et jeo entend que laction bien gist. Et a ceo que ad este dit que laction est personall et pur ceo ne gist, ceo nest issint: car le brefe de ejectione firme et ejectione custodie del terre est maynteynable per lun tenaunte en comen vers lauter. Et si deux tenauntes en comen sont, et lun deux est fait viscount, et lauter que est vicount retorne le brefe serve lou ne fuit serve, en ceo case cestui que perde aura action de disciett envers son companion pur son faux retorne et recovera damages. Auxi un tenaunt en comen aura action pur forger de faux faites envers son companion, sil soit a son disheritance, et recovera damages, et ceo est per estatut ley auxibien [come][11] cest case al barr. Et cest action est port sur[12] lentree et nient solement pur les damages, car lestatute dit que si

[1] le pl. et A. *E.* K. et A. *F.*
[2] cest action. Et sur cest evidence le defendant demurre *F.*
[3] difference *E, R.* [4] *E, F, R.* [5] record *E, R.*
[6] placita *E, F, R.* personall *A.* [7] partie *E, R.*
[8] *E, R.* lun de eux destroy le columbary *F.* [9] *E, R.*
[10] ilz embleont *E.* [11] *E, F.* comen *A.* [12] pur *E,R.*

3.

King's Bench.

An action was brought upon the statute of forcible entry made in 5 Ric. II,[1] and the plaintiff counted that the defendant had entered with force against the statute; the defendant said he had not entered against the form of the statute; and thereupon they were at issue. And the plaintiff gave in evidence to the jury that one William Style was seised of the same land in fee and had issue two daughters, namely Katharine and Alice, and Alice married the defendant, who held in as tenant by the curtesy in all the land, upon which entry the plaintiff brought action upon the statute of 5 Ric. II against the other. That was the question; <and upon this evidence the defendant demurred> .

Morgan, apprentice of Lincoln's Inn,[2] for the defendant, said that the evidence given is not good matter to maintain his action: for I have learned this distinction, that a tenant in common may not have any personal action against his fellow but only real actions. Now, this action is personal and not real, for in this action he is to recover only triple damages and the profits; and the profits are only damages, and the damages are only personal; and so, when the thing to be recovered in the action is personal, this proves that the action is personal; and if the action is personal, then it does not lie between tenants in common. Also, the entry of the action proves that it is personal, for the entry is 'for a plea of trespass and contempt'; therefore triple damages shall be recovered for the trespass, and a fine to the king for the contempt. There is a case in 47 Edw. III which might perhaps be vouched to the contrary,[3] which was that there were two tenants in common of a dovecote, and one of them destroyed all the doves, and the other brought an action of trespass against [him], and it was adjudged for the plaintiff. But I believe that judgment was not in accordance with law. It was agreed in the same case, however, that if there are two tenants in common, and they sow the land, and when the grain is mature one of them takes the whole, and the other brings an action, it cannot lie but [would be] abated: and so etc.

Foster[4] to the contrary. I think the action lies well. As to what has been said that the action is personal and therefore does not lie, that is not so: for the writ of ejectment, and ejectment of ward for land, is maintainable by one tenant in common against the other. If there are two tenants in common, and one of them is made sheriff, and the one who is sheriff returns the writ as served, when it was not served, in this case the one who loses shall have an action of deceit against his fellow for his false return and recover damages. Also, a tenant in common shall have an action for forging false deeds against his fellow, if it is to his disinheritance, and recover damages; that is by statute law, like this case at the bar. And this action is brought upon the entry and not solely for the damages, for the statute says 'if someone enters, where his entry is not given by law, he shall be

[1] 5 Ric. II, stat.2, c. 7.

[2] Richard Morgan, bencher of Lincoln's Inn and serjeant-elect; later C.J.C.P.

[3] YB Mich. 47 Edw. III, fo. 22, pl. 54.

[4] William Forster, bencher of Lincoln's Inn.

ascun entre lou son entre nest don per ley que il serra puny, issint nostre action est port sur lentree a nostre disheritance. Issint moy semble que laction bien gist.

Hales al contrary. Et moy semble que laction port per un tenaunt en comen envers lauter ne gist. Et a ceo prover, est comen maxime que <lactions personalls>[1] ne sont mayntaynable per lun vers lauter tenaunte en comen si laction soit a recover damages solement, mes si soit personal action et soit a recover le [*fo. 1v*] chose en demande et nient solement damages, come en le case de ejectione firme et ejectione custodie, la peradventure est auterment. Et en lestatute de Westm. 2. fuit provision fait que un tenaunt en comen poet aver action de wast, et si ils poient aver ceo devaunt donques lestatute [de W. 2][2] fuit en vaine. Et a prover que cest action est personell et nul chose recover en ceo forsque damages, il est apparant per cest case: le baron prist brefe de forcible entre pur entre fait en les terres que il avoit en droit sa feme, et fuit plede en abatement del brefe pur ceo que le feme ne fuit nosme en le brefe, et le brefe tenus assetes bon pur ceo que le baron en cest action recovera forsque damages, queux serront a son use demesne. Issint ceo prove que cest action est personell; per que [etc.].

[4]

Action de trns. fuit port vi et armis envers J. S. pur ceo que, lou le pl. ad use de toutes temps dont [memory ne court][3] etc. daver un water course per my le terre del defendant, issint que le ewe courge per my le terre le defendant jesque al terre le pl., la avoit le defendant vi et armis fait certen banckes en son terre demesne issint que le ewe ne puit aver son directe course sicome il soleit aver.

Harris. Moy semble que laction ne gist, car home ne puit aver action de trns. envers moy vi et armis pur fesans de un chose en mon soyle demesne. Mes laction de trns. quare vi et armis gist envers estraungers[4] que veignont sur le terre pur prisell de chattels et tiels semble choses. Mes action de trns. ne puit estre vi et armis en cest case, mes il puit aver assize de nusance: come en le case lou un fait un mese joust mon mese issint que il fait mon mese obscure per le erection de novell mese, jeo poet aver un assize de nusance en luy que fait le mese. Et issint icy.

Hales fuit del contrary opinion, mes il ne argua pas.

Hynd. Moy semble que il avera action de trns. sur le case mes [nemi][5] vi et armis. Et a ceo que ad este dit que si un leva un meson al nusance dun auter sur son terre demesne que cesti a que le nusans est fait avera assize de nusans, ceo est veray. Et auxi sil voet il poet [debruser et abater tiel meason issint levy a son

[1] personall actions *E, F, R.*
[2] *E, F, R.*
[3] *E, F, R.*
[4] estr' *E, F, R.* ester *A.*
[5] *E, F.* ne *A.*

punished', and therefore our action is brought upon the entry to our disinheritance. Thus it seems to me that the action lies well.

Hales to the contrary. It seems to me that an action brought by one tenant in common against the other does not lie. To prove that, it is a common maxim that personal actions are not maintainable by one tenant in common against the other if the action is solely to recover damages, but if it is a personal action and is to recover the thing in demand and not solely damages, as in the case of ejectment and ejectment of ward, perhaps it is otherwise. In the statute of Westminster II[1] provision was made that a tenant in common might have an action of waste; and if he could have had it before then, the statute would have been in vain. To prove that this action is personal, and nothing recovered therein except damages, it is apparent by this case: a husband brought a writ of forcible entry for an entry made in the lands which he had in his wife's right, and it was pleaded in abatement of the writ that the woman was not named in the writ, and yet the writ was held perfectly good because the husband in this action shall only recover damages, which will be to his own use. Thus this proves that this action is personal; and so etc.

4.

Common Pleas.

An action of trespass *vi et armis* was brought against John Style because, whereas the plaintiff had used from time whereof memory runneth not etc. to have a watercourse through the defendant's land, so that the water runs through the defendant's land as far as the plaintiff's land, the defendant had with force and arms (*vi et armis*) made certain banks in his own land so that the water could not have its direct course as it was wont to have.

Harris. It seems to me that the action does not lie, for one may not have an action of trespass *vi et armis* against me for doing something in my own soil. The action of trespass *quare vi et armis* lies against strangers who come onto the land to take chattels, and such like things. But an action of trespass cannot be *vi et armis* in this case, though he could have an assize of nuisance: as in the case where someone builds a house next to my house, so that he makes my house dark by the erection of a new house, I may have an assize of nuisance against the person who built the house. Likewise here.

Hales was of the contrary opinion, but he did not argue.

HYNDE. It seems to me that he shall have an action of trespass upon the case, but not *vi et armis*. As to what has been said that, if someone puts up a house to the nuisance of another upon his own soil, the person to whom the nuisance is done may have an assize of nuisance, that is true. Also he may if he wishes break and knock down such a house which has been put up to his nuisance, if he can do it on his own land. But he may not come on the other's land, where the nuisance is done, in order to abate it; and so etc.

[1] Westminster II, c. 14.

nusans sil poet][1] ceo faire sur son terre demesne. Mes il ne puit vener sur le terre lauter ou le nusans est fait dabater[2] ceo; per que [etc.].

Montague et *Broune* fueront de mesme lopinion, per que agarde fuit que le brefe abatera et que il soit bote a son action sur le case.

[5]

Hales mova un case a les justices. Un J. per indenture covenaunt ove un auter que il paiera a luy annuelment durant son vie xx. li. videlicet al feast de Novell ou xx jors apres x. li. et al feast de Pasche ou xx. jours apres x. li., le grauntee avant les xx. jours passes et apres le feast de Pasche devie: si les executors le grantee aura le rent ou nemy?

Et les justices (*Shelley* esteant absent) desoient que il fuit bon case. <Semble que les executors nauront [ceo],[3] pur ceo que nest pas due tanque le xx. jour soit passe.>[4]

[6]

[5]*Hales* vient al barre et monstre a les justices coment un avoit sue un brefe de droit patent, et pendant le brefe le tenant ad fait wast, per que nous priomus brefe de estrepement.

Montague. En quel chose est le wast et estrepement fait?

Hales. En foder pur carbones et lapides, issint que il debrust la terre.

Montague. Les carbones peradventure poet estre tout le proffitt del terre. Donques si nous mittomus brefe de estrepement de prendre les proffittes del terre de le tenant ceo ne fuit resonable. Et mittomus que jeo ay brefe de droit de xx. acres de bois, et le tenant succide eux, poy jeo aver brefe de estrepement pur cell? Moy semble que non.

Hales. Oyel, sir, vous poyes aver brefe de estrepement en vostre case.

Et al darrayne toutes les justices agree que brefe de estrepement serra grant.

[7]

Leas fuit a un pur [terme de][6] xl. ans, le lessee fist son testament, et per ceo devise le terme a J. S. pur terme de sa vie, si il vive tanque le lease soit expire, et

1 *E, F, L, R. Om. by hapolgraphy in A.*
2 *E, F, L.* debat[er] *A, R.*
3 *L.*
4 Quere *E, F, R.*
5 *Runs on in R.*
6 *E, F, R.*

MONTAGUE and BROWNE were of the same opinion, and so it was awarded that the writ should abate and that he be driven to his action upon the case.

5.

Common Pleas.

Hales moved a case to the justices: one J. covenants by indenture with someone else that he will pay him annually during his lifetime £20, namely £10 at Christmas or within twenty days thereafter, and £10 at Easter or within twenty days thereafter, and the grantee dies before the twenty days have passed but after Easter. Shall the executors have the rent, or not?

The justices (SHELLEY being absent) said it was a good case. It seems that the executors shall not have it, because it is not due until the twentieth day has passed.

6.

Common Pleas.

Hales came to the bar and showed the justices how someone had sued a writ of right patent, and pending the writ the tenant had committed waste: and so we pray a writ of estrepement.

MOUNTAGUE. In what thing is the waste and estrepement made?

Hales. In digging for coals and stones, so that he broke the land.

MOUNTAGUE. Perhaps the coal may be the whole profit of the land. If, then, we sent a writ of estrepement to take the profits of the tenant's land it would not be reasonable. Suppose I have a writ of right for twenty acres of wood, and the tenant fells the wood, may I have a writ of estrepement for that? It seems to me that I may not.

Hales. Yes, sir, you may have a writ of estrepement in your case.

In the end all the justices agreed that a writ of estrepement should be granted.

7.

Common Pleas.

A lease was made to someone for forty years; the lessee made his testament, and thereby devised the term to John Style for term of his life, should he live until the lease expired, and should he die before the years expired then the remain-sil devie avant les ans expire donsque le remaynder del ans a un pur terme de sa vie, et sil devie devant les ans determines le remainder des ans al eglise de St James. Si le remainder al dit eglise soit bon ou nemi, pur ceo que les gardeines de eglise nont ascun corporation issint que ils poient prender per ceo graunt?

Montague, Broun et *Hynde* penseyent que le remaynder ne fuit bon a ceux,[1] mes *Shelley* fuit de contrary opinion.

Et *Montague* dit que le primer remaynder ne fuit bon.

[8]

[*fo. 2*] Un bill obligatorie fuit monstre al courte en det port sur ceo, et en le fyne del bill fueront ceux parols: In witnes wherof I have sett to my hand. Et il avoit escrie son nosme ove son proper mane desouth le bill, et avoit mise son seale al bill auxi. Et pur ceo que nul mention fuit fait en le bill dascun seale destre mise al bill, fuit move a les justices si le bill soit bon ou nemi. Et fuit agree per totam curiam que le bill fuit assetes bon.

[9]

Saunders move al barre: si parson fist leas pur lxx.[2] ans de son rectorye reservaunt rent, et apres le patron et ordinarye confirme le leas,[3] si cest confirmation soit bon issint que le lessee aura son terme apres le morte le lessor, ou apres les xxi. expire, ou nemi?

Montague. Moy semble que le lessee aura son terme et le confirmation bon, car si le [parson],[4] patron et ordinarye ussent joyne en le leas il serroit bon, issint cest confirmation est assetes bon, et chescun depart ove ceo que fuit en luy. Et si durant le temps del vacation le patron et ordinarie graunt rent charge, lencumbent apres tiendra ceo charge quant il est present: quod fuit negatum per *Hynde.*

Et *Broune* semble que le lessee naura son terme per cest confirmation.[5]

[10]

Un fuit endicte a Newegate de ceo que il feloniosment vi et armis robb un home in quadam via pedestri regia, scilicet a foote waye, ducente a London usque

[1] eux *E, F, R.*
[2] 80 *E.* xlxx *F.* lxxx *R.*
[3] *E adds* pur 20 ans, *apparently an emendation by Christopher Yelverton.*
[4] *E, F, R.*
[5] *In A only there follows a case of Hil. 11 Eliz., which is obviously an interpolation.*

der of the years to someone for term of his life, and if he should die before the years ended then the remainder of the years to the church of St James. Is the remainder to the said church good, or not, given that the churchwardens are not a corporation such that they may take by this grant?

MOUNTAGUE, BROWNE and HYNDE thought that the remainder to them was not good, but SHELLEY was of a contrary opinion.

MOUNTAGUE said that the first remainder was not good.

8.

Common Pleas. Cf. *OHLE*, vi. 822 n. 26.

A bill obligatory was shown to the court, in an action of debt brought upon it, and at the end of the bill were these words: 'In witness whereof I have set to my hand'. And he had written his name with his own hand beneath the bill, and had set his seal to the bill as well. But because no mention was made in the bill of any seal to be set to the bill, it was moved to the justices whether the bill was good, or not. And it was agreed by the whole court that the bill was perfectly good.

9.

Common Pleas.

Saunders moved at the bar: if a parson makes a lease of his rectory for seventy years, reserving rent, and afterwards the patron and ordinary confirm the lease, is this confirmation good, so that that the lessee would have his term after the lessor's death, or after the 21 years expired, or not at all?

MOUNTAGUE. It seems to me that the lessee shall have his term, and the confirmation is good; for if the parson, patron and ordinary had joined in the lease it would have been good, and therefore this confirmation is perfectly good, and each parts with what was in him. If, during a vacancy, the patron and ordinary grant a rent-charge, the incumbent shall afterwards, when he is presented, hold it charged: which was denied by HYNDE.

BROWNE thought that the lessee should not have his term as a result of this confirmation.

10.

Newgate gaol delivery.

Someone was indicted at Newgate for that he feloniously with force and arms did rob a man *in quadam via pedestri regia*, namely a footway, leading from London to Highgate;[1] and thereupon he was arraigned and found guilty. And before his judgment he prayed his clergy, and prayed a book because he is a clerk.

[1] Islington in *E, F.*

Heighate[1] et sur ceo fuit arraigne et trove culpable. Et avant son judgment il pria son clergie, et pria un liver pur ceo que il est un clerke.

Et les justices de gaole deliverye fueront en doubt sil avera le privelidge del clergie ou nemi, pur ceo que lestatute est si ascun soit prise pur felonie fait en le haut chemyn que il navera son clergie, mes lenditment est en cest case que le felonie fuit fait in via regia pedestri issint que les parols ne sont in alta regia via ne in magna via: car si cest parol pedestri avoit este hors de endictment il navera son clergie clerement.

Et *Chidley*[2] et *Tawe*,[3] justices la, fueront en opinion que cest parol adde al lendictment [fait][4] que il avera son liver et le privelidge de son clergie.

Chomley Cheif Baron fuit del contrary opinion.

Explicit Annus 38. H. 8.

Justices de Communi Banco

E[d]wardus Montague miles
Humfridus Broune
Willelmus Shelley
Johannes Hynde

<Justices de regio Banco

Ricardus Lyster

Capitalis baro

Rogerus Chomley>[5]

Servientes ad legem

Hales. Sanders. Harris.

[1] Highgate *L.* Islington *E, F.* Flington *R.*
[2] Shelley *E only.*
[3] *Blank in E, R.*
[4] *R.*
[5] *Om. E, F, R.*

The justices of gaol delivery were in doubt whether or not he should have the privilege of the clergy, because the statute says that if someone is taken for a felony committed in the highway he shall not have his clergy,[1] whereas the indictment in this case is that the felony was committed *in via regia pedestri*, so that the words are not 'in the highway' (*in alta regia via*), nor *in magna via*. If the word *pedestri* had been left out of the indictment, he would clearly not have his clergy.

Chidley and *Tawe*,[2] justices there, were of opinion that adding this word to the indictment has the effect that he shall have his book and the privilege of his clergy.

CHOLMLEY C.B. was of the contrary opinion.

Here ends the year 38 Hen. VIII

Justices of the Common Bench:

Edward Mountague, knight[3]
Humphrey Browne[4]
William Shelley[5]
John Hynde[6]

Justices of the King's Bench:

Richard Lyster[7]

Chief Baron:

Roger Cholmley[8]

Serjeants at law:[9]

Hales. Saunders. Harris.

[1] 23 Hen. VIII, c. 1.

[2] Robert Chidley, bencher of the Inner Temple and att.-gen. of the First Fruits; John Tawe, bencher of the Inner Temple.

[3] CJCP 1545–53 (not reapp. by Mary I).

[4] JCP 1542–62.

[5] JCP 1526–49.

[6] JCP 1545–50.

[7] Appointed Chief Justice by writ dated 9 Nov. 1545: KB 27/1136, m. 160. The puisne justices were Edmund Mervin, Thomas Bromley and William Portman.

[8] C.B.Exch. 1545–52. The junior barons were John Smith, Nicholas Luke and John Pilbarough.

[9] I.e. James Hales (king's serjeant 1546–49), Edward Saunders and John Harris (king's serjeants 1546–51). The list omits Edmund Molyneux, king's serjeant 1546–50.

DALISON'S REPORTS

1552–1558

De annis Regis Edwardi sexti ex libro manu Willelmi Dallison olim justiciarii conscripto

Michaellis 6 E. 6.

[1]

A, fo. 18v; *L* 111 (Trin. 7 Edw. VI); *D*, fo. 12, pl. 17 (Trin. 7 Edw. VI).

Nota que fuit agree per toutes les justices de Common Banke et per *Por[t]man* Justice que si home devant lestatute novelment fait pur usury ad lone[1] son argent al auter pur x. li. [en][2] le c. li. a endurer pur x ans que ore apres le dit estatute fait nest nul usury de receyver ne de payer les dittz x. li. accordaunt a lour agreament soit ceo per escript ou sauns car lestatute avera resonable construction coment que soit generall.

[2]

A, fo.19; *L* 116 (Trin. 7 Edw. VI); *B*, p. 124; *D*, fo. 13, pl. 26 (Trin. 7 Edw. VI).

Super serra toutes foites <use et entend>[3] pur le ewe come si home levye fyne ou done ses terres quex sont prochein al ewe come Thames ou Trent il serra des terrres super le ewe come Henley super Thamesiam et nemy juxta le Thames. [Subter][4] serra referre al bois come en le cas avandit en done ou fyne des terres purchase al un boys serra [subter] le boys. Juxta serra referr al vylle come de done ou fyne ou feofment des terres en un vill prochien al auter serra juxta Dale et juxta Sale: per *Hales* et *Portman* Justices, et Stanford *Serjeant*, al Serjeantes Inne.

[3]

A, fo. 19[f]; *L* 117[f].

Si home port precipe quod reddat vers auter et le brefe est pur le mannor de Dale en Dale juxta Sale et des xx acres de terre en eadem, ore eadem serra referr al Dale et nemy al Sale car Sale nest nosme forsque come addition: eodem loco et per eosdem.

[1] lend *A, L.* [2] *A, D, L.* [3] entend et referre *A, B.* [4] *A, B, D.* subtus *H.*

[Cases] from the years of King Edward VI, out of a book written in the hand of the erstwhile Justice William Dalison

Michaelmas term, 6 Edw. VI (1552)

1. USURY

Probably in Serjeants' Inn.

Note that it was agreed by all the justices of the Common Bench, and PORTMAN J. [of the King's Bench], that if someone before the statute recently made concerning usury[1] lent his money to another for £10 in the £100, the loan to last for ten years, it is not usury now after the statute to receive or pay the [ten per cent] according to their agreement, whether or not it is in writing, for the statute shall have a reasonable construction even though it is in broad terms.

2. 'SUPER', 'SUBTER' AND 'JUXTA'

Serjeants' Inn.

The word 'upon' (*super*) shall always be used and understood when referring to water: as where someone levies a fine [of] or gives his lands which are next to the water (such as the Thames, or Trent), it shall be of the lands 'upon' the water: for instance, Henley 'upon' Thames, and not 'by' the Thames. The word 'under' (*subter*) shall refer to a wood, so that in the case aforesaid a gift or fine of lands purchased [next to] a wood shall be 'under' the wood. 'Near' or 'by' (*juxta*) refers to the vill, so that a gift, fine or feoffment of lands in one vill near to another shall be 'by Dale' and 'by Sale'. By HALES and PORTMAN JJ., and *Staunford*, serjeant, at Serjeants' Inn.

3. 'EADEM'

Serjeants' Inn.

If someone brings a *praecipe quod reddat* against another, and the writ is for the manor of Dale in Dale by (*juxta*) Sale, and for twenty acres of land 'in the same', the word 'same' refers to Dale and not Sale, for Sale is only named as an addition. In the same place. By the same.

[1] 5 & 6 Edw. VI, c. 20.

[4]

Abr. in *A*, fo. 19^{f}; *L* 118^{f}.

Nota per *Mountague* Cheife Justice del Common Banke, *Portman* et *Cooke* Justices en le <Duchi Chamber>[1] que si home comaund son servant oue auter home a batter J. S. per vertue de quel J. S. est battue et issint battue quil morust ore cestui que comaund cest act est fait accessory al manslaughter.[2] Et issint si per cest comaundment J. S. ust este tue maintenant le comaunder ust este accessory al mort de J. S.

Montague dit que fuit issint adjuge en le cas de Sir Robert Shefeild, Recorder, pur le mort dun Gyrlington.

[5]

A, fo. 19^{f}; *L* 119^{f}; abr. in *B*, p. 124 (foll. pl. 2).

Et fuit agree <per les justices la esteantes [scilicet *Montague, Poort* et *Cooke*][3],>[4] que si un seignor ou chivaler ou auter entendaunt a faire un entree en terres forciblement ou ryotousment et prist les servantes usualles ou accostomables ovesque luy et ne monstra riens al eux de ceo que il voil faire et enter en tyel manner ovesque ses servantes en la terre il serra punye pur loffence per le roye et ses servantes excuses pur le ryott ou forcible entre vers le roy mes sil monstre a ses servantes adevant quil voil faire tyel entree et comaunda eux denter ovesque luy donques tam le master quam les servantes serront punyes vers le roy pur le ryott.

[6]

A, fo. 19v; *L* 122–123; *B*, p. 125.

[*fol. 1v*] Nota que si home soit tenus a payer xx li. al J. S. lobligee a tiel jour et liew et devant le jour lobligor vient al obligee et luy pria dassigne un auter lieu et il issint fait et lobligor vient ovesque largent a cest lieu assigne et la nest nul a receyver largent unquor lobligation est forfait. Issint est sil assigne lobligor de ceo paier al auter jour per paroll sans escript et a cest jour lobligee ne vient a receiver largent lobligation est forfait car le jour en lobligation nest performe. Issint est si home fist feofment en morgage de payer certen argent al feofee al certein jour et devant le jour le feofor vient al feoffe et demaunda de luy ou il voil aver son argent pay et il monstre a luy le liew et al jour le feoffor vient al liew

1 Camera Stellata *A, L.*
2 *Written over this:* i.e. murder.
3 *A.*
4 in camera stellata *B.* la per Mountague Portman et Cooke *L.*

4. ACCESSORIES

Duchy Chamber.

Note, by MOUNTAGUE C.J. of the Common Bench, PORTMAN and COKE JJ., in the Duchy Chamber,[1] that if someone commands his servant (or another man) to beat John Style, by virtue whereof John Style is beaten, and so [badly] beaten that he dies, the person who commanded this act is accessory to manslaughter.[2] Likewise if John Style had been killed immediately by this command, the commander would have been accessory to John Style's death.

MOUNTAGUE said it had been so adjudged in the case of Sir Robert Sheffield, recorder [of London], for the death of one Gyrlington.[3]

5. ACCESSORIES

Duchy Chamber, contd.

And it was agreed by the justices who were there – namely MOUNTAGUE, PORTMAN and COKE[4] – that if a lord or a knight (or anyone else), intending to make an entry into lands forcibly or riotously, takes his usual or accustomed servants with him, and does not disclose to them what he is going to do, and he enters the land in that way with his servants, he shall be punished for the offence by the king, whereas his servants are excused for the riot or forcible entry as against the king. But if he told the servants beforehand that he was going to make such an entry, and commanded them to enter with him, then both the master and the servants shall be punished for the riot as against the king.

6. PERFORMANCE OF CONDITIONS

Serjeants' Inn.

Note that if someone is bound to pay £20 to John Style, the obligee, at such a day and place, and before the day the obligor comes to the obligee and asks him to appoint another place, and he does so, and the obligor comes with the money to this appointed place and there is no one there to receive the money, nevertheless the bond is forfeited. So it is if, by word without writing, he appoints the obligor to pay it on another day, and at that day the obligee does not come to receive the money, the bond is forfeited, for [the condition as to] the day in the bond is not performed. So it is if someone makes a feoffment in mortgage to pay certain money to the feoffee at a certain day, and before the day the feoffor comes to the feoffee and asks him where he wants to have his money paid, and he shows [i.e. appoints] him the place, and at the day the feoffor comes to the

[1] *A* says Star Chamber.
[2] *Written over this:* i.e. murder.
[3] Cf. *OHLE*, vi. 93.
[4] *A* only.

ovesque son argent et la nul est de ceo receyver le condition nest performe. Mes en tiel case si le payment duit estre fait en frument ou malt et le feoffor vient adevant al feoffee et demaund de luy ou il receyvera ses choses en le condition et al certayne jour appoint parenter eux il porta son frument ou malt et nul est la de ceo receyver lobligation est save et le condition performe et ceo est pur le portage. Mes auterment est de payment de argent. Auxi si home soit tenus en obligation al auter de faire al obligee en tiel liew un barne de tyel boys et puis accord est perenter eux que lobligor donera al obligee x li. in recompence ou que il ferroit a luy un auter petit meason ore cest agreament ne savera lobligation nient pluis que si home soit tenus a J. S. de luy enfeoffer del manner de Dale et il per assent fist feoffment del manner de Sale en recompence de ceo cest feoffment ne savera lobligation. Mes uncore en toutes ceux cases si un jour et liew soit appoint per lescript a payer et lobligee ou feoffee en morgage accepta largent al jour en auter liew cest bon et savera lobligation et le penaltie per *Portman* et *James Hales* al Serjantes Inne.

[7]

A, fo. 19[f]; *L* 124[f]; *B*, p. 125[f].

[1]Nota que si home en assise ou precipe quod reddat come tenant pria aide de roy ou demaunda judgment si le roy nient consaile per letters pattentes monstres ore a dire neint parcell ou nient comprise ne sont causes de mister le tenant de son aid le roy pur ceo que laid nest forsque un delay.

[8]

A, fo. 20; *L* 125; *B*, p. 125[f].

Nota auxi eodem tempore per *James Hales* pur clere ley que si soit aiel, pier et fittz, le pier purchase terres tenus in capite et devie, le fittz deins age et vivant layell, que ore [en][2] cest case et auxi en un common persons case le fittz serra en gard tam pro corpore quam pro terris a luy discendus de son pier quar nul per la ley serra preferre en son fittz et heir forsque le pier et il tantum avera son fittz et nul auter. Et uncore per le regester home avera breife de trns. quare filium et heredem ou consanguineum et heredem [*fol. 2*] rapuit, mes ceo est entendue vers estranger et nemy vers le seignor que ad droit et title vers laiell. *Stanford* et *Rookby* serjeantes agreont a luy.

[1] *Runs on in H.*

[2] *Conjectural:* le *erased.*

place with his money and there is no one there to receive it, the condition is not performed. In this case, however, if the payment is to be made in corn or malt, and the feoffor comes to the feoffee in advance and asks him where he wishes to receive his things named in the condition, and at the certain day appointed between them he brings his corn or malt and there is no one there to receive it, the bond is saved and the condition performed. But that is because of the carrying (*portage*); it is otherwise with respect to the payment of money. Moreover, if someone is bound to someone else in a bond to make a barn for the obligee at such and such a place, from such and such wood, and then there is an accord between them that the obligor should give the obligee £10 in recompense, or that he should make him another small house, this agreement shall not save the bond, any more than where someone is bound to John Style to enfeoff him of the manor of Dale, and with his assent he makes a feoffment of the manor of Sale in recompense for it, this feoffment shall not save the bond. Nevertheless in all these cases if a day and place of payment are appointed by writing, and the obligee or feoffee in mortgage accepts the money at the day in another place, this is good and will save the bond and the penalty. By PORTMAN and JAMES HALES at Serjeants' Inn.

7. AID OF THE KING

Probably in Serjeants' Inn.

Note that if someone as tenant in an assize or *praecipe quod reddat* prays aid of the king or demands judgment *si rege inconsulto etc.*, by letters patent shown, 'not parcel' or 'not comprised' are not causes to deprive the tenant of his aid from the king, because the aid is only a delay.

8. WARDSHIP

Serjeants' Inn.

Note also, on the same occasion, by JAMES HALES as clear law, that if there are grandfather, father and son, and the father purchases lands held in chief and dies, the son being under age and the grandfather still living, in this case (and also in a common person's case) the son shall be in ward [to the king] with respect both to the body and to the lands descended to him from his father, for by the law no one shall be preferred in his son and heir except the father, and he alone shall have his son and no other.[1] Yet, by the Register,[2] one shall have a writ of trespass for ravishment of a son and heir or a kinsman and heir; but that is understood to be against a stranger and not against the lord who has right and title against the grandfather. *Staunford* and *Rokeby*, serjeants, agreed with him.

[1] A clue to the meaning is provided by the marginal note: 'fits en gard nient obstant le vy laiel' (son in ward notwithstanding the grandfather's life).

[2] *Registrum Omnium Brevium*, fo. 163 ('De haerede rapto').

[9]

A, fo. 20f; *L* 126–127f.

Nota auxi que la fuit agree per toutes les dittz justices et serjeantes la esteantes que si le roy per ses letters pattentes graunta un mannor al J. S. pur son vie et le patent est date i° Maii i° E. 6. et puis le roy per ses letters patentes recytantes come il ad grant son mannor per ses lettres patentes dates 2° Maii 2° E. 6. al J. S. pur son vie ore graunt le dit mannor ovesque les appurtenaunces al J. D. et a ses heires a toutes jours que ore per le misrecytall de patentes avantdittz le 2 graunte per patent est ousterment void en ley entaunt que le recytall est materiall et il recyta tiel chose lou nul tiel chose est. Nota que toutes patentes le roy portant lour dates le jour que le garrant pur ceo est deliver al chauncellor et cest jour de deliverie serra enter de record en le Chauncery et si le patent port auter date est tenus void en ley per lestatute 18 H. 6. cap. 1.

[10]

Abr. in *A*, fo. 20f; *L* 128f; *B*, p. 125 (foll. pl. 8).

Nota auxi agree per *Portman* et *Hales* que si home pleda les letters patentes le roy et per eux conveia a luy certein terres et le demaundant luy entitle a ceux terrs auxi per letters patentes le roy per puisne date ore il concludera Et issint nient comprise, ou Nient parcell, come le cas requiroit, car les lettres patentes sont cy fortes come record dun fyne ou dun recoverie. Mes si le roy nad ascun chose en les terres en demaunde al temps de son grant mes les terres fueront en le possession et seisin dun estranger al cest temps et ses propres terres ore home poet avoider le patent le roy adire que un estranger fuit seisi des les terres en fee et luy enfeoffe absque hoc quod le roy riens avoit en eux al temps de grant et issint confesser les letters patentes le roye.

[11]

A, fo. 20f; *L* 129f; *D*, fo. 12, pl. 20 (Pas. 7 Edw. VI).

Nota per curiam que en quare impedit nul conusans de[1] ple serra graunt pur ceo que brefe al evesque ne poet estre agard pur le pl. en ascun auter court forsque in court le roy. Issint in brefe de wast semble que nul conusans serra grant entant que brefe denquirer de wast ne poet estre graunt en auter court forsque del roy. Et en brefe dadmeasurement de pasture nul conusans serra graunt pur ceo que donques apres nul breife de superoneratione pasture poet estre agard sils surchargeront apres. En breife de redisseisin nul conusans serra agard pur ceo que donques le deffendant ne poet estre agard al prison accordant al statute sil soit attaint.

[1] *Written twice.*

9. MISRECITAL IN LETTERS PATENT

Serjeants' Inn.

Note also that it was there agreed, by all the said justices and serjeants who were there, that if the king by his letters patent grants a manor to John Style for his life, and the patent is dated 1 May, 1 Edw. VI, and then the king by his letters patent, reciting how he has granted his manor to John Style for life by his letters patent dated 2 May, 2 Edw. VI, grants the said manor with the appurtenances to John Dale and his heirs for ever, now by the misrecital of the aforesaid patent the second grant by patent is utterly void in law, inasmuch as the recital is material, and he recites such and such a thing when there is no such thing. Note that every patent by the king bears date on the day when the warrant for it is delivered to the chancellor, and this day of delivery shall be entered on record in the Chancery, and if the patent bears another date it is held void in law by the statute 18 Hen. VI, c. 1.

10. LETTERS PATENT, contd

Possibly in Serjeants' Inn.

Note also that it was agreed by PORTMAN and HALES that if someone pleads the king's letters patent and thereby entitles himself to certain lands, and the demandant also makes his title to these lands by the king's letters patent of more recent date, he must conclude 'And so not comprised' or 'Not parcel', as the case should require, for the letters patent are as strong as a record of a fine or a recovery. If, however, the king had nothing in the land in demand at the time of his grant, but the lands were in the possession and seisin of a stranger at that time, and were his own lands, then one could avoid the king's patent by saying that a stranger was seised of the lands in fee and enfeoffed him, 'without this, that the king had anything in them at the time of the grant', and thus confess [and avoid] the king's letters patent.

11. COGNIZANCE OF PLEAS

Probably Common Pleas.

Note by the court that in *quare impedit* no cognizance[1] of plea shall be granted, because a writ to the bishop cannot be awarded for the plaintiff in any court other than the king's court. Likewise in a writ of waste it seems that no cognizance shall be granted, inasmuch as a writ to enquire of waste cannot be awarded in any court other than the king's. And in a writ of admeasurement of pasture no cognizance shall be granted, because then no writ of overburdening of pasture could be awarded if they were to overburden the pasture afterwards. In a writ of redisseisin no cognizance shall be awarded, because then the defendant could not be sent to prison in accordance with the statute if he were attainted.

[1] I.e. a claim to jurisdiction made on behalf of an inferior court.

[1][*fol. 2v*] Si conusans de ple soit demaunde et le charter del roy est monstre de ceo portant date devant memorie ore nul conusans serra agard sinon que le chartre et le conusans sur ceo fuit allowe devant les justices en eire ou en quo warranto deins le temps del memory. Et coment que le ple de conusans fuit allowe al ascun temps devant les justices del Common Banke deins le temps del memory sur le dit chartre uncore cest allowance ne voile server sans auter allowance en eire ou en quo warranto car les dittes justices la nont authority de faire allowance: quod nota.

[12]

A, fo. 20v[f]; *L* 130[f].

Nota per *James Hales* et *Portman* Justices que en action sur lestatute 8 H. 6. nest ple adire Non ingressus est contra formam statuti, mes il pledera Rien culpable entant que le breife est vi et armis. Mes en action sur lestatute 5 R. 2. la est bon, car cest breife nest vi et armis et si vi et armis soit soit mise en cest breife le breife abatera. Et vide le breife en le Regestre fo. 182, enter Brevia super Statuta.

[13]

A, fo. 20v[f]; *L* 131[f].

Nota per totam curiam eodem termino que si home en action de trns. ou en auter action pleda que J. S. fuit possesse dun terme pur ans ex dimissione talis abbatis et conventus, que estate il ad, ceo nest ple sans monstre son estate coment il ad ceo, car nul pledera que estate (en barr) dun particuler tenant come pur ans, pur vie ou en taile sans monstre coment. Autrement est de tenant en fee simple, car la home pledera que estate de luy generalment: quod nota.

[14]

A, fo. 20v[f]; *L* 132[f]; *B*, p. 125.

Nota que essoine de service le roy al Calice ne gist mye, mes un protection, car deins le realme et actes faites la serra tries deins le countie de Kent. Mes fuit agree que essoine de service le roy pur un feme quia nutrix filii aut filie regis ou lotrix domini regis gist assettes bien deins le realme per lestatute.

[1] *New paragraph in H.*

If cognizance of plea is demanded, and the king's charter is shown for it, bearing date before memory, no cognizance shall be awarded unless the charter and the cognizance thereon were allowed before the justices in eyre or in quo warranto within time of memory. Even if a plea of cognizance was allowed upon the said charter at some time within time of memory before the justices of the Common Bench, that allowance would not serve without some other allowance in eyre or in quo warranto, for the said justices there [i.e. the Bench] have no authority to make allowance. Note that.

12. PLEADING IN FORCIBLE ENTRY

Serjeants' Inn.

Note, by JAMES HALES and PORTMAN JJ., that in an action on the statute of 8 Hen. VI[1] it is no plea to say 'He did not enter against the form of the statute', but he must plead Not guilty, because the writ is *vi et armis.* But in an action on the statute of 5 Ric. II[2] it is good, for that writ is not *vi et armis,* and if the words *vi et armis* are put into the writ it will abate. See the writ in the Register, fo. 182, among the 'Brevia de Statuta'.[3]

13. PLEADING QUE ESTATE

Common Pleas.

Note by the whole court, the same term, that if someone in an action of trespass (or other action) pleads that John Style was possessed of a term of years by the demise of a certain abbot and convent, 'whose estate he has', this is no plea without showing how he has his estate; for no one shall plead a *que estate* in bar in respect of the estate of a particular tenant – as for years, for life, or in tail – without showing how. It is otherwise of a tenant in fee simple, for there one may plead a *que estate* generally. Note that.

14. CALAIS

Probably in the Common Pleas.

Note that an essoin does not lie in respect of the king's service at Calais, but a protection; for it is within the realm, and acts done there shall be tried in the county of Kent.[4] But it was agreed that an essoin of the king's service lies well enough within the realm, by the statute,[5] for a woman on the grounds that she is the nurse of the king's son or daughter, or the king's laundress.

[1] 8 Hen. VI, c. 9 (forcible entry).

[2] 5 Ric. II. stat. 1, c. 7 (forcible entry).

[3] *Registrum Omnium Brevium,* fo. 182v ('Quod nullus ingrediatur terram alicujus manuforti').

[4] Cf. below, p. 19, pl. 23.

[5] *Modus Calumniandi Essonia* (*SR,* i. 7), once reputed as a statute of Edw. II.

[15]

A, fo. 20v[f]; *L* 133[f]; *B*, pp. 125–126[f]; *D*, fo. 12, pl. 21 (7 Edw. VI).

Nota per *James Hales* eodem termino que si le costome soit deins auncient demesne que les terrs la serront parties enter heires males come en gavell kynd que coment que apres le tenant del terre levia un fyne ou suffer un recoverie de ceux terres al comon ley uncore les terrs serront departies enter les heires males come devant car cest costome quant a departer enter males va ovesque la terr et nient in respect dauncient terrs, car il dit si le seignor dauncient demesne purchase ceux terrs et devie quils serront departes enter ses heires males et uncore en ses mains ne sont auncient demesne mes frankefee mes le costome va ovesque le terre etc.

Mountague Cheif Justice fuit al [*fol. 3*] contrary car il dit que nest semble al costome de gavelkind car la le costome trenche ovesque la terre et est per reason del terre car coment que al commencement les terrs en Kent (ore gavelkyndes) fueront terrs tenus in socage et ore plusors partes del terrs sont tenus per service de chivaler uncore le costome remaina come devaunt, mes en auncien demesne le costome trench al terrs en auncien demesne per reason del auncien demesne et de le nature de cel, s. destre implede la per breife de droit clos, et quant ceux terres ne sont auncien demesne mes al comon ley le partition de eux est auxi change come le costome est, quar ore il ne poet faire le prescription de ceux terres, s. quills sont auncien demesne terrs etc. et ont use destre partes enter heires males, car ore ne sont auncien demesne le fyne ou recoverie esteant en force et nient defete per le seignor per breife de disceite etc.

Browne Justice fuit de loppinion de *Hales* Justice.

Dyer's report of the case

Les Reports (1688 ed.), fo. 72, pl. 4.

Terres deins auncient demesne, queux sont departibles enter heires males, sont aliens per fine levie al common ley. Si per ceo le course de inheritance soit alter et fait discendible al heir al common ley. Quaere, et semble per le meliour opinion que il nest.

[16]

A, fo. 20v[f]; *L* 134[f].

[1]Nota per tout les justices que si le tenant le roy entruda devant office trove pur le roy et puis fist feoffment de ceux et sur ceo levy un fyne ove proclamation et puis le roy pardon toutes entrusions per act de parlament ou autrement et apres le office est trove et toute cest matter et title est trove que ore le feoffee et recognisee per fyne serront discharges auxibein de son ouster le mayne et le primer seisin come lentrusion, en mesme le manner come si le roy pardon leire son

[1] *Runs on in H.*

15. CUSTOMS OF ANCIENT DEMESNE

Common Pleas. Also reported in Dyer, fo. 72b; printed below.

Note, by JAMES HALES, the same term, that if there is a custom in ancient demesne that the lands there should be partitioned between male heirs, as in gavelkind, then even if the tenant of the land afterwards levies a fine or suffers a recovery of these lands at common law, the lands are still partible between the male heirs as before; for this custom as to partibility between males goes with the land, and not [only] in respect of ancient lands. For he said that even if the lord of ancient demesne purchases these lands and dies, they shall still be partitioned between his heirs male even though they are not ancient demesne in his hands but frank-fee, since the custom goes with the land etc.

MOUNTAGUE C.J. to the contrary. For he said that it is not like the custom of gavelkind, for there the custom trenches with the land, and is by reason of the land; and although in the beginning the lands in Kent (now gavelkind) were lands held in socage, and now several parts of the lands are held in knight-service, nevertheless the custom remains as before, whereas in ancient demesne the custom trenches to the lands in ancient demesne by reason of ancient demesne and the nature thereof, namely to be impleaded there by writ of right close, and when these lands are not ancient demesne but at common law the partition thereof is changed also, as the custom is, for now one cannot make prescription in respect of these lands, namely that they are ancient demesne lands etc. and have been used to be partitioned between heirs male; for now they are not ancient demesne while the fine or recovery is in force and undefeated by the lord by writ of deceit etc.

BROWNE J. was of the same opinion as Hales J.

Translation of Dyer's report

Michaelmas term 1552.

Lands within ancient demesne, which are partible between heirs male, are aliened by fine levied at common law. Is the course of inheritance thereby altered, so that it is made descendible to the heir at common law? Query; it seems, according to the better opinion, that it is not.

16. GEORGE FITZWILLIAM'S CASE

Serjeants' Inn. Cf. below, p. 9, pl. 24.

Note, by all the justices, that if the king's tenant intrudes before an office is found for the king, and then makes a feoffment of the lands and thereupon levies a fine with proclamations, and then the king by act of parliament (or otherwise) pardons all intrusions, and afterwards the office is found and all this matter and title is found, now the feoffee and cognizee by fine are discharged not only of the intrusion but also of the ousterlemain and primer seisin, in the same way as where tenant apres le mort son tenant apres lentrusion et devant office cest pardone amount al lyvery en ley et pardona lentrusion: sicut accedit in casu Georgii fittz William de Mawbelthorpe in comitatu Lyncolne.

[17]

A, fo. 20v^{f}; *L* 135^{f}; abr. in *B*, p. 125.

Nota per *James Hales* Justice que entant que nul soit suffer ne oye a demaunder terrs etc. en breife de droit ou autrement per lestatute de lymitation de pluis temps que de 60 ans devant son breife purchase que ore si terrs ou tenementes ou demesnes ount estre lesses per copy de court roll per le space de 60 ans que cest bon prescription et bon copyhoud terre. Et la fuit clerement agree per le dit *Hales* et *Portman* Justice de Banke le Roye que le seignor ne poet ouster son tenant per copy ou costomary tenant quel est tout un per la ley cy longe temps que il fait son service et paie son rent due accordant al costome et son copy tenure. Et ceo fuit al Serjeantes Inne eodem termino. Et ills agreeont la que lestatute de lymitation quant al avowry ou demaunder des services de copyhoud tenantes per le seignor nextenda al copyhoudes quant a cest purpose car lestatute ne serra entendue forsque de freehoudes enter veraie seignor et veray tenant.

[18]

A, fo. 21^{f}; *L* 136^{f}.

[*fol. 3v*] Et fuit dit la per <les dittes justices>[1] clerement que si en <spirituall court>[2] le parson dun esglise sua J. S. pur les dismes [et] J. S. dit que le parson lessa son rectory a luy pur 3. ans, que ore le judge en le court spirituall triera le leas si soit tiel leas ou nemy et si soit pled per covin ou nemy tanque un prohibition vient car autrement null avera ses dismes per tiel feint plee.

[19]

A, fo. 21^{f}; *L* 137^{f}; *B*, p. 126.

Nota auxi per *James Hales* Justice que si terres sont dones al un home et a ses heires males de son corps engendres et il ad yssue 2 fittz, leigne ad yssue file et

[1] Hales *A, L.*
[2] court christien *A, L.*

the king pardons his tenant's heir after his tenant's death, after the intrusion and before office this pardon amounts to a livery in law and pardons the intrusion: as happened in the case of George Fitzwilliam[1] of Mablethorpe in Lincolnshire.

17. COPYHOLD

Serjeants' Inn.

Note, by JAMES HALES J., that since, by reason of the statute of limitation,[2] no one is allowed or heard to demand lands etc. in a writ of right or otherwise for more than sixty years before his writ was obtained, nevertheless if lands, tenements or demesnes have been leased by copy of court roll for a period of sixty years, this is a good prescription and good copyhold land. And it was clearly agreed there by the said HALES, and PORTMAN J. (of the King's Bench), that the lord may not oust his tenant by copy or customary tenant (which is all one in law) so long as he does his service and pays his rent due in accordance with the custom and his copy tenure.[3] This was at Serjeants' Inn the same term. And they agreed there that the statutory limitation with respect to the avowing [upon] or demanding services of tenants[4] by the lord does not extend to copyholds for this purpose, for the statute shall only be understood of freeholds between very lord and very tenant.

18. SPIRITUAL JURISDICTION

Serjeants' Inn, contd.

And it was said there by the said justices, clearly, that if in a spiritual court the parson of a church sues John Style for the tithes, and John Style says that the parson leased his rectory to him for three years, now the judge in the spiritual court shall try the lease – for instance, whether or not there is such a lease, and whether or not it is pleaded by covin – until a prohibition comes, for otherwise by reason of such feigned plea no one would have his tithes.

19. COMMON RECOVERY

Probably in Serjeants' Inn.

Note also by JAMES HALES that if lands are given to someone and his heirs male of his body begotten, and he has issue two sons, and the elder has issue a daugh-

[1] Of Gray's Inn (adm. 1531), probably a son of Sir George Fitzwilliam (d. 1536) of Mablethorpe; J.P. Lincs. from 1554; died *c.* 1559 (P.C.C. 10 Mellershe).

[2] 32 Hen. VIII, c. 2.

[3] This seems to represent a change of judicial opinion: cf. *OHLE*, vi. 649–650 (overlooking this passage), which puts the change a few years later.

[4] The text reads 'copyhold tenants', which does not make sense. The statute does not mention copyholds.

devi, le pier suffer un recovery vers luy ove voucher ouster et devi, leigne fittes devi sans yssue, le file vivant, ore puisne le fittz ne serra barr [per lassetts][1] quar le recompence[2] va al file car ne appert coment le garranty fuit fait. Quere.

[20]

A, fo. 21[f]; *L* 138[f]; *B*, p. 126[f]; *D*, fo. 13, pl. 22 (7 Edw. VI).

Nota que si home a cest jour per son volunt devisa ses terres a 2 fittes eux nosmant per lour nosmes payant ses dettes que les fittes nont que estate pur vie et nemi fee simple, quar quant un[3] volunt est fait et est dobtful coment il serra prise il serra construe pluis beneficiall pur le heire pur saver son inheritance: per *James Hales*, que dit que ceo fuit issint adjuge quant il fuit al barre.

[21]

A, fo. 21; *L* 141.

Nota que fuit tenus per toutes les justices en le Common Bancke que si home fait son darrein testament et devisa ses terrs et tenementes per cest testament al estranger que le testament pur ceux terrs est bon coment que le volunt ne unques fuit prove devant lordenary quar lestatute parle de testamentes fait en escript et nemi del probation devant lordinary.

[22]

A, fo. 21v[f]; *L* 142[f]; *B*, p. 126.

Al Serjeantes Inn fuit tenus per *Hales* Justice que si J. S. soit robbe de ses biens et J. S. agrea ovesque le felon pur certen argent ou auterment et que il ne donera ascun evidence pur cest agreament vers le felon et pur reson de ceo le felon ala quite que J. S. est accessory al felony <entant que est le duty de chescun home a discover felons et ceo per son allegeance et serement pur le>[4] common wealth le realme et le felony ne toucha luy tantsolement mes le roye auxi et son realme et crowne et per cest agreament le felon est encourage al auters felons en derogation del roy et son crowne. Et aydant, confortant, [procurant][5] ou abettant[6] est clere accessory et tiel agreament est un aide et confort al felon. Mes auters fueront al contrary, ideo quere. Mes fuit clerement agree que si apres le robbery

[1] *B*.
[2] assets *A, B, L*.
[3] *B*. quant *inserted with a caret after* un *H*.
[4] per son agreamente et fauxine al *A only*.
[5] *Reads* procurement.
[6] *Altered from*: abettment.

ter <and dies>, and the father suffers a recovery against him with voucher over and dies, and the elder son dies <without issue>,[1] the daughter living, now the younger son shall not be barred by the assets, because the recompense goes to the daughter, for it does not appear how the warranty was made. Query.

20. INTERPRETATION OF WILLS

Probably in Serjeants' Inn, contd.

Note that if someone at this day by his will devises his lands to two sons, naming them by their names, 'paying his debts', the sons have an estate but for life and not fee simple, for when a will is made and it is doubtful how it shall be understood, it shall be construed more beneficially for the heir, so as to preserve his inheritance. By JAMES HALES, who said that it was so adjudged when he was at the bar.

21. UNPROVED WILL OF LAND

Common Pleas.

Note that it was held by all the justices of the Common Bench that if someone makes his last testament and devises his lands and tenements by this testament to a stranger, the testament is good for these lands even though the will was never proved before the ordinary: for the statute[2] speaks of testaments made in writing, but not of probate before the ordinary.

22. ACCESSORIES AND MISPRISION OF FELONY

Serjeants' Inn. Cf. *OHLE*, vi. 578.

At Serjeants' Inn it was held by HALES J. that if John Style is robbed of his goods, and John Style agrees with the felon for certain money (or otherwise) that he will not give any evidence against the felon by reason of this agreement, and by reason thereof the felon is acquitted, John Style is accessory to the felony, inasmuch as it is the duty of everyone to discover felons; and that is by his allegiance, and by the oath for the common wealth of the realm, and the felony touches not only him but also the king and his realm and crown, and by this agreement the felon is encouraged to commit other felonies in derogation of the king and his crown. Aiding, comforting, procuring or abetting is clearly accessory, and such an agreement is an aid and comfort to the felon. But others thought the contrary, so query. It was, however, clearly agreed that if after the robbery John Style

[1] These words are clearly so written but make no sense.

[2] Statute of Wills, 32 Hen. VIII, c. 1.

J. S. pursua le felon et la prist ses biens issint robbes de luy et suffer le felon aler son voy que ceo nest accessory al felony mes un concelement, que nest accessory, come en le cas de treason que le concelement [est] mispresion de treason.

[23]

A, fo. 21v[f]; *L* 143[f]; *B*, p. 126[f].

[*fol. 4*] Nota per *Mountague* Cheif Justice de Common Place que si home fist feoffment en morgage sur payment et non payment ex parte le feoffor que si le feoffee va al Calice ouster le mere et la est al jour de payment que cest aler est un disablement en ley de parte le feoffe a receiver largent et pur ceo le feoffor poet bien enter arere. Quere, car semble que le payment serra sur le terre et la tender, et si nul soit la a receyver le feoffor bein poet enter come si un jour certeine soit expresse en le fait.

Et *Hales* dit clerement que le tender serra al heir esteant al Calice, car Calice est deins le realme et choses la faites serront tries en Kent quel est prochin county a luy et essoine de service le roy ne gist pur un al Calice.

[24]

Abr. in *A*, fo. 22; *L* 148–149.

Nota per *Hales* Justice et auters al Serjeantes Inne et agree per auters la presentes pur clere ley que si tenant le roy entruda et enter en ses terrs apres le mort son auncester et devant ascun office trove, et le roy luy pardona toutes intrusions, que per cest pardon lentrusion est pardon et le livery auxi pur ceo que le roy est entitle a rien devant loffice et nul offence fuit forsque lentrusion, et ceo pardon que est tout. Mes sil intrude apres loffice et donques le roy luy pardon toutes intrusions, ore rien est pardon forsque lentrusion et nemi le liverey pur ceo que les terrs fueront en mains le roy adevant et rien per le pardon est discharge forsque lentrusion, de quel le pardon parle. Et le dit *Hales* et auters la disoient pur ley que si le tenant le roy apres le mort son auncestor enter et entrude et levye fyne devant office ou suffer un recoverie vers luy, que cest fine ou recovery est bon. Mes si tiel fyne ou recoverie fait apres entrusion et apres office donques sont voides, pur ceo que lestatute de Prerogativa Regis dit quod nullum accrescat ei liberum tenementum nec mulieri dos. Uncore per *Hales* si le baron et feme tenants le roy entrude, et le feme devie, le baron ne serra tenant per le curtesie pursues the felon and takes back his goods which were so robbed from him, and suffers the felon to go on his way, this is not accessory to the felony but a concealment, which is not accessory, just as in the case of treason the concealment is misprision of treason.

23. CONDITIONS; CALAIS

Common Pleas.

Note, by MOUNTAGUE C.J. of the Common Place, that if someone makes a feoffment in mortgage upon [condition of] payment and non-payment on the part of the feoffor, and the feoffee goes across the sea to Calais, and is there on a day of payment, this going abroad is a disablement in law on the feoffee's side to receive the money and therefore the feoffor may well enter again. Query. For it seems that the payment should be on the land, and also the tender, and if no one is there to receive it the feoffor may well enter, just as if a certain day were expressed in the deed.

HALES said clearly that the tender must be to the heir, if he is at Calais, for Calais is within the realm and things done there shall be tried in Kent, which is the next county thereto; and an essoin of the king's service does not lie for someone at Calais.[1]

24. INTRUSION

Serjeants' Inn. Perhaps Fitzwilliam's case, contd: cf. above, p. 6, pl. 16.

Note, by HALES J. and others at Serjeants' Inn, and agreed by others there present as clear law, that if the king's tenant intrudes and enters into his lands after his ancestor's death and before any office found, and the king pardons him all intrusions, by this pardon the intrusion is pardoned and also the livery, because the king is entitled to nothing before the office and there was no offence except the intrusion, and that is pardoned, which is everything. If, however, he intrudes after the office, and then the king pardons him all intrusions, nothing is here pardoned save the intrusion, and not the livery, because the lands were already in the king's hands and nothing is discharged by the pardon except the intrusion whereof the pardon speaks. And the said HALES, and others who were there, stated as law that if the king's tenant enters and intrudes after his ancestor's death, and levies a fine before office, or suffers a recovery against himself, this fine or recovery is good; but if such fine or recovery be made after intrusion and after office, then they are void, because the statute Prerogativa Regis says that no free tenement shall accrue to him, nor dower to a woman. Nevertheless, according to HALES, if a husband and wife intrude (being the king's tenants), and the wife dies, the husband shall not be tenant by the curtesy, for the same

[1] See above, p. 5, pl. 14.

per mesme le reason. Et *Hales* dit que lestatute de Prerogative est commen ley et nul estatute, quar sil fuit estatute serroit pris accordant al parolls et issint il nest quar les parolls sont Si mulieres queux tient del roy ascun inheritance mariont sans license le roy ils serront fynes al volunt le roy mes la ley est use contrary a cest jour et ad estre toutes temps. Et si fuit estatute, donques serroit prise al parolls come est prise des dowgiers de tenants le roye.

[25]

A, fo. 22[f]; *L* 150; *B*, p. 127; *D*, fo. 13, pl. 25. In *A*, *B* and *L* this is the last case of Edw. VI.

Nota que si tenant le roy fist un joynture ou estate a son feme pur vie et devie la feme poet marier sans license le roy car el ne serra jure come le tenant en dower serra agrea per toutes.

[*fol. 4v*]

Terminus Hillarii Annis 6 et 7 E. 6

[1]

William Partrige tam pro domina regina quam pro seipso port dett vers John Strange de comitatu Oxonie generosum et Johannem [Croker][1] de Hocknorton in comitatu Oxonie armigerum et demand 80 li. et declare cum per lestatute de parliament 28 Aprilis anno 32° domini Henrici Regis Anglie tenus al Westm' etc. fuit enact que nul person etc. barganizarent, emerent aut venderent ou per ascon voy obteignerent ascun pretense droit ou title seu caperent ascun promise ou graunt a aver le droit dascun al ascun mannours, terrs etc., except que tiel person que issint bargaine etc. ses auncestors ou illi per quos clamat etc. fueront en possession de eisdem ou de le revercione etc. ou perceivont rentes ou profittes inde per spacium unius anni proxime ante predictam barganiam etc. sub pena que il que fait ascun tiel bargaine forfeitera lenteir value des terrs issint etc. et le emptor auxi eundem valorem prout in statuto, et que les deffendantes J. et J. 6 die Julii anno E. 6. quarto messuagium vocatum Genettes et 15 acras terre eidem pertinentes al value 80 li. as Robert Myll et Geffrey Pledall barganisaverunt et ad firmam dimiserunt ad terminum annorum, dex queux tenementes les dittes J. et J. ne nul de lour auncestors ne ceux per queux ils claymont etc. ne fueront en

[1] *Reads*: Oroken. *Name from record in Plowden.*

reason. And HALES said that the statute Prerogativa Regis is common law and no statute, for if it were a statute it would be taken according to the words, and it is not so; for the words are, 'If women who hold any inheritance of the king should marry without the king's licence, they shall be fined at the king's will', and yet the law is used contrary to this at the present day and always has been. Yet if it were a statute it would be taken according to the words – as it is with respect to the dowagers of the king's tenants.

25. WIDOWS OF TENANTS IN CHIEF

Serjeants' Inn, contd.

Note that if the king's tenant makes a jointure or estate to his wife for life, and dies, the woman may marry without the king's licence, for she shall not be sworn – as the tenant in dower shall. This was agreed by everyone.

Hilary term, 6 & 7 Edw. VI (1553)

1. PARTRIDGE v. STRAUNGE and CROKER

Common Pleas. Record: CP 40/1151, m. 522; printed in Plowd. 77. Also reported in Plowd. 78v; Dyer, fo. 74.

William Partridge brought debt both for her majesty the queen and for himself against John Strange of the county of Oxford, gentleman, and John Crocker[1] of Hook Norton in the county of Oxford, esquire, and demanded £80, and declared that, whereas by the statute of the parliament of the lord Henry, king of England, held at Westminster on 28 April [1540], 32 Hen. VIII,[2] it was enacted that no person etc. should bargain, buy or sell or in any way obtain any pretended right or title or take any promise or grant to have anyone's right to any manors, lands, etc., unless such person who so bargains etc., or his ancestors, or those through whom he claims etc. were in possession of the same or of the reversion etc., or received rent or profits therefrom, for the space of one year next before the aforesaid bargain etc., on pain that he who should make any such bargain should forfeit the whole value of the lands so etc. and the buyer also the same value, as is contained in the statute, [nevertheless] the defendants J. and J. on 6 July [1550], 4 Edw. VI, bargained and demised for a term of years a messuage called Genettes, and fifteen acres of land belonging to the same, to the value of £80, to Robert Myll and Geoffrey Pledall, of which tenement neither the said J. and J. nor any of their ancestors or those through whom they claim

1 Or Crokker, of Hook Norton, Oxon.; died *c.* 1568 (P.C.C. 8 Sheffeld; C142/152/118). Plowden gives the name as Croker or Crocker.

2 32 Hen. VIII, c. 9.

possession etc. ne receyveront les rentes etc. per spacium etc. Et sur cest declaration les deffendantes demurront en ley.

Un exception fuit pur ceo que lestatute ne fuit bein recyte, car nest nul tiel acte come il reherse, quar cest parlament commensa al Westm' 28 die Aprill 31 H. 8. et issint ne fuit ascun tiel acte de 32 H. 8. sicome il parle et cest exception fuit a luy allow.

Auter exception fuit prise pur ceo que fuit allege dun mese et 10 acres de terre eidem messuagio pertinentes et nul terre perteigne al mese forsque orchard et gardeine.

Auter: le terre et mese sont alleges in campo de Mynty in Mynty predicta, et issint 2 foites demaund. [Mes] il nest forsque supposell et nul terre en demaund.

Auter: il nalege le certenty des ans en nomber ne quant ils commenceront ne quant ils finieront.

Cooke allowa cest exception, mes *Hales* nemi.

Auter: que le declaration fuit doble quar il est alledge que les deffendantes barganaverunt, granteront et al farme dismiseront, et issint ceux charga ovesque [*fol. 5*] 3. matters.

Cooke dit que fuit double. *Hales* al contrary.

Auter: il nad alleage que le dit bargaine fuit sur pretense title ou sur mayntenance etc. contra formam statuti.

Cooke dit que nest besoigne. *Hales* econtra.

Auter que lanuall value de terre ne fuit allege deins le declaration. [Mes] ne besoigne, entant que il alledge lentier value destre 80 li. que nest deny per les deffendantes.

Nota que le primer exception fuit bein allowe per *Cooke* et *Hales* Justices que entant que les pl. meddla ovesque lestatute et chargera le deffendantes ovesque ceo que lestatue doit estre verament alledge ou auterment nest bon. Mes si le declaration ust este generalment que les deffendantes ont demise ou graunt les dittes terrs contra formam statuti in hoc casu editi et provisi que ceo ust este bon, mes entant que il chargera le deffendantes ovesque lestatute lou nul tiel fuit fait nest bon.

Et *Hales* dit que un statute de parlament generalment fait avera relation al primer jour de session del parlament en quel fuit fait et nemy al jour lassent le roy.

Cooke semble que le declaration fuit double et que le pl. doit monstre les nomber des ans et quant le terme commensa et quant finye entant que il ad prise[1] sur luy conusans del demise pur ans. Et il dit que lesse pur ans est deins lestatute quar il ad estate per la ley. Et auxi graund mischeif serra de prender estate pur ans come un greinder estate.

Mes *Hales* dit que le declaration ne fuit double, neint pluis que en declaration sur lestatute 8 H. 6. que le deffendant entra ovesque force et teigna ovesque force cest bon, et uncore lestatute est que si home entra ovesque force ou reteigna etc.

[1] Prose. *So written below.*

etc. were in possession etc. or received the rents etc. for the period etc. Upon this declaration the defendants demurred in law.

[1] One exception was because the statute was not well recited, for there is no such act as he set out: for that parliament began at Westminster on 28 April [1539], 31 Hen. VIII, and so there was no such act of 32 Hen. VIII of which he spoke. This exception was allowed him.[1]

[2] Another exception was taken because there was alleged to be a house and [fifteen] acres of land belonging to the same messuage, and no land may belong to a house except an orchard and garden.[2]

[3] Another: the land and house are alleged to be in the field of Mynty, in Mynty aforesaid, and thus they are demanded twice. But it is only a supposal, not land in demand.

[4] Another: he does not allege with certainty the number of the years, nor when they commenced or when they will end.

COKE allowed this exception, but HALES did not.

[5] Another: the declaration is double, for it is alleged that the defendant bargained, granted, and let to farm, and thus it charges him with three matters.

COKE said it was double; HALES to the contrary.

[6] Another: he has not alleged that the said bargain was upon a pretended title or upon maintenance etc. against the form of the statute.

COKE said it was unnecessary; HALES to the contrary.

[7] Another: that the annual value of the land was not alleged in the declaration. But it need not be, inasmuch as he alleges the whole value to be £80, which is not denied by the defendants.

Note that the first exception was well allowed by COKE and HALES, for since the plaintiffs meddled with the statute and charged the defendants with it, the statute ought to be truly alleged or else it is not good. But if the declaration had been generally that the defendants demised or granted the said land 'against the form of the statute made and provided in that case', that would have been good; but since he charged the defendants [under a specific] statute, where no such statute was made, it is not good.

HALES said that a statute of parliament generally made shall have relation to the first day of the session of the parliament in which it was made, and not to the day of the king's assent.[3]

COKE thought the declaration was double and that the plaintiff ought to show the number of years, and when the term began and ended, since he has taken upon himself knowledge of the demise for years. And he said that a lessee for years is within the statute, for he has an estate by the law. Also it would be as great mischief to take an estate for years as a greater estate.

But HALES said that the declaration was not double, any more than a declaration upon the statute of 8 Hen. VI,[4] that the defendant entered with force and

[1] Cf. *Wytton* v. *Morgan* (1553) CP 40/1153, m. 428d; sub nom. *Whitton* v. *Marine*, Dyer, fo. 95a.

[2] Cf. below, p. 78, pl. 15; p. 99, pl. 10.

[3] See *OHLE*, vi. 75–76; below, p. 30, pl. 27.

[4] 8 Hen. VI, c. 9 (forcible entry).

en le disjunctive. Et semble [per][1] luy auxi que leas pur ans est deins lestatute, mes entant que il naledge que leas fuit fait de pretensed droit ne pur maintenance semble que nest deins lestatute, quar home bein poit fair leas pur ans rendant rent coment que il ne nul etc. fuit en possession per un an devant si ceo soit fait bona fide. Et dit que si home recover en formdon en descender come heir a son auncester et puis bona fide fit leas de cest terrre pur ans rendant rent, et ceo deins lan, uncore cest bon et nemi deins lestatute.

Et fuit agree per *Cooke* et *Hales* que si home forge faux fait dun terme dans que cestui que est greve avera action sur statute de forgery coment que nest forsque chattell car est un tort et falshood que lestatute entendoit a punisher. Et *Hales* dit que quant al exception des 10 acres apperteignant etc. ceux 10 acres poient estre le orchard et gardein pertinentes al mese etc.

Et quant as toutes [*fol. 5v*] auters exceptions ils fueront rule ouster per tout le court entant que nest forsque supposell en le declaration et nul terre est en demand. Et *Hales* dit que le certenty del ans ne serra mention entant que il ne gist en conusans le pl. nient pluis que si home soit endite pur embler des biens cujusdam hominis ignoti cest enditement est bon, a fortiore icy.

Non audivi vocem *Browne* Justice.

Mountague Chief Justice de Common Banke allowa le primer exception de misrecytall lestatute, quar il dit que fuit tout un de reherse nul estatute come a reherser un statute destre fait en tiel temps lou nul tiell fuit donques fait. Car si home soit endite dun felony fait per statute et lestatute nest bon reherse les justices ne luy arreigneront. Et dit ouster que le ple ne fuit double car si statute dona punishment pur divers choses il poet alleger toutes les choses queux enforceant le punishment et nest double. Et quant al terre perteynant etc. il dit que lententes les parties serront prise: come de fyne levy dun mannor de D. lou sont deux D. ceo passa que est suppose destre lentent les parties a passer, et issint en cest case. Et il dit que un leas poet este deins lestatute si soit fait dun pretended droit ou title, mes nemi de possession, car il dit que il est terre et tenement. Et dit que si le seignor ad terre per eschete ou sur recoverie per disclaymer ou per entry per mortmayne, issint que il ad le terre en le post, ore sil fist leas de eux deins lan uncore ceo nest deins lestatute. Et si home tenant en taile discontinue al feme et devie et puis le feme prist al baron lissue en taile et puis le feme morust sans yssu per son baron et son heire entra, si ore lissue en taile vende son droit et title il serra puny per le statute coment il ad possession pur un an. Et dit que si home soit ouste de son terme pur ans et puis vende son droit de terme al auter cest cybein deins lestatute come franktenement ou inheritance. Et il dit que si home port precipe quod reddat vers le pier que pendant

[1] *Reads* pur.

held with force – which is good even though the statute says, 'if a man enters with force, or detains' etc., in the disjunctive. He also thought that a lease for years is within the statute, but since it is not alleged that the lease was made of a pretended right, or for maintenance, it seems that it is not within the statute; for one may well make a lease for years yielding rent even though neither he nor any etc. was in possession for a year beforehand, provided it is made bona fide. He said that if someone recovers in formedon in the descender as heir to his ancestor, and then bona fide makes a lease of this land for years yielding rent, and this is within the year, it is nevertheless good and not within the statute.

It was agreed by COKE and HALES that if someone forges a false deed of a term of years, the person aggrieved may have an action on the statute of forgery,[1] even though it is only a chattel; for it is a wrong and a falsehood which the statute is intended to punish. And HALES said that, as to the exception concerning the [fifteen] acres 'belonging etc.', these [fifteen] acres might be the orchard and garden belonging to the house etc.

As to all the other exceptions, they were overruled by the whole court, inasmuch as the matters were only supposals in the declaration and no land is in demand. HALES said that the certainty of the years need not be mentioned, since it does not lie in the plaintiff's knowledge. Likewise where someone is indicted for stealing the goods 'of a certain man unknown', this indictment is good: a fortiori here.

I could not hear BROWNE J.'s voice.

MOUNTAGUE C.J. of the Common Bench allowed the first exception, concerning misrecital of the statute, for he said that it was all one to recite no statute and to recite a statute as having been made at a time when none was made. For if someone is indicted for committing a statutory felony, and the statute is not properly recited, the justices will not arraign him. He said furthermore that the plea was not double, for if a statute gives a punishment for various things one may allege all the things that reinforce the punishment and it is not double. As to the land 'belonging etc. ', he said that the intentions of the parties shall be followed: as where a fine is levied of the manor of Dale, and there are two Dales, that one shall pass which it is supposed to have been the intention of the parties to pass; and likewise in this case. And he said that a lease may be within the statute if it is made of a pretended right or title, but not of a possession, for he said that [a lease] is 'land and tenement'. And he said that if the lord has land by escheat, or upon a recovery by disclaimer, or by entry for mortmain, so that he has the land in the *post*, and he makes a lease thereof within the year, this is still not within the statute. And if someone, being tenant in tail, discontinues to a woman and dies, and then the woman marries the issue in tail and dies without issue by her husband, and her heir enters, now if the issue in tail sells his right and title he shall be punished by the statute even if he has had possession for a year. And he said that if someone is ousted of his term of years and then sells his right to the term to someone else, this is just as much within the statute as a freehold or inheritance. And he said that if someone brings a *praecipe quod reddat*

[1] 1 Hen. V, c. 3.

le breife enfeoffa son fittz et heire, ceo ne fuit ne est champertie per lestatute de champertye. Et issint est si le tenant pendant le breife fist feoffment bona fide sans ascun entent de mainteyner. Et issint si feme port appeale de mort son baron, lappellee est trove nient culpable, et enquirie est des abbettors, et trove est que fittz et heire la feme fuit abbettor que fuit fittz auxi al baron, ceo nest abbettment per lestatute coment que il soit generall. Yssint son opinion fuit que home non obstant lestatute poet fair sale de ses terres sil fuit en possession ent per un jour [*fol. 6*] et que les parolls averont relation al prender des rentes per un an tantum et nemi en possession per un an. Et il dit que il ne doit recyter quant le terme commense etc. entant que cest bargaine pur ans generalment est contrary al statute et le pl. est estrange a lour communication yssint que il nad conusans des ans. Et il dit que entant que le declaration est demiseront serra entend que ils fueront seisies et demiseront quar en dett sur leas pur ans il poet declarer que il lessa generalment et ne dira que il fuit seise et lessa nient pluis que en formdon in discender dun done. Et pur cest cause sans averment que le demise fuit sur un pretense title ou pur maintenance contrary al statute laction ne gist vers le deffendantes etc. Quod nota.

[2]

A, fo. 17; *L* 87; B, p. 123; *D*, fo. 11, pl. 9 (7 Edw. VI).

Nota per *Hales* et *Portman* al Serjeantes Inne que si home soit arrest ou emprison pur suspicion de felony ou pur auter felony pur quel home est baylable[1] [per la ley][2] que le viscont ou counstable de la ville ou il fuit prise poet luy bayler per obligation mes nemi per recognisaunce. La cause est pur ceo que ils fueront et ore sont conservators del peace per la ley, et come conservators ils poient lesse a baile. Et lestatute que done power al justices de peace dont un soit de quorum a bailer ne [repugne ne restreigne][3] le power de le viscont et constable quel fuit en eux al commencement.

Mes uncore *Hales* dit que son pier Baron Hales dit a luy que la est un precedent contrary al eux en Banke le Roy en temps de Feneux chief justice, et la fuit un viscont de Kent amercy en graund somme pur lesser un suspect issera a large al baile, et le reson fuit que lestatute que done le power al justices de peace [implicative][4] tolle le power del viscont et auters constables. Quere causam.

[1] mainepernable *L.*
[2] *A, B, D, L.*
[3] *A, B, D, L.* preigne *H.*
[4] *A, B, D, L.*

against a father, who while the writ is pending enfeoffs his son and heir, this was not and is not champerty by the Statute of Champerty.[1] So it is if the tenant, while the writ is pending, makes a bona fide feoffment without any intention of maintaining. Likewise if a woman brings an appeal for the death of her husband, and the appellee is found not guilty, and there is an enquiry as to the abettors, and it is found that the woman's son and heir was abettor, who was also the husband's son, this is not an abetment under the statute[2] even though the wording is general. Thus his opinion was that, notwithstanding the statute, a person may sell his lands if he has been in possession thereof for a day, and that the words relate only to the taking of the rent for a year and not to possession for a year. And he said that he need not recite when the term commenced etc., inasmuch as this bargain for years generally is contrary to the statute and the plaintiff is a stranger to their dealings and therefore has no knowledge of the years. And he said that, since the declaration says 'demised' it shall be presumed that they were seised and demised; for in debt on a lease for years one may declare that he leased, generally, without saying that he was seised and leased – just as in formedon in the descender of a gift [one need count that he was seised and made the gift]. For this reason, the action does not lie against the defendant without an averment that the demise was upon a pretended title or for maintenance, contrary to the statute etc. Note that.

2. POWER TO GRANT BAIL

Serjeants' Inn.

Note, by HALES and PORTMAN at Serjeants' Inn, that if someone is arrested or imprisoned on suspicion of [larceny],[3] or for another felony for which one is bailable by the law, the sheriff or the constable of the vill where he was taken may bail him by bond, but not by recognizance. The reason is because they were (and still are) conservators of the peace by the [common] law, and as conservators they may release on bail. The statute[4] which gives justices of the peace power to grant bail, whereof one justice must be of the *quorum*, does not impugn or restrain the power of the sheriff and constable which was in them previously.

Yet it was said by HALES that his father, HALES B.,[5] told him that there was a precedent contrary to their opinion in the King's Bench in the time of Fyneux C.J.,[6] where a sheriff of Kent was amerced in a great sum for releasing a suspect at large on bail; and the reason was that the statute which gives the power to justices of the peace impliedly takes away the power of the sheriff and the constables. Query the reason.

1 Ordinatio de Conspiratoribus, 33 Edw. I, *SR*, i. 145.
2 Statute of Westminster II, c. 13.
3 Cf. Statute of Westminster I, c. 15.
4 3 Hen. VII, c. 3; see *OHLE*, vi. 514.
5 John Hales, B. Exch. 1522–39.
6 C.J.K.B. 1495–1525.

[3]

Abr. in *A*, fo. 17 (before pl. 2); *L* 86 (sim.); *B*, p. 123; *D*, fo. 10, pl. 8 (7 Edw. VI).

Nota per *Hales* [et *Portman*][1] clerement eodem tempore que si 2 homes soient obligees al auters al estoier al arbiterment de 2 homes issint que ils publishe lour agard en escript devant le primer jour del terme de Saint Hillary, et ils publishont lour agard en escript que port date le primer jour dessoynes, et devant le quarto die, ore cest nul agard, quar le primer jour dessoynes est le primer jour del terme et le quarto die nest forsque jour de grace. Mes si le condition fuit issint que lour agard serra publishe en escript devant le primer jour del plein terme la auterment est car cest un entendment al quarto die que est le primer jour del plein term.

[4]

A, fo. 17v; *L* 96.

[*fol. 6v*] Nota per *Hales* al Serjeantes Inne clerement que si un enfant soit fait executor a un home que prova le volunt que ore il poet doner les beins que il ad come executor ou lesser les terrs a luy devise per le volunt al performer le volunt et auxi faire acquittance pur receite des dettes et duties le testator. Et auxi il dit que si un enfant soit executor et ad un terme pur ans a luy devise per le testator que il poet lesser cest terme, quar il ad power issint a faire per le testatment. Et un executor est toutes temps al age, come un deane del colleadge ou cathedrall esglise, parson dun esglise, ou abbe est.

Mes *Portman* dit que enfant que ad un terme pur ans ou beins come executor poet bein disposer ou deviser eux mes quant il ad le terme pur ans a luy dona per le testament ore quant toutes les dettes sont paies il ad ceo terme en son droit demesne, et pur ceo il ne poet doner ou lesser mes come un enfant. Postea <in ista>[2] pagina.

[5]

A, fo. 17v[f]; *L* 97[f].

Nota per *Hales* auxi et *Portman* que si parson desglise fist leas pur ans de son rectory ou de parcell de son glebe rendant rent et devie, et son successor accepta le rent, cest acceptance ne fait le leas bon come fait lacceptance lissue en taile ou del successor dun abbe ou prior, entant que per le mort le parson le franketenement est en abeyaunce, s. en nulluy, tanque auter soit induct. Mes auter est en lauters cases, quar ils poient fair discontynuance et parson nemye, et pur ceo riens passa de luy forsque durant sa vie tantum.

[1] *A, B, D.* et Porte *H, L.*

[2] *Altered from:* proxima. *A mark in the margin refers to pl. 6, below, which is a continuation.*

3. TERM AND FULL TERM

Serjeants' Inn.

Note, by HALES and PORTMAN clearly at the same time, that if two men are bound to others to stand to the arbitration of two men, provided they publish their award in writing before the first day of Hilary term, and they publish their award in a writing dated on the first essoin-day, but before the *quartus dies*, this is no award: for the first essoin-day is the first day of term and the *quartus dies* is only a day of grace. But if the condition had been that their award should be published in writing before the first day of full term, it would have been otherwise, for it is understood that *quartus dies* is the first day of full term.[1]

4. INFANT EXECUTOR

Serjeants' Inn.

Note, by HALES at Serjeants' Inn, clearly, that if an infant is made someone's executor and proves the will, he may make a gift of the goods which he has as executor, or lease the lands devised to him by the will to perform the will, and also make an acquittance for receipt of the testator's debt and duties.[2] He also said that if an infant is executor, and has a term of years devised to him by the testator, he may lease this term; for he has power so to do through the testament. And an executor is always of age – like a dean of a college or cathedral church, a parson of a church, or an abbot.

But PORTMAN said that an infant who has a term of years, or goods, as executor may well dispose of or devise them; but when he has the term of years given him by the testament, and all the debts are paid, he has this term in his own right, and therefore he may not give or lease it except as an infant. [See] below on page [15].

5. PARSON'S FREEHOLD

Serjeants' Inn, contd.

Note also, by HALES and PORTMAN, that if the parson of a church makes a lease for years of his rectory or parcel of his glebe, yielding rent, and dies, and his successor accepts the rent, this acceptance does not make the lease good – as does an acceptance by the issue in tail, or the successor of an abbot or prior – inasmuch as by the parson's death the freehold is in abeyance, namely in no-one, until another is inducted. It is otherwise in the other cases, for they may make a discontinuance, whereas the parson may not; and therefore nothing passes from him except during his life.

1 Cf. 110 Selden Soc. 223.

2 See *Anon.* (1529) 93 Selden Soc. 133; 121 Selden Soc. 265, 323, 417; below, p. 15, pl. 6.

[6]

A, fo. 17v^{f}; *L* 98^{f}; *B*, p. 124.

Nota per *Portman* que fuit rule en le Common Banke ore tard que si feme ou home esteant deins age soit fait executor que ils poient bein relesser per fait toutes les dettes et duties le testator.

Mes *Hales* doubta de ceo case.

[1]Et ils disoient ouster que si home per volunt devise son term pur ans al estranger que lestranger poet enter en le terme sans livery del executor a son perill sil voille. Et si toutes les dettes le testator soient paies lentry est bon. Auter est de devisees des chattells personalles, quar eux ils ne poient prender nul voy sans deliverie.[2]

[7]

A, fo. 18^{f}; *L* 99^{f}.

[3]Nota que fuit agree per *Portman* et *Hales* al Serjeantes Inn que si home soit possesse dun terme pur ans des terres ou tenementes et per son darrein volunt devisa son terme a son feme et al estranger pur lour vies et voet ouster per le dit volunt que si le feme ou lestranger morust que donques J. S. son fittes avera le terme que donques remayne ou si home yssint possesse per son testament voet que J. [*fol. 7*] S. son fittes avera son terme a luy et a ses heires de son corps et sil devy sans heires de son corps le terme endurant que donques le terme remayner al J. S., ore en ceux cases si les primers devisees grantont les ans et terme al estranger ou ceo vendont que ceux en le remaynder nont remedy, et que le vendition et done est bone entant que nest forsque chattell et le primer devisee ad tout lenterest. Mes si le primer home devie sans ascun done, vendition our leas de ceo en sa vie fait, donques celui a que le remaynder est limitte avera le terme que remayna accordant al volunt <et ils disoient que fuit ore tarde yssint agree et ajudge>.[4]

[8]

Abr. in *A*, fo. 18^{f}; *L* 100^{f}; *B*, p. 124.

Nota auxi que la fuit clerement per ceux agree que si home port action de trns. ou forcible entree vers auter et le deffendant per verditt est trove culpable et devant judgement le pl. relessa al deffendant, que ore entant que le pl. est barre le roy est auxi barre de son fyne. Et si le roy soit entitle al un forfaiture sur un statute dont lenformer avoit le moyty le roy poet bein ceo relesser ou pardoner devant enformation commence, mes apres lenformation commence le roy ne

[1] *New paragraph in H.*
[2] *Written over:* recovery, *which is deleted.*
[3] *Runs on in H.*
[4] et ceo fuit adjudge 6 & 7 Ed. 6. *A*, *L*.

6. EXECUTORS

Serjeants' Inn. Cf. p. 14, above, pl. 4.

Note, by PORTMAN, that it was recently ruled in the Common Bench that if a woman or a man under age is made executor they may well release by deed all the testator's debts and duties.

HALES, however, doubted this case.

They said furthermore that if someone by will devises his term of years to a stranger, the stranger may at his peril enter in the term without livery from the executor, if he wishes, and (if all the testator's debts have been paid) the entry is good. It is otherwise of devises of chattels personal, for he may not take them in any way without delivery.

7. REMAINDER IN A TERM OF YEARS

Serjeants' Inn, contd. Cf. *OHLE*, vi. 641.

Note that it was agreed by PORTMAN and HALES at Serjeants' Inn that if someone is possessed of a term of years in lands or tenements, and by his last will devises his term to his wife and a stranger for their lives, and wills further by the said will that if the wife or stranger should die then John Style (his son) should have the term which then remains; or if someone (being so possessed) by his testament wills that John Style, his son, shall have his term unto him and his heirs of his body, and should he die without heirs of his body while the term endures then the term should remain to John [Dale]: in these cases if the first devisees grant the years and term to a stranger, or sell it, those in the remainder have no remedy, and the sale and gift is good, inasmuch as it is only a chattel and the first devisee has the whole interest. But if the first man dies without any gift, sale or lease thereof made in his lifetime, then the person to whom the remainder is limited shall have the term which remains according to the will. And they said that this was recently so agreed and adjudged.

8. FINE AND FORFEITURE

Serjeants' Inn.

Note also that it was there clearly agreed by them that if someone brings an action of trespass or forcible entry against another, and the defendant is found guilty by verdict, and before judgment the plaintiff releases to the defendant, now, since the plaintiff is barred, the king is also barred of his fine. If the king is entitled to a forfeiture upon a statute, whereof the informer [should have] half, the king may well release or pardon it before an information is commenced; but after the information commenced the king may not pardon anything but his poet pardoner forsque son moitie et nemy le moyty lenformer. Et uncore semble que si lenformer soit nonsue ou discharge laction que le roy navera ascun parte entant que il est entitle per le partie. Nota auxi ils disoent clerement que si home soit endite de felony et pur ceo est arraigne et trove culpable et devant judgement prist luy a son liver et est deliver al ordinarie come clerk convict, que ore il forfait toutes ses beins et chattells coment que il nad judgement, quar icy nul est partie forsque le roy et per le verdit il ad perdue ses beins et per son prisell a son liver il ad luy prise al auter ley, et pur ceo ses beins et chattells sont forfaites. Eodem tempore et loco.

[9]

A, fo. 18[f]; *L* 101[f].

Nota la auxi per *Hales* que si un fait nad son teste en luy, s. in cujus rei testimonium sigillum meum apposui, que ceo nest ascun fait. Et il dit que toutes covenantes, grantes et agreamentes mises en le fait apres le teste ne sont ascun parte del fait ne serront unques pled come parcell del fait.

[10]

A, fo. 18;[f] *L* 102[f]; *D*, fo. 11, pl. 13 (7 Edw. VI).

[*fol. 7v*] Nota per totam curiam (et la allege fuit que issint fuit agree in Banko domini Regis) que si un viscount per venire facias arraigna un pannell quel remayna per default des jurours, et tales est agard, quel est fait et returne per mesme le viscount, si ore les jurours apperont en court et le primer array en le primer pannell est challenge per cause de cosinage le viscount, et issint trove et quashe, que le tales est quashe auxi sans auter tryall. Et issint est si le primer array et pannel fuit fait per un viscount et le tales array per auter viscount, si le primer array soit challenge et issint trove et quashe toutes les tales apres arraies sont quashe auxi sans auter tryall, entant que tout depend sur le dit primer array et pannell que est le principall. Quod nota en Common Banke.

Dyer's report of the case

Les Reports (1688 ed.), fo. 78, pl. 41.

Le return de summons in attaint fuit fait al utas de Saint Michael per un viconte, et sur process fuit continue, videlicet un resummons et distres ove un xx tales, et auxy xvi tales, et return per le novel viconte. Et le grand jury et divers de ambideux les tales appruerunt moiety and not the informer's moiety. Nevertheless it seems that if the informer is nonsuited, or discharges the action, the king shall not have any part inasmuch as he is only entitled through the party. Note also they said clearly that if someone is indicted of felony, and arraigned for it and found guilty, and before judgment takes himself to his book[1] and is delivered to the ordinary as a clerk convict, he forfeits all his goods and chattels, even though he has no judgment, for here no one is party except the king, and by the verdict he has lost his goods, and by taking his book he has taken another law, and therefore his goods and chattels are forfeit. At the same time and place.

9. FORMALITIES OF A DEED

Serjeants' Inn. Cf. *OHLE*, vi. 822 n. 26.

Note there also, by HALES, that if a deed has no witnessing clause, namely 'in witness whereof I have [hereto] placed my seal' (*in cujus rei testimonium sigillum meum apposui*), it is no deed. And he said that all covenants, grants and agreements placed in the deed after the witnessing clause are not part of the deed and shall never be pleaded as part of the deed.

10. LYTTELTON v. HOKELTON

Common Pleas. Record: CP 40/1149, m. 546 (demurrer to second challenge, Mich. 1552; final judgment, Pas. 1554). Also reported in Dyer, fo. 78 (first challenge, Mich. 1552); printed below.

Note by the whole court – and it was there alleged that it was likewise agreed in the King's Bench – that if a sheriff by *venire facias* arraigns a panel which remains through default of jurors, and a *tales* is awarded, which is made and returned by the same sheriff, and then the jurors appear in court and the first array in the first panel is challenged by reason of kinship with the sheriff, and it is so found and the array quashed, the *tales* is now also quashed without any other trial. So it is if the first array and panel were made by one sheriff, and the *tales* arrayed by another sheriff, and the first array is challenged and so found and quashed, all the *tales* arrayed afterwards are also quashed without any other trial, inasmuch as everything depends on the said first array and panel, which is the principal. Note this, in the Common Bench.

Translation of Dyer's report

Mich. 1552.

The return of a summons in attaint was made on the octave of St Michael by a sheriff, and thereupon process was continued, namely a resummons and distress with a twenty *tales*, and also sixteen *tales*, and returned by a new sheriff. And the grand jury and various members of both the *tales* appeared on the octave of St Michael in this present term, at which day the first

[1] I.e. prays benefit of clergy.

al utas de Saint Michael cest present terme, a quel jour le primer panel fuit challenge per le plaintife in lattaint, pur cosinage del primer viconte a un del petite jury, et larray fuit quasse. Ore si larray de les tales soit quasse auxy, ceo fuit moult doubt per curiam, et al darrein, al peril del plaintife, sibien les tales come le principal panel fueront quasses et novel summons agard al viconte. Tamen aliter factum fuit Trin. 14 E. 4. rot. 474 . . .

Record of the case

CP 40/1149, m. 546, Reymond & Poley.

Salopia. Jurata xxiiij[or] militum de visneto de Wooderton venit recognitura si juratores per quos quedam inquisitio nuper summonita fuit coram justiciariis domini regis hic scilicet apud Westmonasterium de loquela que fuit coram eisdem justiciariis per breve domini regis de forma donationis in le descendere inter Edwardum Lyttelton armigerum petentem et Walterum Hokelton tenentem de duobus mesuagiis, quadraginta acris terre, viginti acris prati, quadraginta acris pasture, quadraginta acris bosci et decem solidatis redditus cum pertinenciis in Wooderton que Johannes persona ecclesie de Longmenede et Jacobus de Scolle dederunt cuidam Waltero Hokelton et Johanne uxori ejus et heredibus de corporibus eorum exeuntibus et que[i] post mortem predictorum Walteri et Johanne et Margarete filie et heredis eorundem Walteri et Johanne et Johannis filii et heredis ejusdem Margarete et Hameleti filii et heredis ejusdem Johannis et Willelmi filii et heredis ejusdem Hameleti et Alicie filie et heredis ejusdem Willelmi prefato Edwardo ut filio et heredi ejusdem Alicie et consanguineo et heredi predictorum Walteri et Johanne descendere debent per formam donationis predicte etc. et postmodum capta coram dilectis et fidelibus domini regis Willelmo Portman milite et Johanne Harrys serviente domini regis ad legem, justiciariis ipsius domini regis ad assisas in comitatu predicto capiendas assignatis, per breve domini regis de nisi prius per formam statuti etc. apud Shrewesbury falsum fecerunt sacramentum, sicut idem Edwardus domino regi graviter conquerendo monstravit, necne. Et modo hic ad hunc diem, scilicet in octabis Sancti Hillarii, venit tam predictus Edwardus per Humfridum Dycons attornatum suum quam predictus Walterus Hokelton per Thomam Carpenter attornatum suum. Et Thomas Stury armiger, Ricardus Ley armiger, Johannes Stenton armiger, Willelmus Corbett gent', Thomas Draper gent', Thomas Smyth yoman, Lodowicus Porter yoman, Ricardus Wylliams yoman, Ricardus Wyke yoman, Johannes Draper yoman, Ricardus Mason yoman et Humfridus Twyfort yoman, xij juratores prime inquisitonis predicte per predictum Thomam Carpenter attornatum suum similiter veniunt. Et super hoc tam predictus Walterus Hokelton quam predictus[1] Thomas Stury, Ricardus Ley, Johannes Stenton, Willelmus Corbett, Thomas Draper, Thomas Smyth, Lodowicus Porter, Ricardus Wylliams, Ricardus Wyke, Johannes Draper, Ricardus Mason et Humfridus Twyfort petunt auditum predicti brevis de attincta et eis legitur etc. Petunt etiam auditum recordi unde idem breve emanavit. Et eis legitur in [hec] verba:

> PLACITA APUD WESTMONASTERIUM CORAM EDWARDO MOUNTAGU MILITE ET SOCIIS SUIS JUSTICIARIIS DOMINI REGIS DE BANCO TERMINO PASCHE ANNO REGNI EDWARDI SEXTI DEI GRACIA ANGLIE, FRANCIE ET HIBERNIE REGIS, FIDEI DEFENSORIS ET IN TERRA ECCLESIE ANGLICANE ET HIBERNICE SUPREMUM CAPITIS QUARTO Rotulo Dlvi

1 *Sic.*

panel was challenged by the plaintiff in the attaint, on account of the kinship between the first sheriff and one of the petit jury; and the array was quashed. Now it was much doubted by the court whether the array of the *tales* should also be quashed; and in the end, at the plaintiff's risk, the *tales* as well as the principal panel was quashed, and a new writ of summons awarded to the sheriff. Yet it was done otherwise in Trin. 14 Edw. IV, roll 474 . . .

Translation of the record

Common Pleas, Hilary term 1552.

Shropshire. A jury of 24 knights from the venue of 'Wooderton'[1] comes to make recognition whether or not a false oath was made by the jurors by whom a certain inquest was lately summoned before the lord king's justices here, namely at Westminster, concerning a suit which was before the same justices by virtue of the lord king's writ of formedon in the descender between Edward Lyttelton, esquire,[2] demandant, and Walter Hokelton, tenant, for two messuages, forty acres of land, twenty acres of meadow, forty acres of pasture, forty acres of wood, and ten shillings-worth of rent with the appurtenances in Wooderton, which John, parson of Longmynd church and James de Scolle gave to a certain Walter Hokelton and Joan his wife and the heirs of their bodies, and which after the death of the aforesaid Walter and Joan, and of Margaret, daughter and heir of the same Walter and Joan, and of John, son and heir of the same Margaret, and of Hamlet, son and heir of the same John, and of William, son and heir of the same Hamlet, and of Alice, daughter and heir of the same William, ought to descend to the said Edward as son and heir of the same Alice and kinsman and heir of the aforesaid Walter and Joan, by the form of the aforesaid gift etc., which inquest was afterwards taken before the lord king's well beloved and faithful William Portman, knight, and John Harrys, king's serjeant at law, the selfsame lord king's justices assigned to take the assizes in the county aforesaid, by the lord king's writ of nisi prius, by the form of the statute etc., at Shrewsbury, as the same Edward has shown to the lord king by grievous complaint. And now here at this day, namely in the octaves of St Hilary, come both the aforesaid Edward, by Humphrey Dycons his attorney, and the aforesaid Walter Hokelton, by Thomas Carpenter his attorney. And Thomas Stury, esquire, Richard Ley, esquire, John Stenton, esquire, William Corbett, gentleman, Thomas Draper, gentleman, Thomas Smyth, yeoman, Lewis Porter, yeoman, Richard Wylliams, yeoman, Richard Wyke, yeoman, John Draper, yeoman, Richard Mason, yeoman and Humphrey Twyfort, yeoman, the twelve jurors of the first inquest aforesaid, likewise come, by the aforesaid Thomas Carpenter their attorney. And thereupon not only the aforesaid Walter Hokelton but also the aforesaid Thomas Stury, Richard Ley, John Stenton, William Corbett, Thomas Draper, Thomas Smyth, Lewis Porter, Richard Wylliams, Richard Wyke, John Draper, Richard Mason and Humphrey Twyfort pray oyer of the aforesaid writ of attaint; and it is read to them etc. They also pray oyer of the record out of which the same writ emanated; and it is read to them, in these words:

> PLEAS AT WESTMINSTER BEFORE EDWARD MOUNTAGU, KNIGHT, AND HIS FELLOWS, THE LORD KING'S JUSTICES OF THE BENCH, FOR EASTER TERM [1550] IN THE FOURTH YEAR OF THE REIGN OF EDWARD THE SIXTH, BY THE GRACE OF GOD OF ENGLAND, FRANCE AND IRELAND KING, DEFENDER OF THE FAITH, AND ON EARTH SUPREME HEAD OF THE CHURCH OF ENGLAND AND IRELAND Roll 556

[1] Perhaps Wotton, in the parish of Witton.

[2] Of Pillaton Hall, Staffs., and the Inner Temple (adm. 1518), 1st son of Richard Littleton (bencher of the Inner Temple) and grandson of Sir Thomas Littleton (JCP); knighted 1553; died 1558; alabaster effigy at Penkridge, Staffs.

Salopia. Edwardus Lyttleton armiger per Humfridum Dycons attornatum suum petit versus Walterum Hokelton duo mesuagia, quadraginta acras terre, viginti acras prati, quadraginta acras pasture, quadraginta acras bosci et decem solidatas redditus cum pertinenciis in Wooderton que Johannes persona ecclesie de Longmenede et Jacobus de Scolle dederunt cuidam Waltero Hokelton et Johanne uxori ejus et heredibus de corporibus eorum exeuntibus et que post mortem predictorum Walteri et Johanne et Margarete filie et heredis eorundem Walteri et Johanne et Johannis filii et heredis ejusdem Margarete et Hameleti filii et heredis ejusdem Johannis et Willelmi filii et heredis ejusdem Hameleti et Alicie filie et heredis ejusdem Willelmi prefato Edwardo ut filio et heredi ejusdem Alicie et consanguineo et heredi predictorum Walteri et Johanne descendere debent per formam donationis predicte etc. Et unde dicit quod predicti Johannes et Jacobus dederunt tenementa et redditus predicta cum pertinenciis prefato Waltero Hokelton et Johanne uxori ejus et heredibus de corporibus eorundem legittime procreatis in forma predicta etc. per quod donum iidem Walterus et Johanna fuerunt seisiti de tenementis et redditu predictis cum pertinenciis in dominico suo ut de feodo et jure tempore pacis tempore domini Edwardi nuper Regis Anglie tercii post conquestum capiendo inde expletia ad valenciam etc. et de ipsis Waltero et Johanna descendebat jus per formam etc. cuidam Margarete ut filie et heredi etc. et de ipsa Margareta descendebat jus per formam etc. cuidam Johanni ut filio et heredi etc. et de ipso Johanne descendebat jus per formam etc. cuidam Hameleto ut filio et heredi etc. et de ipso Hameleto descendebat jus per formam etc. cuidam Willelmo ut filio et heredi etc. et de ipso Willelmo descendebat jus per[i] formam etc. cuidam Alicie ut filie et heredi etc. et de ipsa Alicia descendebat jus per formam etc. isti Edwardo qui nunc petit ut filio et heredi ejusdem Alicie et consanguineo et heredi predictorum Walteri et Johanne et que post mortem etc. Et inde producit sectam etc.

Et predictus Walterus Hokelton jam tenens per Thomam Carpenter attornatum suum venit. Et defendit jus suum quando etc. Et dicit quod predictus Edwardus Lyttelton actionem suam predictam versus eum habere non debet, quia dicit quod diu ante predictum tempus quo supponitur donum predictum fieri et antequam predicti Johannes persona ecclesie de Longmenede et Jacobus de Scolle aliquid habuerunt in tenementis et redditu predictis cum pertinenciis in Wooderton predicta quidam Baldewinus de[i] Budlers fuit seisitus de tenementis et redditu predictis cum pertinenciis inter alia in dominico suo ut de feodo, et sic inde seisitus dedit tenementa et redditus predicta cum pertinenciis inter alia cuidam Willelmo Hokelton et Margarete uxori ejus, habendum eisdem Willelmo et Margareta et heredibus de corporibus eorundem Willelmi et Margarete legittime procreatis, cuiusquidem doni pretextu predicti Willelmus et Margareta fuerunt seisiti de tenementis et redditu illis cum pertinenciis in dominico suo ut de feodo talliato per formam doni predicti etc. posteaque predicti Willelmus et Margareta obierunt, post quorum mortem tenementa predicta cum pertinenciis descendebant predicto Walteri Hokelton in dicto brevi nominato ut filio et heredi predictorum Willelmi et Margarete de eorum corporibus legittime procreatorum, per quod idem Walterus Hokelton in tenementa predicta cum pertinenciis intravit et fuit inde seisitus in dominico suo ut de feodo talliato, et sic inde seisitus existens idem Walterus Hokelton apud Wooderton in comitatu predicto cepit in uxorem predictam Johannam in dicto brevi nominatam, et postea de tenementis predictis cum pertinenciis feoffavit predictos Johannem personam ecclesie de Longmenede et Jacobum de Scholl habendum eis et heredibus suis imperpetuum, virtute cujus feoffamenti iidem Johannes et Jacobus fuerunt seisiti de tenementis predictis cum pertinenciis in dominco suo ut de feodo, et sic inde seisiti existentes iidem Johannes persona de Lonmenede et Jacobus dederunt tenementa predicta cum pertinenciis prefatis Waltero Hokelton[i] et Johanne uxori ejus et heredibus de corporibus eorum exeuntibus prout per breve predictum superius supponitur, per quod donum iidem Walterus et Johanna fuerunt seisiti de tenementis pre-

Shropshire. Edward Lyttleton, esquire, by Humphrey Dycons his attorney, claims against Walter Hokelton two messuages, forty acres of land, twenty acres of meadow, forty acres of pasture, forty acres of wood, and ten shillings-worth of rent with the appurtenances in Wooderton, which John, parson of Longmynd church and James de Scolle gave to a certain Walter Hokelton and Joan his wife and the heirs of their bodies, and which after the death of the aforesaid Walter and Joan, and of Margaret, daughter and heir of the same Walter and Joan, and of John, son and heir of the same Margaret, and of Hamlet, son and heir of the same John, and of William, son and heir of the same Hamlet, and of Alice, daughter and heir of the same William, ought to descend to the said Edward as son and heir of the same Alice and as kinsman and heir of the aforesaid Walter and Joan, by the form of the aforesaid gift etc. Whereupon he says that the aforesaid John and James gave the aforesaid tenements and rent with the appurtenances to the said Walter Hokelton and Joan his wife, and the heirs of their bodies lawfully begotten, in form aforesaid etc., by virtue of which gift the same Walter and Joan were seised of the aforesaid tenements and rent with the appurtenances in their demesne as of fee and right in time of peace, in the time of the lord Edward the third since the conquest, late king of England, taking esplees therefrom to the value etc., and from them the said Walter and Joan the right descended by the form etc. to a certain Margaret as daughter and heir etc., and from her the said Margaret the right descended by the form etc. to a certain John as son and heir etc., and from him the said John the right descended by the form etc. to a certain Hamlet as son and heir etc., and from him the said Hamlet the right descended by the form etc. to a certain William as son and heir etc., and from him the said William the right descended by the form etc. to a certain Alice as daughter and heir etc., and from her the said Alice the right descended by the form etc. to this Edward who now claims, as son and heir of the same Alice and as kinsman and heir of the aforesaid Walter and Joan, and which after the death etc. And thereof he produces suit etc.

And the aforesaid Walter Hokelton, now tenant, comes by Thomas Carpenter his attorney. And he denies his right when etc. And he says that the aforesaid Edward Lyttelton ought not to have his aforesaid action against him, because he says that, long before the aforesaid time when the aforesaid gift is supposed to have been made, and before the aforesaid John, parson of Longmynd church, and James de Scolle had anything in the aforesaid tenements and rent with the appurtenances in Wooderton aforesaid, a certain Baldwin de Budlers was seised of the aforesaid tenements and rent with the appurtenances, amongst other things, in his demesne as of fee, and (being thus seised) gave the aforesaid tenements and rent with the appurtenances, amongst other things, to a certain William Hokelton and Margaret his wife, to have unto the same William and Margaret and the heirs of the bodies of the same William and Margaret lawfully begotten, by virtue of which gift the aforesaid William and Margaret were seised of the tenements and rent with the appurtenances in their demesne as of fee tail by the form of the aforesaid gift etc.; and afterwards the aforesaid William and Margaret died; and after their death the aforesaid tenements with the appurtenances descended to the aforesaid Walter Hokelton named in the writ, as son and heir of the aforesaid William and Margaret lawfully begotten of their bodies, whereby the same Walter Hokelton entered into the aforesaid tenements with the appurtenances and was seised thereof in his demesne as of fee tail, and (being thus seised) the same Walter Hokelton at Wooderton in the county aforesaid took as his wife the aforesaid Joan, named in the said writ, and afterwards enfeoffed the aforesaid John, parson of Longmynd church, and James de Scholl of the aforesaid tenements with the appurtenances, to have unto them and their heirs for ever, by virtue of which feoffment the same John and James were seised of the aforesaid tenements with the appurtenances in their demesne as of fee, and (being thus seised) the same John, parson of Longmynd church, and James gave the aforesaid tenements with the appurtenances to the said Walter Hokelton and Joan his wife, and the heirs of their bodies, as is above supposed by the aforesaid writ, by which gift dictis cum pertinenciis in dominico suo ut de feodo talliato prout in narratione predicta superius supponitur, et sic inde seisiti habuerunt exitum inter eos Margaretam in dicto breve nominatam, posteaque predicta Johanna obiit, post cujus quidem Johanne mortem idem Walterus Hokelton apud Wooderton in comitatu predicto cepit in uxorem quandam Janam, et postea iidem Walterus et Jana habuerunt exitum inter eos de eorum corporibus legittime procreatum quendam Willelmum Hokelton, et postea predictus Walterus Hokelton obiit, post cujus mortem predictus Willelmus Hokelton filius Walteri in tenementa illa cum pertinenciis intravit et se intrusit et fuit inde seisitus in dominico suo ut de feodo, et sic inde seisitus existens habuit exitum de corpore suo legittime procreatum quendam Walterum Hokelton, et postea predictus Willelmus Hokelton filius Walteri de tali statu de tenementis illis cum pertinenciis obiit seisitus, post cujus mortem tenementa predicta cum pertinenciis descendebant dicto Waltero Hokelton[i] ut filio et heredi predicti Willelmi Hokelton, per quod idem Walterus in tenementa illa cum pertinenciis intravit et fuit inde seisitus in dominico suo ut de feodo talliato ut in suo remittere virtute predicti primi doni, et de tali statu obiit inde seisitus, post cujus mortem tenementa predicta cum pertinenciis descendebant Johanni Hokelton ut filio et heredi ipsius Walteri de corpore ejusdem Walteri legittime procreato, per quod idem Johannes in tenementa illa cum pertinenciis intravit et fuit inde seisitus in dominico suo ut de feodo talliato, et de tali statu obiit inde seisitus, post cujus mortem tenementa predicta cum pertinenciis descendebant prefato Waltero Hokelton modo tenenti ut filio et heredi predicti Johannis Hokelton de corpore dicti Johannis legittime procreato, per quod idem Walterus modo tenens in tenementa illa cum pertinenciis intravit et fuit et adhuc est inde seisitus in dominico suo ut de feodo talliato. Et hoc paratus est verificare. Unde petit judicium si predictus Edwardus Lyttleton actionem suam predictam versus eum habere debeat etc.

Et predictus Edwardus Lyttleton dicit quod ipse per aliqua preallegata ab actione sua predicta habenda precludi non debet, quia, protestando quod predictus Baldewinus de Budlers non dedit tenementa predicta cum pertinenciis prefato Willelmo Hokelton et Margareta uxori ejus et heredibus de corporibus eorundem Willelmi et Margarete legittime procreatis prout predictus Walterus Hokelton modo tenens superius allegavit, pro placito dicit quod predictus Willelmus Hokelton filius predictorum Walteri Hokelton et Jane uxoris ejus non obiit seisitus de tenementis predictis cum pertinenciis prout predictus Walterus Hokelton[i] jam tenens superius allegavit. Et hoc petit quod inquiratur per patriam. Et predictus Walterus Hokelton jam tenens similiter. Ideo preceptum est vicecomiti quod venire faceret hic in octabis Sancti Michaelis xij etc. per quos etc. et qui nec etc. ad recognoscendum etc. quia tam etc. Ad quem diem hic veniunt partes etc. Et vicecomes non misit breve. Ideo sicut prius preceptum est vicecomiti quod venire faceret hic in octabis Sancti Hillarii xij etc. ad recognoscendum in forma predicta etc. Ad quem diem jurata inter partes predictas de predicto placito posita fuit inde inter eas in respectum hic usque ad hunc diem, scilicet in crastino Sancte Trinitatis <tunc proximo sequente>[i] nisi justiciarii domini regis ad assisas in comitatu predicto capiendas assignati per formam statuti etc. die Veneris in secunda septimana Quadragesime proxima preterita apud Salopiam in comitatu predicto prius venissent. Et modo hic ad hunc diem venit predictus Walterus Hokelton jam tenens per attornatum suum predictum. Et prefati justiciarii ad assisas coram quibus etc. misunt hic recordum suum in hec verba:

the same Walter and Joan were seised of the aforesaid tenements with the appurtenances in their demesne as of fee tail, as is above supposed in the aforesaid count, and (being thus seised) they had issue between them the Margaret named in the said writ, and afterwards the aforesaid Joan died, and after the said Joan's death the same Walter Hokelton at Wooderton in the county aforesaid took as his wife a certain Jane,[1] and afterwards the same Walter and Jane had issue between them, lawfully begotten of their bodies, a certain William Hokelton, and afterwards the aforesaid Walter Hokelton died, and after his death the aforesaid William Hokelton, son of Walter, entered into the tenements with the appurtenances and intruded himself and was thereof seised in his demesne as of fee, and (being thus seised) he had issue of his body lawfully begotten a certain Walter Hokelton, and afterwards the aforesaid William Hokelton, son of Walter, died seised in such estate of the tenements with the appurtenances, and after his death the aforesaid tenements with the appurtenances descended to the said Walter Hokelton as son and heir of the aforesaid William Hokelton, whereby the same Walter entered into the tenements with the appurtenances and was seised thereof in his demesne as of fee tail in his remitter, by virtue of the aforesaid first gift, and died seised thereof in such estate, and after his death the aforesaid tenements with the appurtenances descended to John Hokelton as son and heir of him the said Walter lawfully begotten on the body of the same Walter, whereby the same John entered into the tenements with the appurtenances and was seised thereof in his demesne as of fee tail, and died seised thereof in such estate, and after his death the aforesaid tenements with the appurtenances descended to the said Walter Hokelton, now tenant, as son and heir of the aforesaid John Hokelton lawfully begotten on the body of the said Joan, whereby the same Walter, now tenant, entered into the tenements with the appurtenances and was and still is seised thereof in his demesne as of fee tail. And this he is ready to aver. Whereupon he prays judgment whether the aforesaid Edward Lyttleton ought to have his aforesaid action against him etc.

And the aforesaid Edward Lyttleton says that he ought not to be barred by anything previously alleged from having his aforesaid action, because, protesting that the aforesaid Baldwin de Budlers did not give the aforesaid tenements with the appurtenances to the said William Hokelton and Margaret his wife and the heirs of the bodies of the same William and Margaret lawfully begotten, in the way that the aforesaid Walter Hokelton, now tenant, has above alleged, he says by way of plea that the aforesaid William Hokelton, son of the aforesaid Walter Hokelton and Jane his wife, did not die seised of the aforesaid tenements with the appurtenances in the way that the aforesaid Walter Hokelton, now tenant, has above alleged. And this he prays may be enquired into by the country; and the aforesaid Walter Hokelton, now tenant, likewise. Therefore the sheriff is commanded to cause twelve men etc. to come here in the octave of Michaelmas by whom etc. and who neither etc. to make recognition etc. because both etc. At which day the parties come here etc. But the sheriff did not send the writ. Therefore, as before, the sheriff is commanded to cause twelve men etc. to come here in the octave of St Hilary etc. to make recognition in form aforesaid etc. At which day the jury between the aforesaid parties in respect of the aforesaid plea was therein put in respite between them here until this day, namely the morrow of the Holy Trinity then next following, unless the lord king's justices assigned to take the assizes in the aforesaid county by the form of the statute etc. should first have come to Shrewsbury in the aforesaid county on the Friday [27 Feb. 1551] in the second week of Lent next before then. And now here at this day the aforesaid Walter Hokelton, now tenant, comes here by his attorney. And the said justices of assize before whom etc. have sent here their record in these words:

[1] 'Jana' in Latin, which is unusual before this period. Joan and Jane are the same name (Johanna), but the different spellings may be used here to emphasise the distinction between them. Dr Jones has pointed out that 'Jana' occurs on the monumental brass of Jane Tyrrel (1557): as indeed it also does on Dalison's own brass (frontispiece).

Postea die et loco infracontentis coram Willelmo Portman milite et Johanne Harrys serviente domini regis ad legem, justiciariis ipsius[i] domini regis ad assisas in comitatu Salopie capiendas assignatis per formam statuti etc. veniunt tam infranominatus Edwardus Lyttelton quam infrascriptus Walterus Hokelton in propriis personis suis. Et juratores jurate infraspecificate exacti similter veniunt, qui ad veritatem de infracontentis dicendam electi, triati et jurati, dicunt super sacramentum suum quod infranominatus Willelmus Hokelton filius infraspecificati Walteri Hokelton et Jane uxoris ejus obiit seisitus de tenementis infrascriptis cum pertinenciis prout predictus Walterus Hokelton jam tenens interius allegavit. Ideo consideratum est quod predictus Edwardus Lyttelton nichil capiat per breve suum predictum set sit in misericordia pro falso clamore suo inde, et quod predictus Walterus Hokelton jam tenens eat inde sine die etc.

Quibus lectis et auditis, tam predictus Walterus Hokelton quam predicti Thomas Stury, Ricardus Ley, Johannes Stenton, Willelmus Corbett, Thomas Draper, Thomas Smyth, Lodowicus Porter, Ricardus Wylliams, Ricardus Wyke, Johannes Draper, Ricardus Mason et Humfridus Twyfort petunt quod predictus Edwardus assignaret falsum sacramentum si quod etc. Et super hoc[i] predictus Edwardus dicit quod predicti xij juratores prime inquisitionis predicte falsum fecerunt sacramentum in omnibus que dixerunt, videlicet <in hoc>[i] quod ubi dixerunt quod predictus Willelmus Hokelton filius predictorum Walteri Hokelton et Jane uxoris [ejus] obiit seisitus de tenementis predictis cum pertinenciis, quia idem Edwardus dicit quod predictus Willelmus Hokelton filius predictorum Walteri et Jane uxoris ejus[i] non obiit seisitus de tenementis predictis cum pertinenciis prout predictus Walterus Hokelton jam tenens superius allegavit. Et hoc paratus est verificare per predictam juratam xxiiij^{or} militum predictorum etc.

Et tam predictus Walterus Hokelton quam predicti Thomas Stury, Ricardus Ley, Johannes Stenton, Willelmus Corbett, Thomas Draper, Thomas Smyth, Lodowicus Porter, Ricardus Wylliams, Ricardus Wyke, Johannes Draper, Ricardus Mason et Humfridus Twyfort dicunt quod iidem <xij juratores prime inquisitionis predicte>[i] bonum et legale fecerunt sacramentum in omnibus que dixerunt. Et de hoc ponunt se super juratam xxiiij^{or} militum predictam. Et predictus Edwardus Lyttelton similiter. Ideo jurata xxiiij^{or} militum inde inter eos capiatur etc. Set jurata illa ponitur in respectum hic usque a die Pasche in xv dies pro defectu juratorum jurate xxiiij^{or} militum ille quia nullus venit. Et preceptum est vicecomiti <quod distringat eosdem juratores jurate xxiiij^{or} militum ille per omnes terras etc. et quod de exitibus etc. et quod tunc habeat>[i] corpora [juratorum] ejusdem jurate xxiiij^{or} militum etc. Idem dies datus est tam prefato Edwardo quam prefato Waltero Hukelton et similiter predictis Thome Stury, Ricardo Ley, Johanni Stenton, Willelmo Corbett, Thome Draper, Thome Smyth, Lodowico Porter, Ricardo Wylliams, Ricardo Wyke, Johanni Draper, Ricardo Mason et Humfrido Twyfort hic etc. Ad quam quidem quindenam Pasche hic veniunt tam predictus Edwardus quam predictus Walterus Hokelton, et etiam predicti Thomas Stury, Ricardus Ley, Johannes Stenton, Willelmus Corbett, Thomas Draper, Thomas Smyth, Lodowicus Porter, Ricardus Wylliams, Ricardus Wyke, Johannes Draper, Ricardus Mason et Humfridus Twyfort similiter per attornatos suos predictos etc.[i] Et juratores jurate xxiiij^{or} militum predicte solempniter exacti, quidam eorum veniunt et quidam eorum non veniunt, prout patet in panello etc. Ideo jurata xxiiij^{or} militum illa ulterius ponitur in respectum hic usque in crastino Sancte Trinitatis pro defectu juratorum ejusdem jurate xxiiij^{or} militum etc. Ideo vicecomes sicut prius distringat eosdem juratores jurate xxiiij^{or} militum predicte per omnes terras etc. et quod de exitibus etc. ita quod habeat corpora juratorum ejusdem jurate xxiiij^{or} militum hic ad prefatum crastinum Sancte Trinitatis etc. Et apponat viginti tales etc. Idem dies datus est tam prefato Edwardo quam prefato Waltero Hukelton et similiter predictis Thome Stury, Ricardo Ley, Johanni Stenton, Willelmo Corbett, Thome Draper, Thome Smyth, Lodowico Porter, Ricardo Wylliams, Ricardo Wyke, Johanni Draper, Ricardo Mason et Humfrido Twyfort hic etc. Ad quam quidem crastinum Sancte Trinitatis

Afterwards, at the day and place contained within, before William Portman, knight, and John Harrys, the lord king's serjeant at law, justices of the selfsame lord king assigned to take the assizes in the county of Shropshire by the form of the statute etc., both the within-named Edward Lyttelton and the within-written Walter Hokelton come in their own persons. And the jurors of the within-mentioned jury, having been called, likewise come; and, being chosen, tried and sworn to say the truth concerning the matters contain within, they say upon their oath that the within-named William Hokelton, son of the within-mentioned Walter Hokelton and Jane his wife, died seised of the within-mentioned tenements with the appurtenances in the way that the aforesaid Walter Hokelton, now tenant, has within alleged. Therefore it is awarded that the aforesaid Edward Lyttelton take nothing by his aforesaid writ, but be in mercy for his false claim therein, and that the aforesaid Walter Hokelton, now tenant, go therein without day etc.

These things having been read and heard, not only the aforesaid Walter Hokelton but also the aforesaid Thomas Stury, Richard Ley, John Stenton, William Corbett, Thomas Draper, Thomas Smyth, Lewis Porter, Richard Wylliams, Richard Wyke, John Draper, Richard Mason and Humphrey Twyfort pray that the aforesaid Edward should assign the false oath if any etc. And thereupon the aforesaid Edward says that the aforesaid twelve jurors of the aforesaid first inquest made a false oath in everything that they said, namely inasmuch as they said that the aforesaid William Hokelton, son of the aforesaid Walter Hokelton and Jane his wife, died seised of the aforesaid tenements with the appurtenances, because the same Edward says that the aforesaid William Hokelton, son of the aforesaid Walter and Jane his wife, did not die seised of the aforesaid tenements with the appurtenances in the way that the aforesaid Walter Hokelton, now tenant, has above alleged. And this he is ready to aver by the aforesaid jury of 24 knights etc.

And not only the aforesaid Walter Hokelton but also the aforesaid Thomas Stury, Richard Ley, John Stenton, William Corbett, Thomas Draper, Thomas Smyth, Lewis Porter, Richard Wylliams, Richard Wyke, John Draper, Richard Mason and Humphrey Twyfort say that the same twelve jurors of the aforesaid first inquest made a good and lawful oath in everything that they said. And of this they put themselves upon the aforesaid jury of 24 knights; and the aforesaid Edward Lyttelton likewise. Therefore let the jury of 24 knights be taken therein between them etc. But the jury is put in respite here until the quindene of Easter for default of the jurors of the jury of 24 knights, because no-one came. And the sheriff is ordered to distrain the same jurors of the jury of 24 knights by all their lands etc. and that from the issues etc. and that he should then have the bodies of the jurors of the same jury of 24 knights etc. The same day is given not only to the said Edward but also to the said Walter Hukelton and likewise to the aforesaid Thomas Stury, Richard Ley, John Stenton, William Corbett, Thomas Draper, Thomas Smyth, Lewis Porter, Richard Wylliams, Richard Wyke, John Draper, Richard Mason and Humphrey Twyfort, here etc. At which quindene of Easter both the aforesaid Edward and the aforesaid Walter Hokelton come here. And the aforesaid Thomas Stury, Richard Ley, John Stenton, William Corbett, Thomas Draper, Thomas Smyth, Lewis Porter, Richard Wylliams, Richard Wyke, John Draper, Richard Mason and Humphrey Twyfort likewise come here, by their aforesaid attorneys etc. And, the jurors of the aforesaid jury of 24 knights being solemnly called, some of them come and some of them do not come, as appears in the panel etc. Therefore the jury of 24 knights is further put in respite here until the morrow of the Holy Trinity for default of jurors of the same jury of 24 knights etc. Therefore, as before, let the sheriff distrain the same jurors of the aforesaid jury of 24 knights by all their lands etc. and from the issues etc. so that he has the bodies of the jurors of the same jury of 24 knights here at the said morrow of the Holy Trinity etc. And let him put in twenty *tales* etc. The same day is given both to the said Edward and the said Walter Hukelton, and likewise to the aforesaid Thomas Stury, Richard Ley, John Stenton, William Corbett, Thomas Draper, Thomas Smyth, Lewis Porter, Richard Wylliams, Richard Wyke, John Draper, Richard Mason and Humphrey Twyfort, here etc. At hic veniunt tam predictus Edwardus Lyttelton quam predictus Walterus Hokelton. Et etiam predicti Thomas Stury, Ricardus Ley, Johannes Stenton, Willelmus Corbett, Thomas Draper, Thomas Smyth, Lodowicus Porter, Ricardus Wylliams, Ricardus Wyke, Johannes Draper, Ricardus Mason et Humfridus Twyfort similiter venerunt per attornatos suos predictos. Et juratores jurate xxiiij^or^ militum predicte solempniter exacti, quidam eorum veniunt et quidam eorum non veniunt, prout patet in panello etc. Ideo jurata xxiiij^or^ militum illa ulterius ponitur in respectum hic usque in octabis Sancti Michaelis pro defectu juratorum ejusdem jurate xxiiij^or^ militum etc. Ideo vicecomes sicut pluries distringat eosdem juratores jurate xxiiij^or^ militum predicte per omnes terras etc. et quod de exitibus etc. ita quod habeat corpora juratorum ejusdem jurate xxiiij^or^ militum hic ad prefatas octabas Sancti Michaelis etc. Et apponat sexdecim tales etc. Idem dies datus est tam prefato Edwardo quam prefato Waltero et similiter predictis Thome Stury, Ricardo Ley, Johanni Stenton, Willelmo Corbett, Thome Draper, Thome Smyth, Lodowico Porter, Ricardo Wylliams, Ricardo Wyke, Johanni Draper, Ricardo Mason et Humfrido Twyfort hic etc. Et sciendum est quod justiciarii domini regis hic in curia xviii die Junii isto eodem termino deliberaverunt deputato vicecomitis comitatus predicti breve inde in forma juris exequendum etc. Ad quem diem hic veniunt tam predictus Edwardus Lyttelton quam predictus Walterus Hokelton, et etiam predicti Thomas Stury, Ricardus Ley, Johannes Stenton, Willelmus Corbett, Thomas Draper, Thomas Smyth, Lodowicus Porter, Ricardus Wylliams, Ricardus Wyke, Johannes Draper, Ricardus Mason et Humfridus Twyfort, xij juratores prime inquisitionis predicte, per attornatos suos predictos. Et juratores jurate xxiiij^or^ militum predicte impanellati tam de principali panello quam de viginti tales et de sexdecim tales eidem panello appositis exacti similiter veniunt. Et super hoc idem Edwardus Lyttelton calumpniat arraiamentum predicti principalis panelli quod incipit per Thomam Palmer militem et definit per Thomam Smyth, quia dicit quod panellum illud arraiatum fuit per Andream Corbett militem nuper vicecomitem comitatus predicti, quiquidem nuper vicecomes est et tempore arraiamenti panelli predicti fuit consanguineus predicti Thome Stury armigeri, unius xij juratorum prime inquisitionis predicte, videlicet filius Rogeri Corbett armigeri, filii Roberti Corbett militis, filii Ricardi Corbett militis, filii Rogeri Corbett militis, patris Anne matris Thome Stury, patris predicti Thome Stury unius predictorum xij juratorum prime inquisitionis predicte. Et hoc idem Edwardus Lyttelton paratus est verificare. Unde petit judicium et quod panellum predictum principalis panelli predicti[1] quam de predictis viginti tales et de sexdecim tales cassetur. Quam quidem calumpniam modo et forma predictis factam predictus Walterus dedicit fore veram, super quo postea per Ricardum Lawley armigerum et Edwardum Hopton generosum duos juratores ad hoc electos, triatos et juratos predicta calumpnia modo et forma predictis facta comperta est vera. Ideo tam panellum predicti principalis panelli quam de viginti tales et sexdecim tales predictis omnino amoveatur et cassetur. Et preceptum est nunc vicecomiti quod de novo summoneat per bonos summonitores xxiiij^or^ milites de predicto visneto de Wooderton quod sint hic in crastino Animarum ad faciendum juratam xxiiij^or^ militum predictam etc. Idem dies datus est tam prefato Edwardo quam prefato Waltero Hukelton et similiter predictis Thome Stury, Ricardo Ley, Johanni Stenton, Willelmo Corbett, Thome Draper, Thome Smyth, Lodowico Porter, Ricardo Wylliams, Ricardo Wyke, Johanni Draper, Ricardo Mason et Humfrido Twyfort hic etc. Ad quem diem

[1] pdcm.

which morrow of the Holy Trinity both the aforesaid Edward Lyttelton and the aforesaid Walter Hokelton come here, and the aforesaid Thomas Stury, Richard Ley, John Stenton, William Corbett, Thomas Draper, Thomas Smyth, Lewis Porter, Richard Wylliams, Richard Wyke, John Draper, Richard Mason and Humphrey Twyfort also likewise come by their aforesaid attorneys. And, the jurors of the aforesaid jury of 24 knights being solemnly called, some of them come and some of them do not come, as appears in the panel etc. Therefore the jury of 24 knights is further put in respite here until the octave of Michaelmas [1552] for default of jurors of the same jury of 24 knights etc. Therefore, as often before, let the sheriff distrain the same jurors of the aforesaid jury of 24 knights by all their lands etc. and from the issues etc. so that he have the bodies of the jurors of the same jury of 24 knights here at the said octave of Michaelmas etc. And let him put in sixteen *tales* etc. The same day is given both to the said Edward and the said Walter, and likewise to the aforesaid Thomas Stury, Richard Ley, John Stenton, William Corbett, Thomas Draper, Thomas Smyth, Lewis Porter, Richard Wylliams, Richard Wyke, John Draper, Richard Mason and Humphrey Twyfort, here etc. And it is to be known that the lord king's justices here in court on the eighteenth day of June [1552] this same term delivered the writ therein to the deputy of the aforesaid county to be executed in legal form etc. At which day both the aforesaid Edward Lyttelton and the aforesaid Walter Hokelton come here, and also the aforesaid Thomas Stury, Richard Ley, John Stenton, William Corbett, Thomas Draper, Thomas Smyth, Lewis Porter, Richard Wylliams, Richard Wyke, John Draper, Richard Mason and Humphrey Twyfort, the twelve jurors of the aforesaid first inquest, by their aforesaid attorneys. And the jurors of the aforesaid jury of 24 knights, impanelled both from the principal panel and from the twenty *tales* and sixteen *tales* put into the same panel, being called, likewise come. And thereupon the same Edward Lyttelton challenges the array of the aforesaid principal panel, which begins with Thomas Palmer, knight, and ends with Thomas Smyth, because he says that the panel was arrayed by Andrew Corbett, knight,[1] late sheriff of the aforesaid county, which late sheriff is and was at the time of arraying the aforesaid panel a kinsman of the aforesaid Thomas Stury, esquire,[2] one of the twelve jurors of the aforesaid first inquest, namely the son of Roger Corbett, esquire, son of Robert Corbett, knight, son of Richard Corbett, knight, son of Roger Corbett, knight, father of Anne, mother of Thomas Stury, father of the aforesaid Thomas Stury, one of the aforesaid twelve jurors of the aforesaid first inquest. And this the same Edward Lyttelton is ready to aver. Therefore he prays judgment and that the aforesaid panel, both of the principal panel and of the aforesaid twenty *tales* and sixteen *tales*, be quashed. Which challenge, made in manner and form aforesaid, the aforesaid Walter denies to be true, whereupon afterwards, by Richard Lawley, esquire, and Edward Hopton, gentleman, two jurors chosen, tried and sworn for this purpose, the aforesaid challenge as made in manner and form aforesaid is found to be true. Therefore let the panel, both of the aforesaid principal panel and of the aforesaid twenty *tales* and sixteen *tales*, be utterly withdrawn and quashed. And the present sheriff is ordered that by good summoners he shall newly summon 24 knights of the aforesaid venue of Wooderton to be here on the morrow of All Souls to make the aforesaid jury of 24 knights etc. The same day is given both to the said Edward and to the said Walter Hukelton, and likewise to the aforesaid Thomas Stury, Richard Ley, John Stenton, William Corbett, Thomas Draper, Thomas Smyth, Lewis Porter, Richard Wylliams, Richard Wyke, John Draper, Richard Mason and Humphrey Twyfort, here etc. At which day both the afore-

[1] Of the Middle Temple (where his arms are still in the hall window) and Moreton Corbet, Salop.; MP Shropshire 1555–59; died 1578 (*HPHC 1509–58*, i. 697).

[2] The celebrated covenant case of *Corbet* v. *Stury* (or 'Scurye') (Shrewsbury, 1292) long antedates this alliance: see J. H. Baker and S. F. C. Milsom, *Sources of English Legal History* (1986), p. 282.

hic veniunt tam predictus Edwardus Lyttelton quam predictus Walterus Hokelton, et etiam predicti Thomas Stury, Ricardus Ley, Johannes Stenton, Willelmus Corbett, Thomas Draper, Thomas Smyth, Lodowicus Porter, Ricardus Wylliams, Ricardus Wyke, Johannes Draper, Ricardus Mason et Humfridus Twyfort, xij juratores prime inquisitionis predicte, per attornatos suos predictos. Et predictus nunc vicecomes nichil inde fecit nec breve inde misit. Ideo sicut prius preceptum est eidem nunc vicecomiti quod de novo summoneat per bonos summonitores xxiiij^{or} milites de predicto visneto de Wooderton quod sint hic in octabis Sancti Hillarii ad faciendum juratam xxiiij^{or} militum predictam etc. Idem dies datus est tam prefato Edwardo quam prefato Waltero Hukelton et similiter predictis Thome Stury, Ricardo Ley, Johanni Stenton, Willelmo Corbett, Thome Draper, Thome Smyth, Lodowico Porter, Ricardo Wylliams, Ricardo Wyke, Johanni Draper, Ricardo Mason et Humfrido Twyfort hic etc. Et sciendum quod justiciarii domini regis hic in curia viij die Novembris isto eodem termino deliberaverunt deputato vicecomitis comitatus predicti breve inde in forma juris exequendum etc. Ad quem diem hic veniunt tam predictus Edwardus Lyttelton quam predictus Walterus Hokelton, et etiam predicti Thomas Stury, Ricardus Ley, Johannes Stenton, Willelmus Corbett, Thomas Draper, Thomas Smyth, Lodowicus Porter, Ricardus Wylliams, Ricardus Wyke, Johannes Draper, Ricardus Mason et Humfridus Twyfort, xij juratores prime inquisitionis predicte, per attornatos suos predictos. Et juratores jurate xxiiij^{or} militum predicte de novo impanellati exacti, quidem eorum veniunt et quidam eorum non veniunt, prout patet in panello etc. Et vicecomes modo mandavit quod quilibet eorum juratorum jurate xxiiij^{or} militum summonitus est per Johannem Den, Ricardum Fen, Thomam More et Willelmum Lande etc. Ideo iidem juratores jurate xxiiij^{or} militum predicte resummoneantur quod sint hic a die Pasche in xv dies ad faciendum juratam xxiiij^{or} militum predictam. Idem dies datus est tam prefato Edwardo quam prefato Waltero Hukelton et similiter predictis Thome Stury, Ricardo Ley, Johanni Stenton, Willelmo Corbett, Thome Draper, Thome Smyth, Lodowico Porter, Ricardo Wylliams, Ricardo Wyke, Johanni Draper, Ricardo Mason et Humfrido Twyfort hic etc. Ad quem diem hic veniunt tam predictus Edwardus Lyttelton quam predictus Walterus Hokelton, et etiam predicti Thomas Stury, Ricardus Ley, Johannes Stenton, Willelmus Corbett, Thomas Draper, Thomas Smyth, Lodowicus Porter, Ricardus Wylliams, Ricardus Wyke, Johannes Draper, Ricardus Mason et Humfridus Twyfort, xij juratores prime inquisitionis predicte, per attornatos suos predictos. Et juratores jurate xxiiij^{or} militum predicte de novo impanellati exacti, quidem eorum veniunt et quidam eorum non veniunt, prout patet in panello etc. Et vicecomes modo mandavit quod quilibet eorum juratorum jurate xxiiij^{or} militum resummonitus est per Johannem Doo, Ricardum Roo, Henricum Harte et Ricardum Smarte etc. Ideo iidem juratores jurate xxiiij^{or} militum predicte distringantur quod sint hic in crastino Sancte Trinitatis ad faciendum juratam xxiiij^{or} militum predictam. Idem dies datus est tam prefato Edwardo quam predicto[i] Waltero Hukelton et similiter predictis Thome Stury, Ricardo Ley, Johanni Stenton, Willelmo Corbett, Thome Draper, Thome Smyth, Lodowico Porter, Ricardo Wylliams, Ricardo Wyke, Johanni Draper, Ricardo Mason et Humfrido Twyfort hic etc. Ad quem diem hic veniunt tam predictus Edwardus Lyttelton quam predictus Walterus Hokelton, et etiam predicti Thomas Stury, Ricardus Ley, Johannes Stenton, Willelmus Corbett, Thomas Draper, Thomas Smyth, Lodowicus Porter, Ricardus Wylliams, Ricardus Wyke, Johannes Draper, Ricardus Mason et Humfridus Twyfort, xij juratores prime inquisitionis predicte, per attornatos suos predictos. Et juratores jurate xxiiij^{or} militum predicte de novo impanellati exacti, quidem eorum veniunt et quidam eorum non veniunt, prout patet in panello etc. Et vicecomes modo mandavit quod quilibet eorum juratorum jurate xxiiij^{or} militum manucaptus est per Johannem Doo, Ricardum Roo, Edmundum Hert et Gilbertum Dart. Ideo iidem juratores jurate xxiiij^{or} militum predicte distringantur quod said Edward Lyttelton and the aforesaid Walter Hokelton come here, and also the aforesaid Thomas Stury, Richard Ley, John Stenton, William Corbett, Thomas Draper, Thomas Smyth, Lewis Porter, Richard Wylliams, Richard Wyke, John Draper, Richard Mason and Humphrey Twyfort, the twelve jurors of the aforesaid first inquest, by their aforesaid attorneys. And the aforesaid present sheriff did nothing therein, and has not sent in the writ. Therefore, as before, the same present sheriff is ordered by good summoners newly to summon 24 knights of the aforesaid venue of Wooderton to be here in the octave of St Hilary to make the aforesaid jury of 24 knights etc. The same day is given both to the said Edward and to the said Walter Hukelton, and likewise to the aforesaid Thomas Stury, Richard Ley, John Stenton, William Corbett, Thomas Draper, Thomas Smyth, Lewis Porter, Richard Wylliams, Richard Wyke, John Draper, Richard Mason and Humphrey Twyfort, here etc. And it is to be known that the lord king's justices here in court on the eighth day of November [1552] this same term delivered the writ therein to the deputy of the sheriff of the aforesaid county to be executed in lawful form etc. At which day both the aforesaid Edward Lyttelton and the aforesaid Walter Hokelton come here, and also the aforesaid Thomas Stury, Richard Ley, John Stenton, William Corbett, Thomas Draper, Thomas Smyth, Lewis Porter, Richard Wylliams, Richard Wyke, John Draper, Richard Mason and Humphrey Twyfort, the twelve jurors of the aforesaid first inquest, by their aforesaid attorneys. And the jurors of the aforesaid newly impanelled jury of 24 knights having been called, some of them come and some of them do not come, as appears in the panel etc. And the sheriff has now sent word that each of the same jurors of the jury of 24 knights has been summoned, by John Den, Richard Fen, Thomas More and William Lande etc.[1] Therefore let the same jurors of the aforesaid jury of 24 knights be resummoned to be here at the quindene of Easter [1553] to make the aforesaid jury of 24 knights. The same day is given both to the said Edward and to the said Walter Hukelton, and likewise to the aforesaid Thomas Stury, Richard Ley, John Stenton, William Corbett, Thomas Draper, Thomas Smyth, Lewis Porter, Richard Wylliams, Richard Wyke, John Draper, Richard Mason and Humphrey Twyfort, here etc. At which day both the aforesaid Edward Lyttelton and the aforesaid Walter Hokelton come here, and also the aforesaid Thomas Stury, Richard Ley, John Stenton, William Corbett, Thomas Draper, Thomas Smyth, Lewis Porter, Richard Wylliams, Richard Wyke, John Draper, Richard Mason and Humphrey Twyfort, the twelve jurors of the aforesaid first inquest, by their aforesaid attorneys. And the jurors of the aforesaid newly impanelled jury of 24 knights having been called, some of them come and some of them do not come, as appears in the panel etc. And the sheriff has now sent word that each of the same jurors of the jury of 24 knights has been resummoned, by John Doo, Richard Roo, Henry Harte and Richard Smarte etc. Therefore let the same jurors of the aforesaid jury of 24 knights be distrained to be here at the morrow of the Holy Trinity to make the aforesaid jury of 24 knights. The same day is given both to the said Edward and to the aforesaid Walter Hukelton, and likewise to the aforesaid Thomas Stury, Richard Ley, John Stenton, William Corbett, Thomas Draper, Thomas Smyth, Lewis Porter, Richard Wylliams, Richard Wyke, John Draper, Richard Mason and Humphrey Twyfort, here etc. At which day both the aforesaid Edward Lyttelton and the aforesaid Walter Hokelton come here, and also the aforesaid Thomas Stury, Richard Ley, John Stenton, William Corbett, Thomas Draper, Thomas Smyth, Lewis Porter, Richard Wylliams, Richard Wyke, John Draper, Richard Mason and Humphrey Twyfort, the twelve jurors of the aforesaid first inquest, by their aforesaid attorneys. And the jurors of the newly impanelled jury of 24 knights having been called, some of them come and some of them do not come, as appears in the panel etc. And the sheriff has now sent word that each of the jurors of the jury of 24 knights has been mainprised, by John Doo, Richard Roo, Edmund Hert and Gilbert Dart.

[1] The names suggest that the summoners and mainpernors in the record are fictitious.

sint hic in octabis Sancti Michaelis ad faciendum juratam xxiiij^{or} militum predictam. Idem dies datus est tam prefato Edwardo quam predicto[i] Waltero Hukelton et similiter predictis Thome Stury, Ricardo Ley, Johanni Stenton, Willelmo Corbett, Thome Draper, Thome Smyth, Lodowico Porter, Ricardo Wylliams, Ricardo Wyke, Johanni Draper, Ricardo Mason et Humfrido Twyfort hic etc. Ad quem diem hic veniunt tam predictus Edwardus Lyttelton quam predictus Walterus Hokelton, et etiam predicti Thomas Stury, Ricardus Ley, Johannes Stenton, Willelmus Corbett, Thomas Draper, Thomas Smyth, Lodowicus Porter, Ricardus Wylliams, Ricardus Wyke, Johannes Draper, Ricardus Mason et Humfridus Twyfort, xij juratores prime inquisitionis predicte, per attornatos suos predictos. Et juratores jurate xxiiij^{or} militum predicte de novo impanellati exacti, quidem eorum veniunt et quidam eorum non veniunt. Et super hoc predictus Edwardus Lyttelton calumpniat arraiamentum panelli illius de novo impanellati quia dicit quod panellum illud arraiatum fuit per Ricardum Maynwaryng militem vicecomitem comitatus predicti, qui quidem vicecomes duxit in uxorem Elizabeth filiam Roberti Corbett militis, filii Ricardi Corbett militis, filii Rogeri Corbett militis, patris Anne matris Thome Stury patris Thome Stury unius juratorum prime inquisitionis predicte, per quam quidem Elizabeth predictus vicecomes habet exitum Arthurum Maynwaryng militem adhuc superstitem et in plena vita existentem. Et hoc paratus est verificare. Et ea de causa petit quod panellum illud cassetur et amoveatur etc.

Et predictus Walterus ac predicti Thomas Stury, Ricardus Ley, Johannes Stenton, Willelmus Corbett, Thomas Draper, Thomas Smyth, Lodowicus Porter, Ricardus Wylliams, Ricardus Wyke, Johannes Draper, Ricardus Mason et Humfridus Twyfort dicunt quod calumpnia predicta in cassationem arraiamenti panelli predicti de novo impanellati modo et forma predictis placitata et facta minus sufficiens in lege existit ad panellum illud cassandum, quodque ipsi ad calumpniam illam modo et forma predictis factam et placitatam necesse non habent nec per legem terre tenentur respondere. Et hoc parati sunt verificare. Unde pro defectu sufficientis calumpnie ipsius Edwardi Lyttelton in ea parte idem Walterus ac predicti xij juratores prime inquisitionis predicte petunt quod jurata xxiiij^{or} militum inter eos capiatur etc.

Et predictus Edwardus Littelton, ex quo ipse sufficientem materiam in lege in cassatione arraiamenti panelli predicti de novo impanellati superius allegavit, quam ipse paratus est verificare, quam quidem materiam predictus Walterus Hokelton ac predicti xij juratores prime[i] inquisitionis predicte non dedicunt nec ad eam aliqualiter respondent set verificationem illam omnino admittere recusant, petit judicium et quod panellum illud cassetur.

Super quo, visa calumpnia predicta ac per justiciarios hic plenius intellectis [premissis], consideratum est per eosdem justiciarios quod calumpnia illa minus sufficiens in lege existit ad cassandum panellum arraiamenti predicti de novo impanellati set quod jurata xxiiij^{or} militum predicta inter prefatum Edwardum Lyttelton et predictum [Walterum] Hokelton ac predictos xij juratores prime inquisitionis predicte capiatur etc. Super quo quidam eorundem juratorum xxiiij^{or} militum hic comparentium, videlicet Lodowicus Jones armiger, Ricardus Moreton armiger, Franciscus Kynnaston armiger, Ricardus Brocton gent', Johannes Leveson gent', Thomas Forster armiger, Thomas Ketylby gent', Humfridus Conysby armiger, Willelmus Byllyngley gent', Edwardus Williams gent', Johannes Walcote gent', Humfridus Conysby de Nyne Sollers, Egidius Covert armiger, Edwardus Lewys gent', Ricardus Harryngton gent', Arthurus Makworth gent', Fulco Crumpton armiger, Ricardus

Therefore let the same jurors of the aforesaid jury of 24 knights be distrained to be here in the octave of Michaelmas to make the aforesaid jury of 24 knights. The same day is given both to the said Edward and to the aforesaid Walter Hukelton, and likewise to the aforesaid Thomas Stury, Richard Ley, John Stenton, William Corbett, Thomas Draper, Thomas Smyth, Lewis Porter, Richard Wylliams, Richard Wyke, John Draper, Richard Mason and Humphrey Twyfort, here etc. At which day here come both the aforesaid Edward Lyttelton and the aforesaid Walter Hokelton, and also the aforesaid Thomas Stury, Richard Ley, John Stenton, William Corbett, Thomas Draper, Thomas Smyth, Lewis Porter, Richard Wylliams, Richard Wyke, John Draper, Richard Mason and Humphrey Twyfort, the twelve jurors of the aforesaid first inquest, by their aforesaid attorneys. And the jurors of the aforesaid newly impanelled jury of 24 knights having been called, some of them come and some of them do not come. And thereupon the aforesaid Edward Lyttelton challenges the array of the newly impanelled panel, because he says that the panel was arrayed by Richard Maynwaryng, knight, sheriff of the aforesaid county, which sheriff has taken to wife Elizabeth the daughter of Robert Corbett, knight, son of Richard Corbett, knight, son of Roger Corbett, knight, father of Anne, mother of Thomas Stury, father of Thomas Stury, one of the jurors of the aforesaid first inquest, by which Elizabeth the aforesaid sheriff has issue Arthur Maynwaryng, knight,[1] still surviving and being in full life. And this he is ready to aver. And for that reason he prays that the panel be quashed and withdrawn etc.

And the aforesaid Walter and the aforesaid Thomas Stury, Richard Ley, John Stenton, William Corbett, Thomas Draper, Thomas Smyth, Lewis Porter, Richard Wylliams, Richard Wyke, John Draper, Richard Mason and Humphrey Twyfort say that the aforesaid challenge as pleaded and made in manner and form aforesaid to quash the array of the aforesaid newly impanelled panel is insufficient in law to quash the panel, and that they have no need and are not bound by the law of the land to answer to that challenge as made and pleaded in manner and form aforesaid. And this they are ready to aver. Wherefore, for want of a sufficient challenge by him the said Edward Lyttelton in this behalf, the same Walter and the aforesaid twelve jurors of the aforesaid first inquest pray that the jury of 24 knights be taken between them etc.

And the aforesaid Edward Littelton, since he has above alleged sufficient matter in law to quash the array of the aforesaid newly impanelled panel, which he is ready to aver, which matter the aforesaid Walter Hokelton and the aforesaid twelve jurors of the aforesaid first inquest do not deny, nor do they in any way answer the same, but utterly refuse to admit the averment, prays judgment and that the panel be quashed.

Whereupon, the aforesaid challenge having been looked into and the foregoing matters having been fully understood by the justices here, it is awarded by the same justices that the challenge is insufficient in law to quash the array of the newly impanelled panel, but that the aforesaid jury of 24 knights should be taken between the said Edward Lyttelton and the aforesaid Walter Hokelton and the aforesaid twelve jurors of the aforesaid first inquest etc. Whereupon some of the same jurors of 24 knights here appearing, namely Lewis Jones, esquire, Richard Moreton, esquire, Francis Kynnaston, esquire, Richard Brocton, gentleman, John Leveson, gentleman, Thomas Forster, esquire, Thomas Ketylby, gentleman, Humphrey Conysby, esquire, William Byllyngley, gentleman, Edward Williams, gentleman, John Walcote, gentleman, Humfridus Conysby of Neen Sollers,[2] Giles Covert, esquire, Edward Lewys, gentleman, Richard Harryngton, gentleman, Arthur Makworth, gentleman, Fulke Crumpton, esquire, Richard Crumpton, gentleman, Richard Hussey, esquire, John

[1] Of Gray's Inn (adm. 1542) and Ightfield, Salop., 1st son of Sir Richard Mainwaring (d. 1558); died 1590: *HPHC 1558–1603*, iii. 2.

[2] Grandson of Sir Humphrey Conyngesby J.K.B.; died 4 April 1559 (incised slab at Hope under Dinmore, Herefordshire): 27 Harleian Soc. 43; 15 Harleian Soc. N.S. 180; *HPHC 1509–1558*, i. 680.

Crumpton gent', Ricardus Hussey armiger, Johannes Powes gent', Petrus Banaster gent' et Henricus Twyford gent' in juratam predictam jurati existunt. Et quidam juratores xxiiij^{or} [militum] modo hic similiter comparentes, videlicet Willelmus Acton gent', Johannes Persall armiger, Humfridus Hanmer [gent'], Willelmus Mynde gent' et Thomas Lawley gent', pro eo quod ipsi inter partes predictas suspectuosi inventi existunt, a panello inde penitus extrahuntur. Ideo jurata xxiiij^{or} militum predicta ulterius ponitur in respectum hic usque in crastino Animarum pro defectu juratorum xxiiij^{or} militum etc. Ideo vicecomes sicut pluries distringat eosdem juratores xxiiij^{or} militum etc. Idem dies datus est tam prefato Edwardo quam predicto Waltero Hukelton et similiter predictis Thome Stury, Ricardo Ley, Johanni Stenton, Willelmo Corbett, Thome Draper, Thome Smyth, Lodowico Porter, Ricardo Wylliams, Ricardo Wyke, Johanni Draper, Ricardo Mason et Humfrido Twyfort, xij juratoribus prime inquisitionibus predicte hic etc. Ad quem diem hic veniunt tam predictus Edwardus Lyttelton quam predictus Walterus Hokelton, et etiam predicti Thomas Stury, Ricardus Ley, Johannes Stenton, Willelmus Corbett, Thomas Draper, Thomas Smyth, Lodowicus Porter, Ricardus Wylliams, Ricardus Wyke, Johannes Draper, Ricardus Mason et Humfridus Twyfort, xij juratores prime inquisitionis predicte, per attornatos suos predictos. Et vicecomes nichil inde fecit nec breve inde misit. Ideo jurata xxiiij^{or} militum predicta ulterius ponitur in respectum hic usque in octabis Sancti Hillarii pro defectu juratorum ejusdem jurate xxiiij^{or} militum etc. Ideo vicecomes sicut pluries distringat eosdem juratores xxiiij^{or} militum etc. Idem dies datus est tam prefato Edwardo quam predicto Waltero Hukelton et similiter predictis Thome Stury, Ricardo Ley, Johanni Stenton, Willelmo Corbett, Thome Draper, Thome Smyth, Lodowico Porter, Ricardo Wylliams, Ricardo Wyke, Johanni Draper, Ricardo Mason et Humfrido Twyfort, xij juratoribus prime inquisitionibus predicte hic etc. Ad quem diem hic veniunt tam predictus Edwardus Lyttelton quam predictus Walterus Hokelton, et etiam predicti Thomas Stury, Ricardus Ley, Johannes Stenton, Willelmus Corbett, Thomas Draper, Thomas Smyth, Lodowicus Porter, Ricardus Wylliams, Ricardus Wyke, Johannes Draper, Ricardus Mason et Humfridus Twyfort, xij juratores prime inquisitionis predicte, per attornatos suos predictos. Et vicecomes nichil inde fecit nec breve inde misit. Ideo jurata xxiiij^{or} militum predicta ulterius ponitur in respectum hic usque a die Pasche in xv dies pro defectu juratorum ejusdem jurate xxiiij^{or} militum etc. Ideo vicecomes sicut pluries distringat eosdem juratores xxiiij^{or} militum etc. Idem dies datus est tam prefato Edwardo quam predicto Waltero Hukelton et similiter predictis Thome Stury, Ricardo Ley, Johanni Stenton, Willelmo Corbett, Thome Draper, Thome Smyth, Lodowico Porter, Ricardo Wylliams, Ricardo Wyke, Johanni Draper, Ricardo Mason et Humfrido Twyfort, xij juratoribus prime inquisitionibus predicte hic etc. Et sciendum est quod justiciarii domine regine hic in curia isto eodem termino deliberaverunt breve inde deputato vicecomitis comitatus predicti in forma juris exequendum etc. Ad quem diem hic veniunt tam predictus Edwardus Lyttelton quam predictus Walterus Hokelton, et etiam predicti Thomas Stury, Ricardus Ley, Johannes Stenton, Willelmus Corbett, Thomas Draper, Thomas Smyth, Lodowicus Porter, Ricardus Wylliams, Ricardus Wyke, Johannes Draper, Ricardus Mason et Humfridus Twyfort, xij juratores prime[i] inquisitionis predicte, per attornatos suos predictos. Et juratores jurate xxiiij^{or} militum predicte de novo impanellati exacti similiter veniunt, quia ad veritatem de premissis dicendam electi, triati et jurati dicunt super sacramentum suum quod predicti xij[i] juratores prime inquisitionis predicte bonum et legale fecerunt sacramentum in omnibus que dixerunt prout predictus Walterus et predicti Thomas Stury, Ricardus Ley, Johannes Stenton, Willelmus Corbett, Thomas Draper, Thomas Smyth, Lodowicus Porter, Ricardus Wylliams, Ricardus Wyke, Johannes Draper, Ricardus Mason et Humfridus Twyfort, juratores prime inquisitionis predicte, superius allegarunt. Ideo consideratum est quod predictus Edwardus Lyttelton nichil capiat per breve suum predictum, et quod[i] tam predictus Walterus Hokelton quam predicti xij juratores prime inquisitionis predicte eant inde sine die etc., et quod predictus Edwardus Lyttelton capiatur etc.

Powes, gentleman, Peter Banaster, gentleman, and Henry Twyford, gentleman, were sworn into the aforesaid jury. And some of the jurors of 24 knights now likewise here appearing, namely William Acton, gentleman, John Persall, esquire, Humphrey Hanmer, gentleman, William Mynde, gentleman, and Thomas Lawley, gentleman, were completely withdrawn from the panel therein, forasmuch as they were found to be suspicious between the aforesaid parties. Therefore the aforesaid jury of 24 knights is further put in respite here until the morrow of All Souls for default of jurors of 24 knights etc. Therefore let the sheriff, as often before, distrain the same jurors of 24 knights etc. The same day is given both to the said Edward and to the aforesaid Walter Hokelton, and likewise to the aforesaid Thomas Stury, Richard Ley, John Stenton, William Corbett, Thomas Draper, Thomas Smyth, Lewis Porter, Richard Wylliams, Richard Wyke, John Draper, Richard Mason and Humphrey Twyfort, the twelve jurors of the aforesaid first inquest, here etc. At which day both the aforesaid Edward Lyttelton and the aforesaid Walter Hokelton come here, and also the aforesaid Thomas Stury, Richard Ley, John Stenton, William Corbett, Thomas Draper, Thomas Smyth, Lewis Porter, Richard Wylliams, Richard Wyke, John Draper, Richard Mason and Humphrey Twyfort, the twelve jurors of the aforesaid first inquest, by their aforesaid attorneys. And the sheriff did nothing therein and has not sent in the writ. Therefore the aforesaid jury of 24 knights is further put in respite here intil the octave of St Hilary [1554] for default of jurors of the same jury of 24 knights etc. Therefore let the sheriff, as often before, distrain the same jurors of 24 knights etc. The same day is given both to the said Edward and to the aforesaid Walter Hukelton, and likewise to the aforesaid Thomas Stury, Richard Ley, John Stenton, William Corbett, Thomas Draper, Thomas Smyth, Lewis Porter, Richard Wylliams, Richard Wyke, John Draper, Richard Mason and Humphrey Twyfort, the twlve jurors of the aforesaid first inquest, here etc. At which day here come both the aforesaid Edward Lyttelton and the aforesaid Walter Hokelton, and also the aforesaid Thomas Stury, Richard Ley, John Stenton, William Corbett, Thomas Draper, Thomas Smyth, Lewis Porter, Richard Wylliams, Richard Wyke, John Draper, Richard Mason and Humphrey Twyfort, the twelve jurors of the aforesaid first inquest, by their aforesaid attorneys. And the sheriff did nothing therein and did not send in the writ. Therefore the aforesaid jury of 24 knights is further put in respite here until the quindene of Easter for default of jurors of the same jury of 24 knights etc. Therefore let the sheriff, as often before, distrain the same jurors of 24 knights etc. The same day is given both to the said Edward and to the aforesaid Walter Hukelton, and likewise to the aforesaid Thomas Stury, Richard Ley, John Stenton, William Corbett, Thomas Draper, Thomas Smyth, Lewis Porter, Richard Wylliams, Richard Wyke, John Draper, Richard Mason and Humphrey Twyfort, the twelve jurors of the aforesaid first inquest, here etc. And it is to be known that the lady queen's justices here in court this same term have delivered the writ therein to the deputy of the sheriff of the aforesaid county to be executed in legal form etc. At which day both the aforesaid Edward Lyttelton and the aforesaid Walter Hokelton come here, and also the aforesaid Thomas Stury, Richard Ley, John Stenton, William Corbett, Thomas Draper, Thomas Smyth, Lewis Porter, Richard Wylliams, Richard Wyke, John Draper, Richard Mason and Humphrey Twyfort, the twelve jurors of the aforesaid first inquest, by their aforesaid attorneys. And the jurors of the aforesaid newly impanelled jury of 24 knights, having been called, likewise come, and, having being chosen, tried and sworn to say the truth concerning the foregoing, say upon their oath the the aforesaid twelve jurors of the aforesaid first inquest made a good and lawful oath in everything that they said, as the aforesaid Walter and the aforesaid Thomas Stury, Richard Ley, John Stenton, William Corbett, Thomas Draper, Thomas Smyth, Lewis Porter, Richard Wylliams, Richard Wyke, John Draper, Richard Mason and Humphrey Twyfort, the jurors of the aforesaid first inquest, have above alleged. Therefore it is awarded that the aforesaid Edward Lyttelton take nothing by his aforesaid writ, and that not only the aforesaid Walter Hokelton but also the aforesaid twelve jurors of the aforesaid first inquest shall go therein without day etc., and that the aforesaid Edward Lyttelton be taken etc.

[11]

A, fo. 18^{f}; *L* 103^{f}.

Nota auxi que fuit dit per curiam que si le feme dun ducke, earle, <seignor ou chivall[er]>[1] apres le mort son baron prist auter baron, come gent[leman] ou esquier, que ore el ad perdue son nosme dun dame ou lady et que en action port vers baron et luy el ne serra nosme dame ne lady mes solement come uxor son baron, come les comon breifes sont: sicut accidit in casu Domine Powis in partitione facienda versus heredem Ducisse Suff' et alias: eodem tempore et loco.

Dyer's report of the case

Les Reports (1688 ed.), fo. 79b, pl. 51 only (continued in pl. 52).

Brief de partition fuit port vers le Duke de Suff. et sa feme et auters per Ranulphum Howard armigerum et dominam Annam Powes uxorem ejus, et issint el fuit nosme in le brief, et lexception fuit pris de misnosmer, eo que el duist aver estre nosme tantum per le nosme de son baron, et nemy auterment. Et per lopinion de *Mountague,* Chief Justice, et *Hales,* Justice, lexception est bone, eo que per la ley de dieu el est sub potestate viri, et auxy sa nosme de dignity serra change, accordant al degree son baron, nient obstant le curtesie de les dames de honor et court: sur que les plaintifes portont novel brief ad respondendum Ranulpho H. et Annae uxori suae, nuper uxori domini Powes defuncti . . .

[12]

A, fo. 18^{f}; *L* 104^{f}; *B*, p. 124.

Nota auxi que la fuit agree per curiam que en toutes escriptes et faites <le feme dun duke, earle ou viscount ou seignor>[2] serra nosme lady mes la feme dun chivaler serra nosme dame: eodem tempore et loco.

[13]

A, fo. 18^{f}; *L* 105^{f}; *B*, p. 124^{f} (runs on from pl. 12).

Nota auxi que si home prist un enheritrix des terres al feme que port armes et le baron ne unques dona ou porta armes que ore il ne ses heires apres luy ne doneront larmes sa feme. Et auxi si home prist al feme la file dun graund ou meinder home que nest inheritrix des ses terres que ore le baron durant la vie

[1] ou baron *A*.

[2] les femes de dukes, erles ou viscountes *A*. les femes de dukes, countees or viscounts *L*.

11. LADY ANNE POWYS v. DUKE OF SUFFOLK

Common Pleas. But note that pl. 13, which is said to be in the same place, is in Serjeants' Inn. Also reported in Dyer, fo. 79b (Mich. 1552); printed below; BL MS. Harley 1624, fo. 59; see *OHLE*, vi. 619.

Note also that it was said by the court that if the wife of a duke, earl, lord or knight, after her husband's death marries a gentleman or esquire she has now lost her name of Dame or Lady; and that in an action brought against her husband and herself she should not be named Dame or Lady but only as wife of her husband, as the common writs are. This happened in the case of Lady Powys, in *partitione facienda* against the heir of the duchess of Suffolk and others.[1] At the same time and place.

Translation of Dyer's report

Hilary term 1553.

A writ of partition was brought against the duke of Suffolk and his wife, and others, by Ranulph Howard, esquire, and 'the Lady Anne Powes his wife', and so she was named in the writ, and exception was taken for misnomer, in that she ought to have been named only by the name of her husband and not otherwise. And by the opinion of MOUNTAGUE, Chief Justice, and HALES, Justice, the exception is good, inasmuch as by the law of God she is under the control of her husband (*sub potestate viri*), and also her name of dignity shall be changed according to the degree of her husband, notwithstanding the courtesy [titles] of the ladies of honour and [of the] court: whereupon the plaintiffs brought a new writ 'to answer unto Ranulph Howard and Anne his wife, late the wife of the Lord Powes, deceased' . . .[2]

12. TITLES OF 'LADY' AND 'DAME'

Common Pleas, contd. But note that pl. 13, which is said to be in the same place, is in Serjeants' Inn.

Note also that it was there agreed by the court that in all writings and deeds the wife of a duke, earl, viscount or lord shall be named Lady; but the wife of a knight shall be named Dame. At the same time and place.

13. HUSBAND'S RIGHT TO WIFE'S ARMS

Serjeants' Inn.

Note also that if someone marries an heiress of lands who bears arms, and the husband never gave or bore arms, neither he nor his heirs after him may give his wife's arms. Moreover, if someone marries the daughter of a great or lesser man who is not an heiress of his lands, the husband during his said wife's lifetime may

[1] The action was brought in the names of Ranulph Howard, esq., and Lady Anne Powys, his wife: Dyer.

[2] Dyer's report continues on another point.

sa dit feme donera les armes del auncestor la feme sil devant dona armes, mes apres le mort sa feme ne il ne ses heires ne quarteront ou doneront les dittes armes per son feme: per *Hales* al Serjeantes Inne eodem tempore et loco.

[14]

A, fo. 18[f]; *L* 106[f]; *B*, p. 124[f].

Nota que il est clerement agree a cest jour et issint use que home poet levier fyne des terres ou tenementes al recognisee en la fyne directment pur xx. ans our c. ans come ils sont agrees rendant rent annuelment, sans ascun grant ou render devant, come fuit use avant ceux heures. Mes *Hales* et *Portman* disoent que le [*fol. 8*] clerer et meleux voy est en cest case [de] aver fyne sur grant et render pur les dittes ans, car ils disoient auterment que si les terres sont entayles lissue en taile avoydera le leas pur ans coment que il fuit [per][1] fyne entant que lestate contynue en taile non obstant le fyne et lestatute 32 H. 8. ne barra lissue en taile sinon que un franktenement passa del tenant en taile al maynes. Quod nota al Serjeantes Inne.

[15]

A, fo. 18v;[f] *L* 107[f]; *D*, fo. 11, pl. 14 (7 Edw. VI).

Et la auxi ils disoient que lentent del leas per indenture serra prise et poet per ascun resonable voy estre construe. Come si home per indenture fist leas pur ans rendant rent al 2 feastes et si le rent soit arere per space de xii. jours al ascun des dittes feastes que donques le lessor entra et oustera le lessee, ore cest paroll al ascun des dittes feastes serra prise apres les dittes feastes per construction en ley. Come si home fist leas per indenture et les parolls sont que J. S. ad demise et al farm lett al J. D. tout son mannor de D. en D., uncore per common parlaunce serra entend pur son mannor demesne et donques les leas serra a nul effect en ley. Mes entant que cest le comon forme de faire indentures pur ans et lentent fuit que le mannor fuit al J. S. le lessor il serra yssint prise ou auterment sont forsque petites leases bons en Engliterr.

[16]

A, fo. 18v[f]; *L* 108[f].

Nota per *Hales* clerement eodem tempore que si soit agree per indenture perenter 2 homes que J.S. et J.D. apres estate al eux execute des terres etc. serront

[1] *Reads* pur.

give[1] the arms of his wife's ancestor if he gave arms before; but after his wife's death neither he nor his heirs shall quarter or give the said arms through his wife. By HALES at Serjeants' Inn, at the same time and place.[2]

14. FINAL CONCORD OF A TERM

Serjeants' Inn.

Note that it is clearly agreed at the present day, and so used, that one may levy a fine of lands or tenements to the conusee in the fine directly for twenty years, or a hundred years (as they agree), yielding rent annually, without any previous grant or render, as was used in former times. But HALES and PORTMAN said that the clearer and better way in this case is to have a fine *sur grant et render* for the said years, for they said that otherwise if the terms are entailed the issue in tail may avoid the lease for years even though it was by fine, inasmuch as the estate continues in tail notwithstanding the fine, and the statute 32 Hen. VIII[3] does not bar the issue in tail unless a freehold at least passes from the tenant in tail. Note this, at Serjeants' Inn.

15. INTERPRETATION OF LEASES

Serjeants' Inn.

They also said that the intention of a lease by indenture shall be followed; and it is to be construed in any reasonable way. For instance, if someone by indenture makes a lease for years yielding rent at two feasts, and provides that if the rent is in arrear for a period of twelve days 'at any of the said feasts' the lessor might then enter and oust the lessee, these words 'at any of the said feasts' shall be understood by a construction in law to mean 'after the said feast'. Then again, if someone makes a lease by indenture, and the words are that John Style has demised and let to farm to John Dale all 'his' manor of Dale in Dale, in common speech this would be understood as [John Dale's] own manor,[4] and thus the lease would be of no effect in law; but since it is the common form in making leases for years, and the meaning is that the manor belongs to John Style (the lessor), it shall be so understood – or else there would be very few good leases in England.

16. USE IN TAIL

Serjeants' Inn.

Note clearly, by HALES on the same occasion, that if it is agreed by indenture between two men that after an estate in land has been executed to John Style

[1] Here meaning, presumably, impale.
[2] This evidently refers to pl. 11–12, which seem, however, to be in court.
[3] 32 Hen. VIII, c. 36.
[4] I.e. by assuming that 'his' refers to the last antecedent.

seisies al use dun des parties en lendenture en taile etc. et que le dit tenant en taile poet faire leases pur xl ans a son pleasure, et les dittes feoffees serront seisies al dittes uses, que ore nient obstant lestatute duses les leases yssint faites sont bons, et lestatute ne altera ceo. Quod nota.

[17]

Abr. in *A*, fo. 18v[f]; *L* 109[f]; *B*, p. 124 (foll. pl. 14); *D*, fo. 11, pl. 15 (7 Edw. VI).

Nota per *Mountague* et *Hales* eodem tempore que si home fait leas per indenture des terres pur ans et est agree per indenture que si le lessee fait tiel act que il forfeytera son [terme][1] ou son leas, ore sil face tiel act ceo est forfeyture de son [terme][2] et leas car lendenture est le fait et parlance dambideux parties. Yssint est si fuit per indenture que le lessee ne ferra tiels choses come aliener sans assent le lessor ou faire wast sur paine de forfayture, ore sil fait contrary cest un forfaiture de son leas.

[18]

A, fo. 18v[f]; *L* 110[f]; *D*, fo. 11, pl. 16 (7 Edw. VI).

[*fol. 8v*] Nota per *Hales* Justice que si home a cest jour prist terre en morgage s. pur 4 ans purchase ou x ans purchase al covetouse entent destre gayner ceo per lestatute est usury clerement mes si home prist terre en morgage bona fide sans tiel covin pur xx ans ou xviii ans purchase ceo nest usury per lestatute.

[19]

A, fo. 18v[f]; *L* 112 (foll. pl. 20).

Nota que fuit clerement agree per *Hales* et *Portman* que estranger esteant en le revertion auxibein en fee come pur vie poet auxibein enter pur un condition enfreint come le patentee le roy poet des terres perteignantes al monasteries et que lestatute est generall pur toutes terrs et homes 32 H. 8.

[1] *D.* indenture *H.*
[2] *D.* indenture *H.*

and John Dale they shall be seised to the use of one of the parties to the indenture, in tail etc., and that the said tenant in tail may make leases for forty years at his pleasure and the said feoffees shall be seised to the said uses: the leases so made are good, notwithstanding the Statute of Uses,[1] and the statute does not alter that. Note that.

17. FORFEITURE OF LEASE

Serjeants' Inn.

Note, by MOUNTAGUE[2] and HALES on the same occasion, that if someone makes a lease of lands for years by indenture, and it is agreed by the indenture that if the lessee commits such and such an act he will forfeit his term or his lease, now if he commits such an act it is a forfeiture of his term and lease: for the indenture is the deed and wording of both parties. Likewise if it was provided by indenture that the lessee should not do certain things, such as alienating without the lessor's assent, or committing waste, upon pain of forfeiture, and he does the contrary, it is a forfeiture of his lease.

18. MORTGAGES AND USURY

Probably in Serjeants' Inn.

Note, by HALES J., that if someone at the present day takes land in mortgage, namely for four years' purchase or ten years' purchase, with the covetous intention of gaining it, by the statute[3] this is clearly usury. But if someone takes land in mortgage bona fide, without such covin, for twenty or eighteen years' purchase, this is not usury by the statute.

19. MONASTIC LANDS

Serjeants' Inn.

Note that it was clearly agreed by HALES and PORTMAN that a stranger in reversion, whether in fee or for life, may enter for a condition broken in respect of lands belonging to monasteries just as well as the king's patentee may; and that the statute of 32 Hen. VIII[4] applies generally to all lands and men.

[1] 27 Hen. VIII. c. 10. The point is that the statute does not convert the estate tail in use into an ordinary legal entail, but the special power of leasing is preserved.

[2] A member of Serjeants' Inn, Fleet Street: Dyer, fo. 59; above, pp. xxi–xxii.

[3] 5 & 6 Edw. VI, c. 20.

[4] 32 Hen. VIII, c. 28.

[20]

A, fo. 18v[f]; *L* 113 (foll. pl. 18) ; *B*, p. 124.

Nota que fuit tenus clerement per *Hales* Justice al Serjeantes Inne que si un disseisor soit des terres que est ouste per force per le disseysee et le disseisor luy endite de ceo sur lestatute 8 H. 6. et est restore al possession per breife de restitution per le viscount et sur cest entree del disseisor per breife le disseissee avera assise car il est un disseisor vers le disseisee quant al franktenement et le breife ne luy remitta forsque al possession, et si son title ne soit bon il enter a son perill car lestatute nentendoit a doner le disseisor title vers le disseisee mes solement a luy punisher pur le force vers le roy per fyne. Mes *Portman* fuit contrary a luy.

Mes fuit agree per *Portman* et *Hales* que si home ad le peaceable possession des terres per 3 ans que il poet tener et occuper les terrs ovesque force apres le 3 ans cybein vers le roy pur ascun enditement come vers ascun auter person et ceo per lestatute. Et auxi ils disoient que si home ad le possession per 3 ans et puis secrement un auter luy ouste et entra que ore cestui issint ouste poet maintenant entre sur luy ovesque force car auterment ils disoient que lestatute nest forsque de petit effect quere car lestatute est que tiel home [aiant][1] le possession pur 3 ans poet bein reteygner ovesque force et ne parle dentry ovesque force.

[21]

Abr. in *A*, fo. 19[f]; *L* 114–115[f]; *B*, p. 124[f]; *D*, fo. 12, pl. 18 (7 Edw. VI).

Nota que le condition dun obligation serra toutes foites prise accordant a lentent obligor et si jeo soi tenus en obligation de xx li. al J. S. et sur le dorse de obligation sont ceux parolls, Memorandum quod predictus obligor conservabit lobligee indemnem et [ne] monstra de quel ne vers que uncore cest bon condition et lobligor ou obligee poient averrer lentent de ceo condition. Issint si soit endorse, Memorandum que lobligor solvet al obligee ou al estranger a tiel jour [*fol. 9*] x li., cest bon condition sans pluis dire per *Hales, Portman* et auters. Nota auxi que [si] soit tenus en obligation de c li. al J. S. sur condition to stand to thaward and arbiterment of two other ita quod arbitrium deliberetur partibus infrascriptis avant tiel jour partibus hoc peten[ti]bus cest bon condition. Et si les arbitrators deliveront lour agard en escript devant le jour et devant que les parties ceo demaund ceo nest bon devant le demaund les parties car ceux parolls partibus hoc petentibus font le condition conditional: per *Hales, Portman* et auter[s] all Serjeantes Inne.

[1] eeant *H.* que ad *A, L.*

20. FORCIBLE ENTRY AND DISSEISIN

Serjeants' Inn. Cf. Bendl. 37, pl. 68 (Pas. 1554).

Note that it was held clearly by HALES J. at Serjeants' Inn that if there is a disseisor of lands, who is ousted by force by the disseisee, and the disseisor indicts him for it upon the statute of 8 Hen. VI[1] and is restored to possession by the sheriff under a writ of restitution, upon this entry of the disseisor by writ the disseisee shall have an assize: for he is a disseisor as against the disseisee with respect to the freehold, and the writ does not remit him to anything but the possession, and if his title is not good he enters at his peril; for the statute did not intend to give the disseisor a title as against the disseisee, but only to punish the disseisee by fine for the force as against the king. PORTMAN, however, was against him.

But it was agreed by PORTMAN and HALES that, if someone has peaceable possession of lands for three years, he may hold and occupy the lands with force after the three years, as well against the king (with respect to any indictment) as against any other person; and this is by the statute. They also said that if someone has possession for three years and then another secretly ousts him and enters, the person so ousted may now immediately enter upon him with force, for otherwise they said the statute would be of only slight effect. Query this, for the statute says that such a man, having the possession for three years, may well *retain* it with force, but it says nothing about an entry with force.

21. INTERPRETATION OF CONDITIONS

Serjeants' Inn.

Note that the condition of a bond shall always be understood according to the intention of the obligor. If I am bound in a bond for £20 to John Style, and on the dorse of the bond are these words, 'Be it remembered that the aforesaid obligor shall indemnify the obligee', without saying in respect of what or against whom, this is nevertheless a good condition and the obligor or the obligee may aver the intention of this condition. Likewise if it is endorsed, 'Be it remembered that the obligor shall pay £10 to the obligee, or to a stranger, on such and such a day', without saying more. By HALES, PORTMAN, and others. Note also that if someone is bound to John Style in a bond for £100 upon condition 'to stand to the award and arbitration of two others, so that the arbitration be delivered to the within-mentioned parties before such and such a day, the parties so requesting', this is a good condition; and if the arbitrators deliver their award in writing before the day, and before the parties request it, this is not good before the parties' demand: for these words 'the parties so requesting' make the condition conditional. By HALES, PORTMAN and others at Serjeants' Inn.

[1] 8 Hen. VI, c. 9 (forcible entry).

[22]

A, fo. 19; *L* 120; *B*, pp. 124–125; *D*, fo. 12, pl. 19 (7 Edw. VI).

Nota que fuit agree per *Hales* et toutes auters en Serjeantes Inne que si home fist leas de ses terres en 2 counties per un indenture reservant un rent ovesque condition de payment et non payment que le lessor en cest case ne poet aver action de dett sur le dit leas mes il puit distreyner ou fair son demaund pur le rent en quel des counties que il voile ou en ambideux ou en lun a son pleasure et cest demaund en lun county est sufficient a reenter.

[23]

A, fo. 19[f]; *L* 120 (contd from pl. 22); *D*, fo. 12, pl. 18 (7 Edw. VI).

Et per *James Hales* si le lessor graunt le revertion de ses terres en un county ove xx s. rent ove cest revertion[1] a que le tenant atturna que per cest atturnment cest graunt del revertion ove le dit rent et atturnment le tenant est bon. Mes cest grauntee de le revertion ne poet enter apres pur le non payment del rent per lestatute 32 H. 8. eo quod il nad forsque parte del revertion et nemi toute le revertion [Veies mon report in 14 et 15 Eliz. de ceo][2].

[24]

A, fo. 19v[f]; *L* 120 (contd from pl. 23).

Et per *Hales* auxi si home fist leas pur ans en un county reservant rent et graunta le revertion des x acres al estranger en fee a que le tenant atturne que ore le grauntee navera nul parte de rent <le rent >[3] incident a cest revertion, mes le lessor avera tout le rent incident a cest revertion que en luy remayna come si home seisie des xx acres de terre a que advowson est appendant et enfeoffa un estranger de xv de les dittes xx acres en fee sans pluis dire ore le feoffee navera rien de ladvowson mes ceo remayna appendant al auters acres que remayna et cest bon ley sed quere de lauter case quar *Portman* fuit contrary pur le rent quar il dit que le rent poet estre apportion quia severall et yssint ne poet ladvowson quia entier. <Et Dyar accorde ovesque Portman in 14 et 15 Elizabeth.>[4]

[1] Condition *deleted.*

[2] *Obviously added* Vide M. 14 Eliz. le case de Sir William Wintor cont *D.*

[3] *Perhaps written in error.*

[4] *Evidently an interpolation.*

22. RENT FOR LAND IN TWO COUNTIES

Serjeants' Inn.

Note that it was agreed by HALES and all others in Serjeants' Inn that if someone makes a lease of his land in two counties, by an indenture reserving one rent, upon condition of payment and non-payment, the lessor in this case may not have an action of debt upon the said lease; but he may distrain, or make his demand for the rent, in whichever of the counties he wishes, in both or one of them at his pleasure; and this demand in one of the counties is sufficient to re-enter.

23. ATTORNMENT

Serjeants' Inn, contd.

According to JAMES HALES, if a lessor grants the reversion of his lands in one county, and 20*s.* rent with this reversion, and the tenant attorns [to the grantee], by this attornment this grant of the reversion with the said rent and the tenant's attornment is good. But this grantee of the reversion may not enter afterwards for non-payment of the rent, by the statute of 32 Hen. VIII,[1] inasmuch as he only has part of the reversion and not the whole reversion.

<See my report of this in 14 & 15 Eliz.>[2]

24. REVERSION

Serjeants' Inn, contd.

Also, according to HALES, if someone makes a lease for years in one county, reserving rent, and grants the reversion of ten of the acres to a stranger in fee, to whom the tenant attorns, the grantee shall have no part of the rent incident to this reversion, but the lessor shall have all the rent as incident to the reversion which remains in him. Similarly, if someone seised of twenty acres of land to which an advowson is appendant enfeoffs a stranger of fifteen of the said twenty acres, in fee, without saying anything more, the feoffee shall have nothing of the advowson, but it shall remain appendant to the other acres which remain. That is good law; but query concerning the other case, for PORTMAN was contrary as to the rent; for he said that the rent may be apportioned, because it is severable, whereas an advowson cannot be, because it is entire.

<Dyer [C.J.] agreed with Portman in 14 & 15 Eliz. [1572].>[3]

1 32 Hen. VIII, c. 34.

2 Evidently an interpolation. The case is identified in the printed ed. as *Sir William Winter's Case* (1572), which it says was 'cont[ra]'.

3 Evidently another interpolation.

[25]

A, fo. 19v[f]; *L* 121[f]; *B*, p. 125.

[*fol. 9v*] Nota que fuit agree per *Hales* Justice en le Comen Banke que si lessee pur term de son vie accepta de son lessor un leas pur ans cest surrender de son leas pur vie coment que lestate pur vie est greinder en ley come si home ad estate pur xx ans de terre et accepta estate de son lessor de le dit terre lesse pur x ans ou un an cest clerement un surrender des primiers ans car tout est un lou il accepta un meynder estate que il ad al comencement ou greinder estate: quod nota. Et si leas pur ans fuit fait per paroll al primier lesse ceo fuit auxi un surrender per mesme le reason.

[26]

A, fo. 21; *L* 139; *B*, p. 126; *D*, fo. 13, pl. 23 (7 Edw. VI).

Si abbe et son covent font un leas per indenture southe lour covent seale al J. S. pur terme de son vie sans ascun livery et puis per auter fait ils recytantes le primier indenture grauntont le revertion des terres lesse al J. D. pur xxi ans a commencer puis le morte J. S. ou [apres lexpiration],[1] forfyture ou determination de primer indenture [ou auterment][2] il fuit agree per le court que le primer lessee nad forsque estate al volunt. Uncore le meleux opinion fuit que J. D. avera bon estate pur xxi ans puis le mort de J. S. pur ceo que un act graunt ou fait ne serra prise pur void si poet per ascun meane estre prise pur bon. Mes semble al *Hales* Justice que le graunt al J. D. serra void entant que est [le][3] graunt dun revertion pur xxi ans quel ne poet estre bon sur un estate a volunt. Et fuit clerement agree que le recytall del primer leas ne fait ceo estre bon a toutes ententes ne fait ceo estre en meleux condition que fuit adevaunt quar le primer lessee est estranger al second fait yssint que il ne poet prender advantage de ceo. Et per le meleux opinion le recytall dun fait nest materiall ne nul conclusion.

[27]

Nota per *Hales* clerement que un acte que ad nul jour certein en luy lymitte quant il comensera naver relation al primer jour de parlament ne al jour de lassent le roy mes al primer jour del sessions de parlament et de cest parlament en quel fuit fait et a nul auter jour avera relation.

[1] *A, D, L.* per *H.*
[2] *A, D, L.* ore coment que *H.*
[3] de, *altered from* un.

25. IMPLIED SURRENDER OF A GREATER ESTATE

Common Pleas.

Note that it was agreed by HALES J. in the Common Bench that if a lessee for term of his life accepts from his lessor a lease for years, this is a surrender of his lease for life, even though the estate for life is greater in law. Similarly, if someone has an estate in land for twenty years, and accepts from his lessor an estate in the said leased land for ten years, or one year, this is clearly a surrender of the first years;[1] for it is all one whether he accepts a lesser estate than he had to begin with, or a greater. Note that. And if a lease for years is made by parol to the first lessee, this is also a surrender, for the same reason.

26. RECITAL IN A DEED

Common Pleas.

If an abbot and his convent make a lease, by indenture under their convent seal, to John Style for term of his life, without any livery, and then by another deed (reciting the first indenture) they grant the reversion of the lands so leased to John Dale for 21 years, to commence after the death of John Style, or after the expiry, forfeiture or determination of the first indenture, it was agreed by the court that the first lessee has only an estate at will: and yet the better opinion was that John Dale would have a good estate for 21 years after the death of John Style, because an act, grant or deed shall not be taken as void if by any means it can be taken as good. Nevertheless, it seemed to HALES J. that the grant to John Dale should be held void, since it is the grant of a reversion for 21 years, which cannot be good upon an estate at will. It was clearly agreed that the recital of the first lease does not make it good for all purposes, and does not cause it to be in a better condition than it was before; for the first lessee is a stranger to the second deed, and therefore cannot take advantage of it. And, by the better opinion, the recital of a deed is immaterial and is no conclusion.[2]

27. RELATION OF ACTS OF PARLIAMENT

Common Pleas or Serjeants' Inn.

Note, by HALES, clearly, that an act [of parliament] which has no certain day limited therein when it shall commence shall not relate back to the first day of the parliament, nor to the day of the king's assent, but to the first day of the session of the parliament in which it was made, and shall have relation to no other day.[3]

[1] *Whytney* v. *Gough* (1557) CP 40/1166, m. 140; Dyer, fo. 140.
[2] I.e. estoppel.
[3] See *Partridge* v. *Straunge* (1553), above, p. 11, pl. 1; below, p. 33, pl. 36; *OHLE*, vi. 75–76.

[28]

A, fo. 21 (foll. pl. 26); *L* 140 (sim.); *B*, p. 126.

Nota per *Hales* et *Portman* en Serjeantes Inn que si breife de precipe quod reddat vient al viscount et al jour del returne le viscount ne fist ascun returne de ceo breife, le tenant appiert gratis et pleda ovesque le demaundant et perde per verditt ou auterment, ore le tenant avera breife derrour pur non returne le breife car il est come nul breife ne nul breife est pendant devant que il soit returne per le viscount. Nota.

[29]

A, fo. 21v; *L* 144; *B*, p. 126.

[*fol. 10*] Nota que si le viscount returne en destres sur un venire facias que quant al parte des jurors il ad distreyne et al remnant il ad maunde al baylief de libertie al eux destreyne cest nul returne mes le viscount serra amercye mes en capias sur action de dett vers plusors si le vicount returne que il ad prise 2 et quant al 3 que il ad maund al baylief de libertie qui respondit etc. cest bon returne quod nota per *Hales*.

[30]

A, fo. 21v[f]; L 145[f]; *B*, p. 126 [f]; *D*, fo. 13, pl. 24 (7 Edw. VI).

Nota auxi per *Hales* clerement en Serjeantes Inne que si home fist leas pur ans s. 2 ans pur commenser al M[ichaelmas] rendant x li. rent durant le dit terme al feast de Peter ad Vincula al[ias] Lammas et Purification Beate Marie Virginis per egall portions ore pur le rent due le darreine jour apres le terme fynie s. al Candelmas le lessor navera action de dette ne nul remedy per le comen ley entant que le rent est reserve durant le terme yssint per les parolls del leas le rent doit estre due deins le terme et nemy apres le terme. Et issint serra [arect][1] le folly le lessor a faire tiel reservation: mes si le leas fuit en fourm avaundit pur 2 ans reservaunt x li. al feast[s] de Lammas et Candelmas generalment sans dire durant le terme en cest case le lessor avera action de dett pur le rent due le darrein jour apres le finye del terme entant que est generalment reserve et lessor poet auxibein reserver le rent apres le terme come deins le terme sil voet generalment. Nota.

[1] *L.* rette *A.* errect *D* (i.e. arrette). dit *H.*

28. ERROR IN NOT RETURNING WRIT

Serjeants' Inn.

Note, by Hales and Portman in Serjeants' Inn, that if a writ of *praecipe quod reddat* comes to the sheriff, and at the return-day the sheriff makes no return of this writ but the tenant appears gratis and pleads with the demandant, and loses by verdict or otherwise, the tenant shall have a writ of error for non-return of the writ: for [an unreturned writ] is as no writ, and no writ is pending until it has been returned by the sheriff. Note that.

29. SHERIFF'S RETURN

Contd from last.

Note that if the sheriff returns in a *distringas* upon a *venire facias* that, as to part of the jurors he has distrained, and as to the rest he has sent to the bailiff of a liberty to distrain them, this is no return, but the sheriff shall be amerced. On the other hand, in a *capias* upon an action of debt against several persons, if the sheriff returns that he has taken two, and as to the third that he has sent to the bailiff of a liberty, who has answered etc., this is a good return. Note that, by Hales.

30. INTERPRETATION OF LEASES

Serjeants' Inn.

Note also, by Hales, clearly, at Serjeants' Inn, that if someone makes a lease for years, namely two years to commence at Michaelmas, yielding £10 rent during the said term at the feasts of St Peter ad Vincula (otherwise Lammas) and the Purification of the Blessed Virgin Mary, in equal portions, the lessor shall not have an action of debt – nor any [other] remedy by the common law – for the rent due on the last day after the term ended, namely Candlemas,[1] inasmuch as the rent is reserved 'during the term', so that by the words of the lease the rent ought to be due within the term and not after the term. Thus it shall be reckoned the folly of the lessor to make such a reservation. If, however, the lease was made in the form aforesaid for two years, reserving £10 at the feasts of Lammas and Candlemas generally, without saying 'during the term', in that case the lessor would have an action of debt for the rent due on the last day after the end of the term, since it is reserved generally, and a lessor may as well reserve a rent after the term as within the term, if he does so in general terms. Note that.

[1] I.e. the feast of the Purification.

[31]

A, ff. 21v–22[f] *L* 146[f]; *B*, p. 127[f].

Nota auxi per *Hales* eodem tempore et loco que si le roy ou auter estranger fist leas pur ans reservant rent, corne, barbittes ou laynes[1] annuelment durant le terme, et puis le roy ou lestranger lessa le dit rent issint reserve al auter home pur ans pur rent en argent ore si les dittes rentes de corne barbites ou lanyes sont arrere et denye destre paies per le tenant que doit eux paier le lessee des dittes rentes nad ascun remedy a luy compeller de eux paier entant que it nad le revertion a que ils sont incidentes.

[32]

A, fo. 22[f]; *L* 147[f].

Nota que fuit agree clerement al Serjeantes Inne que si home en pledant dit que son pier fuit seisie des terrs et per protestation morust seisie apres quel mort il entra etc. cest pleder nest bon mes il doit dire que son pier fuit seisie et per protestation morust apres quel mort etc. et nemi per protestation morust seisie: quod nota.

[33]

A, fo. 17; L 88; *B*, p. 123; *D*, fo. 11, pl. 11.

Nota per totam curiam in Communi Banco en le case de John Wyburne en attaynt que si le jurye en attaint soit parte jure et parte nemy et yssint remayna et al auter jour un de eux que fuit primes jure est challenge, cestui que luy challenge ne monstra cause maintenant de puisne temps tanque le pannell soit peruse, donques il monstra assettes per temps.

[34]

A, fo. 17[f]; L 89[f]; *B*, p. 123[f]; *D*, fo. 11, pl. 10.

[*fol. 10v*] Et la fuit auxi agree per les justices que si home fist leas dun mannor pur ans exceptant le boys et suboys ore toutes ceux boys queux son conus per le nosme de boys et yssint uses et le soyle <de [south][2] ceux boyes>[3] sont except et horse de leas mes si ne soit boys ensemble [cressant][4] mes hedgegroves[5] la le soyle nest pas except ne le harbage en ceo quod nota.

[1] lambes *A, L.* lammes *B.*
[2] *D, L.*
[3] de ceux *A.*
[4] *A, D, L.*
[5] hedgrowes *A, L.*

31. LEASE OF RENT IN KIND

Serjeants' Inn.

Note also, by HALES at the same time and place, that if the king (or another stranger) makes a lease for years, reserving corn, sheep or wool as rent annually during the term, and then the king or the stranger leases the said rent so reserved to someone else for years, for a money rent, and the said rents of corn, sheep or wool are in arrear and refused to be paid by the tenant who ought to pay them, the lessee of the said rents has no remedy to compel him to pay them since he does not have the reversion to which they are incident.

32. PROTESTATION

Serjeants' Inn. Cf. *Vivion* v. *St Abyn* (1554) Dyer, fo. 107a.

Note that it was clearly agreed at Serjeants' Inn that if someone says in pleading that his father was seised of lands, and (by protestation) died seised, after whose death he entered etc., this pleading is not good; but he must say that his father was seised, and (by protestation) died, after whose death etc., and should not say by protestation that he died seised. Note that.

33. WYBURNE'S CASE

Common Pleas.

Note by the whole court in the Common Bench, in the case of John Wyburne in an attaint, that if the jury in attaint is part sworn and part not, and so they remain, and at another day one of those who was first sworn is challenged, the person who challenges him need not immediately show cause of more recent time, until the panel is used up, and then it will be time enough to do so.

34. INTERPRETATION OF LEASES; 'WOOD'

Common Pleas.

It was also agreed there by the justices that if someone makes a lease of a manor for years, excepting the wood and underwood, all the woods which are known by the name of 'wood' and so used, and the soil beneath those woods, are excepted and outside the lease. If, however, there is no wood growing together, but only hedgerows, there the soil is not excepted, nor the herbage therein. Note that.

[35]

A, fo. 17[f]; *L* 90[f].

Nota la auxi agree et per nully deny que en attaint le pl. ne donera nul evidence al graund jury forsque ceo que fuit done primerment en evidence al petit jury sinon que il soit tiel chose que repose toute en le notice del pays mes le deffendant en attaint et le petit jury poient porter en le court wittness[e]s et deponentes a enforcer lour primer verditt estre voyer auters que ceux que fueront primerment jures etc.

[36]

Abr. in *A*, fo. 17[f]; *L* 91[f].

Nota que la fuit auxi agree per curiam lou le parlament commensa le 16 jour de January et la contynua al primer jour de Aprill 33 H. 8. en quel fuit le court de surveyors establishe et ordeine coment ils ferront lour leases per warrantes al chauncellor de terre al value de vi li. xiii s. iiiid. et ouster ou de southe le dit value come per lact appeiert que si en Marche seiant le parlament et devant le fyne de ceo les surveiors font leas de southe lour seales come devant le dit acte ils usont de faire cest leas est void eo que lacte de parlament avera relation al primer jour del session de ceo si ne soit auterment expresse.

[37]

A, fo. 17[f]; *L* 92[f]; *B*, p. 123.

Nota per *Hales* et *Portman* al Serjeantes Inne que les justices de peace bein poient enquirer de murder ex malicia precogitata cybein come de manslaughter et arrayna cestui que est endite devant eux et luy pender ou acquiter per le comission de le peace et les justices de le goale deliverie poient issint arrayner home devant eux que est yssint endite de murder devant les dittes justices de peace, loppinion de Fitzher[bert] en son liver de Justice de Peace non obstante, et issint est lexperience et opinion des toutes les justices: quod nota.

35. EVIDENCE IN ATTAINT

Common Pleas. Cf. other decisions to the same effect: Dyer, fo. 129; *OHLE*, vi. 371 n. 178.

Note that it was also agreed there, and by no-one denied, that in attaint the plaintiff shall not give any evidence to the grand jury besides what was first given in evidence to the petty jury, unless it is something which reposes wholly in the notice of the country. But the defendant in attaint, and the petty jury, may bring witnesses and deponents[1] into court to enforce their first verdict as true, besides those who were sworn before etc.

36. RELATION OF ACTS OF PARLIAMENT

Common Pleas. This was a point in *Partridge* v. *Strange* (1553), above, p. 11, pl. 1; Plowd. 77 at fo. 84; above, p. 30, pl. 27; *OHLE*, vi. 75.

Note that it was also agreed by the court that, whereas a parliament began on 16 January and continued until 1 April [1542], 33 Hen. VIII, in which was established the Court of Surveyors,[2] and it was ordained how they should make their leases by warrant to the chancellor for land of the value of £6. 13*s.* 4*d.* and above, or below the said value, as appears from the act, if the Surveyors made a lease in March, while the parliament was sitting but before the end thereof, under their seals which they used before the said act, this lease is void[3] inasmuch as the act of parliament relates back to the first day of the session thereof unless it is otherwise expressed.

37. JURISDICTION TO TRY MURDER

Serjeants' Inn.

Note, by HALES and PORTMAN at Serjeants' Inn, that justices of the peace may well enquire of murder of malice aforethought, just as they may of manslaughter, and may arraign the person indicted before themselves and hang him, or acquit him, by reason of the commission of the peace. And the justices of gaol delivery may likewise arraign someone before themselves who has been thus indicted of murder before the said justices of the peace, notwithstanding the opinion of Fitzherbert (in his book on justices of the peace).[4] That is the experience, and the opinion of all the justices: note that.

[1] Probably meaning depositions.
[2] 33 Hen. VIII, c. 39.
[3] I.e. because they could only have used the new seal ordained by the statute of 1542, even though it was not then in fact in existence.
[4] A. Fitzherbert, *The Newe Boke of Justices of the Peas* (1538), fo. 13v.

[38]

A, fo. 17[f]; L 93[f]; *B*, p. 123[f]; *D*, fo. 11, pl. 12 (7 Edw. VI), garbled.

Nota per *Portman* et *Hales* que home poet estre accessory al un rape ou auter felony fait per un statute auxibein come al un felony fait al comen ley nient obstant que opinions ont estre al contrary entant que chescun estatute penall serra prise stricti juris accordant al parolls et nemy auterment. Et uncore entant que lestatute fait lact felony il ceo fist tiell felony come fuit al common ley al toutes ententes.

[39]

A, fo. 17[f]; *L* 94[f].

Nota per totam curiam in Communi Banco que si home fist leas pur vie [et le][1] lessee graunta son estate ouster al estranger que estranger levy un fyne sur conusans de droit come ceo que il ad de son done al auter en fee ovesque proclamation les cynque ans passont et puis le lessee pur vie devie et cestui en revercion entra deins lan apres son mort ore lentry de cestui en le revercion nest pas bon mes il per statute est barre entant que le title accrue al cestui en le revercion maintenant per le fyne et ceo fuit un forfayture de son estate pur vie quot nota.

[40]

A, fo. 17[f]; *L* 95[f]; *B*, p. 124.

[*fol. 11*] Nota per *Hales* Justice que les justices de gaole deliverie poient enditer un home un jour de felony, murder ou treson et mesme le jour luy arrayna de mesme loffence. Mes les justices de peace ne poient issint faire tout al un jour mes doient daver un jour meane al meyns per lordinance: quod nota.

[41]

A, fo. 15v; L 81; *D*, fo. 9, pl. 5 (7 Edw. VI).

Nota [que fuit agree][2] per *Portman* et *Hales* al Serjeantes Inne que si home per son volunt devisa terre a ses 2 files estre egalment devides enter eux et a lour heires a toutes jours et sils deviont devant lour age de xxi ans sans heires de lour corps engendres que la terre remaynera al auter estranger ou al devisor en fee ou serra vendus per ses executors ore les 2 files sont tenants en comen dun estate en fee simple et nemi en taile car ceux parolls et si etc. font estate en fee estre conditionall. Mes ils disoient que si home dona terre ou devisa al estranger

[1] *Conjectural.*

[2] *A, D, but not L.*

38. ACCESSORY TO STATUTORY FELONIES

Serjeants' Inn.

Note, by PORTMAN and HALES, that one may be accessory to a rape or other felony created by statute as well as to a felony at common law. Although there have been opinions to the contrary, on the grounds that every penal statute shall be construed strictly according to the words, and not otherwise, nevertheless when a statute makes an act felony, it makes it the same kind of felony as [a felony] at common law, for all purposes.

39. FINAL CONCORDS

Common Pleas.

Note, by the whole court in the Common Bench, that if someone makes a lease for life, and the lessee grants his estate over to a stranger, and the stranger levies a fine *sur conusance de droit come ceo que il ad de son done* to someone else in fee, with proclamations, and the five years pass, and then the lessee for life dies, and the reversioner enters within a year after his death, the entry of the reversioner is not good, but he is barred by statute,[1] since the title accrues to the reversioner immediately by the fine, and that was a forfeiture of his estate for life. Note that.

40. INDICTMENT AND TRIAL

Common Pleas or Serjeants' Inn. Cf. Yorke's notebook, 120 Selden Soc. 203, no. 301 (assembly of judges in 1531/33).

Note, by HALES J., that the justices of gaol delivery may indict someone on one day for felony, murder or treason, and arraign him on the same day for the same offence. Justices of the peace, however, may not do this all on one day, but there must be at least a day between, by the ordinance. Note that.

41. INTERPRETATION OF WILLS

Serjeants' Inn.

Note that it was agreed by PORTMAN and HALES at Serjeants' Inn that if someone by his will devises land to his two daughters, to be equally divided between them, and to their heirs for ever, and if they should die before their age of 21 years without heirs of their bodies begotten the land should remain to a stranger (or to the devisor) in fee, or should be sold by his executors, the two daughters are now tenants in common of an estate in fee simple and not in tail; for the words 'and if etc.' cause an estate in fee to be conditional. But they said that if someone

[1] 4 Hen. VII, c. 24.

a luy et a ses heires sur condition dun si contingat que [si][1] le donee ou devisee devie sans heires de son corps que la terre revertera al donour ou remaynera[2] al estranger en fee que ore le donee ou devisee ad estate taile et nemy en fee car cest condition est annex al estate en la terre et va ovesque la terre mes en la primer case le condition est annex al aige del person et nemi al terre et pur ceo les 2 files ont estate dun fee simple en comen per ceux parolls egallment devides ovesque le condition de lour mortes deins age sans heire de lour corps quod nota.

[42]

Abr. in *A*, fo. 15v–16^{f}; *L* 82^{f}; *B*, pp. 122–123.

Trns. fuit port per Thomam Benger vers Johannem Pert in custodia mariscalli pur prisel hors de son possession xx old ryalls, 60 demy soveraignes, 80 demy angells et 6 double duckettes et ne counta de valencia de eux etc. <car fuit agree per toutes>[3] que il ne besoign entant que argent et le valew de ceo est conus. Le deffendant dit que longe temps devant le trns. un John Kyrckhed[4] fuit possesse des dittes beins come ses beins propers et issint possesse fist son testament et fait ses executors George Ireland et M. son feme et le feme le dit John K. et puis le feme le dit testator prist al baron le dit Thomas Benger per reson de quel le [dit] Thomas et auters les executors fueront ent possesse et ils esteantes yssint possesse le dit John Piert prist les dittes beins en son possession et mains hors de lour possession et puis le dit George Ireland relessa per son fait al dit deffendant J. P. toutes trns. et actions personalls et demaunda judgement etc. et sur ceo ple en barr les pl. demurre pur deux causes. Lun pur ceo que cest ple ne gist pur argent pur ceo que ne poet estre conus. Et lauter pur ceo que en le barr il ne traversa sans ceo que il prist les beins ou argent le pl.

Et al primer exception *Portman* Justice dit que le barr fuit bon car money nest tiel chose mes que poet estre conus. Et pur [ceo] si home robbe auter de son argent et puis il sue appeall lappeallee poet gager battaile, lappellor dira que lappelle fuit prise ovesque le maynor ovesque largent, et ouster en appeale de robbery pur argent lappellee [*fol. 11v*] est trove culpable lappellor avera restitution de son argent. Et auxi il voucha un liver ou les executors portant trns. de

[1] *A, D, L.*
[2] returnera *A, L.* enurera *D.*
[3] tenus que *A, B, L.*
[4] Doubtless misreading Byrkned: record.

gives or devises land to a stranger, unto him and his heirs, on condition (with a 'si contingat') that if the donee or devisee should die without heirs of his body the land should revert to the donor, or remain to a stranger in fee, the donee or devisee here has an estate tail and not in fee; for this condition is annexed to the estate in the land and goes with the land, whereas in the first case the condition is annexed to the age of the person and not the land. Therefore the two daughters have an estate of fee simple in common (by virtue of these words 'equally divided'), with the condition of their deaths under age without heirs of their bodies. Note that.

42. BENGER v. PERT

King's Bench. Record: KB 27/1162, m. 89 (demurrer, Pas. 1552, c.a.v. to Hil. 1553); printed below. Cf. KB 27/1161, m. 60 (beginning of the declaration in trespass), m. 89 (debt on a bond as administrator of Margaret Benger, alias Bryckett, widow of John Bryckett esq.; *non potest dedicere*); KB 27/1162, m. 134 (demurrer to bill of assumpsit).

Trespass was brought by Thomas Benger[1] against John Pert,[2] in the custody of the marshal, for taking out of his possession 20 old ryals, 60 half sovereigns, 80 half angels and six double ducats, and he did not count of the value thereof etc., for it was agreed by all that he need not do so since it is money and its value is known. The defendant said that long before the trespass one John [Byrknede] was possessed of the said goods, as his own goods, and (being so possessed) made his testament and appointed as his executors George Ireland and his wife [Elizabeth], and the wife of the said John Byrknede, and then the said testator's wife [Margaret] married the said Thomas Benger, by reason whereof the said Thomas and the other executors were possessed thereof, and (they being so possessed) the said John Pert took the said goods into his possession and hands out of their possession, and then the said George Ireland released by his deed to the defendant John Pert all trespasses and personal actions, and he demanded judgment etc.; and upon this plea in bar the plaintiff demurred for two reasons. One was because the plea does not lie for money, because it cannot be known; and the other was because he does not in the bar traverse 'without this, that he took the goods or money of the plaintiff'.

As to the first exception, PORTMAN J. said that the bar was good, for money is not something which cannot be known. For instance, if a man robs another of his money and then he sues an appeal, the appellee may wage battle, and the appellor shall say that the appellee was taken with the mainour, [namely] with the money; and moreover in an appeal of robbery for money, if the appellee is found guilty the appellor shall have restitution of his money. He also vouched a book where executors brought trespass for goods carried away in the testator's

[1] For whom see below, p. 132. Sir Thomas Benger is not known to have married a widow called Birkenhead: see *HPHC 1558–1603*, i. 427.

[2] Perhaps the auditor and receiver of the Augmentations, who served as M.P. in 1547: *HPHC 1509–58*, ii. 88 (which says he died 1549/51).

bonis asportatis in vita etc. et declaront parte dargent et parte dauters beins et adjuge bon. Et al auter exception il dit que ne besoigne ascun traverse entant que est forsque un supposell et le coulor a ceo respondit.

Bromeley Justice a mesme le entent et il semble que al ascun respect money ne poet estre conus uncore al parties et priveis al tort il bein poet estre conus. Et un replegaire ne gist pur argent ou money et cest pur ceo que le viscount que est estranger [ne][1] doit faire deliveraunce de ceo ne ou il est car poet estre en chest locke et il ne poet ceo debruser et ascuns disoent que breife de detynue ne gist de argent entant que il ne poet aver mesme le chose deliver arere mes semble que breife de detynue sur un baylement gist assettes bein entant que il est enter parties et privies. Et le deffendant serra distreine tanque que il ad fait deliveraunce del chose car il gist en son notyce assettes bein. Et home avera appeale de robbery dargent et si lauter soit trove culpable il serra restore a son argent arere quel prova que il poet bein estre conus. Et si home deliver argent al J. S. pur deliver ouster al estranger lestranger avera accompt pur cest money et recovera mesme largent. Yssint ycie, cest argent poet bein estre conus et prise pur mesme largent que le pl. luy complayna. Et al auter exception il dit que ne besoigne ascun travers entant que nest forsque supposell come en replegiare le deffendant poet bien pleder done per un estranger sans travers. Et en assise le pl. dit que le deffendant luy disseisa le deffendant pleda que un stranger fuit ent seisie et luy enfeoffe et done coulor ore il ne prendra traverse que il ne disseisa le pl. car il nest forsque supposell. Et en assise de mordauncester le tenant dit que launcester le pl. et le tenant fueront joyntenants en fee et que apres le morte launcestor il entra per survivor cest bon sans traverser le mor[ant] seisie launcestor le pl. Et 11 H. 8. replegiare pur un nief ovesque son tackell le deffendant dit que le pl. et un estranger fueront joyntment possesse et lestranger done toute ceo que a luy [appent][2] al deffendant per que il occupie en comen ovesque le pl. apres le morte lestranger et en son vie et ceo fuit bon sans traverse quil est le nief le pl. tantum. Auxi un barre bon al common entent est bon mes declaration et title doit toutes foites estre en certeine.

Mervin Justice fuit al contrary opinion et denya le case dassise de mordauncestor car il dit que traverse doit estre prise sur le morant seisie del pier le pl.

Chomley Cheif Justice[3] dit que le ple ne serra bon sans traverse car il dit que ne fuit mere supposell et il ne responde a luy mes per un argument. Et al auter point il dit que le ple est bon entant que le pl. ne recovera nul money come en

[1] *Reads* le.
[2] *Reads* appiert.
[3] Baron *A.*

lifetime etc. and declared partly for money and partly for other goods, and it was adjudged good.[1] As to the other exception, he said that there was no need for any traverse since it is only a supposal and the colour answers it.

BROMLEY J. to the same effect. And it seemed to him that although in some respects money cannot be known, nevertheless to the parties and privies to the wrong it may well be known. A replevin does not lie for silver or money, and that is because the sheriff (who is a stranger) is not bound to make deliverance of it and may not have access to it, for it might be in a locked chest and he may not break into it. Some say that a writ of detinue does not lie for money, since he cannot have the same thing delivered again; but it seems that a writ of detinue lies well enough on a bailment [of money], since it is between parties and privies, and the defendant shall be distrained until he has made deliverance of the thing, for it lies in his notice well enough. One may have an appeal of robbery for money, and if the other is found guilty he shall be restored to his money again: which proves that it may well be known. If someone delivers money to John Style to deliver over to a stranger, the stranger shall have account for this money and shall recover the money itself. Likewise here, this money may well be known and taken for the same money of which the plaintiff complains against him. As to the other exception, he said there was no need for any traverse, since it is only a supposal: as in replevin, the defendant may well plead a gift by a stranger without a traverse. And in an assize the plaintiff says that the defendant disseised him, and the defendant pleads that a stranger was seised thereof and enfeoffed him, and gives colour; the defendant shall not traverse 'that he did not disseise the plaintiff', for that is only a supposal. And in an assize of mort d'ancestor the tenant may say that the plaintiff's ancestor and the tenant were joint tenants in fee, and that after the ancestor's death he entered by survivorship, and this is good without traversing the dying seised of the plaintiff's ancestor. In 11 Hen. VIII,[2] in replevin for a boat with its tackle, the defendant said that the plaintiff and a stranger were jointly possessed and the stranger gave all that belonged to him to the defendant, as a result of which he occupied in common with the plaintiff after the stranger's death and in his lifetime; and this is good without traversing that it is the ship of the plaintiff alone. Moreover, a bar which is good to a common intent is good, whereas a declaration and title ought always to be certain.

MERVIN J. was of the contrary opinion, and denied the case of the assize of mort d'ancestor, for he said that a traverse ought to be taken upon the dying seised of the plaintiff's father.

CHOLMLEY C.J.[3] said that the plea shall not be good without a traverse, for he said that it was not mere supposal and he does not answer him save by an argument. As to the other point, he said that the plea is good, since the plaintiff is

[1] The reference may be to YB Mich. 11 Hen. IV, fo. 3, pl. 8, where executors brought trespass (on the statute 4 Edw. III, c. 7) for money taken in the testator's lifetime, and for breaking the testator's close, though there is no reference to goods.

[2] Not traced; it cannot refer to a printed report.

[3] *A* says Chief Baron, a position he had held until becoming C.J.K.B. on 21 May 1552.

replegiare [*fol. 12*] et detinue mes damages tantum et mesme le reson que le pl. avera action de trns. pur son money pur mesme le reson de deffendant pledera son justification en barre car si le ley dona al home un chose il dona auxi a luy libertie a pleder mesme le chose come la ley ceo a luy dona: quod nota.

Record of the case

KB 27/1162, m. 89.

Hertf'. Memorandum quod alias, scilicet termino Sancti Hillarii ultimo preterito coram domino rege apud Westmonasterium, venit Thomas Benger armiger per Ricardum Heywood attornatum suum. Et protulit hic in curia domini regis tunc ibidem quendam billam suam versus Johannem Pert in custodia marrescalli etc. de placito transgressionis. Et sunt plegii de prosequendo, scilicet Johannes Doo et Ricardus Roo. Quequidem billa sequitur in hec verba:

Hertf'. Thomas Benger armiger queritur de Johanne Pert in custodia marrescalli marescalcie domini regis coram ipso rege existentis de eo quod vicesimo die Julii anno regni domini regis nunc Edwardi sexti quinto vi et armis etc. viginti pecias auri vocatas old ryalles, sexaginta pecias auri vocatas half soveraignes, octoginta pecias auri vocatas halfe angelles, sexaginta coronas aureas, octo angelos aureos, et sex pecias auri vocatas dubble duckettes, ipsius Thome apud Berkhampsted in comitatu predicto inventos cepit et asportavit, et alia enormia ei intulit, ad dampnum ipsius Thome ducentarum mercarum et contra pacem dicti domini regis. Et inde producit sectam etc.

Et modo ad hunc diem, scilicet diem Mercurii proxime post quindenam Pasche isto eodem termino, usque quem diem predictus Johannes habuit licenciam ad billam predictam interloquendi et tunc ad respondendum, coram domino rege apud Westmonasterium veniunt tam predictus Thomas per attornatum suum predictum quam predictus Johannes per Franciscum Sandbache attornatum suum. Et idem Johannes defendit vim et injuriam quando etc. Et dicit quod predictus Thomas actionem suam predictam inde versus eum manutenere non debet quia, protestando quod narratio predicta ac materia in eadem contenta minus sufficiens in lege existit ad quas[1] necesse non habet nec per legem terre tenetur respondere, pro placito tamen dicit quod diu ante tempus transgressionis predicte fieri supposite quidam Johannes Byrknede apud Croxton in comitatu Cestrie fuit possessionatus de predictis viginti peciis auri vocatis old ryalles, sexaginta peciis auri vocatis half soveraignes, octoginta peciis auri vocatis halfe angelles, sexaginta coronis aureis, octo angelis aureis, et de predictis sex peciis auri vocatis dubble duckettes in narratione predicta specificatis ut de bonis suis propriis, et sic inde possessionatus idem Johannes Byrkned quarto die Julii anno regni domini regis nunc quarto[i] apud Croxton in comitatu predicto condidit testamentum suum et per idem testamentum constituit quosdam Georgium Irelond et Elizabeth uxorem suam et Margaretam uxorem predicti Johannis Byrkned executores suas[2] et obiit apud civitatem Cestrie, post cujus mortem predicte viginti pecie auri vocate old ryalles, sexaginta pecie auri vocate half soveraignes, octoginta pecie [auri] vocate halfe angelles, sexaginta corone auri, octo angeli[3] auri, et sex pecie auri vocate dubble duckettes apud Croxton predictam devenerunt ad manus et possessionem predictorum

[1] *Sic, though* sufficiens . . . existit *are in the singular.*
[2] Sic, evidently ignoring George.
[3] angelis.

not to recover any money, as in replevin and detinue, but only damages. And for the same reason that the plaintiff shall have an action of trespass for his money, so for that reason shall the defendant plead his justification in bar; for if the law gives someone a thing it also gives him liberty to plead the same thing in the way that the law gave it to him. Note that.

Translation of the record

King's Bench, Pas. 1552.

Hertfordshire. Remember that heretofore, namely in Hilary term last past, Thomas Benger esquire came before the lord king at Westminster by Richard Heywood his attorney. And he proffered here in the court of the lord king, then being there, a certain bill of his against John Pert in the custody of the marshal etc. in a plea of trespass. And there are pledges for prosecuting, namely John Doo and Richard Roo. Which bill follows in these words:

Hertfordshire. Thomas Benger, esquire, complains of John Pert, in the custody of the marshal of the lord king's marshalsea before the selfsame king, for this, that on the twentieth day of July [1551] in the fifth year of the reign of the present King Edward VI, with force and arms etc. took and carried away 20 pieces of gold called old ryals, 60 pieces of gold called half sovereigns, 80 pieces of gold called half angels, 60 golden crowns, 80 golden angels, and six pieces of gold called double ducats, belonging to him the said Thomas, found at Berkhamstead in the county aforesaid, and inflicted other outrages upon him, to the damage of him the said Thomas 200 marks, and against the peace of the said lord king. And thereof he produces suit etc.

Now at this day, namely the Wednesday [4 May 1552] next after the quindene of Easter this same term, until which day the aforesaid John had leave to imparl to the aforesaid bill and then to answer, both the aforesaid Thomas by his attorney aforesaid and the aforesaid John by Francis Sandbache[1] his attorney come before the king at Westminster. And the same John denies the force and wrong when etc. And he says that the aforesaid Thomas ought not to have his aforesaid action against him therefor, because, protesting that the aforesaid count and the matter contained in the same are insufficient in law, to which he has no need and is not bound by the law of the land to answer, he nevertheless says by way of plea that, long before the time when the aforesaid trespass is supposed to have been done, a certain John Byrknede[2] at Croxton in the county of Chester was possessed of the aforesaid 20 pieces of gold called old ryals, 60 pieces of gold called half sovereigns, 80 pieces of gold called half angels, 60 golden crowns, 80 golden angels, and of the aforesaid six pieces of gold called double ducats specified in the aforesaid count, as of his own goods, and (being so possessed) the same John Byrkned on the fourth day of July [1550] in the fourth year of the reign of the present lord king at Croxton in the county aforesaid made his testament and by the same testament appointed a certain George Irelond and Elizabeth his wife and Margaret, wife of the aforesaid John Byrkned, his executors, and died at the city of Chester; after whose death the aforesaid 20 pieces of gold called old ryals, 60 pieces of gold called half sovereigns, 80 pieces of gold called half angels, 60 golden crowns, 80 golden angels, and six pieces of gold called double ducats at Croxton aforesaid came to the

1 Secondary of the King's Bench. The surviving remembrance rolls of this office begin in 1552: KB 167/1.

2 Clerk of the crown and prothonotary of the Common Pleas in the county palatine of Lancaster, second justice of Lancaster, and recorder of Chester. According to his grant of arms, he was of Crowton (not Croxton): BL MS. Harley 5846, fo. 11v (Byrkhned). In KB 27/1161, m. 89, the name is spelt Bryckett; but it is a form of Birkenhead.

Georgii, Elizabeth et Margarete, virtute cujus ipsi iidem Georgii, Elizabeth et Margareta fuerunt inde possessionati, et sic inde possessionati existentes predicta Margareta apud Berkhamsted in comitatu Hertf' cepit in virum predictum Thomam, pretextu cujus iidem Thomas et Margareta, Georgius et Elizabeth fuerunt de predictis viginti peciis auri vocatis old ryalles, sexaginta peciis auri vocatis half soveraignes, octoginta peciis auri vocatis halfe angelles, sexaginta coronis auri, octo angelis auri, et sex peciis auri vocatis duble duckettes possessionati, et sic inde possessionati existentes idem Johannes Pert cepit predictas viginti pecias auri vocatas old ryalles, sexaginta pecias auri vocatas half soveraignes, octoginta pecias auri vocatas halfe angelles, sexaginta coronas auri, octo angelos auri, et sex pecias auri vocatas duble duckettes, et postea scilicet vicesimo die Januarii anno regni domini regis nunc quinto apud Chyldwall in comitatu Lancastrie idem Georgius per scriptum suum sigillo ipsius Georgii sigillatum, hic in curia prolatum, relaxavit prefato Johanni Perte omnes transgressiones et actiones personales quas predictus Georgius aliquo modo sive ratione habuit versus predictum Johannem. Que omnia et singula idem Johannes paratus est verificare. Unde petit judicium si predictus Thomas Benger actionem suam predictam versus eum habere seu manutenere debeat etc.

Et predictus Thomas Benger dicit quod ipse per aliqua per predictum Johannem Pert superius placitando allegata ab actione sua predicta versus ipsum Johannem habenda precludi non debet, quia dicit quod placitum predictum modo et forma predictis superius placitatum minus sufficiens in lege existit, ad quod idem Thomas necesse non habet nec per legem terre tenetur aliquo modo respondere. Unde pro defectu sufficientis responsionis in hac parte idem Thomas petit judicium et dampna sua predicta occasione transgressionis predicte sibi adjudicari etc.

Et predictus Johannes Perte dicit quod placitum predictum modo et forma predictis superius placitatum bonum et sufficiens in lege existit ad predictum Thomam ab actione sua predicta versus ipsum Johannem habenda precludendum, quod quidem placitum materiamque in eodem contentam idem Johannes paratus est verificare, ad quod predictus Thomas hucusque non respondit nec illud aliqualiter dedicit. Ideo petit judicium et quod predictus Thomas ab actione sua predicta versus ipsum Johannem habenda precludatur etc.

Et quia curia domini regis hic de judicio suo de et super premissis reddendo non dum advisatur, dies inde datus est partibus predictis coram domino rege apud Westmonasterium usque diem Veneris proxime post crastinum Sancte Trinitatis de judicio suo de et super premissis audiendo etc. eo[i] quod curia domini regis hic inde non dum etc. Ad quem diem hic coram domino rege apud Westmonasterium veniunt partes predicte per attornatos suos predictos. Et quia curia domini regis hic de judicio suo de et super premissis reddendo non dum advisatur, dies inde datus est partibus predictis coram domino rege apud Westmonasterium usque diem Lune proxime post octabas Sancti Michaelis de judicio suo de et super premissis audiendo etc. eo quod curia domini regis hic inde non dum etc. Ad quem diem hic coram domino rege apud Westmonasterium veniunt partes predicte per attornatos suos predictos. Et quia curia domini regis hic de judicio suo de et super premissis reddendo non dum advisatur, dies inde datus est partibus predictis coram domino rege apud Westmonasterium usque diem Lune proxime post octabas Sancti Hillarii de judicio suo de et super premissis audiendo etc. eo quod curia domini regis hic inde non dum etc.

[*See opposite*]

hands and possession of the aforesaid George, Elizabeth and Margaret, by virtue whereof the same George, Elizabeth and Margaret were thereof possessed, and while they were so possessed thereof the aforesaid Margaret at Berkhamstead in the county of Hertford married the aforesaid Thomas, by reason whereof the same Thomas and Margaret, George and Elizabeth were possessed of the aforesaid 20 pieces of gold called old ryals, 60 pieces of gold called half sovereigns, 80 pieces of gold called half angels, 60 golden crowns, 80 golden angels, and six pieces of gold called double ducats, and while they were so possessed the same John Pert took the aforesaid 20 pieces of gold called old ryals, 60 pieces of gold called half sovereigns, 80 pieces of gold called half angels, 60 golden crowns, 80 golden angels, and six pieces of gold called double ducats; and afterwards, namely on the twentieth day of January [1552] in the fifth year of the reign of the present lord king, at Childwall in the county of Lancaster, the same George by his writing sealed with the seal of the selfsame George, put forward here in court, released to the said John Pert all trespasses and personal actions which the aforesaid George in any way or for any reason had against the aforesaid John. All and singular which things the same John is ready to aver. Wherefore he prays judgment whether the aforesaid Thomas Benger ought to have or maintain his aforesaid action against him etc.

And the aforesaid Thomas Benger says that he ought not to be barred by anything above alleged in pleading by the aforesaid John Pert from having his aforesaid action against the selfsame John, because he says that the aforesaid plea above pleaded in manner and form aforesaid is insufficient in law, to which the same Thomas has no need and is not bound by the law of the land in any way to answer. Wherefore, for want of a sufficient answer in that behalf, the same Thomas prays judgment and his aforesaid damages by reason of the aforesaid trespass to be awarded to him etc.

And the aforesaid John Pert says that the aforesaid plea above pleaded in manner and form aforesaid is good and sufficient in law to bar the aforesaid Thomas from having his aforesaid action against him the said John: which plea, and the matter contained in the same, the same John is ready to aver, and the aforesaid Thomas has not yet answered or in any way denied it. Therefore he prays judgment, and that the aforesaid Thomas be barred from having his aforesaid action against him the said John etc.

And because the lord king's court here is not yet advised of its judgment to be given upon and concerning the foregoing, a day is given therein to the parties aforesaid before the lord king at Westminster until the Friday next after the morrow of the Holy Trinity for hearing their judgment upon and concerning the foregoing, forasmuch as the lord king's court here is not yet etc. At which day the parties aforesaid come here before the lord king at Westminster by their aforesaid attorneys. And because the lord king's court here is not yet advised of its judgment to be given upon and concerning the foregoing, a day is given therein to the parties aforesaid before the lord king at Westminster until the Monday next after the octaves of Michaelmas for hearing their judgment upon and concerning the foregoing, forasmuch as the lord king's court here is not yet etc. At which day the parties aforesaid come here before the lord king at Westminster by their aforesaid attorneys. And because the lord king's court here is not yet advised of its judgment to be given upon and concerning the foregoing, a day is given therein to the parties aforesaid before the lord king at Westminster until the Monday [23 Jan. 1553] next after the octaves of Hilary for hearing their judgment upon and concerning the foregoing, forasmuch as the lord king's court here is not yet etc.

[*No judgment is entered*]

[43]

Abr. in *A*, fo. 16[f]; *L* 83[f]; *B*, p. 123;[f] *D*, fo. 9, pl. 6 (7 Edw. VI).

Nota per *Gasnold* de Graies Inne, sollicitor le roy, per son report a *Carrell*, attorney le roy de son duchie de Lancaster, al request del dit atturney, que loppinion des justices fuit en le case de duke de Norf. quant il fuit son sollicitor que quant devant le duke de Lancastar dona al abbe et ses successors en frankealmoigne un mannor ove les appurt[en]aunces rendant al dit duke et ses heires xx li. annuelment et puis le dissolution del meason le Roy H. 8. dona le dit meason et toutes les possessions al dit duke de Norff. et a ses heires rendant al dit roy et ses heires et successors en son Court de Augmentations les dittes xx li. et puis le chancellor de la duchie demaund a son court les dittes xx li. come parcell del duchye et que le roy ne poet doner ceo sinon southe le seale del duchye et que ne fuit extinct entant que le roy nad ceo rent forsque come duke et en droit son duchie mes pur ceo que il dit que le roy come un comen[1] person ad le rent et le possession del terre en ses maynes tout al un temps il fuit agree per les justices que le graunt et reservation fuit bon [a] le court avaundit et que le duke fuit discharge en le duchie vers le roy: quod nota per son report al Serjeantes Inne gate in Fletestreet, London.

[44]

A, fo. 16[f]; *L* 84[f]; *B*, p. 123[f].

Nota per *Hales* est felony per common ley auxibein lembler des pissons[2] en un severall ponde esteant come en un trunke et auxibein come de jeunes pygeons esteant en le dovehouse en lour nides entant que tiels pissons sont estemes et acceptes ovesque toutes homes et sont profitables et poient estre prises al volunt des parties en lour poundes. Et nest semble al un stoune come dyamound ou tiel queux pur ceo que ils [ne][3] sont estimes en prise ovesque toutes gentes lembler de eux ne fuit felony al commen ley mes pissons sont come auters comen choses: quod nota. Et vowcha 18 E. 4. pur cest matter.

[1] mesme *A, B, D, L.*
[2] pisces *A.* pishes *B.* poisons *L.*
[3] *A, B, L.*

43. DUKE OF NORFOLK'S CASE

At Serjeants' Inn gate, Fleet Street.

Note, by *Gosnold* of Gray's Inn,[1] the king's solicitor-general, by his report to *Caryll*,[2] the king's attorney of his duchy of Lancaster, at the request of the said attorney, that the opinion of the justices in the duke of Norfolk's case, when he was the duke's solicitor, was that, whereas the duke of Lancaster in earlier times gave a manor with the appurtenances to an abbot and his successors in frankalmoin, yielding to the said duke and his heirs £20 annually, and after the dissolution of the house King Henry VIII gave the said house and all the possessions to the said duke of Norfolk and his heirs, yielding to the said king and his heirs and successors the said £20 in his Court of Augmentations; and then the chancellor of the duchy demanded the said £20 in his court, as parcel of the duchy, the king could not give it away except under the seal of the duchy, and that it was not extinct, since the king only had this rent as duke and in right of his duchy; but because he said that the king has the rent and the possession of the land in his hands all at one time, like a common person, it was agreed by the justices that the grant and reservation were good at the court aforesaid, and that the duke was discharged in the duchy as against the king. Note that: by his report at Serjeants' Inn gate in Fleet Street, London.

44. LARCENY OF FISH, BIRDS AND DIAMONDS

Probably in Serjeants' Inn. Cf. 94 Selden Soc. *317–318*, *322*; *OHLE*, vi. 33, 565.

Note, by HALES, it is felony at common law to steal the fish in a several pond as well as in a trunk, or young pigeons while in the dovehouse in their nests, since such fish are esteemed [of value] and accepted amongst all men and are profitable, and may be taken at the will of the parties in their ponds. It is not like a stone, such as a diamond or the like, for however much they are esteemed in price amongst all men, the stealing of them was not felony at common law. But fish are like other common things. Note that. And he vouched 18 Edw. IV,[3] for this matter.

1 Of Shrubland, Suffolk; bencher of Gray's Inn; solicitor-general 1552–53; died 1554: *HPHC 1509–58*, ii. 237–238.

2 Of Warnham, Sussex, son of Mr Serjeant Caryll; bencher of the Inner Temple; attorney of the duchy 1544–66; died 1566: *HPHC 1509–58*, i. 390; R. Somerville, *The Duchy of Lancaster* (1963), pp. 408, 458.

3 Perhaps YB Pas. 8 Edw. IV, fo. 5, pl. 16 (wild animals not valued); or Mich. 18 Hen. VIII, fo. 2, pl. 11 (peacocks in same category as domestic fowl). There is no reference to diamonds or precious stones in the year-book cases. In the 1526 case it was argued, unsuccessfuly, that peacocks were 'birds more for pleasure than for profit'.

[45]

A, ff. 16v–17[f]; *L* 85 [f]; *D*, ff. 9–10, pl. 7 (7 Edw. VI).

John [Bridges][1] chivaler port action sur le case verse <John Warnfard>[2] en Banco Regis pur ceo que le deffendant avoit overtment dit et publishe al gentes de pays that at Perton[3] ther is a great nest of theves and Sir John Burghe is a mainteyner[4] of them and he is a stronge theife him self [*fol. 12v*] et counta que il fuit damnifie (come il devoit) al damnum 350 li. Le deffendant dit que il parle auters parolls et monstra queux absque hoc que il parle ceux parolls etc. et sur ceo fueront al yssue et lenquest trove que le deffendant parla toutes les parolls avandittes forsque cest paroll (stronge) et assessa damages al 350 li. et costs al xx. markes et trova ouster que le deffendant ne parla cest paroll strong in manner et forme etc. Et ore si cest verdit soit trove [vers] le pl. ou pur le pl. ou si soit void ceo fuit debate.

Et pur le pl. fuit dit que le verdit est bon car cest paroll (stronge) nest materiall ne le substaunce del matter mes est come un adjective et nient auterment et le substance des les parolls queux ont le force est trove que le pl. est mayntenor de theves et cest un cause de action et que il est un laron et cest auxi cause daction. Et fuit dit que cest action est en nature dun trns. de close debruse, herbes pues et boys coupe et pur beins prises, si le defendant plede rien culpable et il est [trove][5] culpable de parte et de parte acquite le pl. avera son judgement pur ceo que est trove. Et per mesme le reson serra ycie coment que ils ont trove que il ne parle cest paroll (stronge) uncore pur le residue le pl. avera son judgement.

Et al contrary en arrest de judgement fuit dit que le verdit ne voile serve le pl. pur deux causes. Lun pur ceo que le jury ne poet doner lour verdit a large, car per lestatute W. 2. ca. 30. in fyne appiert que les justices al comen ley ne poient prender verdit en assise a large mes precisement come lissue fuit. Et per cest statute ore ils poient et per equity del dit statute en toutes cases lou lissue est joyne sur point del breife come appiert 15 H. 7. t[itulo] Verditt 44. et 22. H. 6, [Judgement][6] 30. Mes si lissue fuit joyne hors del point del breife sur collaterall matter come en assise de un feoffment sur un disceite ou sur un releas le jury ne donera verditt a large ne les justices ceo receiveront. Et en dett sur un

[1] *A, D, L.* Burgh *H.*
[2] Henrie Vavasor *A, L.*
[3] Rippon *A, D, L.*
[4] Master *D.* M[r] *L.* maynte[ner] *over a correction in A.*
[5] *A, D, L.*
[6] *A, D, L.* verditt *H.*

45. BRYDGES v. WARNFORD

King's Bench. Also reported in Dyer, fo. 75, sub. nom. *Brugis* v. *Warenford* (Mich. 1552). Record: KB 27/1160, m. 172 (postea, Mich. 1552; c.a.v.; judgment, Pas. 1553); printed below.

John Brydges, knight,[1] brought an action on the case against John Warnford[2] in the King's Bench because the defendant had openly said and published to the local people that 'at Purton there is a great nest of thieves, and Sir John Brydges is a maintainer of them, and he is a strong thief himself' and counted (as he ought) that he was damaged to the extent of £350. The defendant said that he spoke other words, and set them out, 'without this, that he spoke those words etc.', and thereupon they were at issue, and the inquest found that the defendant spoke all the words aforesaid except the word 'strong', and assessed damages at £350 and costs at 20 marks, and found further that the defendant did not speak this word 'strong' in manner and form etc. It was now debated whether this verdict was found against the plaintiff, or for the plaintiff, or was void.

For the plaintiff it was said that the verdict is good, for the word 'strong' is not material and is not the substance of the matter, but is like an adjective and not otherwise; and the substance of the words, which have the force, has been found, [namely] that the plaintiff is a maintainer of thieves, and that is a cause of action, and that he is a thief, and that also is a cause of action. It was said that this action is in the nature of an action of trespass for breaking a close, trampling grass and cutting wood, and taking goods, if the defendant pleads not guilty and is found guilty of part and acquitted of part, the plaintiff shall have his judgment for that which is found [for him]. For the same reason it shall be so here; even though they have found that he did not speak the word 'strong', the plaintiff shall nevertheless have his judgment for the rest.

In arrest of judgment, it was said to the contrary that the verdict would not serve the plaintiff, for two reasons. One was because the jury may not give their verdict at large, for by the Statute of Westminster II, c. 30, at the end, it appears that the justices at common law could not take a verdict at large in an assize but only precisely as the issue was. They may do so now, by the statute, and by equity of the said statute in all cases where the issue is joined upon a point of the writ: as appears in Trin. 15 Hen. VII, 'Verdict', 44, and 22 Hen. VI, 'Judgement', 30.[3] But if the issue was joined outside the point of writ, upon collateral matter, as in an assize concerning a feoffment upon a deceit, or upon a release, the jury shall

[1] Of the Middle Temple (sued 1552) and Coberley, Glos.; knighted 1513; created Lord Chandos of Sudeley 1554; died 1558 (*HPHC 1509–1558*, i. 533–4; *ODNB*).

[2] Of the Inner Temple and Sevenhampton, Wilts. (heads visitation pedigree in 64 Harleian Soc. 191); attorney of the Common Pleas by 1535; appealed of murder in Wilts. 1541 (Dyer, fo. 50). In *A*, the name is unaccountably altered to Henry Vavasour. A Henry Vavasour, ninth son of Sir Peter Vavasour, was admitted to the Middle Temple in 1554. He was probably a Yorkshireman and father of Sir Thomas Vavasour M.P. The place-name is also altered, to Ripon (Yorks.).

[3] 15 Hen. VII, Fitz. Abr., *Verdict*, pl. 44 (identified in the margin as YB Mich. 9 Hen. VII, fo. 13, pl. 8); *Judgement*, pl. 30 (YB Mich. 22 Hen. VI, fo. 33, pl. 50).

obligation le defendant plede que il ne fuit [literate][1] et que fuit lye a luy en lewe dacquittance et yssint nient son fait et sur ceo al yssue et le jury trove que le defendant bein cognovit que il fuit son fait et que bein fuit [lie][2] a luy et ceo fuit nul verditt pur ceo que a lardge et le jury la fuit compell adire precisement sil fuit son fait ou nemi. 3 H. 6, Verditt 3.[3] Et issint ycie. Et pur auter cause entant que cest action vary del auters actions car est foundue sur le case et matter et le matter[4] est entier. Et pur ceo que tout ne soit trove est trove vers le pl. come en case home port tiel action pur appeller luy villaine regardaunt a son mannor de D. le defendant dit rien culpable et le jury trove [*fol. 13*] que le defendant luy appell villayne mes nemi regardant cest trove encounter le pl. Mes si action fuit pur luy appeller vyllen generallment et le jury trove que le defendant luy appell villaine regardant cest trove pur le pl. car le surplusage est void. En dett sur contract de 2 chivalls le defendant plede luy rien doit et ils trove que le contract fuit pur 3 chivalls ou pur un chivall ceo nest trove pur le pl. Yssint si le jury trove que le deffendant et un estranger fesoient le contract. En action pur appeller le pl. faux laron le jury trove que il luy appell laron mes nemy faux ore le pl. navera judgement. Veies bons causes titulo Verditt 47 E. 3. 20 et 11 E. 3. 26. Et quant a ceux parolls que le pl. est mayntener des larons ne font ascun cause daction car home poet bein mainteigner et herbeger larons que a luy ne sont conus come larons etc.

Et postea eodem termino judgement fuit done per bone advisement pur le pl. sur le dit verditt. Et le case de villenage regardant devant mise fuit denye per *Portman* Justice: quod nota. Et yssint fuit le case de appeller faux theife mise devant deny per luy auxi car laron ymplie tant come faux laron. Nota per *Portman* eodem tempore que si home appell auter extortioner et que il ad emblee les beins de J. S. et il port action sur le case lauter plede ryen culpable ou que il ne parla ceux parolls et sur ceo sont al yssue et le jury trove que le deffendant luy appell extortioner mes que il ne dit que lauter ad emblee les beins J. S. cest verdit est encounter le pl. car toutes ceux parolls sont materialls et bein reduce et prove lun lauter mes yssint nest ycy car cest paroll (stronge) nest materiall mes theife ceo ymplie. Quod nota bene. Et yssint theife ymplia faux.

Record of the case

KB 27/1160, m. 172, Rooper and Heywode.

Wiltes' Memorandum quod die Lune proxime post quindenam Sancti Michaelis isto eodem termino coram domino rege apud Westmonasterium venit Johannes Brydges miles per Ricardum Heywoode attornatum suum. Et protulit hic curie domini regis tunc ibidem

[1] *Reads* liberate. [2] *A, D, L.* lre *H.*
[3] 3° *A.* 31 *L.* [4] linjury *A, D, L.*

not give a verdict at large, nor shall the justices receive it. In debt on a bond, the defendant pleaded that he was illiterate and that the bond was read to him as an acquittance, and so Not his deed, and thereupon they were at issue, and the jury found that the defendant well knew that it was his deed and that it was properly read to him, and this was no verdict because it was at large, and the jury there was compelled to say precisely whether it was his deed or not: 3 Hen. VI, 'Verdict', [30].[1] Likewise here. There is another reason, since this action varies from other actions, for it is founded upon the case and the [special facts], and the facts are entire: therefore, because everything is not found, it is found against the plaintiff. Similarly in the case where someone brings such an action for calling him a villein regardant to his manor of Dale, the defendant says Not guilty, and the jury finds that the defendant called him villein but not regardant, this is found against the plaintiff. But if there was an action for calling him a villein generally, and the jury found that the defendant called him a villein regardant, that is found for the plaintiff, for the surplusage is void. In debt on a contract for two horses, if the defendant pleads *Nil debet* and they find that the contract was for three horses, or for one horse, this is not found for the plaintiff. Likewise if the jury finds that the defendant and a stranger made the contract. In an action for calling the plaintiff a false thief, if the jury finds that he called him a thief but not 'false', the plaintiff shall still not have judgment. See good cases in the title 'Verdict', 47 Edw. III, 20, and 11 Edw. III, 26.[2] As to the words that the plaintiff is a maintainer of thieves, they do not make any cause of action, for one may well maintain and lodge thieves if they are not known to him as thieves etc.

Afterwards in the same term judgment was given for the plaintiff, upon the said verdict, by good advisement. And the case of villeinage regardant, which is put above, was denied by PORTMAN J.: note that. The case of calling someone false thief, also previously put, was likewise denied by him, for 'thief' implies as much as 'false thief'. Note by PORTMAN, on the same occasion, that if someone calls another 'extortioner' and says he has stolen the goods of John Style, and he brings an action on the case, and the other pleads Not guilty (or pleads that he did not speak the words) and thereupon they are at issue, and the jury finds that the defendant called him extortioner but that he did not say that he had stolen the goods of John Style, this verdict is against the plaintiff, for all these words are material and well reduced, and the one proves the other. But it is not so here, for this word 'strong' is not material, in that 'thief' implies it. Note that well. Likewise 'thief' implies 'false'.

Translation of the record

King's Bench, Michaelmas term 1551.

Wiltshire. Remember that on the Monday next after the quindene of Michaelmas this same term, Sir John Brydges came before the lord king at Westminster by Richard Heywoode his attorney. And he proffered here to the lord king's court, then being there, a certain bill of

[1] Probably Mich. 3 Hen. VI, Fitz. Abr., *Verdict*, pl. 30.

[2] Fitz. Abr., *Verdict*, pl. 20 (YB Hil. 47 Edw. III, fo. 19, pl. 41) and pl. 26 (Trin. 11 Edw. III).

quandam billam suam versus Johannem Warnford in custodia marrescalli etc. de placito transgressionis super casum. Et sunt plegii de prosequendo scilicet Johannes Doo et Ricardus Roo. Quequidem billa sequitur in hec verba.

Wiltes' Johannes Brydges miles queritur de Johanne Warnford in custodia marrescalli marescalcie domini regis coram isto rege existentis pro eo videlicet quod cum idem Johannes Brydges verus ligeus domini regis nunc existit et ut verus ligeus dicti domini regis et progenitorum suorum absque ullo crimine falsitatis, felonie et murdri a tempore nativitatis sue hucusque se gesserit et habuerit et hujusmodi status, conversationis et honestatis apud universos fideles subditos dicti domini regis a quacumque criminosa, nequisia, falsitatis, felonie et murdri ac cujusvis insigni doli aut alicujus hujusmodi criminis immaculatus acceptatus et vociferatus fuerat necnon apud serenissimum principem dominum regem nunc Edwardum Sextum dei gracia Anglie, Francie et Hibernie Regem, fidei defensorem, et in terra ecclesie Anglicane et Hibernice supremum caput, ut verus et fidelis subditus acceptatus et reputatus existerat, et ea occasione in diversis arduis negotiis ipsius domini regis nunc per longum iam retroactum tempus ex mandato ipsius domini regis ut hujusmodi verus subditus dicti domini regis versatus fuerat ac apud omnes proceres et magnatos dicti domini regis rectores et gubernatores ac apud omnes alios subditos dicti domini regis cujuscumque status per totum tempus predictum ut hujusmodi verus et[i] ut prefertur immaculatus subditus dicti domini regis nunc acceptatus fuerat, predictus tamen Johannes Warnford, premissorum non ignarus, ex sua perversa et malivola voluntate, machinans dictum Johannem Brydges de omni[i] hujusmodi credencia sua, honestate et reputatione ac de omnibus terris, tenementis, bonis et catallis suis falso, subdole et nequiter deprivare et ut idem Johannes Brydges penitus periret et destrueretur, primo die Aprilis anno regni[i] dicti domini regis nunc quinto, hec falsa mendacia et scandalosa verba de prefato Johanne Brydges apud Sevenhampton in comitatu Wiltes' in presencia diversorum fidedignorum subditorum dicti domini regis dixit et propalavit videlicet, There ys a grete nest of theves at Pyrton and Syr John Brydges dictum Johannem Brydges modo querentem innuendo ys the maynteyner of them and he ys a strong thefe hym selfe: quorum quidem falsorum et scandalosorum verborum locutionis et propalationis pretextu predictus Johannes Brydges non solum diversa magna expensa, onera et custagia pro declaratione sua in hac parte habenda perpessus est, verum etiam idem Johannes Brydges in magnam diffidenciam apud vicinos suos incidit et inductus ac in corpore suo ea occasione maxime gravatus existit. Unde dicit quod deterioratus est et dampnum habet ad valenciam mille librarum. Et inde producit sectam etc.

Et predictus Johannes Warnford per Johannem Payne attornatum suum venit et defendit vim et injuriam quando etc. Et dicit quod predictus Johannes Brydges actionem suam predictam versus eum habere seu manutenere non debet quia dicit quod diu ante predictum tempus dictionis et propalationis predictorum Anglicanorum verborum in narratione predicta superius fieri supposite quidam Thomas Fyssher de More, Agnes Martyn de Cott, vidua, Willelmus Aldworth de Meghenden, Amicia Sawnders de Lydyard vidua, Willelmus Martyn de Shawe, Dominus Johannes Hays, rector de Lydyard, Benedictus Jay de Pyrton, Johannes Bradley inhabitans apud le Churche Soyle de Pyrton predicta, Willelmus Cuffe de Pyrton Stoke, [*blank*] Buck de Yewen, [*blank*] Blanford de Somerford Keynes, [*blank*] Norbourne de Brynkworth, Johannes Ymbrydge de Castell Eton, Willelmus Mores de Wescott, et diversi alii honesti et fideles dicti domini regis nunc subditi in predicto comitatu Wiltes' false, felonice et burgulariter de bonis et catallis suis in separalibus propriis domibus et mancionibus per diversos felones illuc tempore nocturno confluentes, habentes facies suas velaminibus Anglice dictis vysardes coopertas, ad diversas vices spoliati fuerunt, de quibusquidem felonibus[1] quidam Ricardus Newman de Pyrton predicta, husbondman,

[1] *Sic, presumably for* feloniis.

his against John Warnford, in the custody of the marshal etc., concerning a plea of trespass on the case. And there are pledges for prosecuting, namely John Doo and Richard Roo. Which bill follows in these words:

Wiltshire. John Brydges, knight, complains of John Warnford, in the custody of the marshal of the lord king's marshalsea before the king himself, forasmuch as, whereas the same John Brydges is a true liege of the present lord king, and has borne and conducted himself since the time of his birth until now as a true liege of the present lord king and of his forebears, without any crime of falseness, felony and murder, and has been accepted and known among all the faithful subjects of the said lord king as being of such condition, conversation and honesty, untainted with any crime, evil, falseness, felony and murder, or of any mark of deceit or any similar crime, and also accepted and reputed as a true and faithful subject of that kind by the most serene prince, our present lord King Edward the Sixth, by the grace of God king of England, France and Ireland, defender of the faith, and supreme head on earth of the English and Irish Church, and by reason thereof has been employed for a long time past on various difficult affairs of him the said lord king, by command of the selfsame lord king, and has been accepted by all the peers and great men who are rulers and governors of the said lord king and by all other subjects of the said lord king of whatever estate, throughout the time aforesaid, as a true and untainted subject of the present lord king, as aforesaid: nevertheless the aforesaid John Warnford, being not unaware of the foregoing, of his perverse and evil will, scheming falsely, fradulently and wickedly to deprive the said John Brydges of all such credit, honesty and reputation, and of all his lands, tenements, goods and chattels, and that the said John Brydges should utterly perish and be destroyed, on the first day of April [1551] in the fifth year of the reign of the present lord king, spoke and published these false lies and slanderous words concerning the said John Brydges, at Sevenhampton in the county of Wiltshire in the presence of various trusty subjects of the said lord king, namely, 'There is a great nest of thieves at Purton, and Sir John Brydges (meaning the said John Brydges now plaintiff) is the maintainer of them, and he is a strong thief himself'; and by virtue of the speaking and publication of these false and slanderous words the aforesaid John Brydges has not only suffered various great expenses, charges and costs for clearing himself in that behalf, but the same John Brydges has also fallen into great discredit among his neighbours and has been greatly troubled in his body. Whereupon he says that he is the worse, and has suffered damage to the extent of £1,000. And thereof he produces suit etc.

And the aforesaid John Warnford comes, by John Payne his attorney, and denies the force and wrong when etc. And he says that the aforesaid John Brydges ought not to have or maintain his aforesaid action against him, because he says that, long before the aforesaid time when the aforesaid English words specified in the aforesaid count were supposed to have been spoken and published, a certain Thomas Fyssher of 'More', Agnes Martyn of Coate, widow, William Aldworth of 'Meghenden', Amy Saunders of Lydiard, widow, William Martyn of Shawe, Mr John Hays, rector of Lydiard, Benet Jay of Purton, John Bradley living at the Church Soil of Purton aforesaid, William Cuffe of Purton Stoke, [*blank*] Buck of Ewen, [*blank*] Blanford of Somerford Keynes, [*blank*] Norbourne of Brinkworth, John Ymbrydge of Castle Eaton, William Mores of 'Wescott', and various other honest and faithful subjects of the said present lord king in the aforesaid county of Wiltshire have been on various occasions falsely, feloniously and burglariously robbed of their goods and chattels, in their own several houses and mansions, by various felons coming together at that time at night, having their faces covered with visors, among which felons a certain Richard Newman of Purton aforesaid, husbandman, George Kechyner of the same, weaver, John

Georgius Kechyner de eadem, wever, Johannes Davys nuper de eadem, yoman, et alii de separalibus feloniis et burglariis predictis per totum comitatum predictum fuerunt vehementer suspecti, et pro eo quod eedem diverse felonie et burgularie fuerunt comisse et perpetrate infra limites et partes ubi dictus Johannes Brydges fuit commorans et inhabitans ac prope mansionem ipsius Johannis Brydges, pro eo etiam quod idem Johannes Brydges tunc fuit unus justiciariorum dicti domini regis ad pacem in dicto comitatu Wiltes' conservandam necnon ad diversa felonias, transgressiones et alia malefacta in eodem comitatu audienda et terminanda assignatorum, et vicinior omnibus aliis justiciariis ejusdem comitatus locus ubi felonie et burgularie predicte fuerunt facte, predicti Ricardus Newman, Georgius Kechyner [et] Johannes Davys, felones existentes inde ut prefertur suspecti, per Robertum Shurtmore et Willelmum Cuffe ad predictum Johannem Brydges et coram eodem Johanne Brydges virtute officii sui predicti per dictos Robertum Shurtmore et Willelmum Cuffe de feloniis et burgulariis predictis examinandi capti et adducti fuerunt, videlicet apud Bluntesden Andrewe in comitatu Wiltes' predicto, ac idem Johannes Warnford dicit in facto quod per bonos honestos et sufficientes testes coram eodem Johanne Brydges approbatum et testificatum fuit quod predicti Ricardus Newman, Georgius Kechyner, Johannes Davys et alii felones predicti fuerunt culpabiles de diversis feloniis et burgulariis predictis, quo non obstante predictus Johannes Brydges apud Bluntesden Andrewe predictam permisit felones illos transire ad largum quo voluerunt, ob quod predictus Johannes Warnford[i] predicto tempore quo supponitur dictionem et propalationem predictorum Anglicanorum verborum in narratione sua superius specificatorum fieri apud Sevenhampton predictam dixit et propalavit hec Anglicana verba sequentia vel hiis veresimilia et ejusdem sensus et significationis, videlicet, Rychard Newman of Pyrton, husbondman, George Kechyner of the same, wever, and John Davys late of the same, yoman, and many other persons late servauntes to Syr Edmond Brydges, knyght, were and be openly famed and comenly escryed in the countrey there of the commyttyng of certen robberyes and burglaries uppon Thomas Fyssher of More, Agnes Marten of Coott, wydowe, William Aldeworth of Meghenden, Amy Saunders of Lydyard, William Martyn of Shawe, Sir John Hays, parson of Lydyard, Bennett Jay, John Bradley att the Church Soyle at Pyrton, William Cuffe of Pyrton Stoke, [*blank*] Buk of Yewen, [*blank*] Blanford of Somerford Keynes, [*blank*] Norbourne of Brynkworth, John Ymbrydge of Castell Eaton, William Morres of Wescott, and many mo, and the nest of them was <or ys>[i] found out in or nere about the dwellyng howse of Sir Edmond Brydges in Pyrton aforeseyd, and the nest of the seyd theves was or ys very well broken, and I marvell (consyderyng the seyd Syr John Brydges hath so jolly a witt and considering he understandyth that such lewde and yvyll dysposyd persons were drawen and hangyng about the seyd Sir Edmond Brydges hys sonne and heyre apparant) why the seyd Syr John Brydges dyd or doth nott faythfully hys dylygence to see the seyd felons punysshed wherby all suche felons myght be a feerd to drawe nere about the seyd Sir Edmond and Sir John Brydges and wherby men myght have good opynyon of them and myght perceve that the seyd Sir John Brydges and Sir Edmond wold not favour, cloke nor colour any suche vyle persons, and I also marvell why the seyd Sir John Brydges and Sir Edmond Brydges or there adherentes wold showe ther unlawfull favour towardes the seyd felons wythout the[i] fere of the kynges highnes and the daunger of the lawes, and I feare muche least the crafty, false and disseytfull conveyaunce and doynges of the seyd Sir John Brydges wold or wyll manifestly prove hym to be very accessary to dyverse of the seyd fellons, and I have learned the lawes to be that every accessary to fellony ys a very thefe, and therfore for a grete number of causes whych I ernestly noted and marked in the seyd Sir John Brydges and hys unlawfull doynges I vehemently suspected and yet vehemently suspect the seyd Sir John Brydges to be accessary to diverse of the seyd felounes and ther fellonyes, and so I suspect hym self therof to be a strong theff, and I thynke in my hert the same to be very true, but, syrs, I prey you bere me record I do not sey precyselye he ys a thefe because he doth not make me prevey when or howe he intendeyth to do anny such feate, and by my feyth I do thinke

Davys lately of the same, yeoman, and others, were vehemently suspected throughout the aforesaid county of the several felonies and burglaries aforesaid, and inasmuch as the same various felonies and burglaries were committed and perpetrated in the region and parts where the said John Brydges was dwelling and inhabiting, and near the mansion-house of the selfsame John Brydges, and forasmuch also as the same John Brydges was then one of the said lord king's justices assigned to keep the peace in the said county of Wiltshire and to hear and determine the various felonies, trespasses and other misdemeanours in the same county, and a closer neighbour than all the other justices of the same county to the place where the aforesaid felonies and burglaries were done, the aforesaid Richard Newman, George Kechyner and John Davys, being suspected felons as above, were arrested by Robert Shurtmore and William Cuffe and brought before the aforesaid John Brydges to be examined before the same John Brydges by virtue of his aforesaid office, namely at Blunsdon St Andrew in the aforesaid county of Wiltshire; and the same John Warnford says in fact that it was proved and testified by good, honest and sufficient witnesses before the same John Brydges that the aforesaid Richard Newman, George Kechyner, John Davys, and the other aforesaid felons, were guilty of the various felonies and burglaries aforesaid, notwithstanding which the aforesaid John Brydges at Blunsdon St Andrew aforesaid allowed the felons to go at large, wherever they wished, as a result of which the aforesaid John Warnford, at the aforesaid time when the aforesaid English words specified in his count above are supposed to have been spoken and published, at Sevenhampton aforesaid, spoke and published (as he was fully entitled to do) these English words following, or something like them and of the same sense and meaning, namely, 'Richard Newman of Purton, husbandman, George Kechyner of the same, weaver, and John Davys late of the same, yeoman, and many other persons, late servants to Sir Edmund Brydges, knight, were and be openly famed and commonly escried in the country there of the committing of certain robberies and burglaries upon Thomas Fyssher of 'More', Agnes Marten of Coate, widow, William Aldworth of 'Meghenden', Amy Saunders of Lydiard, William Martyn of 'Shawe', Sir John Hays, parson of Lydiard, Bennett Jay, John Bradley at the Church Soyle at Purton, William Cuffe of Purton Stoke, [*blank*] Buck of Ewen, [*blank*] Blanford of Somerford Keynes, [*blank*] Norbourne of Brinkworth, John Ymbrydge of Castle Eaton, William Morres of 'Wescott', and many more, and the nest of them was or is found out in or near about the dwelling house of Sir Edmund Brydges in Purton aforesaid, and the nest of the said thieves was or is very well broken, and I marvel (considering the said Sir John Brydges hath so jolly a wit, and considering he understandeth that such lewd and evil disposed persons were drawn and hanging about the said Sir Edmund Brydges's son and heir apparent) why the said Sir John Brydges did or doth not faithfully his diligence to see the said felons punished, whereby all such felons might be afraid to draw near about the said Sir Edmund and Sir John Brydges, and whereby men might have good opinion of them and might perceive that the said Sir John Brydges and Sir Edmund would not favour, cloak nor colour any such vile persons, and I also marvel why the said Sir John Brydges and Sir Edmund Brydges or their adherents would show their unlawful favour towards the said felons without the fear of the king's highness and the danger of the laws, and I fear much lest the crafty, false and deceitful conveyance and doings of the said Sir John Brydges would or will manifestly prove him to be very accessory to divers of the said felons; and I have learned the laws to be that every accessory to felony is a very thief, and therefore for a great number of causes which I earnestly noted and marked in the said Sir John Brydges and his unlawful doings I vehemently suspected and yet vehemently suspect the said Sir John Brydges to be accessory to divers of the said felons and their felonies, and so I suspect himself thereof to be a strong thief, and I think in my heart the same to be very true, but, sirs, I pray you bear me record I do not say the seyd Sir John Brydges hym self was not in proper person at eny of the seyd robberys, neverthelesse I wyll when I see tyme and place convenyent by order of lawe lay hys mayntenaunces and other onlawfull doinges so sore unto hys charge as he shalbe more afeard of the rope then ever he was of the rodd in hys youth, prout ei bene licuit, quequidem verba sunt eadem <verba et>[i] propalationes que predictus Johannes Warnford locutus fuit et ex quibus predictus Johannes Brydges actionem suam predictam modo concepit, absque hoc quod idem Johannes Warnford dixit et propalavit predicta Anglicana verba in narratione predicta superius specificata modo et forma prout predictus Johannes Brydges superius[i] se modo queritur. Et hoc paratus est verificare. Unde petit judicium si predictus Johannes Brydges actionem suam predictam inde versus eum habere seu manutenere debeat etc.

Et predictus Johannes Brydges dicit quod ipse per aliqua per predictum Johannem Warnford superius placitando allegata ab actione sua predicta versus ipsum Johannem Warnford habenda precludi non debet, quia dicit quod predictus Johannes Warnford dixit et propalavit predicta Anglicana verba in narratione predicta superius specificata, videlicet, There ys a grete nest of theves at Pyrton and Sir John Brydges ys the maynteyner of them and he ys a strong thefe hym self, modo et forma prout ipse in narratione sua predicta superius allegavit. Et hoc petit quod inquiratur per patriam. Et predictus Johannes Warnford similiter. Ideo veniat inde jurata coram domino rege apud Westmonasterium die Lune proxime post octabas Sancti Hillarii et qui nec etc. ad recognoscendum etc. quia tam etc. Idem dies datus est partibus predictis ibidem etc.

Ad quem diem coram domino rege apud Westmonasterium veniunt tam predictus Johannes Brydges quam predictus Johannes Warnford in propriis personis suis. Et vicecomes non misit breve. Ideo sicut alias veniat inde jurata coram domino rege apud Westmonasterium die Jovis proxime post quindenam Pasche et qui nec etc. ad recognoscendum etc. quia tam etc. Idem dies datus est partibus predictis ibidem etc. Postea, continuato inde processu inter partes predictas de placito predicto per juratas positas inde inter eas in respectum coram domino rege apud Westmonasterium usque diem Lune proxime post octabas Sancti Michaelis extunc proxime sequentes nisi justiciarii domini regis ad assisas in comitatu predicto capiendas assignati ut prius die Jovis, videlicet xiiij[to] die Julii, apud Novam Sarum in comitatu [infraspecificato][1] per formam statuti etc. venerint per defectum juratorum etc. Ad quem diem <coram domino rege apud Westmonasterium>[i] veniunt partes predicte per attornatos suos predictos. Et prefati justiciarii coram quibus etc. miserunt hic recordum suum coram eis habitum in hec verba:

> Postea, die et loco infracontentis, coram Humfrido Browne milite et Jacobo Hales milite, justiciariis domini regis ad assisas in comitatu Wiltes' capiendas assignatis per formam statuti etc. veniunt tam infranominatus Johannes Brydges quam infrascriptus Johannes Warnford in propriis personis suis. Et juratores jurate infraspecificate exacti similiter veniunt, qui ad veritatem de infracontentis dicendam electi, triati et jurati dicunt super sacramentum suum quod predictus Johannes Warnford dixit et propalavit omnia infrascipta Anglicana verba in narratione infrascripta specificata excepto illo verbo stronge in eadem narratione similiter specificato modo et forma prout predictus Johannes Brydges inde interius allegavit. Et assident dampna ipsius Johannis Brydges occasione illa ultra misas et custagia sua circa sectam suam in hac parte apposita ad trescentos et quinquaginta libros et pro misis et custagiis illis ad viginti marcas. Et ulterius juratores predicti dicunt super sacramentum suum quod predictus Johannes Warnford non dixit nec propalavit illud verbum stronge in narratione predicta specificatum modo et forma prout predictus Johannes Warnford interius allegavit.

Et quia curia domini regis hic de judicio suo de et super premissis reddendo nondum advisatur dies inde datus est partibus predictis in statu quo nunc coram domino rege apud Westmonasterium usque diem Lune proxime post octabas Sancti Hillarii de judicio suo de

[1] *Reads* tuo.

precisely he is a thief, because he doth not make me privy when or how he intendeth to do any such feat, and by my faith I do think the said Sir John Brydges himself was not in proper person at any of the said robberies, nevertheless I will when I see time and place convenient by order of law lay his maintenances and other unlawful doings so sore unto his charge as he shall be more afeared of the rope then ever he was of the rod in his youth', which words are the same words and publishings which the aforesaid John Warnford spoke and upon which the aforesaid John Brydges has now conceived his action aforesaid, without this that the same John Warnford spoke and published the aforesaid English words specified above in the aforesaid county, in the manner and form in which the aforesaid John Brydges above complains. And this he is ready to aver. Whereupon he prays judgment whether the aforesaid John Brydges ought to have or maintain his aforesaid action against him therefor etc.

And the aforesaid John Brydges says that he ought not to be barred from having his aforesaid action against him the said John Warnford by anything alleged above in pleading by the aforesaid John Warnford, because he says that the aforesaid John Warnford spoke and published the aforesaid English words specified above in the aforesaid county, namely, 'There is a great nest of thieves at Purton and Sir John Brydges is the maintainer of them and he is a strong thief himself', in manner and form as he has above alleged in his aforesaid count. And this he prays may be enquired into by the country; and the aforesaid John Warnford likewise. Therefore let a jury come before the lord king at Westminster on the Monday next after the octaves of Saint Hilary [1552], who neither etc., to make recognition etc., because both etc. The same day is given to the parties aforesaid there etc.

At which day both the aforesaid John Brydges and the aforesaid John Warnford come before the lord king at Westminster in their own persons. And the sheriff did not send the writ. Therefore, as before, let a jury come before the lord king at Westminster on the Thursday next after the quindene of Easter [1552] who neither etc. to make recognition etc. because both etc. The same day is given to the aforesaid parties there etc. Afterwards, the process therein being continued between the parties aforesaid in the aforesaid plea by the juries therein between them being put in respite before the lord king at Westminster until the Monday next after the octaves of Michaelmas then next following, unless the lord king's justices assigned to takes the assizes in the aforesaid county should first have come to Salisbury in the county aforesaid by the form of the statute, namely on Thursday 14 July [1552], for want of jurors etc. At which day the aforesaid parties come before the lord king at Westminster by their aforesaid attorneys. And the said justices before whom etc. have sent here their record, [made] before them, in these words:

> Afterwards, at the day and place mentioned within, before Humphrey Browne, knight, and James Hales, knight, the lord king's justices assigned to take the assizes in the county of Wiltshire by the form of the statute etc., both the within-named John Brydges and the within-mentioned John Warnford come in their own persons. And the jurors of the jury mentioned within, having been called, likewise come, and, being chosen, tried and sworn to say the truth concerning the matters within, they say upon their oath that the aforesaid John Warnford did speak and publish all the within mentioned English words specified in the within-mentioned count, except for the word 'strong' (likewise specified in the same count), in manner and form as the aforesaid John Brydges has within alleged therein; and they assess the damages of him the said John Brydges on that account, beyond the outlay and costs laid out by him about his suit in that behalf, as £350, and for the outlay and costs 20 marks. The jurors further say upon their oath that the aforesaid John Warnford did not speak or publish the word 'strong' specified in the aforesaid count, in manner and form as the aforesaid John Warnford has within alleged.

And because the lord king's court here is not yet advised concerning the giving of their judgment of and upon the foregoing, a day is given therein to the parties aforesaid before the lord king at Westminster in the same state as now until the Monday next after the et super premissis inde audiendo eo quod curia domini regis hic inde non dum etc. Ad quem diem coram domino rege apud Westmonasterium veniunt partes predicte per attornatos suos. Et quia curia domini regis hic de judicio suo de et super premissis reddendo non dum advisatur dies inde datus est partibus predictis in statu quo nunc coram domino rege apud Westmonasterium usque diem Mercurii proxime post quindenam Pasche de judicio suo de et super premissis inde audiendo eo quod curia domini regis hic inde non dum etc. Ad quem diem coram domino rege apud Westmonasterium veniunt partes predicte per attornatos suos predictos. Super quo, visis et per curiam domini regis hic plenius intellectis omnibus et singulis premissis, maturaque deliberatione superinde habita, consideratum est quod predictus Johannes Brydges recuperet versus predictum Johannem Warneford dampna sua predicta per juratores predictos in forma predicta asssessa. Et predictus Johannes Warneford in misericordia etc.

Dampna – ccclxiij li. vj s. viij d. unde clericis ccclxiij s. iiij d.

[De termino Pasche anno septimo Edwardi 6][1]

[1]

A, fo. 15; *L* 73 (Pas. 7 Edw. VI); *B*, p. 122 (Pas. 7 Edw. VI); *D*, fo. 8, pl. 1 (7 Edw. VI).

Nota per *Bromeley*[2] Justice et *Portman* Justice pur clere ley que si un comen carier preigna un packe de stuff de J. S. pur carier al Lincolne et en un comen inne[3] per le voy le packe est [prise et][4] emblee de le carier hors del inne que ore le owner s. J. S. avera action vers [le] hostler pur les beins et nemi le carier car ils ne sont les beins de le carier ne il nest charge ouster al J. S. entant que il est compellable per la ley a carier choses. Mes si un estranger que nest comen carier prist beins generalment a carier et il est yssint spoyle[5] des beins il serra charge al owner pur son generall prisell del eux a carier car il ne fuit compellable issint a faire. Et en cest case il avera laction en respect de son charge ouster. Auterment est en le primer case quot nota bene etc. Vide M. 2 H. 4 en hostler 13. que si le servant soit yssint spoile des beins son maister en un comen inne que le maister avera laction. Et coment que nest nul direct breife pur le maister en cest case en le Regester uncore per lestatute si les clerkes del Chauncery agreont et font tiel breife ceo est bon. *Hales* fuit de mesme loppionion al Serjeantes Inne.

1 *A, immediately before the next case.* Pas. vii^o Ed. vi *in the same position in L.*
2 Browne *A, B, D, L.*
3 hostry *A, B, L.*
4 *A, B, D, L.* ale ou *H.*
5 robbe *A, B, L.*

octaves of St Hilary [1553] for hearing their judgment of and upon the foregoing, inasmuch as the lord king's court here is not yet therein etc. At which day the aforesaid parties come before the lord king at Westminster by their [aforesaid] attorneys. And because the lord king's court here is not yet advised concerning the giving of their judgment of and upon the foregoing, a day is given therein to the parties aforesaid before the lord king at Westminster, in the same state as now, until the Wednesday next after the quindene of Easter [1553] for hearing their judgment of and upon the foregoing, inasmuch as the lord king's court here is not yet therein etc. At which day the aforesaid parties come before the lord king at Westminster by their aforesaid attorneys. Whereupon, all and singular the foregoing having been looked into and fully understood by the lord king's court here, and mature deliberation thereupon had, it is awarded that the aforesaid John Brydges do recover against the aforesaid John Warnford his aforesaid damages as assessed by the aforesaid jurors in form aforesaid; and the aforesaid John Warnford is in mercy etc.

Damages – £363. 6*s.* 8*d.*, whereof 363*s.* 4*d.* to the clerks

[Easter term, 7 Edw. VI (1553)][1]

1. CARRIERS AND INNKEEPERS

Serjeants' Inn. Cf. *OHLE*, vi. 761–762.

Note, by BROMLEY J. and PORTMAN J., as clear law, that if a common carrier takes a pack of stuff from John Style to carry to Lincoln, and in a common inn on the way the pack is taken or stolen from the carrier out of the inn, the owner (namely John Style) shall have an action for the goods against the innkeeper, and not against the carrier, for they are not the carrier's goods, nor is he chargeable over to John Style inasmuch as he is compellable by the law to carry things. If, however, a stranger (who is not a common carrier) takes goods generally[2] to carry, and he is similarly despoiled of the goods, he shall be charged to the owner by his general taking of them to carry; for he was not compellable so to do. In that case he shall have an action in respect of his charge over. It is otherwise in the first case: note that well etc. See Mich. 2 Hen. IV in 'Hostler', [4],[3] that if a servant is thus despoiled of his master's goods in a common inn, the master shall have the action. And even though there is no direct writ in the Register for the master in this case, nevertheless by statute if the clerks of the Chancery agree and make such a writ it is good.[4] HALES was of the same opinion, at Serjeants' Inn.

[1] Heading in *A* only.
[2] I.e without special terms.
[3] Fitz. Abr., *Hostler*, pl. 4 (YB Mich. 2 Hen. IV, fo. 7, pl. 31).
[4] Statute of Westminster II, c. 24, *In consimili casu.*

[2]

A, fo. 15[f]; *L* 74[f].

[*fol. 13v*] Nota per *Bromeley* et *Portman* [clerement][1] eodem anno et loco quod breife de wast ne gist vers executors pur le wast fait en temps lour testator mes solement pur wast fait en lour temps demeasne pur ceo que est un personall action et le wronge morust cum le person auxibein del parte le lessee come del parte le lessor quod nota clerement et sans question.

[3]

A, fo. 15[f]; L 75–76[f]; *B*, p. 122 (Pas. 7 Edw. VI); *D*, fo. 9, pl. 2–3 (7 Edw. VI).

Nota per *Bromeley* clerement eodem anno et loco, et ne fuit mult deny per *Portman*, que si breife yssist per default pur enquirer de wast et enquiry doit estre fait per xii homes al meins per lexpresse parolls del statute et le jury issint ympannell devant le viscount poet trover nul wast fait per le defendant quar auter[ment] ils serront perjuries sills serront compelles a trover wast. Mes si le defendant en trns. soit condempne per default et breife yssist pur enquirer des damages la si le viscount returna que le jury ad trove nul dammages ou que le deffendant nest culpable ceo nest bon returne car cest breife denquirer des dammages est agard tantum al enquirer des damages entant que le deffendant est attaint de trns. devaunt per son default yssint que le trns. per la ley est adevant adjuge al pl. et le breife yssist solement pur enformer le court des damages et ascuns damages ils doient trove mes en lauter case le breife issuist al enquirer del toute le wast etc. et nemy des damages pur le wast come si le wast fuit confes: quod nota. Et si devant que le breife yssist denquirer del wast le pl. surmitta al court que le deffendant tient ad terminum annorum et ne monstra le certenty des ans ceo est bon. 2 H. 5. Wast 55. [*Hales* agrea.][2]

[4]

A, fo. 15[f]; L 77[f] (Pas. 7 Edw. VI); B, p. 122[f].

Nota per les dittes *Bromeley* et *Portman* eodem anno et loco que si en ascun action en court de record les parties sont al yssue que ore devant lenquest soit prise le pl. ou defendant poet monstre cause al court que lissue est misjoyne et jeofaile et pria repleder et que lissue soit quasse lestatute de jeofailes nient obstant. Mes ils disoent clerement que tiel exception devant les justices de nisi prius devant que

[1] *A*.
[2] *A only*.

2. A WRONG DIES WITH THE PERSON

Serjeants' Inn.

Note, by BROMLEY and PORTMAN, clearly, in the same year and place, that a writ of waste does not lie against executors for waste committed in the time of their testator, but only for waste committed in their own time, because it is a personal action and the wrong dies with the person[1] – on the lessee's side as well as the lessor's. Note that, clearly and without question.

3. WRIT OF ENQUIRY

Serjeants' Inn, contd.

Note, by BROMLEY, clearly, in the same year and place, and not much denied by PORTMAN, that if a writ issues after a default to enquire as to waste, the enquiry ought to be made by twelve men at least, by the express words of the statute,[2] and the jury thus impanelled before the sheriff may find no waste to have been committed by the defendant, for otherwise they might be perjured if they were compelled to find waste. But if the defendant in trespass is condemned by default, and a writ issues to enquire of the damages, and the sheriff returns that the jury has found no damages, or that the defendant is not guilty, that is not a good return, for this writ to enquire of the damages is awarded only to enquire into damages, inasmuch as the defendant has been attainted of the trespass already by his default, so that the trespass has already by law been adjudged for the plaintiff, and the writ issues solely to inform the court of the damages, and some damages they must find. But in the other case the writ issues to enquire of all the waste etc., and not merely of the damages for the waste (as if the waste were confessed): note that. If, before the writ issued to enquire of the waste, the plaintiff surmised to the court that the defendant held for a term of years, and did not show the certainty of the years, that would be good. 2 Hen. V, 'Waste', 55.[3] HALES agreed.[4]

4. JEOFAILS

Serjeants' Inn.

Note, by the said BROMLEY and PORTMAN, in the same year and place, that if in any action in a court of record the parties are at issue, the plaintiff or defendant may before the inquest is taken show cause to the court that the issue is misjoined and a jeofail, and pray a repleader, and that the issue be quashed, notwithstanding the statute of jeofails.[5] But they said clearly that such an excep-

[1] Cf. below, p. 48, pl. 3; p. 55, pl. 12.

[2] Statute of Westminster II, c. 14.

[3] Fitz. Abr, *Wast*, pl. 55 (YB Trin. 2 Hen. V, fo. 9, pl. 8).

[4] *A* only.

[5] 32 Hen. VIII, c. 30.

lenquest soit prise nest bon car ils nont power de allower cest exception devant eux nient pluis ore que devant le estatute. Car cest exception fuit toutes foites referr al justices queux doneront judgement de le matter et devant eux en arrest de judgement lexception fuit toutes foites prise devant le dit estatute de jeofailes et per statute lexception apres le verditt est ale mes en arrest del enquest devant ascun nisi prius issera lexception bein poet estre prise et hors del dit statute de jeofailes. Et per ceo appiert bein que les justices de nisi prius nont auter power forsque a prender lenquest et a trier larray et les challenges al jurors et al eux judger mes nemy dallower ou disalower ascun auter chose car le resceit dun feme ou de cesty en le revertion ils ne poient allower ne protection ne assoyne.

[De termino Trinitatis anno septimo E. 6][1]

[1]

A, fo. 15^{f}; L 78^{f} (Trin. 7 Edw. VI); *D*, fo. 9, pl. 4 (7 Edw. VI).

[*fol. 14*] Nota per tout le court en le Comen Place que si un port breife de dett sur obligation <et declara lobligation estre fait en la countie ou il port laction>[2] et le defendant dit que il seala et delivera cest fait al D. en auter county et que puis le pl. debrusa le seale et fixa novel seale a ceo en mesme le county et monstra liew ou il ceo delivera et issint nient son fait. Ore le venire facias et le triall serra en le county ou laction est port car le matter monstre devant nest forsque evidence a prover le fait rien et lissue est tout sur le fait.

[2]

A, fo. 15^{f}; *L* 79^{f}.

Nota per *Hales* et *Cooke* clerement que si home en faux emprisonment justefie per force dun precept direct a luy per le viscount hors dun capias soit il baily errant ou auter baylie ore le pl. poet bein dire de son tort demesne sans tiel cause entant que il ne justefie per force del matter de record mes del precept. Mes auter est si le viscount mesme ust justefie per reson del proces a luy direct hors del court de record quar la il <doit responder al matter de record>.[3]

1 *A, immediatelty before the next case.* Trin. vii Ed. vi *before the next case in L.*

2 en London ou ceo fuit fait *A, L.*

3 viendra a le recorde *A.* respondra a le record *L.*

tion is not good before the justices of nisi prius before the inquest is taken, for they have no power to allow this exception before them – no more now than before the statute. For this exception was always referred to the justices who gave judgment of the matter, and before the said statute of jeofails the exception was always taken before them in arrest of judgment, and by the statute the exception is taken away after verdict; but in arrest of the inquest, before any nisi prius issues, the exception may well be taken, and it is outside the said statute of jeofails. Hereby it clearly appears that the justices of nisi prius have no other power except to take the inquest, and to try the array and the challenges to the jurors, and to adjudge them, but not to allow or disallow anything else; for they may not allow the receipt of a wife, or a reversioner, or a protection or essoin.

<Trinity term, 7 Edw. VI (1553)>[1]

1. VENUE IN A PLEA OF NON EST FACTUM

Common Pleas.

Note, by the whole court in the Common Place, that if someone brings a writ of debt on a bond and declares that the bond was made in the county where he brings the action, and the defendant says that he sealed and delivered this deed at Dale in another county, and that afterwards the plaintiff broke the seal and affixed a new seal to it in the same county, and shows the place where he delivered it, 'and so not his deed', the *venire facias* and the trial shall be in county where the action is brought: for the matter set out before is only evidence to prove the deed naught and the issue is all upon the deed.[2]

2. REPLICATION DE INJURIA

Probably in the Common Pleas.

Note, by HALES and COKE, clearly, that if someone in false imprisonment justifies by virtue of precept directed to him by the sheriff under a *capias*, whether he is a bailiff errant or other bailiff, the plaintiff may well say 'of his own wrong, without such cause', since he does not justify by virtue of the matter of record but by virtue of the precept. It would be otherwise, however, if the sheriff himself had justified by reason of the process directed to him out of a court of record, for there he must answer to the matter of record.

[1] Heading in *A* only. This date, however, is at odds with that given at the end of pl. 5.
[2] Cf. below, p. 81, pl. 25.

[3]

Abr. in *A*, fo. 15v[f]; *L* 80[f].

Nota auxi per *Bromeley* et *Hales* que si home en execution sur recognizance condempnation ou estatute et en custodie del gardeine de Fleete ou auter gaoiler et puis escapa hors del custodye per negligence ou voluntariment per lassent le gaoiler et le gardein ou gaoiler morust que ore ses executors ne serront charges[1] en dett pur le tort del testator.

[4]

Nota per *Bromeley* auxi et affirme per toutes que si home tient del roy en soccage en cheif et morust son heir al plein age que ore le heire suera livery et payera primer seisin pur cest terre solement et nemy pur ses auters terrs auxi sicome il doit si la terre fuit tenus en service de chivaler en cheife coment que les parolls del statute de Prerogativa sont generall de eo qui tenet in capite car lestatute serra entend del tenure del chivaler en capite et nemi de soccage in capite.

[5]

En replegiare le deffendant avowa come bayly al J. S. et que le dit J. S. fuit seisie del certein terres dont le liew etc. fuit parcell en son demsne come de fee et pur damage feasant il come bayly avowa. Le pl. dit que longe temps devant que le dit J. S. rien avoit un J. D. fuit seisie des dittes tenementes cum pertinentiis en fee et lessa al pl. pur ans et que il fuit possesse et mist eins ses avers et le deffendant eux prist etc. ceo nest ple sans travers que le dit J. S. nad fee. Yssint est en trns. si le deffendant luy entitle per feoffment de J. S. il doit travers le feoffment J. S. Et en trns. si le deffendant dit que le pier le pl. enfeofe le pier le deffendant en fee et que son pier devie ent seisie et il enter ore le pl. poet luy entitler et traverser le feofment son pier sans responder al [*fol. 14v*] discent entant que le deffendant conveia del pier le pl. Mes si en trns. ou replegiare le deffendant justefie ou avowa per reson que J. S. fuit seisie en fee et luy enfeoffa et le pl. dit que le pl. fuit seisie en fee et lessa les terres al J. S. pur son vie et ils fist le feofment al defendant per que il entra pur le fortaiture etc. ceo est bon ple sans traverser que J. S. nad fee en les terres pur ceo que ceo est matter en ley sil ad fee per le feofment: yssint

[1] chargable *A*, *L*.

3. A WRONG DIES WITH THE PERSON

Probably in Serjeants' Inn.

Note also, by BROMLEY and HALES, that if someone in execution upon a recognizance, condemnation, or statute [merchant], is in the custody of the warden of the Fleet or other gaoler and then escapes out of this custody through negligence, or voluntarily by the consent of the gaoler, and the warden or gaoler dies, his executors shall not be charged in debt for their testator's wrong.[1]

4. LIVERY AND PRIMER SEISIN

Probably in Serjeants' Inn. Cf. below, p. 89, pl. 17 (under Mich. 1554), which is another version of the same report.

Note also by BROMLEY, and affirmed by everyone, that if someone holds of the king in socage in chief and dies, his heir of full age, the heir shall sue livery and pay primer seisin for this land only, and not for his other lands also, as he ought to if the land were held in knight-service in chief, even though the words of the statute Prerogativa Regis are in general terms, 'of him who holds in chief': for the statute shall be understood of knight-service in chief and not of socage in chief.

5. TRAVERSES IN PLEADING

Serjeants' Inn, Mich. 1552.

In replevin the defendant avowed as bailiff to John Style, and said that the said John Style was seised of certain lands whereof the place etc. was parcel, in his demesne as of fee, and he avowed as bailiff for damage feasant. The plaintiff said that, long before the said John Style had anything, one John Dale was seised of the said tenements with the appurtenances in fee and leased to the plaintiff for years, and that he was possessed and put in his cattle, and the defendant took them etc. This is no plea without a traverse that the said John Style had fee. It is likewise in trespass if the defendant entitles himself by feoffment of John Style, he must traverse the feoffment of John Style. And in trespass, if the defendant says that the plaintiff's father enfeoffed the defendant's father in fee, and that his father died seised thereof, and he entered, now the plaintiff may entitle himself and traverse his father's feoffment without answering to the descent, since the defendant traced title from the plaintiff's father. But if in trespass or replevin the defendant justifies or avows by reason that John Style was seised in fee and enfeoffed him, and the plaintiff says that the plaintiff was seised in fee and leased the lands to John Style for his life, and they made the feoffment to the defendant, as a result of which he entered for the forfeiture etc., this is a good plea without traversing that John Style had no fee in the lands, because that is a matter in law, whether he has fee by the feoffment. Likewise in replevin, if the

[1] For the principle that wrongs die with the person see above, p. 46, pl. 2; below, p. 55, pl. 12.

en replegiare si le deffendant avowa pur rent charge quel J. S. luy granta en fee hors des terres dont le [dit] J. S. fuit seisie en fee le pl. poet dire que le dit J. S. nad riens en les terres forsque pur son vie de son lease et puis morust apres quel mort le pl. entra et tient discharge etc. sans ascun travers al estate J. S. car ryen est la a responder forsque le graunt et ceo est confesse et avoid. Agree per toutes en Serjeantes Inne M. 6 E. 6.

[Finis secundum Dalison Justice del Banck de Roy][1]

Gulielmus Lamberdus transcripsit 1569

[1] *A, fo. 22, foll. pl. 25 on p. 10, above (the last case of Edw. VI in A). L, fo. 15v, in the same position.*

defendant avows for a rent-charge which John Style granted him in fee out of the lands whereof the said John Style was seised in fee, the plaintiff may say that the said John Style had nothing in the lands except for his life, by his lease, and then died, after whose death the plaintiff entered and held discharged etc., without any traverse to the estate of John Style, for there is nothing to answer except the grant and that is confessed and avoided. Agreed by all in Serjeants' Inn, Mich. 6 Edw. VI.

[The end, according to Dalison, Justice of the King's Bench[1]]

William Lambarde transcribed this in 1569.

[1] Explicit in *A*, between the cases of Edw. VI and Mary I.

[*fol. 15*] Termino Michelis Anno regni Regine Marie primo 1553 e libro manu Willelmi Dalison olim conscripto

[1]

A, fo. 27v (Trin. 1 & 2 Phil. & Mar.); *L* 205 (sim.); *D*, fo. 18, pl. 11 (1 & 2 Phil. & Mar.).

Nota per *Bromeley* ore Justice, *Portman* et *Hales* al Serjeantes Inne que en breife daccompt si le defendant vient eins le primer jour et confesse laction ou denia laction en point le breife et ceo est trye vers luy per jury que le defendant accompta en gard et serra comitt al prison quar per la ley nient plus que le deffendant poet accompter sur parcells mes sur tout nient pluis poet le defendant auterment accompter que en gard mes poet estre lesse al mainprise al discretion le courte.

[2]

A, fo. 27v[f]; *L* 205 (contd); *D*, fo. 18, pl. 12 (1 & 2 Phil. & Mar.).

Et en accompt ils disoent que le pl. ne recovera dammages coment que il declare de dammage pur le non certenty de son demaund. Mes *Hales* dit que [les][1] livers sont agrees que si le defendant devant auditors plede ple en discharge de son accompt come payment et sur ceo sont all yssue et trove pur le pl. que ore il recovera dammages entant que cest tryall est sur collaterall matter ou le certenty est primes conus per les auditors.

[3]

A, fo. 27v[f] (first case of Mich. 2 & 3 Phil. & Mar.); *L* 206[f] (sim.); *D*, fo. 18, pl. 1 (2 & 3 Phil. & Mar.).

Nota que si home a cest jour ou devant grant al auter per son fait que en consideration de son bon service que il ad fait ou a faire a luy ou en consideration que son file marier ove moye ou mon fittes que il avera tout le terre en un ville et cest graunt est per fait et nient enrolle que ore nul use est alterate sur cest

[1] *A.*

Michaelmas term in the first year
of the reign of Queen Mary 1553,
from a book written some while ago
in the hand of William Dalison

1. WRIT OF ACCOUNT

Serjeants' Inn.

Note, by BROMLEY, now [Chief] Justice,[1] PORTMAN and HALES at Serjeants' Inn, that in a writ of account if the defendant comes in on the first day and confesses the action, or denies the action in the point of the writ and it is found against him by the jury, the defendant shall account in ward and shall be committed to the prison, for by the law just as the defendant may not account bit by bit, but upon the whole, so the defendant may not account otherwise than in ward. But he may be released on mainprise at the court's discretion.

2. DAMAGES IN ACCOUNT

Probably in Serjeants' Inn, contd.

And they said that in account the plaintiff shall not recover damages, even though he declares of damage, because of the uncertainty of his demand. But HALES said that the books are in agreement that if the defendant pleads a plea before the auditors in discharge of his account, such as payment, and thereon they are at issue, and it is found for the plaintiff, he shall now recover damages, inasmuch as this trial is upon a collateral matter where the certainty is already known by the auditors.

3. USES WITH AND WITHOUT CONSIDERATION

Serjeants' Inn: cf. pl. 4.

Note that if someone at the present day (or before) grants to someone else by his deed that, in consideration of his good service that he has done or is to do for him, or in consideration that his daughter should marry me or my son, he should have all the land in a vill, and this grant is by deed and not enrolled, no

[1] Appointed C.J.Q.B. on 4 Oct. 1553; formerly J.K.B.

graunt entant que il va per voy de graunt et done et prist nul perfection[1] tanque le done soit execute per liverey de seisin et lenrollemnt ne [servera][2] en cest case car est hors del case destatute anno 27 H. 8. et uncore si home done a moy xx li. in consideration que il avera mon terre pur son vie ore il ad use [en] mon terre pur son vie devant liverey et seisin pur le certentie del consideration et en present temps.

[4]

Runs on from pl. 3 in *A, L* and *D.*

Et si home a cest jour per indentures de covenant perenter luy et auter de enfeoffer ou a doner xx li. en terre per an en consideration dun mariage destre ewe enter le fittes lun et le file lauter que ore sans ascun enrolment apres tiel mariage luse est alterate accordant al covenant sans ascun auter enrolement ou livery de seisin entant que cest va en covenant et nemy per graunt ou done: per *Bromeley,* [*Portman*][3] et *Hales* at Serjeantes Inne eodem termino.

[5]

A, ff. 27v–28[f]; *L* 207[f]; *D,* ff. 18–19, pl. 2 (2 & 3 Phil. & Mar.).

Nota per *James Hales* et *Portman* Justice que si home soit seisie dun mannor que extend en 2 counties ou 2 ou 3 villes a que un advouson est appendant et graunt et done son mannor en un countie ou en un ville ove les appurtenances que ore comment que rien passe per le done ou graunt [forsque][4] cest parte de le mannor en cest countie ou en cest ville ou le graunt est uncore tout lentier advowson passa al feofee [*fol. 15v*] ou grauntee entant que le grauntor ad graunt son mannor per cest nosme et il est conclude a dire le contrary mes que il ad graunt tout son mannor. Come si home ad mannor que extend a 3 villes et graunt tout son mannor que il ad en un ville, tout le mannor passa quar le grauntor nad ore mannor en les auters 2 villes mes avera les rentes et services come services et rentes en grosse. Mes auterment est sil ad done ou graunt le 3 parte ou le moytie de son mannor en Dale ove les appurtenance: la rien passa [per le graunt de ladvowson que le][5] moity remayna uncore al donor. Et ils toutes clerement agreeont que si home soit seisie dun mannor a que un advowson est appendant il per son feofment dun acre de le dit mannor ove le dit avowson ferra ladvowson appendant al dit acre si soit issint expresse mes si ne soit expresse et nosme

[1] effect *D.*
[2] *D.* serra *H.*
[3] *D, L.* Port *A.*
[4] *D, L.* que *H.*
[5] del advowson passera per le grant solement del *A, D, L.*

use is altered upon this grant inasmuch as it goes by way of grant and gift and takes no effect until the gift is executed by livery of seisin. And an enrolment would not serve in this case, for it is outside the case of the statute of the year 27 Hen. VIII;[1] and yet if someone gives me £20 in consideration that he shall have my land for his life, now he has a use in my land for his life before livery and seisin, because of the certainty of the consideration and the present tense.

4. USES ALTERED BY COVENANT

Serjeants' Inn, contd from pl. 3.

And if someone at the present day, by indentures of covenant between him and another, makes a feoffment or gives £20 in land a year in consideration of a marriage to be had between the son of the one and the daughter of the other, after such marriage the use is altered in accordance with the covenant, without any other enrolment or livery of seisin, inasmuch as this goes in covenant and not by grant or gift. By BROMLEY, PORTMAN and HALES at Serjeants' Inn the same term.

5. APURTENANCY AND APPENDANCY

Serjeants' Inn.

Note, by JAMES HALES and PORTMAN J., that if someone is seised of a manor which extends into two counties (or two or three vills), to which an advowson is appendant, and he grants and gives his manor in one county or in one vill 'with the appurtenances', now even though nothing passes by the gift or grant except that part of the manor in that county or in that vill where the grant is made, nevertheless the entire advowson passes to the feoffee or grantee inasmuch as the grantor has granted his manor by that name and he is concluded[2] from gainsaying that he has granted all of his manor.[3] Similarly, if someone has a manor which extends into three vills and grants all that his manor which he has in one vill: the whole manor passes, for the grantor now has no manor in the other two vills, but he shall have the rents and services as services and rents in gross. It would be otherwise, however, if he had given or granted the third part or the moiety of his manor of Dale with the appurtenances: there nothing of the advowson passes, because a moiety still remains with the donor.[4] They all clearly agreed that if someone is seised of a manor to which an advowson is appendant, he may by his feoffment of one acre of the said manor with the said advowson make the advowson appendant to the said acre, if it is so expressed; but if it is not expressed and stated in words, namely 'with the advowson', the

[1] Statute of Enrolments, 27 Hen. VIII, c. 16.
[2] I.e. estopped.
[3] Cf. above, p. 29, pl. 24.
[4] Garbled text corrected from *D*.

per parolls s. ove ladvowson [come devant][1] ladvowson remayna ove le feoffor entant que il ad le mannor eodem termino al Serjeantes Inne.

[6]

A, fo. 28[f]; *L* 208[f].

Nota que fuit agree per *Bromeley* et *Portman* et *Hales* Justices et auters serjeantes la esteantes que si la baron et feme ont un mannor al eux assure et a les heires le baron de que mannor un estraunger tient ses terres per service de chivaler et devie et puis le baron devie devant seisir de corps ou del terres et fait ses executors que la feme avera le gard de corps et de terre et nemy lexecutors le baron quar come per done fait al baron et feme des terres pur ans joyntment per le morte le baron le feme avera tout sinon que le baron ceo done ou graunt al estranger per mesme le reson icy pur cest guard que est done per ley. Et <mesme la ley est>[2] si baron fuit sole seisie de dit mannor en droit son feme. Et mesme le ley ils tiendront dadvowson que happa void que est appendant al dit mannor en le vie le baron et le baron devie devant presentment le feme presentera et nemy les executors. Et hoc accidit in casu Frye eodem termino al Serjeantes Inne et tout <un si seisir fuit>.[3]

[7]

A, fo. 28[f]; *L* 209[f].

Et per *Hales* clerement que si home ad villaine en droit sa feme ou evesque en droit son esglise le villaine purchase teres en fee si le baron ou evesque enter etc. ils naveront les dittes terres en fee mes en droit le feme et lesglise come ont le villaine adevant. Auter est de villen lesse al auter pur ans ou pur vie et il purchase terre le lessee avera fee. Eodem termino.

[8]

A, fo. 28r–v (foll. pl. 11); *L* 213 (sim.); *D*, fo. 19, pl. 4 (2 & 3 Phil. & Mar.).

Nota per toutes les justices agree que si home pled Nul tiel record sur un recoverye ou acte de parlament pled et ad jour a porter eins le record et il port eins un record ou acte al jour de south le graund seale testefiant le dit record estre voier accordant a son plee que ore tout soit en fait que la soit nul tiel record ou

[1] *A, D.*
[2] issint fuissoit *A, L.*
[3] est un si nul seisure fuissoit fait *A, L.*

advowson remains with the feoffor, inasmuch as he has the manor. The same term at Serjeants' Inn.

6. FRYE'S CASE

Serjeants' Inn.

Note that it was agreed by BROMLEY, PORTMAN, and HALES JJ., and other serjeants being there, that if a husband and wife have a manor assured unto them and the heirs of the husband, of which manor a stranger holds his lands by knight-service and dies, and then the husband dies before seizing the body or the lands, and makes his executors, the wife shall have the wardship of the body and the land, and not the husband's executors; for just as by a gift of lands made jointly to a husband and wife for years, the wife shall have the whole on her husband's death, unless the husband gives or grants it to a stranger, so the same reason applies here to this wardship which is given by law. The law is the same if a husband is sole seised of the said manor in right of his wife. And they held the law to be the same of an advowson which is appendant to the said manor and becomes void in the husband's lifetime, and the husband dies before making a presentation, the wife shall present and not the executors. This occurred in the case of Frye the same term at Serjeants' Inn. And it is all one if there was [no] seizure made.

7. VILLEIN IN RIGHT OF ANOTHER

Serjeants' Inn, contd.

And according to HALES, clearly, if someone has a villein in right of his wife, or a bishop has one in right of his church, and the villein purchases lands in fee, and the husband (or bishop) enters etc., he shall not have the said lands in fee but in right of the wife (or church), in the same way as they had the villein before. It is otherwise if a villein leases to another for years, or for life, and he purchases land [in fee]: the lessor shall have fee. The same term.

8. DUKE OF NORFOLK'S CASE

Chancery, and Serjeants' Inn, Mich. 1553. See also p. 55, below, pl. 14. Also reported in Dyer, fo. 93 (Mich. 1553); printed below.

Note that it was agreed by all the justices that if someone pleads No such record upon a recovery or act of parliament, and has a day to bring in the record, and at the day he brings in a record or act under the great seal witnessing the said record to be true according to his plea, now even if in fact there is no such record or no such act of parliament, the plea and certificate are nevertheless good in law and shall bind the person against whom the plea is pleaded, inasmuch as it is thus certified under the great seal to be true, and that cannot and nul tiel act de parlament uncore le plee et certificat sont bons en ley et lya cestui vers que le plee [*fol. 16*] est plede entant que il est issint certifie de southe le graund seale estre voier que ne poet estre ne serra adjuge auterment que voier quar cest seale serra toutes foites creditt. Et sic accidit in casu Thomas Duke de Norff. lou lexemplification de son attainder per act de parlament fuit certifie desouthe le graund seale estre fait per les Seigniors, les Comons, et per lassent le roy ou en fait le roy ne vient en cest parlament mes done son power al auters per ses lettres pattentes southe son graund seale a doner pur luy a cest acte son royall assent que commission done al dit seignors fuit fyle al dit acte dattaynder fait anno 38 H. 8. que commission fuit omitt en lexemplification et fuit tenus que per lexemplification fait il serra adjuge bon acte de parlament issint que le duke nad auter remedy a adnuller le dit exemplification que per lacte de parlament ou per aucthorytye de le chauncellor Dengliterre a causer les dittes parties <a ducer>[1] ove eux le dit exemplification arrere en le Chauncery la a estre cancel ou remayner quousque[2] etc. M. 1. Marie Regine Anglie en le Chauncery et Serjeantes Inne. Mes auterment fuit tenus de exemplification desouthe le seale de le Comen Bank, Exchequer ou le Banke le Roy, car eux nont ascun tiel force en eux ne emporter en eux tiel verity come fuit tenus per eux toutes.

Dyer's report of the case

Les Reports (1688 ed.), fo. 93, pl. 23–24.

Memorandum quod in ultimo Parliamento Regis H. 8. un bill de petition fuit exhibite per les Seigniors et commons al Roy pur lattainder del Duke de North. de haut treason, le quel fuit pas per ambideux measons, ove le contentment des Seigniors primes, et endoce (soit baile aux commons) et ove lassent des commons et endoce (les commoners sont assentus). Et quant il soit pas, le Roy per ses Letters Patents portant date 27 Januarii Anno 38 Regni sui recitant le dit Bill, fait in forme dun act et concluded and assented unto per les Seigniors et Commons regium assensum et consensum suum eidem bille ac omnibus in eadem specificatis duxit adhibendum et prebendum per tielx parolz Sciatis igitur etc. que il aver[3] done power et authority a 4. de les Seigniors, ou 3. a doner assent et consent in son nosme, ratifiant ceo que ilz ferront in ceo. Et les Letters Patents purport le signe, s. Henry Rex, manuel del Roy. Et auxy av[oient] le grand seal a ceo mis. Et cest commission fuit annex al dit Bill. Et le Bill fuit auxy endoce per ceux parolx, soit fait come est desire. Et si ceo fuit un perfect act fuit moult debate inter Justic[iarios]. Et ceux queux averont purchase les terres del Roy que fueront le Dukes, procure un certiorari direct a 2. clerks del Parliament a certifier le tenor dun act de Parliament concernaunt le attainder le dit Duke, fait tiel an. Et lun des Clerks tantum fist le certificat del nude bil sans les circumstances &c. Et si le certificat fuit bone, fuit move, eo que lun de eux tantum naver ascun garrant de certifier. Et pur ceo que les purchasors avoient procure certiorari, et le tenor del act, sans parler de commission destre exemplie in le Chancery, Le Duke procure le very original record del

1 de amesner *A, L.*
2 ove ceo *A, L.*
3 *Sic, presumably for:* avoit.

shall not be adjudged other than true, for this seal must always be believed. It so befell in the case of Thomas, duke of Norfolk, where an exemplification of his attainder by act of parliament was certified under the great seal to be made by the Lords, the Commons, and the assent of the king, whereas in fact the king did not come to this parliament but gave his power to others, by his letters patent under his great seal, to give his royal assent to this act on his behalf.[1] This commission given to the said lords was filed to the said act of attainder made in the year 38 Hen. VIII, but the commission was omitted in the exemplification; and it was held that by the exemplification made it shall be adjudged a good act of parliament, so that the duke has no other remedy to annul the said exemplification other than by act of parliament, or by authority of the chancellor of England to cause the said parties to bring with them the said exemplification into the Chancery again, there to be cancelled or to remain until etc. [This was decided in] Michaelmas term in the first year of Mary, queen of England, in the Chancery and Serjeants' Inn. But it was held otherwise of an exemplification under the seal of the Common Bench, Exchequer, or King's Bench,[2] for those do not have any such force in themselves and do not import in themselves such truth: as was held by them all.

Translation of Dyer's report

Les Reports (1688 ed.), fo. 93, pl. 23–24.

It is to be remembered that in the last parliament of King Henry VIII a bill of petition was exhibited to the king by the Lords and Commons for the attainder of the duke of Norfolk of high treason, which was passed by both houses, first with the contentment of the Lords, and endorsed 'Soit bailé aux commons', and then with the assent of the Commons and endorsed 'Les commoners sont assentus'. When it was passed, the king, by his letters patent bearing date 27 Jan. [1547], in the 38th year of his reign, reciting the said bill made in form of an act concluded and assented unto by the Lords and Commons, thought fit to put and give his royal assent and consent to the same bill, and to everything therein specified, by these words, 'Know ye therefore etc.' that he had given power and authority to four of the lords, or three, to give assent and consent in his name, ratifying what they did therein. And the letters patent bore the king's sign manual, namely 'Henry Rex', and also had the great seal set to them. And this commission was annexed to the said bill. The bill was also endorsed with these words, 'Soit fait come est desiré'. And it was much debated among the justices whether this was a perfect act. Those who had purchased from the king lands which were the duke's procured a *certiorari* directed to the two clerks of the parliament to certify the tenor of an act of parliament concerning the attainder of the said duke, made in such a year; and one of the clerks only made the certificate of the bare bill, without the circumstances etc. And it was moved whether the certificate was good, because there was no warrant for one of them only to certify. And because the purchasers had procured a *certiorari*, and the tenor of the act, without speaking of the commission having been exemplified

[1] The commission was sealed on the day the king died. It appeared to bear the sign manual, but was thought in fact to be stamped: Dyer said it was too well written for a man on his deathbed (below).

[2] Dalison at first retains the name King's Bench under Queen Mary, but in Pas. 1554 adopts Queen's Bench (below, p. 64); after the accession of King Philip he reverts to King's Bench.

act destre port per Spilman le Clarke del Parliament devant les Justices a Serjeants Inne. Et nota que per grand proof et presumption le Roy ne avoit mis son signe manuel: primes in tant que ceo fuit escript desouth le teste del patent, ou il soloit estre supra caput. Item le scripture fuit cye perfecte, que ne poit escrie per un home si malady et pres mort que le Roy fuit, car il morust mesme le nute etc. Item ascuns diont que ceo fuit le stampe. Et vide pur cest assent, le statute de 33 H. 8. ca. 21. Et postea le dit act dattainder fuit declare per le Parliament destre void et irrite, Quaere actum ipsum.

[9]

A, fo. 28 (foll. pl. 7); *L* 210 (sim.).

Et fuit dit per *Hales* Justice al Serjeantes Inne mesme le terme que si home soit seisie de terre en droit sa feme ou en joynture ovesque son feme et emblea les terres ove graine et devie devant severance que les executors le baron averont lemblementes et nemy le feme entant que les emblementes vient per son industry demesne et sont que un person en ley.

[10]

A, fo. 28[f]; *L* 211[f].

Nota per *Bromeley* Cheif Justice et *Hales* que en assise le tenant ne serra essoine devant apparance ne apres mes le pl. en assise serra essoine devant apparance et apres apparance nemi et lestatute serra entendue de querente et non de tenente en assise. Vide lestatute W. 1. ca. 42 et W. 2 ca. 28. Eodem termino al Serjeantes Inne.

[11]

A, fo. 28[f]; *L* 212[f]; *D*, fo. 19, pl. 3 (2 & 3 Phil. & Mar.).

Nota per *Hales* et auters agree clerement que si home soit seisie dun mannor en que sont divers copihouders pur ans ou pur vie en droit son feme ou durant le minority dun heire esteant deins age ou en taile ou [en fee][1] esteant issint seisie de tiel mannor et surrender est fait per un tiel copihoulder al dit seignor al opes dun auter et copie est fait accordant al custome que cest est bon clerement et lya cestui en le revertion le heire et la feme pur ceo que ils sont obliges en droit issint a faire: quod nota eodem tempore.

[1] *A, D, L.* enfant *H.*

in the Chancery, the duke procured the very original record of the act to be brought by Spelman,[1] the clerk of the parliament, before the justices at Serjeants' Inn. And note that by great proof and presumption the king had not set his sign manual. First, inasmuch as it was written beneath the *teste* of the patent, whereas it had used to be written above the head. Also, the writing was so perfect that it could not have been written by a man so ill and near to death as the king was, for he died the same night etc. Also, some say that it was the stamp. See, for this assent, the statute of 33 Hen. VIII, c. 21. Afterwards the said act of attainder was declared by the parliament to be null and void. Look for the act itself.

9. EMBLEMENTS

Serjeants' Inn, Mich. 1553.

And it was said by HALES J. at Serjeants' Inn the same term that if someone is seised of land in right of his wife, or in jointure with his wife, and sows the land with grain and dies before reaping, the husband's executors shall have the emblements and not the wife, inasmuch as the emblements come through his own industry and they are but one person in law.

10. ESSOINS IN AN ASSIZE

Serjeants' Inn, Mich. 1553.

Note, by BROMLEY C.J. and HALES, that in an assize the tenant shall not be essoined before appearance or after, whereas the plaintiff in an assize may be essoined before appearance, though not afterwards: and the statute shall be understood of the plaintiff, not the tenant, in an assize. See the Statute of Westminster I, c. 42, and Westminster II, c. 28. The same term, at Serjeants' Inn.

11. SURRENDER AND ADMITTANCE OF COPYHOLD

Serjeants' Inn, Mich. 1553 (but dated 1555 in *D.*).

Note that it was agreed by HALES[2] and others, clearly, that if someone is seised of a manor in which there are various copyholders for years or for life, in right of his wife, or during the minority of an heir under age, whether in tail or in fee, and being thus seised of such manor a surrender is made by a certain copyholder to the said lord to the use of another, and a copy is made according to the custom, this is clearly good and shall bind the reversioner, the heir and the wife, because they are bound in right to do it. Note that. On the same occasion.

[1] Francis Spelman of Stow Berden, Norfolk, and Gray's Inn (sued for dues in 1556); clerk of the parliaments 1551–74 (73 E.H.R. 82).

[2] Hales was reappointed J.C.P. on 4 Oct. 1553, but immediately fell into disfavour. Gardiner refused to give him the oath of office and he was soon afterwards imprisoned. On 4 Aug. 1554 he drowned himself in a stream near Canterbury. His last appearances in Dalison are in pl. 11–12.

[12]

Abr. in *A*, fo. 28; *L* 214.

[*fol. 16v*] Nota per les Justices *Brom*[*eley*], *Port*[*man*] et *Hales* clerement agree que si haut treson soit perpetrate et fait al roy E. le 6. en sa vie ou al roy H. 8. en sa vie que apres le mort les dittes royes et le crowne vient al roigne Mary que ore est que le treson uncore remayne punishable en temps cest roigne come fuit devant entant que cest treson est al crowne et al realme quel ne unques morust. Come si home comitta un murder manslaughter robbery ou felony en temps dauter roy entant que ceo est enconter coronam et dignitatem suam quel ne morust pas car le roy ne unques morust en respect de le royalty mes per son morte en person il dimitta le crowne al auter person. Mes uncore si trns. soit fait al un home come battery a son person ou per entry en ses terres per le mort lun [ou] lauter le trns. est ale quar moritur cum persona et ceo nest que un singuler dammage al un person mes treason towcha lestate de tout le realme que remayne. Al Serjeantes Inne eodem termino Michaelis.

[13]

A, fo. 28v[f]; *L* 215[f]; *D*, fo. 19, pl. 6 (2 & 3 Phil. & Mar.), garbled.

Nota que fuit clerement agree per toutes les dittes justices que si home fait un leas pur ans al estranger et puis fist feofment al auter de ceux terres lesses en fee et deliver possession et seisin al feoffee la lessee la esteant present et agreant al livery et seisin que cest est nul surrender de le terme quar nest que un assent dadmitter le feoffee en possession des terres. Eodem termino.

[14]

A, ff. 28–29[f]; *L* 216[f]; *D*, fo. 20, pl. 7 (2 & 3 Phil. & Mar.).

Nota per *Brom*[*eley*] Cheif Justice et *Port*[*man*] Justice que si un clerke de son teste demesne enter un judgement en Comen Banke ou Banke le Roy contrary al droit s. pur le pl. ou il doit estre pur le defendant que sur cest nul brefe derrour gist car nest null errour quia est contrary a ceo que ils fesoient come justices. Yssint est si les Seignors et Commons sont agrees dun acte de parlament et puis le clerke enter ceux parolls enter auters billes sur cest bill (que le roy le voet) (ou soit fait come ils desireont) coment que le roy ne fuit la present uncore ceo est bon acte de parlament per la ley. Et ils disoent que le roy doit doner son assent a le dit acte in proper person ou per ses lettres pattentes signes ove son maine et que auters ne poient doner son assent per ses lettres pattentes sicut accidit in

12. TREASON IN THE TIME OF A FORMER KING

Serjeants' Inn, Mich. 1553.

Note that it was clearly agreed by BROMLEY, PORTMAN and HALES JJ. that if high treason is perpetrated and committed against King Edward VI in his lifetime, or against King Henry VIII in his lifetime, and after the death of the said kings the crown comes to the present Queen Mary, the treason remains still punishable in the time of this queen as it was before, inasmuch as this treason is against the crown and the realm, which never dies. So it is if someone commits murder, manslaughter, robbery or felony in the time of another king, inasmuch as it is 'against his crown and dignity' (*contra coronam et dignitatem suam*), which do not die: for the king never dies, in respect of the regality, albeit by his death in person he demises the crown to another person. Nevertheless, if a trespass is committed against someone, such as a battery to his person, or by entering in his lands, on the death of either party the trespass is gone, for it dies with the person (*moritur cum persona*)[1] and is only a singular damage to one person, whereas treason touches the estate of the whole realm, which remains in being. At Serjeants' Inn, the same Michaelmas term.

13. ATTORNMENT BY A TERMOR

Probably in Serjeants' Inn, Mich. 1553.

Note that it was clearly agreed by all the said justices that if someone makes a lease for years to a stranger, and then makes a feoffment to someone else in fee of these lands leased, and delivers possession and seisin to the feoffee, the lessee being there present and agreeing to the livery and seisin, this is no surrender of the term: for it is nothing but a consent to admit the feoffee into possession of the lands. The same term.

14. ERROR; ROYAL ASSENT

King's Bench or Serjeants' Inn, Mich. 1553 (but dated 1555 in *D*).

Note, by BROMLEY C.J. and PORTMAN J., that if a clerk on his own initiative (*de son teste demesne*) enters a judgment in the Common Bench or King's Bench contrary to right, that is, for the plaintiff where it ought to be for the defendant, no writ of error lies for this: for it is not error, since it is contrary to what they did as justices. So it is if the Lords and Commons are agreed upon an act of parliament, and then the clerk enters on this bill (amongst other bills) the words 'Le roy le voet', or 'Soit fait come ils desiront': even though the king was not there present, this is still a good act of parliament by the law. And they said that the king ought to give his assent to the said act in his own person, or by his letters patent signed with his hand, and that others may not give his assent by his letters

[1] Cf. above, p. 46, pl. 2; p. 48, pl. 3.

casu Thome Duke Northff. in eodem termino apud le parlament (quere). Mes si le commons assent al un bill et mittont cest bill al Seignors ore si les Seignors mitta a cest bil un proviso et le roy assent a cest bill ove le proviso a ceo annex et ceo sans remaunder arere al commons al assenter al dit proviso ore cest est void acte de parlament: sicut accidit en casu domini [D]acres de Northe.

[*fol. 17*]

Hillarii primo Regine Marie

[1]

A, fo. 28[f] (still Mich. 2 & 3 Phil. & Mar.); *L* 217[f] (sim.).

Nota per tout les Justices de Banke le Roy que si le disseisie enter sur le feoffee ou sur le lessee le disseisor que il s. le disseisie apres son entree navera action de trns. pur le trns. mesne vers le lessee ou feoffee de le disseisor entant que il tient eins per title et al comen ley devant lestatute de Glouc' nul damages pur le mesne occupation mes auterment fuit ou serra recoverie vers le feoffee ou lessee le disseisor come appiert per lestatute et cest case fuit en trns. enter John Sare Junior vers John Sare Senior al Sessions en comitatus Buck.

[2]

Nota auxi fuit agree per les justices et auters al Serjeantes Inne eodem termino que si home fist leas per indenture al un pur ans ou pur vie a fest de Saint Michaell rendant rent annuelment al feastes de Saint Michaell et al Annunciation Beate Marie per equall portions que ore le lessor navera nul rent al feast del Annunciation prochein ensuant quar per sa folly demesne et son reservation il ad perde le demye an rent pur cest an et avera nul rent pur cest an mes solement pur le demy an al feast de Saint Michaell prochein apres le dit feast de Saint Michaell finye donques le lessor avera le rent annuellment accordant a lour agreament en lendenture. Mes ore il est adjuge al contrary en le Comen Banke 3 et 4 Philippi et Marie 1556.

patent: as happened in the case of Thomas, duke of Norfolk, in the same term at the parliament (query).[1] But if the Commons assent to the bill and send this bill to the Lords, and the Lords add to this bill a proviso, and the king assents to this bill with the proviso annexed to it, without sending it back to the Commons to assent to the said proviso, this is a void act of parliament:[2] as happened in the case of Lord Dacre of the North.

Hilary Term in the first year of Queen Mary (1554)

1. SARE v. SARE

King's Bench, Hil. 1554.

Note, by all the justices of the King's Bench, that if a disseisee enters upon the disseisor's feoffee, or upon the disseisor's lessee, the disseisee shall not after his entry have an action of trespass for the mesne trespass against the disseisor's lessee or feoffee, inasmuch as he held in by title; and at common law, before the Statute of Gloucester,[3] there were no damages for the mesne occupation; but it was otherwise where there was a recovery against the disseisor's feoffee or lessee, as appears by the statute. This case was in trespass between John Sare, junior, against John Sare, senior, at the sessions in Buckinghamshire.

2. RENT PAYABLE 'ANNUALLY'

Serjeants' Inn, Hil. 1554. Cf. Bendl. 33, pl. 54 (Pas. 1550); Plowd. 30.

Note also that it was agreed by the justices and others at Serjeants' Inn, the same term, that if someone makes a lease to someone by indenture, for years or for life, from the feast of Michaelmas, yielding rent 'annually' at the feasts of Michaelmas and the Annunciation of the Blessed Mary in equal instalments, the lessor shall have no rent at the feast of the Annunciation next following: for by his own foolishness by this reservation he has lost the half-year's rent for this year and shall have no rent for this year except for the half-year ending at Michaelmas next after the said feast of Michaelmas, for [only] then shall the lessor have the rent 'annually' according to their agreement in the indenture. (But it has now been adjudged the contrary in the Common Bench, 3 & 4 Phil. & Mar., 1556.[4])

[1] See above, p. 62, pl. 8.
[2] Cf. *OHLE*, vi. 75.
[3] Statute of Gloucester 1278, c. 1.
[4] See *Granado* v. *Dyer* (1556) below, at p. 86; *Hill* v. *Grange* (1556) below, at p. 107.

[3]

A, fo. 29 (foll. pl. 1); *L* 218 (sim.).

Nota per *Bromeley* Cheef Justice et *Portman* que si home soit arrayne sur endictment de felony pur embler beins al valewe de vi s. et le jury dit sur lour verditt que cestui que fuit yssint arraine est culpable de lembler de les dittes beins mes disoent que les beins ne vault que xi d. et cest est bon verdict et les justices devant que etc. mitteront luy a ses penances come pur petit larceny. En mesme le manner est si home soit arrayne de wilfull murder le jury trove luy culpable de manslaughter et nemi de wilfull murder cest verdict est bon et sur cest verdict cestui que fuit arraine avera son judgement de morte come si fuit arraine sur indictment de felony sur manslaughter: quod nota per *Portman*, et ceo fuit lopinion des toutes les justices.

[4]

A, fo. 29 (foll. pl. 5); *L* 220 (sim.); *D*, fo. 20, pl. 9 (2 & 3 Phil. & Mar.).

Nota auxi per eux eodem termino que si home soit trove culpable [dun felony][1] devant les justices de gaole deliverie et les justices donont judgement de morte de luy et chargeont le viscount de veyer execution estre fait et apres le viscount respite lexecution et puis apres un novell commission de gaole deliverye vient et devant eux justices cestui que ad judgement de mort vient et [*fol. 17v*] plede son pardon generall de toutes felonies et executions que ore les dittes justices nont power dallower cest pardon mes le record de son arraynment et enditement per certiorare doit estre remove devant les justices de Banco Regis ove le corps le prisonner cum corpus cum causa et [la][2] le pardon serra allowe et nemy aliours quar le power les primers justices fuit determyne per le primer comission et les second justices nont power a viewer le record ou amayner le prisonner devant eux entant que le judgement fuit done mes si nul judgement fuit done sur luy mes remayne executory donques les second justices poient allower son pardon ou a doner judgement vers luy come les primers justices poient et ceo per lestatute anno primo E. 6. ca. 7°. [fait pur continuance dactions puis le mort le roy mes devant ceo estatute semble que ils ne puissoient aver done judgment en ceo cas.][3]

[5]

A, fo. 29 (foll. pl. 3); *L* 219 (sim.); *D*, fo. 20, pl. 8.

Nota per *Bromley* et *Portman* eodem termino clerement tenus que si home esteant seisie en fee de terre [ent][4] fait feoffment a cest jour en fee a divers persons al

[1] *A, D, L.*
[2] *A, D, L.*
[3] *A, , D, L.*
[4] *A, D, L.*

3. PARTIAL VERDICTS IN CASE OF FELONY

King's Bench or Serjeants' Inn, Hil./Pas. 1554.

Note, by BROMLEY C.J. and PORTMAN, that if someone is arraigned upon an indictment of felony for stealing goods to the value of 6*s*., and the jury say [as] their verdict that the person so arraigned is guilty of stealing the said goods but that the goods are only worth 11*d*., this is a good verdict, and the justices before whom [he is arraigned] shall set him to his punishment as for petit larceny. It is the same if someone is arraigned of wilful murder, and the jury find him guilty of manslaughter and not of wilful murder, this verdict is good, and upon this verdict the person arraigned shall have his judgment of death as if he were arraigned upon an indictment of felony for manslaughter.[1] Note that, by PORTMAN. And this was the opinion of all the justices.

4. COMMISSIONERS OF GAOL DELIVERY

King's Bench or Serjeants' Inn, Hil./Pas. 1554. Dated 1555 in *D*.

Note also by them, the same term, that if someone is found guilty of a felony before the justices of gaol delivery, and the justices give judgment of death upon him and charge the sheriff to see execution done, and afterwards the sheriff respites the execution, and then afterwards a new commission of gaol delivery comes, and before these [new] justices the person who had judgment of death comes and pleads his general pardon of all felonies and executions, the said justices have no power to allow this pardon; but the record of his arraignment and indictment ought to be removed by *certiorari* before the justices of the King's Bench, with the body of the prisoner and a *corpus cum causa*, and there the pardon shall be allowed and not elsewhere: for the power of the first justices was determined by the first commission, and the second justices have no power to view the record or to bring the prisoner before them, inasmuch as judgment was already given. If, however, no judgment was given upon him, but it remained executory, the second justices could then allow his pardon or give judgment against him, as the first justices could have done; and that is by the statute of 1 Edw. VI, c. 7,[2] [made for continuance of actions after the king's death; but before this statute it seems that they could not have given judgment in this case].[3]

5. CONTINGENT USES

King's Bench or Serjeants' Inn, Hil./Pas. 1554. Dated 1555 in *D*. This closely resembles a case which arose on the Midland Circuit in Lent 1555: Dyer, fo. 99; Dyer's notebook, 110 Selden Soc. 400, pl. 2. Cf. also *Anon.* (1556) Dyer, fo. 133, in the Court of Wards.

Note that it was clearly held by BROMLEY and PORTMAN, the same term, that if someone being seised of land in fee makes a feoffment thereof at the present

[1] Cf. below, p. 59, pl. 9.
[2] 1 Edw. VI, c. 7.
[3] These words are in the printed *D* only.

use de sa feme pur sa vie et apres la mort son feme al use les heires del corps le dit feoffor loyalment engendres que si la feme devie et puis le feoffor s. le baron fist leas pur ans et devie que ore son heire de son corps navoidera le leas issint fait quar entant que home ne poet aver heires en son vie issint que la fuit nul al temps le mort le feme a prender per le remaynder a son heire de son corps cest limitation fuit void et le feoffor avera fee et pur tant le leas bon et liera ses heires. Come en case leas est fait pur vie le remainder al droit heires J. S. que donques est en vie, si le lessee devie vivant cest J. Stile et puis J. S. devie ses heires navera la terre mes le terre revertera arere al lessor ou donor et ses heires. Mes auterment serra peradventure dun devise per testament en tiel case.

[6]

A, fo. 29v; *L* 221.

Nota per eux auxi que la ley est clere a cest jour coment auncient livers sont al contrary que si home esteant deins age come heire a son auncestor sue appeall de mort son auncestor que le paroll ne demurre per le nonage lappellor entant que lappellant ad fait un tort come est suppose de le mort dun home que vient de son tort demeasne et de son tort nul avera advantage.

[7]

A, fo. 29v[f]; *L* 222[f].

Nota auxi clerement agree per *Portman* et auters que si home soit endite que il tiel lieu et an felonyously plaga J. S. sur que plage J. S. morust et sic il felonice predictum J. S. murdravit contra pacem et coronam et ne parle ne rien dit en lenditement ex sua malicia precogitata felonice [*fol. 18*] murdravit uncore cest enditement est bon enditement de wilfull murder car cest paroll murdravit ymplia wilfull murder ex malicia precogitata. Mes si lenditement ust estre et sic ille felonice predictum J. S. interfecit ou occidit la lenditement nextend al wilfull[1] murder mes al un manslaughter ou chauce medley pur que il avera son clergie.

[1] voluntarie *A*.

day to various persons in fee to the use of his wife for her life, and after his wife's death to the use of the heirs of the said feoffor's body lawfully begotten, and the wife dies, and then the feoffor (that is, the husband) makes a lease for years and dies, his heir of his body shall not now avoid the lease so made, for, inasmuch as a man may not have heirs in his lifetime, and therefore there was no-one at the time of the wife's death to take by the remainder to his heir of his body, this limitation was void and the feoffor shall have fee, and thus the lease is good and shall bind his heirs. Similarly in the case where a lease is made for life, remainder to the right heirs of John Style, who is then alive, and the lessee dies while this John Style is living, and then John Style dies, his heirs shall not have the land, but the land shall revert back to the lessor or donor and his heirs. But perhaps it would be otherwise of a devise by testament in such a case.

6. APPEAL OF DEATH BY A MINOR

King's Bench or Serjeants' Inn, Hil./Pas. 1554.

Note by them also that the law is clear at the present day – although old books are to the contrary – that if someone under age sues an appeal of death as heir to his ancestor, the parol does not demur by the minority of the appellor, because the [appellee] has committed a wrong (as is supposed) in respect of a man's death, which comes from his own wrong, and he shall not take advantage of his own wrong.

7. WORDING OF INDICTMENTS FOR MURDER

King's Bench or Serjeants' Inn, Hil./Pas. 1554.

Note also that it was clearly agreed by PORTMAN and others that if someone is indicted that in such and such a place and year he feloniously wounded John Style, from which wound John Style died, and thus he feloniously murdered the aforesaid John Style against the peace and the crown, and there is nothing said in the indictment to the effect that he 'feloniously murdered of his malice aforethought' (*ex sua malicia praecogitata felonice murdravit*), this is nevertheless a good indictment of wilful murder; for the word *murdravit* implies wilful murder of malice aforethought. But if the indictment had been 'and thus he feloniously killed (*interfecit*) or slew (*occidit*) the aforesaid John Style', the indictment would not have extended to wilful murder, but only to manslaughter or chance medley, for which he could have his clergy.

[8]

A, fo. 22 (first case of 1 Mar.); *L* 151 (sim.); *B*, p. 127 (sim.); *D*, fo. 14, pl. 1; Keil. 204.

Nota per *Bromley* Cheife Justice et *Portman*[1] clerement que si le fittes occide son pier ou son mier ou le fittes en ley occide son pier ou son mier en ley que cest est murder ou manslaughter come le case est et nemy petit treason declare per lestatute anno 25 E. 3. quar lestatute declare mes pur servantes et le fittes nest servant. Mes si le servant occide son mistres soit el covert de son baron ou widow cest est petit treason coment que lestatute parle solement de le master car cest est tout un et le baron et le feme sont en ley un person. Et ils disoent que si le pier ou le pier en ley done a son fittes ou fittes en ley manger boyer et vesture et il fait ove luy necessary service ore si tiel fittes occide son pier ou pier en ley et est endite pur cest come per nomen servientis quod proditorie occidit son pier existentis in servitio suo que cest est petit treason coment que il nad auters gages de luy.

[9]

A, fo. 22r–v[f]; *L* 152[f]; *B*, p. 127[f]; *D*, fo. 14, pl. 2 (1 Mar.).

Auxi ils disoent que si home soit endite de petit treson, felony ou murder et est arraine et plede non culpable et le jury trove luy culpable come accessory que cest verditt est void coment que fuit certenement trove coment fuit accessory quar le verdit est dauter chose que ils fueront charge quar ils fueront charges que de le principall. Mes si home soit arraine de wilfull murder et le jury luy trove culpable de manslaughter cest est bon verdit ou luy trove culpable seipsum defendendo cest est bon verdit auxi ceux verdittes sont ensuantes et dependantes tout sur un et declaront coment il vient a son mort mes en lauter case nest my pursuant mes contrariant.

[10]

Nota auxi per eux clerement que si 3 homes sont endites de felony ou murder et deux auters come accessories a cest offence, 2 de les principals sont present et les accessories auxi et 3 principall nest my present mes est ale, les 2 principals plede sur lour arraynment nient culpable que les accessories puissoient estre mises ore a responder coment que le 3 principall fait default quar ils sont accessories a chescun de eux et lour felony ou murder coment que fuit fait tout al un temps uncore il est severall felonies en chescun de eux quar en appeale versus 2

[1] *D (only) adds* Browne.

8. PETIT TREASON: CHILDREN AND SERVANTS

King's Bench or Serjeants' Inn, Hil./Pas. 1554.

Note, by BROMLEY C.J. and PORTMAN, clearly, that if a son kills his father or his mother, or a son in law kills his father in law or his mother in law, this is murder or manslaughter (as the case is) but not petit treason as declared by the statute of 25 Edw. III,[1] for the statute only mentions servants and the son is not a servant. But if a servant kills his mistress, and she is married (*covert de son baron*) or widowed, this is petit treason, even though the statute speaks only of masters: for this is all one, and husband and wife are in law one person. But they said that if a father or father in law gives his son or son in law food, drink and clothing, and he performs necessary services for him, and such a son kills his father or father in law and is indicted for this by the name of 'servant', that 'he traitorously slew his father, being in his service', this is petit treason even though he has no other wages from him.

9. PARTIAL AND CONTRADICTORY VERDICTS

Contd from pl. 8.

They also said that if someone is indicted of petit treason, felony or murder, and is arraigned and pleads Not guilty, and the jury finds him guilty as accessory, this verdict is void, even though it was found with certainty of detail how he was accessory: for the verdict is something different from what they were charged with, for they were only charged with the principal. If, however, someone is arraigned of wilful murder, and the jury finds him guilty of manslaughter, this is a good verdict;[2] or if they find him guilty in self-defence, this is a good verdict also. These verdicts are wholly pursuant to or dependent upon one [matter] and clarify how he came he came to his death, whereas in the other case it is not pursuant but contradictory.

10. PRINCIPAL AND ACCESSORY

Contd from pl. 9.

Note also by them, clearly, that if three men are indicted of felony or murder, and two others as accessories to this offence, and two of the principals are present, and the accessories also, while the third principal is not present but has gone, and the two principals plead Not guilty upon their arraignment, the accessories may be put to answer now even though the third principal makes default: for they are accessories to each of them, and to their felony or murder, and even though it was all done at one time [the offences] are nevertheless separate felonies in each of them; for in an appeal of murder against two, if the appellor makes a

[1] Treason Act 1351, 25 Edw. III, stat. 5, c. 2. Cf. below, p. 68, pl. 25.

[2] Cf. above, p. 57, pl. 3.

de murder coment que lappellor releas al un uncore ceo nextend al auter [*fol. 18v*] coment que en breife de trns. vers 2 et releas est fait al un cest est discharge al ambideux. Et sic si les 2 principalls sont troves culpable ou un de eux est trove culpable et les accessories auxi ore les accessories serra mises a lour judgement et execution mes si les principalls sont acquites ore les accessories remayna tanque le tierce soit utlage ou auterment attaint ou acquite pur ceo que ils poient estre accessories a luy sil soit attaint. Et issint si les deux principals sont attaintes et les accessories acquites uncore les accessories remayna tanque le 3 soit attaint ou utlage car poet estre accessory a luy et nemy a les auters.

[11]

A, fo. 22v (foll. pl. 9); *L* 153 (sim.); abr. in *B*, p. 127.

En assise de terre le tenant dit que le pier le pl. fuit seisie de le terre et pur xl li. nomine finis et grossom[e] bargaine et vende la terre al tenant pur term de son vie devant lestatute de uses rendant le rent al lessor s. le bargaynor et ses heires de xl li. per que le pier le pl. fuit seisie al son use pur vie et apres lestatute duses il fuit ent seisie come de francktenement pur son vie et done coulor et demaund judgement si lassise. Et cest plee per *Portman* Justice et *Gawdy* Serjeant fuit tenus bon plee en barr et le bargaine bon et cest consideration alter le use en le terre coment que la est un rent reserve devant lestatute et per le statute le possession vient al use come luse est declare: quod nota [quar][1] cest est le greinder opinion de toutes.

[12]

Abr. in *A*, fo. 22[f]; *L* 154[f]; *B*, p. 127[f]; *D*, fo. 14, pl. 3 (1 Mar.).

Nota per *Bromley* et *Portman* auxi que si home soit attaint de treason [or felony][2] et puis le roy luy pardon et le roy puis done a luy et a ses heires terres ou auter home done a luy terres en fee et apres il prist feme et ad yssue et devie sans auter restitution de sanke uncore son yssue yssint ewe avera le terre come heire a luy car ore entant que il fuit pardon ne bosoigne auter restitution quar il poet prender et est enable a prender et a purchase de chescun et issint en ley restore a son sanke per le pardone pur terre done puis le pardon et cest reason tient lieu auxi coment que il avoit yssue devant lattainder quar en cest case cest yssue enherite a luy per le pardon et le [ ][3] puis le pardon: mes si nul pardon fuit auterment est, ou si pier et fittes sont le fittes est attaint de treason ou felony ore coment le fittes ad son pardon et le pier devie uncore le fittes nest per cest

1 que *H.* et *A.*
2 *A, D, but not B or L.*
3 *Blank in H. Sentence om. A, B, D, L.*

release to one of them, this does not extend to the other, although in a writ of trespass against two a release made to one is a discharge to both of them. So it is if two of the principals are found guilty, or one of them is found guilty, and the accessories also, the accessories shall be put to their judgment and execution; but if the [two] principals are acquitted, the accessories remain until the third is outlawed or otherwise attainted or acquitted, because they may be accessories to him if he is attainted. So it is if the [two] principals are attainted and the accessories acquitted: the accessories shall still remain until the third is attainted or outlawed, for they may be accessory to him and not to the others.

11. EXECUTION OF USES

Probably in Serjeants' Inn, Hil./Pas. 1554.

In an assize for land, the tenant says that the plaintiff's father was seised of the land and for £40, in the name of a fine and gersum,[1] bargained and sold the land to the tenant for term of his life before the Statute of Uses,[2] yielding £40 rent to the lessor (namely, the bargainor) and his heirs, as a result of which the plaintiff's father was seised to his use for life, and after the statute he was seised thereof as of freehold for his life, and gives colour, and demands judgment whether the assize should be taken. And this plea was held a good plea in bar by PORTMAN J. and *Gawdy*, serjeant, and the bargain good; and this consideration alters the use in the land even though there is a rent reserved before the statute; and by the statute the possession comes to the use in the same way that the use is declared. Note that, which is the greater opinion of all.[3]

12. PARDON AND RESTORATION IN BLOOD

Probably in Serjeants' Inn, Hil./Pas. 1554.

Note, by BROMLEY, and PORTMAN also, that if someone is attainted of treason or felony, the king pardons him, and then the king gives lands to him and his heirs, or someone else gives him lands in fee, and afterwards he marries and has issue and dies without any other restoration of the blood, nevertheless his issue (so had) shall have the land as heir to him, for since he was pardoned there is no need for other restoration. This is because he may take and is enabled to take and to purchase from everyone, and thus in law is restored to his blood by the pardon, with respect to land given after the pardon: and this reason also holds good even if he had issue before the attainder, for in this case this issue inherits from him by virtue of the pardon and the [death] after the pardon. But it would have been otherwise if there had been no pardon. Or if there be father and son, and the son is attainted of treason or felony, even though the son has his pardon,

[1] A fine or premium: *NED*, gersum.

[2] 27 Hen. VIII, c. 10.

[3] Presumably meaning a majority: cf. below, p. 79.

restore ne avera la terre come heire a son pier car le pardon nest restitution a luy en sanke a demaunder come heire al auter. Et issint est si aiell pier et fittes sont le pier est attaint de treason ou felony et devie ore le fittes ne demaundera le terre come heire a son aiell coment que son pier fuit pardon per le roy car le bridge est enfreint quar nient pluis que le pier poet demaunder come heire nient pluis le fittes. Mes en le primer case quant le pier apres son attainder ad son pardon la est nul impediment a son fittes et heire a [*fol. 19*] demaunder come heire a luy apres le pardon pur les terres purchases ou a luy dones puis le pardon car quant al eux nul bridge est enfreint quod nota per eux agree.

[13]

Nota per *Portman* Justice clerement agree que en petit treason la est nul accessories nient pluis que en hault treason mes toutes les aydors come les actors sont principalls et il dit que fuit agree et adjudge in Banco Regis a tard que si feme occide son baron que ore le heire le baron navera vers le feme de mort son pier nul appeall entant que il est treason que touche le roy et pur ceo si le roy pardon le treason per cest pardon la feme est tout oustrement discharge vers toutes en le monde de ceo offence. Quere tamen des accessories en petit treason.

[14]

A, fo. 22v (foll. pl. 12); *L* 155 (sim.).

Nota auxi per luy que si feme occide son baron per poysoninge que sil soit endite de cest offence come pur treason per cest paroll proditorie que ore ceo est petit treason. Et sil soit endite de wilfull murder il est murder et issint il[1] 2 offences come il poet ou est trove per enditement quar lestatute anno 1 E. 6. ca. 12 ne tolla loffence de treason mes ceo confirme et fuit wilfull poysoninge wilfull murder et issint per son opinion lestatute fait cest offence en cest case 2 offences come il est use en le enditement s. un offence come fuit adevant remayna et cest petit treason et lauter offence est per lestatute avauntdit wilfull murder.

Bromeley Cheife Justice doubta en le case.

[1] *Sic, but otiose.*

and the father dies, the son is nevertheless not thereby restored and shall not have the land as heir to his father, for the pardon is not a restoration to him in blood to demand as heir to another. So it is if there be grandfather, father, and son, and the father is attainted of treason or felony, and dies, the son shall not demand the land as heir to his grandfather, even though the father was pardoned by the king, for the bridge is broken: for, just as the father may not demand as heir, nor may the son. In the first case, however, when the father had his pardon after his attainder, there is no impediment for his son and heir to demand as heir to him after the pardon, with respect to lands purchased or given to him since the pardon, for as to them no bridge is broken. Note that: agreed by them.

13. PETIT TREASON

Serjeants' Inn, Hil. 1554. Cf. below, p. 68, pl. 25.

Note that it was clearly agreed by PORTMAN J. that in petit treason there are no accessories, any more than in high treason, but all the aiders are as much principals as the actors. And he said that it was agreed and adjudged in the King's Bench recently that, if a woman kills her husband, the husband's heir shall have no appeal against the woman for the death of his father inasmuch as it is treason, which touches the king; and therefore if the king pardons the treason the woman is utterly discharged by this pardon against the whole world for this offence. Query, nevertheless, concerning accessories in petit treason.

14. PETIT TREASON

Contd from pl. 13.

Note also, by him, that if a woman kills her husband by poisoning and is indicted for this offence as treason, by the word 'traitorously' (*proditorie*), this is now petit treason. But if she is indicted for wilful murder, it is murder. Thus there are two offences, [depending on how] it is found by indictment. For the statute of 1 Edw. VI, c. 12,[1] does not take away the offence of treason but confirms it, and wilful poisoning was wilful murder, and so in his opinion the statute makes this offence in the present case two offences, depending on how the indictment is drawn, namely an offence which remains as it was before (petit treason) and another offence under the aforesaid statute (wilful murder).

BROMLEY C.J. doubted this case.

[1] Presumably the section concerning poisoning: 'that all wilful killing by poisoning of any person or persons . . . shall be adjudged, taken and deemed wilful murder of malice prepensed'. The intention here was probably to remove the year-and-day limitation in case of poisoning, since it is not clear what other doubt there could have been about wilful poisoning. Cf. the first section: 'no act, deed or offence being by act of parliament or statute made treason or petit treason . . . shall be taken, had, deemed and adjudged to be high treason or petit treason, but only such as be treason or petit treason in or by the act of parliament [of 25 Edw. III]'. Cf. further p. 68, below, pl. 25.

[15]

A, fo. 22v[f]; *L* 156[f]; *B*, p. 127 (foll. pl. 12).

Un fieri facias sur un judgement sur det ou trns. fuit agard en Comen Banke, le viscount returne que il ad prise[1] toutes beins a quel le det ou damages amounta queux en ses maines remaine per default des emptors et devant cest returne un breife derrour a reverser le judgement vient a les judges a remover le record et uncore per bon advise des justices breife ad venditionem exponas fuit direct al vicount a faire sale des beins issint prises et prayses quar ceo nest forsque al executer lexecution devant agard et nemy le judgement: quod nota bene.

Dyer's report of the case

Les Reports (1688 ed.), ff. 98v–99, pl. 57.

<Inter Milton et Eldrington>[2] Un fieri facias fuit direct al viconte de Midd', que returne, quod cepit bona et catalla defendentis al value de part del det, et quod remanent in custodia sua pro defectu emptorum, et quod ante returnum hujus brevis, breve de Non molestando fuit direct, quod de ulteriori executione supersedeas, le quel brief il returne annex al fieri facias, et cest brief de Non molestando fuit agard in Banco, per reason dun brief derror la port per le defendant. Mes le record ne fuit uncore remove, eo que le returne del brief derror fuit, Crastino Ascensionis, et non ante, et fieri facias returne xv. Paschae. Et fuit bien debate, si breve de venditione exponenda, serroit agard in cest case ou nemy, eo que le brief de execution ne fuit servy, ne le property des biens altered, nient obstant le seisure. Et tamen tandem le brief de venditione exponenda fuit agard per *Saunders* et *Brown.*

[16]

A, ff. 22v–23;[f] *L* 157[f]; *D*, fo. 14, pl. 4 (1 Mar.).

Nota que al Serjeantes Inne un graunde question fuit propone enter les justices et serjeantes le roygne et auters esteantes de sa fee. Si ascun patent ou breife de sommons de le parlament ou auters breifes quel touchant le roigne mesme intermittant (supremum caput) sont bones ou nemy. Et per lopinion de Justice *Bromley* Cheife Justice et toutes auters, savant *Portman* Justice, *Wyddon* Justice et *Dallison* serjeant al ley, fuit agree que les lettres patentes sont bons entant que lestatute anno 26 H. 8. et lestatute 37 H. 8. vaont [tant][3] solement en laffirma-

[1] levye *A, L.*
[2] Margin.
[3] *A, D.* toute *H.*

15. MILTON v. ELDRINGTON

Common Pleas, Pas. 1554. Also reported in Dyer, fo. 98b (Pas. 1554); printed below.

A *fieri facias* upon a judgment in debt or trespass was awarded in the Common Bench, the sheriff returned that he had taken all the goods to which the debt or damages amounted, and that they remained in his hands for want of buyers, and before this return a writ of error to reverse the judgment came to the judges to remove the record: nevertheless, by good advice of the justices, a writ *ad venditionem exponas* was directed to the sheriff to make sale of the goods so taken and appraised, for that is but to execute the execution already awarded and not the judgment. Note that well.

Translation of Dyer's report

Easter term 1554.

A *fieri facias* was directed to the sheriff of Middlesex, who returned that he had taken the goods and chattels of the defendant to the value of part of the debt, and that they remained in his keeping for want of buyers, and that before the return of this writ a writ of *non molestando* was directed [to him] 'that you stay further execution', which writ he returned annexed to the *fieri facias*; and this writ of *non molestando* was awarded in the [King's] Bench, by reason of a writ of error brought there by the defendant, but the record was not yet removed, because the return of the writ of error was on the morrow of the Ascension, and not before, and the *fieri facias* was returned at the quindene of Easter. And it was well debated whether a writ of *venditioni exponas* should be awarded in this case, or not, inasmuch as the writ of execution was not served, nor the property of the goods altered, notwithstanding the seizure. Yet in the end the writ of *venditioni exponas* was awarded by SAUNDERS and BROWNE.

16. QUEEN'S STYLE OF 'SUPREME HEAD'

Serjeants' Inn, Pas. 1554. Also reported in Dyer, fo. 98 (Pas. 1554); printed below; cf. *OHLE*, vi. 63.

Note that a great question was propounded at Serjeants' Inn among the justices and queen's serjeants, and others of her fee: whether any patent or writ of summons for the parliament, or other writs which touch the queen herself, leaving out 'supreme head' (*supremum caput*) [of the Church of England], are good, or not. Any by the opinion of BROMLEY C.J. and all others, save for PORTMAN J., WHIDDON J. and *Dalison*, serjeant at law,[1] it was agreed that the letters patent are good, inasmuch as the statute of 26 Hen. VIII,[2] and the statute [35] Hen.

[1] Dyer also names Hare, Browne and Caryll as being of this contrary opinion.

[2] 26 Hen. VIII, c. 1: 'that the king our sovereign lord, his heirs and successors, kings of this realm, shall be taken, accepted and reputed the only supreme head in earth of the Church of England, called *Anglicana Ecclesia*, and shall have and enjoy, annexed and united to the imperial crown of this realm, as well the title and style thereof as all honours, dignities . . .'.

tive et nemy en le negative que sils font auterment ils serront ajudges void et per tant ne obligent le royne come lestatute est quod duo justiciarii seu servientes jurati [*fol. 19v*] essent justiciarii ad assisas etc. et non alii, ore si ceus parolls (non alii) ne fueront en lestatute auters poient estre mises eins per le roigne mes [ceux negative parols oblige le royne mes][1] esteant regard al breifes originalles et auters proces enter partie et partie ceux parolls (supremum caput) doient estre mises eins ou auterment ils abattera car lestatute en laffirmative oblige toutes subjectes mes nemy le roigne sil ne soit per expresse parolls oblige ou en le negative: quod nota.

Dyer's report of the case

Les Reports (1688 ed.), fo. 98, pl. 50.

Un graund doubt fuit move inter les Justices et Serjeants, si les briefs le Roigne del summoner de cest Parliament, in queux le title ou stile de supremum caput Ecclesiae Anglicanae etc. fuit omit, fueront bones et sufficients, ou que tout est voide etc. eo que le dit stile est unite et annexe per les estatutes de 26 et 35 H. 8. al imperial crown de cest Realm, ut ibidem patet, et per lopinion de *Bromley, Baker, Brook, Saunders, Dyer, Stamford, Lattorney*, et *Solicitor*, que il est assets bone, car supremum caput nest parcel del nosme le Roigne, mes addition etc. Et les parols de lestatute sont tantum in laffirmative, et nemy ascun negative, que le stile serra de necessity issint escry per le Roigne etc. Sed *Hare, Portman, Brown, Whiddon* et *Carel* al contrary, et cest doubt fuit auterfoits move in primo Parliamento Reginae Eliz. et fuit resolve per grand deliberatioon, ut supra, primo.

[17]

A, fo. 23^{f}; *L* 158^{f}; *B*, p. 127 (foll. pl. 15); *D*, fo. 14, pl. 5 (1 Mar.).

Nota per *Bromeley* Cheife Justice et *Portman* Justice et auters agree[2] que si 3 ou plusours enter se conspiront a faire un commotion ou levy gwer encounter le roigne en son realm pur alter le religion ou la ley etc., si null act ensua sur cest conspiracy est nul treason per lestatute anno 25 E. 3. Mes si un de eux apres levye gwerr encounter le roigne per reson de cest conspiracy et les auter seiant a lour meases sans auter [act fair][3] ils toutes sont traytors per le dit statute apres le commotion issint fait per un de eux quar cest procurement est un acte quar per cest ils sont adherantes et aydantes enemies le roygne et en treason nul acces-

1 *A, D.*
2 clerement *A, B, D.*
3 *D.* act fait *A, L.* act *B.* fait ou act *H.*

VIII,[1] go solely in the affirmative and not in the negative – i.e. that if [patents] are otherwise they shall be adjudged void – and for that reason they do not bind the queen. Similarly a statute says 'that two justices or serjeants sworn should be justices to take the assizes, and not others';[2] if these words 'and not others' were not in the statute others might be put in [commission] by the queen, [but these negative words bind the queen].[3] But with regard to original writs and other process between party and party, these words *supremum caput* ought to be put in or else they will abate; for a statute in the affirmative binds all subjects, though not the queen – unless she is bound by express words, or by words in the negative.[4] Note that.

Translation of Dyer's report

Easter term 1554.

A great matter of doubt was moved among the justices and serjeants, whether the queen's writs for summoning this parliament, in which the title or style of 'supreme head of the Church of England etc.' was omitted, were good and sufficient, or whether the whole is void etc. because the said style is united and annexed by the statutes of 26 Hen. VIII [c. 1] and 35 H. 8 [c. 3] to the imperial crown of this realm, as there appears. And by the opinion of BROMLEY, *Baker*, BROKE, SAUNDERS, *Dyer*, *Staunford*, *the attorney [general]*, and *solicitor [general]*, it is perfectly good, for 'supreme head' is not parcel of the queen's name but an addition etc. And the words of the statute are solely in the affirmative, and there is no negative, that the style shall of necessity be so written by the queen etc. But HARE, PORTMAN, BROWNE, WHIDDON and *Caryll* to the contrary. This doubt was moved again in the first parliament of Queen Elizabeth, and was resolved by great deliberation as first above.

17. R. v. CROFTE

London Guildhall, 28 April 1554. Record: Baga de secretis, KB 8/29 (Croftes).

Note that it was agreed by BROMLEY C.J., PORTMAN J., and others, that if three or more conspire amongst themselves to make a commotion or to levy war against the queen in her realm, to alter religion or the law etc., and no act follows upon this conspiracy, it is no treason by the statute of 25 Edw. III.[5] But if one of them afterwards levies war against the queen by reason of this conspiracy, and the others sit at home without doing anything further, they are all traitors by the said statute after the commotion thus made by one of them: for this procurement is an act, inasmuch as they are thereby adhering to and aiding the queen's enemies. And in treason there are no accessories, but all are principals, by the

[1] The text says 37 Hen. VIII, but the reference is to 35 Hen. VIII, c. 3. Dyer gives the correct citation. The statute provides that the style 'of the Church of England, and also of Ireland, in earth the supreme head' should be 'annexed for ever to the imperial crown of his highness realm of England'. The statutes were repealed by 1 & 2 Phil. & Mar., c. 8.

[2] A paraphrase of 14 Edw. III. stat. 1. c. 16.

[3] These words are in *A* and *D*.

[4] For an example of a writ of Mary I using the title Supreme Head, see below, p. 94.

[5] Treason Act 1351, 25 Edw. III, stat. 5, c. 2.

sory mes toutes principalls per lexpresse parolls de le dit statute. Ceo fuit agree al arraynment de Sir James Crofte al Guyld Hall in London isto eodem termino Pasche et primo Marie pur estre conspirator ove Wyatt. Et sic nota que lestatute de repell de treasons et felonies fait anno 1° Regine ne repelle cest treason quar est deins le statute anno 25 E. 3.

[18]

A, fo. 23^{f}; *L* 159^{f}; *B*, p. 127^{f}; *D*, fo. 14, pl. 6 (1 Mar.).

Nota que il fuit adjuge en Banke le Roygne per bon advise mesme cest terme que si un office soit traverse en le Chauncery encounter le roigne et sur cest latturney le roygne replia et sont al yssue et le transcript le dit record est amesne en Bank le Roygne a tryer lissue que est trove vers le roygne mes pur ceo que toutes les pointes en loffice ne sont traverses cestui que tenda le travers fuit compell a repleader et que il repleder en Banke le Roygne et nemy en le Chauncery coment que rien est certify en le dit Banke que le transcript et le very record remayne en le Chauncery entant que le court est un foites seisie de le dit record et cest repleder [n]est que a fortefier le dit record et a tryer et a ensuer lissue en le dit travers estre le melior et le pluis [tost][1] estre trye issint que droit soit fait al parties. Et hoc accidit in casu Edmundi[2] Claxton[3] que traverse loffice trove apres le mort Johannis Melstron que trove que le dit John fuit seisie et morust seisie etc. et que il morust 22[4] die Julii anno 28 H. 8. son heire esteant ideott et Claxton convey lestate de Melstron a luy et a ses heires per recoverie et assureance fait a luy anno 22[5] H. 8. et traverse toutes les pointes en loffice forsque le mort Melstron le dit 22 die Julii 28 le roy H. 8. et donques [Melstron][6] fuit morte al temps le dit assurance et issint falsifier le title Claxton pur que cause Claxton pray al court a repleder la en cest court et fuit [*fol. 20*] issint admitt. Et vide pur cest matter P. 13 E. 4. fo. 8. bon matter et precedent pur cest matter a repleder en cest court fuit monstre en cest court per le clerke le Corone en temps H. le 6.

[1] *A, B.* toft *L.* lose *D.* teste *H.*
[2] Egidii *A, D, L. om. B.*
[3] Clayton *A, D.* Clampton *B.* Clopton *L.*
[4] *Altered to or* from 20. 20 *D.*
[5] 20 *D only.*
[6] Westron *H.*

express words of the said statute. This was agreed at the arraignment of Sir James Crofte at the Guildhall, London, this same Easter term in the first year of Mary, for being a conspirator with Wyatt.[1] Thus note that the statute of repeal of treasons and felonies, made in the queen's first year,[2] does not repeal this treason, for it is in the statute of 25 Edw. III.

18. RE MELSTRON, ex parte CLAXTON

Queen's Bench, Pas. 1554.

Note that it was adjudged in the Queen's Bench by good advice this same term that [where] an office is traversed in the Chancery against the queen, and thereupon the queen's attorney replies and they are at issue, and the transcript of the said record is brought into the Queen's Bench to try the issue, and it is found against the queen, nevertheless, because all the points of the office are not traversed, the person who tendered the traverse is compelled to replead. And [it was held] that he should replead in the Queen's Bench and not in Chancery, even though nothing has been certified in the said Bench but the transcript, and the true record remains in the Chancery, inasmuch as the court is already seised of the said record and this repleader is only to fortify the said record, and to try and to follow the issue in the said traverse to make it better and more ready to be tried, so that right may be done to the parties. This happened in the case of Edmund Claxton,[3] who traversed the office found after the death of John Melstron,[4] which found that the said John was seised, and died seised etc., and that he died on 22 July [1536], 28 Hen. VIII, his heir being an idiot, and Claxton traced the estate from Melstron to him and his heirs by a recovery and assurance made to him in the year 22 Hen. VIII, and traversed all the points in the office except the death of Melstron on the said 22 July, 28 Hen. VIII, so that Melstron was dead at the time of the assurance, and Claxton's title is thus falsified; and for this reason Claxton prayed the court to replead there in that court, and was admitted to do so. See for this matter Pas. 13 Edw. IV, fo. 8,[5] where good matter, and a precedent for this matter of repleading in this court, was shown in this court by the clerk of the crown in the time of Henry VI.

[1] Sir James Croft (d. 1590) of Croft Castle and Shobdon, Herefs.; M.P. Herefs. 1542–89; knighted 1547; tried on 28 April 1554 and condemned to death; pardoned 16 Feb. 1555: *HPHC 1509–58*, i. 724–725. For Wyatt see below, p. 99.

[2] 1 Mar. I, sess. 1, c. 1, which was in substantially the same terms as 1 Edw. VI, c. 12, quoted above, p. 61, n. 1.

[3] Probably of Clement's Inn (sued for dues 1525–26; outlawry proclaimed in Lincs.); died in the 1550s (C142/110/127, Notts.). *A* and the printed edition give the name as Giles Clayton; *H* says Edmund Clayton; *L* says Edmund Clopton.

[4] There is no such name in the PRO index of inquisitions post mortem.

[5] YB Pas. 13 Edw. IV, fo. 8, pl. 1.

[19]

Abr. in *A*, fo. 23[f]; *L* 160[f]; *D*, fo. 15, pl. 7 (1 Mar.).

Nota per *Portman* [clerement],[1] et ne fuit mult deny per *Bromley* Cheife Justice, [que] si un ou plusors sont electes per breife destre coroners deins un county et apres cest election le roy morust que uncore ils et cestui issint elect per breife esteant nul discharge per breife remayne coroners ou coroner come il ou ils fueront tanque ils ont lour discharge per breife ou per mort, le mort le [roy][2] nient obstant, entant que ils vient eins per election sur le breife et nemy tout soulement per le breife que breife remayna et fuit direct al vicount et en son custodi[e] remayna et nemy en lour custodie queux sont electes et puis est returne en le Chauncery per le viscount. Mes toutes commissions de peace, commissions al justices, commissions al viscounts et escheators per le mort le roy sont determines et per consequens le power de le commissioners [en eux nosmes][3] quar ils ont lour power per le commission tantum et ceo al volunt le roy et ceo est determine per mort le roy mes coroner ad estate per election pur son vie sil nad auter discharge per breife apres pur causes.

[20]

A, fo. 23v[f]; *L* 161[f]; *B*, pp. 127–128 (foll. pl. 18); *D*, fo. 15, pl. 8 (1 Mar.).

Nota auxi per bon advise des justices de Banke le Roygne que si home soit endict de forcible entree sur lestatute 8 H. 6. et lenditement est que lendictee ad forciblement enter en un tenement en Dale et de ceo ad expulse et disseise lendictor contra formam statuti que ore lendictor navera sur cest indictment breife de restitution pur le non certeinty, issint lendictment est void, quar tenementum ad auxibein relation al un mese ou un cotage come al terres, prate ou pasture yssint les justices ne le viscount ne poient estre ascertein a metter luy en possession ou en quel liew. Come en breife de dower unde nihil habet le breife est de libero tenemento suo in D. si le tenant fist default le demaundant navera[4] graunde cape devant il declare al court le certenty de son demaund. Yssint est en assise le breife est general de libero tenemento et si lassise soit agard per default de le tenant en lassise uncore le pl. doit declare en fesant son pleint le certenty de son demaund et sil ne fait yssint lassise ne serra agard ne il unques ne avera judgement: quod nota per *Bromley*, *Portman* et *Wyddon* Justices la esteant cest temps per advise.

1 *A only.*
2 roigne *H.*
3 mesmes *A, L.* mesures *D.*
4 *Interlined later.*

19. OFFICE OF CORONER

Probably in the Queen's Bench, Pas. 1554.

Note, by PORTMAN, and not much denied by BROMLEY C.J., that if one or more are elected by writ to be coroners within a county, and after this election the king dies, they (or he) having been so elected by writ – and there being no discharge by writ – still remain coroners (or coroner) as they were before, until they have their discharge by writ, or by death, notwithstanding the king's death, inasmuch as they came in by election upon the writ and not solely by the writ, which writ remains and was directed to the sheriff, and remains in his keeping and not in the keeping of those who were elected, and is then returned into the Chancery by the sheriff. On the other hand, all commissions of the peace, commissions to be justices, and commissions to sheriffs and escheators, are determined by the king's death, and in consequence the power of the commissioners therein named [is also determined], for they have their power through the commission only, and that is at the king's will, which is determined by the king's death, whereas a coroner has an estate for his life by election, unless there is some other discharge afterwards by writ, for cause.

20. PARTICULARS OF LAND IN DEMAND

Queen's Bench, Pas. 1554. Cf. Bendl. 37, pl. 68 (Common Pleas, 1554); Dyer, fo. 122 (Mich. 1555).

Note also, by good advice of the justices of the Queen's Bench, that if someone is indicted of forcible entry upon the statute of 8 Hen. VI,[1] and the indictment is that the indictee has forcibly entered into a 'tenement' in Dale and has therefrom expelled and disseised the indictor, against the form of the statute, the indictor shall not have a writ of restitution upon this indictment because of the uncertainty, and thus the indictment is void: for 'tenement' might refer just as well to a house or a cottage as to lands, meadow or pasture, and therefore neither the justices nor the sheriff can be certainly informed for the purpose of putting him in possession, or in what place. Similarly, if in a writ of dower *unde nihil habet* the writ says 'of his free tenement in Dale', and the tenant makes default, the demandant shall not have a grand *cape* before he has declared to the court the certain detail of his demand. So it is in an assize: the writ is in general terms 'of a free tenement', and if the assize is awarded by default of the tenant in the assize the plaintiff ought nevertheless to declare in making his plaint the certain detail of his demand, and if he does not do so the assize shall not be awarded and he shall never have judgment. Note that: by BROMLEY, PORTMAN and WHIDDON JJ., being there at this time, by advice.

[1] 8 Hen. VI, c. 9 (forcible entry).

[21]

Abr. in *A*, fo. 23v[f]; *L* 162[f]; *B*, p. 128[f].

Nota auxi per *Portman* que en haute treason que towcha le roygne mesme come a son person come compasser son morte ou levier gwerre vers luy ou aydant a ses enemies ou a subverter les leyes del terre en ceux cases le judgement serra que ils serront trahes, pendues et quarters [*fol. 20v*] et bowelled etc. Mes en haute treason que ne toucha le roigne mesme come a son person come a tuer ses justices, fauxer le seale le roy, le coyne le roye, ou le coyne del auter roy, signet ou privey seale, coment que ceux sont haut treasons, uncore le judgement serra que ils serra trahes et pendues tantum entant que ils ne towchant le person le roy. Mes *Bromley* Cheife Justice dit que en fait yssint fuit use mes il ne scavoit pas ascun reason pur que il serroit issint quar il dit quant il fuit serjeant al roy un Egerton fuit arraine pur filer le graund seale le roy que fuit adevant al un auter patent al novell pattent et cest fuit tenus treson et il ad son judgement estre trahe, pendue et quarter etc. Et donques *Portman* dit que en fait il poet estre issint et lauter voy al discretion des justices devant queux etc. Come si un feme soit indicta de treason sur lestatute de anno 26 H. 8. per parolls contra le roy et trove culpable el poet estre adjudge destre combure le comon course est al un feme pur treason ou destre trahue et pendue tout per discretion: et issint fuit use al Lincolne tempore Luke Justice dassise la et Whorwood.

[22]

Abr. in *A*, fo. 23v[f]; *L* 163[f]; *B*, p. 128[f].

Nota en petit treason come feme a tuer sa baron, le servant son master, le moigne son abbott ou prior, ou le servant son mistres, le judgement serra trahe et pendue tantum et toutes foites pur un feme en tiel case estre trahe et arse. En ceux cases de petit treason leschete apperteigne al seignors et nemy al roy forsque les terres de luy tenus, et en hault treason le roy avera leschete auxibein des les terres de luy tenus come des auters come appiert per lestatute anno 7 E. 3. de proditionibus.

21. JUDGMENTS FOR TREASON

Queen's Bench, Pas. 1554.

Note also, by Portman, that in high treason which touches the queen herself with respect to her person, such as compassing her death or levying war against her or aiding her enemies or subverting the laws of the land, in these cases the judgment shall be that they be drawn, hanged and quartered and disembowelled etc. But in high treason which does not touch the queen herself as to her person, such as killing her justices, falsifying the king's seal, the king's coin, or the coin of another king, or the signet or privy seal, even though these are high treasons, the judgment nevertheless shall be only that they be drawn and hanged, inasmuch as they do not touch the king's person. But Bromley C.J. said that, although in fact this is the practice, he knew of no reason why it should be so. For he said that when he was the king's serjeant one Egerton was arraigned for attaching the king's great seal, which was already in being on another patent, to a new patent, and this was held treason and he had his judgment to be drawn, hanged and quartered etc.[1] Then Portman said that in fact it may be this way or the other at the discretion of the justices before whom etc. Similarly if a woman is indicted of treason upon the statute of 26 Hen. VIII,[2] for words against the king, and found guilty, she may be adjudged to be burned, as the common course is for a woman for treason, or to be drawn and hanged, all by discretion: and that was used at Lincoln in the time of Luke, justice of assize there, and Whorwood.[3]

22. PETIT TREASON

Contd from pl. 21.

Note that in petit treason, as where a wife kills her husband, a servant his master, a monk his abbot or prior, or a servant her mistress, the judgment shall be to be drawn and hanged only, and for a woman in such cases always to be drawn and burned. In these cases of petit treason the escheat belongs to the lord and not the king, except for lands held of the king, whereas in high treason the king shall have the escheat both of the lands held of him and of those held of others: as appears by the statute of 7 Edw. III, concerning treasons.[4]

[1] This was Ralph Egerton, servant to Lord Audley L.C.: see E. Hall, *Chronicle*, p. 841; BL MS. Add. 25168, fo. 354v; *OHLE*, vi. 588, 615. Cf. *R.* v. *Overton* (1556) below, p. 100.

[2] 26 Hen. VIII, c. 33; *OHLE*, vi. 585–586.

[3] Walter Luke and William Whorwood (Att.-Gen.) were justices of assize on the Midland circuit 1541–44. Cf. 121 Selden Soc. 469–470.

[4] There was no parliament in 7 Edw. III. The reference is presumably to the Treason Act 1351, 25 Edw. III, stat. 5, c. 2.

[23]

A, fo. 23v[f]; *L* 164[f]; *B*, p. 128[f].

Nota que si le declaration en ascun action ne warrant le breife mes est contrariant a ceo coment ceo soit admit uncore nest bon coment un verditt passe: come en breife de dett sur obligation le pl. declare et appiert sur son declaration que le jour nest uncore venus de payment de le debt et ceo nient obstant le deffendant plede Nient son fait et trove est per verditt son fait le pl. navera judgement et sil ad il est errour. Issint est en trns. le pl. declare que le trespas fuit fait a tiel jour que est apres le jour le date le breife de trespas le deffendant plede Rien culpable et il est trove culpable per verditt uncore le pl. navera judgement et sil ad tout est errour quar son breife ore ne garrant le declaration et le declaration est son fait demeasne que est contrary a son breife et tout est un de faire nul declaration come a faire de- [*fol. 21*] claration contrary a la ley et a son breife. Et si le pl. declare en debt solonque le fourme de trns. de close debruser le defendant plede rien culpable et est trove culpable nul judgement serra pur le pl. Yssint serra si home declare en le court de Comen Banke sans breife originall coment que verditt passe pur le pl. uncore nul judgement pur luy et yssint per *Bromley* Cheif Justice si le pl. port breife de debte en le debet et detinet et declare come executor pur le debte due a son testator et trove est pur le pl. per verdit nul judgement pur le pl. car ceo est ore come nul breife et per son declaration demeasne le breife abate. Come si en debt sur obligation le defendant dit que il fist le fait et ceo enseale et deliver le fait al estranger come son fait al deliver al pl. sur condition et devant le condition perfourme lestranger deliver le fait al pl. et yssint nient son fait, et trove est per verditt nient son fait uncore judgement serra done pur le pl. sur son confession car il ad confesse devant per son plee que cest fuit son fait. Ceux cases ne sont remedies per lestatute de jeofailes, mes si le declaration ad en luy conteyne le substance de le matter accordant a la ley et fault course ou fourme la apres verditt ceo est remedy per lestatute come en debt sur obligation en son count il ne declare ou lobligation fuit fait ou en trns. le declaration est gererall et ne monstre le jour de trns. et lissue est trove pur le pl. per verditt ore il avera judgement per lestatute: et coment que ascun mesne proces fayle, ou le garrant datturney faile, uncore lestatute remedy ceux matters: per *Bromley* et *Portman* Justices de Banke le Roy.

23. ERRORS IN DECLARATIONS

Probably in the Queen's Bench, Pas. 1554.

Note that if the declaration in any action does not warrant the writ, but contradicts it, this is not good even if it is admitted, and even though a verdict has passed. Thus in a writ of debt on a bond, if the plaintiff declares and it appears upon his declaration that the day for payment of the debt has not yet come, and despite this the defendant pleads 'Not his deed', and it is found by verdict to be the defendant's deed, the plaintiff shall not have judgment: and if he has, it is error. Likewise in trespass, if the plaintiff declares that the trespass was done on a certain day which is after the date of the writ of trespass, and the defendant pleads Not guilty, and he is found guilty by verdict, the plaintiff shall still not have judgment, and if he does have judgment everything is error: for his writ does not now warrant the declaration, and the declaration is his own act, which in contrary to his writ, and it is all one to make no declaration and to make a declaration contrary to the law and to his writ. If a plaintiff declares in debt according to the form in trespass for breaking a close, and the defendant pleads Not guilty and is found guilty, no judgment shall be given for the plaintiff. Likewise if someone declares in the court of Common Bench without an original writ, even though a verdict passes for the plaintiff, still no judgment can be given for him. Likewise, according to BROMLEY C.J., if a plaintiff brings a writ of debt in the *debet et detinet* and declares as an executor for the debt due to his testator, and it is found for the plaintiff by verdict, no judgment shall be given for the plaintiff, for this is now as no writ, and the writ is abated by his own declaration.[1] Likewise if the defendant in debt on a bond says that he made the deed and sealed it and delivered the deed to a stranger as his deed to deliver to the plaintiff upon condition, and before the condition was performed the stranger delivered the deed to the plaintiff, 'and so not his deed', and it is found by verdict not to be his deed, judgment shall nevertheless be given for the plaintiff upon his confession: for he has confessed before by his plea that this was his deed. These cases are not remedied by the statute of jeofails.[2] If, however, the declaration contains the substance of the matter according to the law, and merely lacks course or form, it is remedied by the statute after verdict: as in debt on a bond, when in his count he does not declare where the bond was made, or in trespass when the declaration is in general terms and does not show the day of the trespass, and the issue is found for the plaintiff by verdict, he shall now have judgment by reason of the statute. Even if some mesne process is lacking, or the warrant of attorney is lacking, the statute nevertheless remedies these matters. By BROMLEY and PORTMAN JJ. of the King's Bench.

[1] I.e. because a writ of debt by an executor should be in the *detinet* only, and should not say *debet*.

[2] 32 Hen. VIII, c. 30.

[24]

Abr. in *A*, fo. 24[f]; *L* 165[f]; *B*, p. 128[f].

Nota per *Bromley* et *Portman* que si home fait un obligation ou auter escript al J. S. et deliver le fait at J. S. come un escrowe sur condition que ore ceo est son fait maintenant et averment ne poet estre alledge encounter le dit fait que il fuit deliver al J. S. come escrowe sur condition etc. et yssint nient son fait quar donques per cest voy home avera nude[1] averment versus chescun fait deliver al partie que serra inconvenient mes un poet aver averment a dire que il deliver cest fait al estranger come escrowe a deliver al J. S. sur condition que deliver ceo al J. S. devant le condition perfourme et yssint nient son fait quar la le fait ne fuit deliver al partie mesme mes al estranger versus que un averment poet estre fait come le deliverie fuit: quod nota bein et issint adjuge t[ermino] P. 19 H. 8. fo. 8.

[25]

A, fo. 24[f]; *L* 166[f]; *B*, p. 128[f]; *D*, fo. 16, pl. 11 (1 Mar.).

[*fol. 21v*] Nota auxi per *Bromeley* et *Portman* que petit treason emplia en luy mesme murder et pluis, yssint que petit treason est murder et pluis, et a cest treason ils semblont que la poet este accessory et al meanes accessory al murder mes ne poet [estre][2] accessory al hault treason mes toutes sont principalls. Yssint ils disoent que si home procure un feme a murder son baron et el fait accordant cestui que procure poet bein estre endite come accessory al murder et ils semblont que poient estre accessories al petit treason et si fuit yssint endite il est bon. Et auxi ils disoent que si le feme et un estranger occide le baron le feme que cest petit treason en la feme et murder en le stranger et [nemy] petit treason en luy quar les parolls lestatute anno 25 E. 3. ne extend mes al feme et servantes et issint le fittes que occide son pier est hors del case de petit treason. Mes ils disoent que si la feme et lestranger fueront [joine][3] en un endictment que ils proditorie et felonise murderaverunt le baron per cest (felonise) lenditement bon quant al murder pur le dit estranger. Et yssint si la feme fuit endite que el proditorye et felonise occide son baron et que lestranger felonice et proditorie luy procure a ceo faire que cest est bon a fair luy accessory al murder ou al treason come la ley voet: quod nota bene. Quere de accessory al petit treason, si poet estre.

1 *Or* inde.
2 *A, B, D, L.*
3 *A, D, L.* endictes *H.*

24. NON EST FACTUM

Probably in the Queen's Bench, following the case put in pl. 23.

Note, by BROMLEY and PORTMAN, that if someone makes a bond or other writing in favour of John Style, and delivers the deed to John Style as an escrow, upon condition, this is his deed at once and an averment may not be alleged against the said deed that it was delivered to John Style as an escrow upon condition etc., 'and so not his deed', for in that way one might have a bare averment against every deed delivered to a party, which would be inconvenient; but one may have an averment to say that he delivered this deed to a stranger as an escrow, to deliver to John Style upon condition, which stranger delivered it to John Style before the condition performed, 'and so not his deed';[1] for there the deed was not delivered to the party himself but to a stranger, against whom an averment may be made how the delivery was. Note that. It is so adjudged in Pas. 19 Hen. VIII, fo. 8.[2]

25. PETIT TREASON

Probably in the Queen's Bench, Pas. 1554. The facts, however, closely resemble those of the case of Lady Smith at Warwick assizes 1555, which was discussed by the justices in Trin. 1555: Dyer's circuit notebook, 110 Selden Soc. 404, pl. 12.

Note also, by BROMLEY and PORTMAN, that petit treason implies in itself murder and more, so that petit treason is murder and more; and to this treason they thought there could be an accessory, or at least accessory to the murder, even though there cannot be an accessory to high treason but all are principals. Therefore they said that if a man procures a woman to murder her husband, and she does so accordingly, the procurer may well be indicted as accessory to the murder; but they thought that there could be accessories to petit treason, and if he was so indicted it would be good. They also said that if a woman and a stranger kill the woman's husband, this is petit treason in the woman and murder in the stranger, but not petit treason in him, for the words of the statute of 25 Edw. III[3] extend but to the wife and servants, and for this reason the son who slays his father is outside the case of petit treason.[4] But they said that if the woman and a stranger are joined in an indictment that they 'traitorously and feloniously murdered' the husband, by this word 'feloniously' the indictment is good against the said stranger with respect to the murder. Likewise if the woman is indicted that she 'traitorously and feloniously slew' her husband, and that the stranger 'feloniously and traitorously procured' her to do it, this is good to make him accessory to the murder, or to the treason, as the law wills. Note that well. Query whether there can be accessory to petit treason.[5]

[1] See above, p. 67, pl. 23.
[2] YB Pas. 19 Hen. VIII, fo. 8, pl. 12.
[3] Treason Act 1351, 25 Edw. III, stat. 5, c. 2.
[4] Above, p. 59, pl. 8.
[5] Cf. above, p. 61, pl. 13.

[26]

A, fo. 24[f]; *L* 167[f]; *B*, p. 128[f].

Nota auxi que il fuit agree per eux que si le feme occide[1] son barron que le heir avera appeall de murder vers luy que ymplia murder mes si la feme fuit primes endict come de petit treason et soit de ceo trove culpable et ad son chartre de roy ore le heire apres cest pardon navera appeall de murder vers luy entant que el fuit adevant endicte de petit treason et sur ceo attaint et pardon que est le pluis hault offence et per tant discharge de toutes de pluis base nature. Mes si el fuit endict de murder et trove culpable ou acquite uncore deins lan lappell vers luy gist quar lappell est foundue tout sur un offence. Mes auterment est en lauter case et tout fuit un sel fuit acquite de le petit treason entant que el est acquite de le pluis hault offence etc. Et ceo ils diont fuit adjuge en Banco Regis ore tarde quant ils fueront serjeantes et fueront al barre en counsell ovesque le matter: quod nota bein.

[27]

A, fo. 24[f]; *L* 168[f]; *B*, p. 128[f].

Nota per *Bromley* Cheife Justice que un coroner super visum corporis poet enquire de petit treason et ceo trove et sur cest enditement le partie serra arrayne et mise a son respons come si feme tua son baron ou le servant son master pur ceo que entant que son authority est a seyer [*fol. 22*] sur le vewe del corps occide et a enquirer coment il vient a son mort per mesme le reason il poet trover tout le veretye et le facte et bon'[2] cum circumstantiis. Mes Porteman fuit al contrary et il dit que il poet faire enquiry de murder et manslaughter mes nemy de petit treason quar son power nextend al enquirer de cest offence et il nad unques viewe que il enquire de treason per nul voy. Mes semble a moy si loffence fuit petit treason per le comen ley yssint que lestatute de anno 27 E. 3. est en affirmance de le comen ley donques il bein poet enquirer de cest auterment nemy. Mes *Bromley* et *Portman* agrea que le coroner poet enquirer des accessories al murder queux fueront devant le felony et murder mes nemy puis le murder et felony quar laccessory devant fueront le cause del morte le home, et issint ne fueront laccessories puis le mort. Et ils disoent auxi que le coroner poet enquire si cestui que tua le home fua pur le felony ou nemy et si soit yssint trove devant luy toutes ses beins serront forfaites sur cest record coment que en fait il ne unques fua pur le felony et il navera unques remedy ou traverse a reverser ou defeter cest record.

[1] tua *A, B, L.*
[2] *Meaning unclear.*

26. PETIT TREASON

Contd from pl. 25. Cf. above, p. 61, pl. 14.

Note also that it was agreed by them that if a woman kills her husband, the heir shall have an appeal of murder against her, which implies murder; but if the woman was first indicted as for petit treason, and found guilty thereof, and had her charter [of pardon] from the king, the heir shall not have an appeal of murder against her after this pardon, inasmuch as she was already indicted of petit treason and thereupon attained and pardoned, which is the higher offence, and she was thereby discharged of all offences of a lower nature. If, however, she had been indicted of murder, and found guilty or acquitted, an appeal would still lie against her within the year, for the appeal is founded wholly on the [same] offence; but it is otherwise in the other case. And it would be all one if she were acquitted of the petit treason, inasmuch as she is acquitted of the higher offence etc. And they said that this was adjudged in the King's Bench recently, when they were serjeants,[1] and were at the bar as counsel in the matter. Note that well.

27. JURISDICTION OF THE CORONER

Probably in the Queen's Bench, contd from pl. 26.

Note, by Bromley C.J., that a coroner *super visum corporis* may enquire of petit treason, and find it, and upon this indictment the party shall be arraigned and put to his answer – as where a woman kills her husband, or a servant his master – because his authority is to sit upon the view of the body slain, and to enquire how he came to his death, and so by the same reason he may find the whole truth and the facts, with the circumstances. But Portman was to the contrary, and he said that he may make enquiry into murder and manslaughter but not petit treason, for his power does not extend to enquiring into this offence: and he has never seen a coroner enquire into treason in any way. But it seems to me that if the offence was petit treason by the common law, so that the statute of [25] Edw. III[2] is [merely] in affirmation of the common law, then he may well enquire into this; otherwise not. But Bromley and Portman agreed that the coroner may enquire as to accessories to murder who were before the felony and murder, but not to accessories after the murder and felony; for the accessories before were the cause of the man's death, whereas the accessories after the death were not. They also said that the coroner may enquire whether the person who killed the man fled for the felony, or not, and if it is so found before him all his goods shall be forfeited upon this record, even if in fact he never fled for the felony; and he shall have no remedy or traverse to reverse or undo this record.[3]

[1] I.e. 1540/46.

[2] The text says 27 Edw. III, but this is evidently a reference to the Treason Act 1351, 25 Edw. III, stat. 5, c. 2.

[3] Cf. below, p. 73, pl. 3.

[28]

A, fo. 24[f]; *L* 169[f]; *B*, pp. 128–129[f]; *D*, fo. 16, pl. 9 (1 Mar.).

Nota que les privileges des courtes ne serra allowe en nulles courtes forsque en Banco Regis sans breife de previledge a eux devant direct a tiel entent que le court poet estre ascertein per breife de record de le previledge [mes][1] en Banco Regis le previledge serra demaund per ple sans breife quar nul breife de previledge poet estre direct al roy ou roygne mes le previledge le parlament serra demaund per breife en Banke le Roy pur ceo que cest court de parlament est le pluis hault court en la terre: quod nota per *Bromeley* et *Portman*.

[29]

A, fo. 24v[f]; *L* 170[f]; *D*, fo. 16, pl. 10 (1 Mar.).

Nota per *Bromeley* et *Portman* [clerement agree][2] si lessee pur terme de x.[3] ans graunt ouster son estate al estranger et puis le rent est arere que le lessor avera action de dett vers le grauntee et nemy vers le lessee quar cest contract va ovesque la terre. Mes auterment est si home vende beins ou terre al auter que vende ceux choses ouster ore laction serra port vers le primer [vendee][4] quar cest contract va ovesque le person.

[30]

A, fo. 24v[f;]; *L* 171[f]; *B*, p. 128 (foll. pl. 28; the last case in *B*).

Nota auxi per eux agree que si home fist leas pur ans de 2 acres de terre rendant rent et le lessee graunt ouster son estate dun acre que le rent ne serra apportion mes le lessor poet charge le lessee de toute le rent per distres ou debt.

[31]

A, fo. 24v[f]; *L* 172[f].

Et si home fist leas des terres et barbites pur terme de x ans rendant rent et le lessee graunt ouster les barbittes al estranger que ore le rent ne serra apportion mes tout le rent est issuant hors de le terre et le terre serra [*fol. 22v*] charge de tout le rent. Et issint il semble que si le lessor fist ses executours et devie que ore le revertion des barbittes va al executours le lessor et le revertion del terre al heire le lessor et uncore le heire per cause de cest revertion avera tout le rent quia est yssuant de la terre.

[1] *A, B, D, L.* et *H.*
[2] *A, B.*
[3] xx. *A, L.* 60 *B.*
[4] *A, D, L.* vende *B.* vendor *H.*

28. CLAIMING PRIVILEGES OF COURTS

Probably in the Queen's Bench, Pas. 1554.

Note that the privileges of courts shall not be allowed in any court except the King's Bench without a writ of privilege previously directed to them, to the intent that the court may be given certain knowledge of the privilege by a writ of record. In the King's Bench, however, the privilege shall be demanded by plea without writ, for no writ of privilege may be directed to the king or queen; but the privilege of parliament shall be demanded by writ in the King's Bench, because the court of parliament is the highest court in the land. Note that, by BROMLEY and PORTMAN.

29. ASSIGNMENT

Probably in the Queen's Bench, Pas. 1554.

Note, by BROMLEY and PORTMAN, clearly agreed, that if a lessee for a term of ten years grants his estate over to a stranger, and then the rent is in arrear, the lessor shall have an action of debt against the grantee and not against the lessee, for this contract goes with the land. But it is otherwise if someone sells goods or land to another, who sells these things over: now the action shall be brought against the first vendee, for this contract goes with the person.

30. APPORTIONMENT OF RENT

Contd from pl. 29.

Note also that it was agreed by them that if someone makes a lease of two acres of land, yielding rent, and the lessee grants over his estate in one acre, the rent shall not be apportioned, but the lessor may charge the lessee with the whole rent by distress or action of debt.

31. APPORTIONMENT OF RENT

Contd from pl. 30.

And if someone makes a lease of lands and sheep for a term of ten years, yielding rent, and the lessee grants over the sheep to a stranger, the rent shall not be apportioned; for the whole rent is issuing out of the land, and the land shall be charged with the whole rent. Likewise, it seems, if the first lessor makes his executors and dies, the reversion of the sheep goes to the lessor's executors and the reversion of the land to the lessor's heir, and yet the heir by reason of this reversion shall have all the rent, for it is issuing from the land.

[32]

Abr. in *A*, fo. 24v^f^; *L* 172 (contd).

Semble auxi al eux si home fist leas des barbittes tantum rendant rent que en dett pur cest le lessee des barbittes gager sa ley sil voet quar nest que mere contract come vende des beins ou chatteux. Mes de leas de terre et barbittes rendant rent en action de det pur cest rent vers [le] lessee il ne gager son ley pur nul ley quar sont vient horse de la terre et la terre est tout charge ovesque cest rent.

[33]

A, fo. 24v^f; *L* 173^f.

Nota auxi ils disoent que si 2 ont estate et a les heires de lun de eux en terres et tenementes et ils 2 font leas pur ans al estranger que fist wast ore en action de wast ils covient joynder et le breife serra que lessee ad fait wast des terres a luy lesse per eux al disinheritance lun de eux s. al exheredition cestui que ad fee. Et ils disoent que si lessee pur vie fist leas pur ans al estranger que fist wast en les tenementes que ore le lessee pur vie navera nul wast vers luy coment que le leas soit per indenture quar la est nul novell revertion gayne per cest leas quar nest discontynuance come leas pur vie de le lessee est yssint que le revertion de fee remayne toutes dittes en le primer lessor ou cestui que ad le primer revertion issint que sur lespecial matter monstre per le lessee pur ans en tiel action de wast le breife abate.

[Finis del primer anne del Royne Marie
De termino Trinitatis 1° et 2° Phillippi et Marie][1]

[34]

A, ff. 24v–25^f; *L* 174^f; *D*, fo. 16, pl. 1 (1 & 2 Phil. & Mar.).

Nota al arraignement en Banke le Roigne de le Seignor John Graye un des fittes puisnes le Marques Dorsett pur treason per luy fait ove son frere et heire Henry jades duke de Suffolke jades attaint de hault treason et execute pur rebellor et conspirator ove le graunde traytor Wyatt et auters, et pur cest semble treason cest John fuit endite et arrayne et al comencement le terme le dit John plede Non culpable al indictment. Et fuit endite en la vie son frere Henry en le com. de Leycester et avoit jour tanque al fyne le terme s. le Monday devant le fyne de cel et donques il vient eins et dit que le marques Dorcett fuit tayle a ses heires males et il est heir male per lattaynder et mort son frere Henry et son frere Robert et issint il est marques de Dorsett et il come marques doit estre arrayne

[1] *A, immediately before pl. 34, but seemingly in the wrong place: cf. heading in H (p. 72).*

32. WAGER OF LAW

Contd from pl. 31.

It also seemed to them that if someone makes a lease of sheep alone, reserving rent, in debt for this rent the lessee of the sheep shall wage his law if he wishes, for it is merely a contract, like a sale of goods and chattels. But where there is a lease of land and sheep, yielding rent, in an action of debt for this rent against the lessee he shall not wage his law, for any law,[1] for it comes out of the land and all the land is charged with this rent.

33. WHO MAY BRING WASTE

Contd from pl. 32.

Note that they also said that if two have an estate in lands and tenements, and to the heirs of one of them, and they both make a lease for years to a stranger, who commits waste, in an action of waste they must join; and the writ shall say that the lessee has committed waste of the lands leased to him by them, to the disinheritance of one of them (that is, to the disinheritance of the one who has fee). And they said that if the lessee for life makes a lease to a stranger, who commits waste in the tenements, the lessee for life shall not have waste against him, even though the lease was by indenture, for there is no new reversion gained by this lease; for it is not a discontinuance, as in the case of a lease for the lessee's life, since the reversion remains always in the first lessor or the first reversioner, so that upon the special matter shown by the lessee for years in such an action of waste the writ will abate.

34. R. v. LORD JOHN GREY

Queen's Bench, Pas. 1554. (Dated Trin. 1554 in *A* and on p. 100, below.)

Note that at the arraignment in the Queen's Bench of the Lord John Grey, one of the younger sons of the marquess of Dorset, for treason committed by him with his brother and heir Henry, late duke of Suffolk[2] – lately attainted of high treason and executed, as a rebel and conspirator with the great traitor Wyatt and others, and for this similar treason John was indicted and arraigned at the beginning of the term – the said John pleaded Not guilty to the indictment. He was indicted in the lifetime of his brother Henry in the county of Leicester, and had day until the end of term, namely the Monday before the end thereof; and then he came in and said that the marquessate of Dorset was entailed to the heirs male and that he is heir male by the attainder and death of his brother Henry and his brother Robert, and is therefore marquess of Dorset and ought to be arraigned

[1] Meaning unclear.

[2] See below, p. 72, pl. 35. For Wyatt see below, pp. 98–99.

et trye per ses piers et pria son tryall destre issint. Et entant que il [*fol. 23*] aver plede Non culpable a lenditement generalment issint que il ad prist son tryal sur le pais per son generall plee de rien culpable il ad perde le benefitt de cest tryall per ses piers quar un pier sil voet poet relinquishe son benefitt de cest tryall per ses piers et luy mitta sur le pais sil voet per le justices de Banke le Roigne. Mes sil ne avoit luy mitta sur le pais sur le dit plee de rien culpable sil avera son tryall donques per ses piers sil ceo challenge quere. Semble a moy et auters quod sic entant que lestate dignitye et nosme de marques per lattainder et mort de son freres Henry et Robert discend a luy puis son indictment et devant son arraignment. Quere tamen si per lattainder de ses freres le sanke nest yssint corrupt que il ne poet claymer come heire al eux et semble al ascuns que tenant en taile ne forfeytera rien mes pur son vie demeasne per le novell statute de rebelles de treason fait anno primo Marie. Mes semble si le fittes et heire dun seignor de le parlament soit endicta de treason et devant son arraygnement son pier devie que ore le fittes serra trye per ses peirs sil ceo pryer quar en cest est nul ympediment per corruption de sanke come en case devant.

[35]

Nota que le dit Henry duke de Suffolke fuit arraigne, condempne et execute per decollation pur son treason et son frere Roberte auxi tempore Quadragesime Anno primo Marie. 1554.

Termino Michaelis anno regni Philippi et Marie Regis et Regine primo et secundo 1554

[1]

A, fo. 25; *L* 176; *D*, ff. 16–17, pl. 2 (1 & 2 Phil. & Mar.).

Nota per *Portman* et auters al Serjeantes Inne que si un jury apres que ils sont jures et charge et devant ou apres que ils sont agrees de lour verdict boyeront ou mangeront de lour costes demeasne ou ascun de eux issint boyer ou manger et puis done lour verditt que ceo ne fait le verditt void mes est un [act][1] que est fyneable al roy et ne fait le verditt void mes le verditt estoiera bon mes si eux ou

[1] *A, D.*

and tried as a marquess by his peers: and he prayed that his trial might be so. But since he had pleaded Not guilty to the indictment generally, so that he had taken his trial by the country by his general plea of Not guilty, he had lost the benefit of this trial by his peers; for, if he wishes, a peer may relinquish his benefit of this trial by his peers and put himself upon the country if he wishes: by the justices of the Queen's Bench. If, however, he had not put himself upon the country upon the said plea of Not guilty, query whether he would then have had his trial by his peers if he claimed it. It seemed to me and others that he should, inasmuch as the estate, dignity and name of marquess descended to him through the attainder and death of his brothers Henry and Robert after his indictment and before his arraignment. Query nevertheless whether by the attainder of his brothers the blood is not corrupted, so that he may not claim as heir to them; and it seemed to some that a tenant in tail shall not forfeit anything except for his own life, by the new statute of repeals of treason made in the first year of Mary.[1] But it seems that if the son and heir of a lord of the parliament is indicted for treason, and before his arraignment his father dies, the son shall be tried by his peers if he prays it, for in that case there is no impediment by corruption of blood as in the former case.

35. R. v. DUKE OF SUFFOLK

Contd from no. 34, referring to a special commission, 17 Feb. 1554, and its outcome. Record: KB 8/28. Also reported in Dyer's notebook, 109 Selden Soc. 10; *Chronicles of Queen Mary* (Camden Soc., 1850), p. 60.

Note that the said Henry, duke of Suffolk, was arraigned, condemned and executed by beheading for his treason, and his brother Robert also, in time of Lent in the first year of Mary.

Michaelmas term in the first and second year of the reign of King Philip and Queen Mary (1554)

1. MISCONDUCT BY JURORS

Serjeants' Inn, Mich. 1554. Cf. *OHLE*, vi. 366.

Note, by PORTMAN and others at Serjeants' Inn, that if a jury after they are sworn and charged, and before or after they are agreed upon their verdict, drink or eat at their own costs, or any of them so drinks or eats, and then they give their verdict, this does not make the verdict void but is an [offence] which is finable to the king, and does not make the verdict void, but the verdict shall stand as good.

[1] 1 Mar, sess. 1, c. 1. Cf. below, p. 100, pl. 13.

ascun de eux boyer ou manger al costes dascun des parties ou lour amies devant que ils fueront agrees ou apres et dona le verditt pur cest partie a que cost ils issint fesoent ou changeont lour verditt apres lour agreament per cest cause et corruption que ore per cest acte lour verditt est void en la ley et cest difference il dit fuit agree divers foites et il fuit en experience [*fol. 23v*] ove le dit matter: et *Gawdy* affirme que il ad estre sovent foytes rule.

[2]

A, fo. 25;[f] *L* 177[f]; *D*, fo. 17, pl. 3 (1 & 2 Phil. & Mar.).

Nota que si un home suffer un recovery per garrant datturney et le recovery est ewe al primer returne de le terme et apres le primer jour et devant quarto die le tenant devie uncore le recovery est bon et nient void quar le judgement avera relation al primer jour del returne le breife. Et *Browne* Justice dit issint et fuit rule et adjuge en Comen Banke devant ceux heures.

[3]

A, fo. 25[f]; *L* 178[f].

Nota que fuit agree per *Bromeley*, *Portman* et auters que si home soit endite de felony ou murder et trove est per mesme lenditement que il fua pur le felony et puis il ad son chartre de pardon ou acquite auterment que ore ses beins ne sont forfaites mes si fuit present devant le coroner super visum corporis que il fua et puis ad son chartre de pardon ou auterment est discharge ou sur lenditement avaunt dit il est arrayne et trove nient culpable et que il fua pur le murder ou felony ore ses beins serra forfaites. Yssint nota que les beins de nullx serra forfaites sur nude surmise en court sans matter de record a ceo prover devant le coroner ou sur larraynment quod nota. Et nota sur ceux recordes sur le trover le fuer sur larraynement ou sur presentment devant le coroner nul avera travers a reverse ceux recordes per nul meanes: quod nota per toutes agrees.

[4]

A, fo. 25;[f] *L* 179[f]; *D*, fo. 17, pl. 4 (1 & 2 Phil. & Mar.).

Nota que la ley ore est et yssint rule que un gard quant al corps per soy auxibein le corps come la terre le heire poet estre graunt per le seignior al estranger

If, however, they or any of them drink or eat at the cost of any of the parties, or their friends, before they are agreed or afterwards, and give the verdict for that party at whose cost they did so, or change their verdict after their agreement by this cause and corruption, by this act their verdict is void in law. And this distinction, he said, had been agreed on several occasions, and he had experience of the said matter.

Gawdy affirmed that it had often been so ruled.

2. RELATION OF JUDGMENTS

Common Pleas or Serjeants' Inn, Mich. 1554. Cf. *Mildmay* v. *Talbot* (1581) 110 Selden Soc. 387.

Note that if someone suffers a recovery by warrant of attorney, and the recovery is had at the first return of the term, and after the first day and before the *quartus dies* the tenant dies, the recovery is still good and not void, for the judgment relates back to the first day of the return of the writ.

BROWNE J. said that it was so, and that it had been ruled and adjudged in the Common Bench before these times.

3. FORFEITURE OF GOODS FOR FELONY

Probably in Serjeants' Inn, Mich. 1554.

Note that it was agreed by BROMLEY, PORTMAN and others that if someone is indicted of felony or murder, and it is found by the same indictment that he fled for the felony, and then he has his charter of pardon or is otherwise acquitted, his goods shall not now be forfeited. But if it was presented before the coroner *super visum corporis* that he fled, and then he has his charter of pardon or is otherwise discharged, or he is arraigned upon the indictment aforesaid and found not guilty, and it is found that he fled for the murder or felony, his goods shall be forfeited. Note, therefore, that no-one's goods shall be forfeited upon a bare surmise in court without matter of record to prove it before the coroner or upon the arraignment. Note that. And note upon these records that when the flight is found upon the arraignment, or upon presentment before the coroner, no-one shall have a traverse to reverse these records by any means. Note that: agreed by all.[1]

4. WARDSHIP GRANTED BY PAROL

Probably in Serjeants' Inn, Mich. 1554.

Note that the law now is, and it was so ruled, that where there is a wardship of the body by itself, the body as well as the land of the heir may be granted by the

[1] Cf. above, p. 69, pl. 27.

auxibein per fait come per paroll sans fait en mesme le fourme come le gard de corps et de terre poient estre graunt ouster per paroll sans escript. Et uncore si home ad villaine pur ans le villen ne poet estre graunt ouster per le lessee sans fait quar le villen est derive hors del estate denheritance mes yssint nest le gard de corps.

[5]

A, fo. 25[f]; *L* 180[f].

Nota si un abbott et son covent ou master et ses confreres dun colledge ont fait leas pur 50 ans desouth lour covent ou chapter seale et puis le dit abbe et covent master et confreres fist auter leas desouth lour seales al dit lessee pur 50 ans a comencer ymmediatment et le second leas est fait deins le an le primer jour de parlament in anno 31 H. 8. que dona al dit roy et ses heires religiouse measons et colledges que ore per le proviso deins le dit estatute le lessee ad estate pur xxi ans de le temps le dit leas s. de le temps que le second leas prist son perfection et esse[1] coment que lestatute et proviso diont: Soe that the said leas [*fol. 24*] [ ][2] xxi yeres quar ceux parolls averont relation a lans lymitt per le dit statute: et cest fuit agree issint per toutes les justices en Banke le Roy s. *Bromley*, *Portman* et *Wyddon* in casu Fulmerston vesus Steward en trns. in comitatu Northff. ou Suffolke.

[6]

A, fo. 25[f]; *L* 181[f].

Nota la fuit clerement agree que si home plede un acte de parlament que il ne besoigne a [pleder et][3] recyter toute lacte ove les [provisoes][4] mes tantum cest parte de lacte que fait pur son purpose coment que lacte soit entier en soy.

[1] essens *A, L.*
[2] *Blank in H.*
[3] *A, L.*
[4] *A, L.* provisicions *H.*

lord to a stranger, either by deed or by parol without a deed, in the same way that the wardship of the body and land may be granted over by word without writing. Nevertheless, if someone has a villein for years, the villein may not be granted over by the lessee without a deed, for the villein is derived out of the estate of inheritance; but that is not so of the wardship of the body.

5. FULMERSTON v. STEWARD

King's Bench, Mich. 1554. Record: KB 27/1156, m. 78 (*venire facias*); KB 27/1162, m. 162 (demurrer); printed in Plowd. 102. Also reported in Plowd. 102; Dyer, fo. 102 (Mich. 1554); BL MS. Harley 1691, fo. 90 (Mich. 1554). There are further notes from this case below, this term, pl. 6–9, 12.

Note that if an abbot and his convent, or a master of a college and his brethren,[1] made a lease for fifty years under their convent seal, or chapter seal, and then the abbot and convent (or master and brethren) made another lease under their seals to the said lessee for fifty years, to commence immediately, and the second lease is made within a year of the first day of the parliament in 31 Hen. VIII, which gave religious houses and colleges to the said king and his heirs,[2] by the proviso within the said statute the lessee has an estate for twenty-one years from the time of the said lease, namely from the time when the second lease took its perfection and being, even though the statute and proviso say, 'so that the said lease [or leases exceed not][3] twenty-one years', for those words relate to the years limited by the said statute.[4] This was so agreed by all the justices of the King's Bench, namely BROMLEY, PORTMAN and WHIDDON, in the case of Fulmerston[5] against Steward,[6] in trespass in the counties of Norfolk and Suffolk.[7]

6. FULMERSTON v. STEWARD, contd

King's Bench, Mich. 1554. Cf. Plowd., fo. 105.

Note that it was clearly agreed there that if someone pleads an act of parliament there is no need to plead and recite the whole act with the provisos, but only that part of the act which serves his purpose, even though the act is entire in itself.[8]

1 The case concerned a lease by Rushworth College, Norfolk.
2 31 Hen. VIII, c. 13; below, pp. 89–91.
3 Blank in MS.
4 I.e. the statute operates to cut down a longer lease to 21 years rather than to invalidate leases for more than 21 years.
5 Richard Fulmerston (d. 1567) of Thetford, Norfolk, of Ipswich, Suffolk, and of Clifford's Inn. He practised as an attorney before becoming comptroller of the duke of Somerset's household (1548–52); he was knighted in 1560.
6 Simon or Simeon Steward (or Styward) (d. 1568) of Soham, Cambs.
7 The record shows that the case was continued for advisement until Mich. 1561.
8 Cf. below, p. 77, pl. 12.

[7]

A, fo. 25v^{f}; *L* 182^{f}.

Nota auxi la fuit clerement agree que si home plede que le master et ses confreres ou le deane et chapter fueront seisies en lour demeasne come de fee et ne dit (in jure domus sive collegeii) que ceo est bon pledinge coment que le course est auterment quar ne poet estre auterment entendue. Mes si un parson desglise ou deane ou prebendary plede que il fuit seisie en son demeasne come de fee de possession son esglise etc. ceo nest bon sinon que il declare in jure ecclesie etc. quar ceo poet estre auterment entendue etc.

[8]

A, fo. 25v^{f}; *L* 183^{f}.

Nota auxi per *Bromeley* Cheife Justice que si home fist leas dun mannor pur ans except un acre parcell de ceo ou ladvowson que ore lacre et ladvowson ne sont nul parcell del mannor durant cest leas pur ans. Et si apres durant cest leas pur ans feoffment est fait de le mannor per le seignor ou lessor lacre ou ladvowson ne passa. Et uncore il agrea si le seignor le mannor ust demise parte de les demeasnes de le mannor al estranger pur ans ou pur vie et puis levie fyne de le mannor al estranger ou fist feoffment de ceo le reversion passa per cest quar le reversion est parte de le mannor: quod *Porteman* concessit, et dit que en le primer case ladvowson et acre de terre remayne parte de le mannor auter est leas pur vie. <Vide pur ceo Plowdens report en le case Fulmerston et Stwerde.>[1]

[9]

A, fo. 25v^{f}; *L* 184^{f}.

Nota auxi pur bon ley per *Bromeley* que si tenant per le curtesy alien le terre etc. ove garrantie et devie et son fittes port vers le terre tenant assise de mordauncestor de le seisin sa mier per lestatute Glouc' ca. 4. et recover per cause <la sunt>[2] nul assettes a luy discend per le pier et puis assettes discend et devene de le pier ore le tenant avera scire facias per le dit estatute vers le dit heire et recover la terre arrere que son pier primes ad vendue a luy et nemi le terre que est discend en assettes et ceo per le dit estatute. Et uncore si tenant en taile alien ove garrantie et devie et son heire recover en formdon quia nul assettes est a luy descend [*fol. 24v*] de son pier en fee et puis assettes a luy discend a son pier ore le tenant

[1] *Evidently an interpolation.*
[2] que *A, L.*

7. FULMERSTON v. STEWARD, contd

King's Bench, Mich. 1554. Cf. Plowd., fo. 102.

Note also that it was clearly agreed there that if someone pleads that a master and his brethren, or a dean and chapter, were seised in their demesne as of fee, and does not say 'in right of the house (or college)', this is good pleading, even though the practice is otherwise, for it cannot be otherwise understood. If, however, the parson of a church, or dean, or prebendary, pleads that he was seised in his demesne as of fee of a possession of his church etc., this is not good unless he declares 'in right of the church etc.', because this could be otherwise understood etc.

8. FULMERSTON v. STEWARD, contd

King's Bench, Mich. 1554. Cf. Plowd., fo. 104.

Note also, by Bromley C.J., that if someone makes a lease for years of a manor, excepting an acre (parcel thereof) or the advowson, the acre and the advowson are no longer any part of the manor during this lease for years; and if a feoffment of the manor is made afterwards, during this lease for years, by the lord or lessor, the acre or advowson does not pass. Nevertheless he agreed that if the lord of a manor had demised part of the demesnes of the manor to a stranger for years, or for life, and then levied a fine of the manor to the stranger, or made a feoffment thereof, the reversion would thereby have passed, for the reversion is part of the manor: which Portman granted. And he said that in the first case the advowson and acre of land remain part of the manor, but it is otherwise of a lease for life.

<For this see Plowden's report in the case Fulmerston v. Steward.>[1]

9. FULMERSTON v. STEWARD, contd

King's Bench, Mich. 1554. Cf. Plowd., fo. 110.

Note also as good law, by Bromley, that if tenant by the curtesy alienates the land etc. with warranty and dies, and his son brings an assize of mort d'ancestor against the terre-tenant upon the seisin of his mother, under the Statute of Gloucester, c. 4, and recovers, inasmuch as there are no assets descended to him through the father, and then assets descend and come from the father, the tenant shall have a *scire facias* by the said statute against the said heir and recover back the land which the heir's father had previously sold to him (but not the land which has descended as assets): and that is by the said statute. Nevertheless, if a tenant in tail alienates with warranty and dies, and his heir recovers in formedon, inasmuch as no assets have descended to him in fee from his father, and

[1] This is an interpolation. Plowden was first published 1571.

avera scire facias et recover per cest vers le dit heire le terre descend en assettes et nemi le terre primes recover et puis lassettes est alien, donques son issue avera formdon et recovera arere vers le tenant et per cest cause le terre en valewe serra restore per le scire facias. Et issint il dit lestatute de W. 2. ca. 21. dona cessavit pur les seignors et pro herede petentis super heredem tenentis et uncore le heire le seignor navera nul cessavit pur cesser des rentes et services son pier mes lestatute avera un resonable construction et ceux cases il mise sur lexposition de le dit proviso de lestatute anno 31 H. 8. pur leases.

[10]

Nota auxi per *Portman* et deny per nully que si deux joyntenants sont de terre et lun fist leas pur ans de son parte que cest leas nest severans de joynture mes le joynture estoit, cest leas nyent obstant mes auterment est en leas pur vie fist per lun joyntenant ceo est un playne severance de joynture et il dit que si home fist leas de son mannor pur ans exceptant ou savant ladvowson que ladvowson est devenus en grosse pro tempore mes la est difference perenter cest case et le case de terre mes non dixit causam.

[11]

Nota il fuit adjuge ultimo termino en Banke le Roy que la ou action est commence que est tam pro seipso quam pro domino rege et le roy avera ascun parte de le demaund que en ceux cases nul dammages ne costages serra recoveres. Sicome action soit pursued vers priest pur prisell des farmes ou vers auters sur lestatute de vender des titles ou maintenances la nul damages serra recoveres mes tantum le penalty quar le roy ne recovera unques dammages ne costes mes lou le recoverie est done tantum a le partie la dammages serra recovers ove costes. Come sur lestatute 8 H. 6. pur forcible entree ou home port action de dett sur lestatute vers le viscount ou son officer que prist les beins cestui que est arrest pur felony devant que il est attaint ore il recovera le treble value pur le then assets descend to him from his father, the tenant shall now have a *scire facias* and thereby recover against the said heir the land descended as assets (and not the land first recovered), and if the assets were afterwards alienated his issue would have formedon and recover against the tenant again, and for this reason the land in value shall be restored by the *scire facias.* Likewise, he said, the Statute of Westminster II, c. 21, gave *cessavit* for lords 'and for the demandant's heir upon the tenant's heir' (*et pro haerede petentis super haeredem tenentis*), and yet the lord's heir shall not have a *cessavit* for a cesser of his father's rents and services; for the statute shall have a reasonable construction. He put these cases upon the exposition of the said provisos in the statute of 31 Hen. VIII, for leases.[1]

10. JOINT TENANTS

Probably in the King's Bench, Mich. 1554.

Note also, by PORTMAN and denied by no-one, that if there are two joint tenants of land, and one of them makes a lease for years of his share, this lease is not a severance of the jointure, but the jointure stands notwithstanding this lease. It is otherwise, however, where a lease for life is made by one of the joint tenants: that is a plain severance of the jointure. And he said that if someone makes a lease of his manor for years, excepting or saving the advowson, the advowson has become in gross for the time being;[2] but there is a difference between this case and the case of land – though he did not explain the reason why (*non dixit causam*).

11. COSTS IN STATUTORY ACTIONS

King's Bench, Trin. 1554.

Note that it was adjudged last term in the King's Bench that where an action is commenced which is 'both for himself and for the lord king', and the king is to have any part of the demand, in these cases no damages or costs shall be recovered. Thus if an action is sued against a priest for taking farms,[3] or against others upon the statute of selling titles, or maintenance,[4] no damages shall be recovered but only the penalty: for the king shall never recover damages or costs. Where, however, the recovery is given solely to the party, damages shall be recovered with costs: for instance, upon the statute of 8 Hen. VI, for forcible entry,[5] or where someone brings an action of debt upon the statute against the sheriff or his officer who took the goods of someone arrested for felony before he is attainted, he shall recover the triple value for the debt and also his damages

1 31 Hen. VIII, c. 13.
2 See above, p.75.
3 21 Hen. VIII, c. 13.
4 Statute of Westminster II, c. 49.
5 8 Hen. VI, c. 9.

debt et ses dammages et costes auxi car lestatute done laction al partie tantum pur son recoverie a son opes demesne.

[12]

A, ff. 25v–26 (foll. pl. 9); *L* 185 (sim.).

Nota que luse et experience est a cest jour en Comen Banke que sur laction sur lestatute de non residence ou pur prisel des farmes per spirituall home le pl. en son action ne reherse tout lestatute ove les provisions mes tantum cest parte que fait pur son action et uncore un recoverie [*fol. 25*] ou auter record ove les circumstances serront reherses ou auterment nest bon, mes luse et experience fist le ley en lauter cas. Et uncore si fyne soit levye de 2. acres de terre et grant et render est fait per mesme le fyne al recognisor pur terme de son vie le remainder dun acre a J. S. le remainder de lauter acre al J. D. ore apres le mort le recognisor J. S. auera scire facias al executer le fyne pur son acre en le remainder et supposer le fyne destre levy tantum de cest acre sans faire mention de lauter acre entant que il est come estranger al auter acre mes en cest case si le remainder dambideux acres sont tantsolement a un home la le scire facias ferra mention dambideux coment que lun acre est en son possession et executed accordant al dit fyne et tout cest fuit declare per *Bromeley* en le case de Fulmerston avandit.

[13]

A, fo. 26;[f] *L* 186[f]; *D*, fo. 17, pl. 5 (1 & 2 Phil. & Mar.).

Nota que lusage et ley est per reason de lestatute fait anno 35 H. 8. ca. 7. a prender et de faire le jury plein de circumstantibus auxibein deins citties et villes corporates esteant counties en eux mesmes come en auters counties et shires et cest per le justices de nisi prius accordant al dit estatute le proviso deins mesme lestatute nient obstant car cest proviso extende forsque pur returner tiels persons deins lour villes et cities en pannelles et enquestes come [devant][1] ils puissoent et nextend a repeller le power des justices de nisi prius a prender juries de circumstantibus deins les dittes cities et villes et ceo fuit mis [en experience per *Brooke* Chief Justice][2] de Comen Bank al nisi prius al Guyldhall, London, et auxi

[1] *A, D, L.*
[2] *A, D, L.*

and costs, for the statute gives the action to the party alone, for his recovery to his own use.[1]

12. FULMERSTON v. STEWARD, contd

King's Bench, Mich. 1554, contd from pl. 9.

Note that the practice and experience in the Common Bench at the present day is that in an action upon the statute of non-residence, for taking farms by spiritual persons,[2] the plaintiff in his [declaration] does not recite the whole statute with the provisos but only that part which supports his action.[3] Nevertheless a recovery or other record must be set out with the circumstances or else it is not good; but the practice and experience makes law in the other case. If, however, a fine is levied of two acres of land, and a grant and render is made by the same fine to the conusor for term of his life, the remainder as to one acre to John Style, and the remainder as to the other acre to John Dale, after the consusor's death John Style shall have a *scire facias* to execute the fine for his acre in remainder, and shall allege that the fine was levied of this acre only, without mentioning the other acre, inasmuch as he is like a stranger as to the other acre. But if in this case the remainder in both acres was made only to one man, the *scire facias* should mention both acres, even though only one of the acres is in his possession, and execution shall be according to the said fine. All this was declared by BROMLEY in the case of Fulmerston aforesaid.

13. TALES DE CIRCUMSTANTIBUS

Probably in the Common Pleas, Mich. 1554.

Note that the usage and law by reason of the statute made in the year 35 Hen. VIII, c. [6], is to take and fill up the jury with bystanders (*de circumstantibus*) as well within cities and incorporated towns which are counties in themselves as in other counties and shires; and this is by the justices of nisi prius, in accordance with the said statute, notwithstanding the proviso within the same statute,[4] for this proviso extends only to returning such persons within their towns and cities in panels and inquests, as they could before, and does not extend to repealing the power of the justices of nisi prius to take juries *de circumstantibus* within the said cities and towns. This was put in practice by BROOKE C.J. of the Common Bench

[1] 1 Ric. III, c. 3. The statute says 'double', not 'triple'.

[2] 21 Hen. VIII, c. 13; previous case.

[3] Cf. above, p 74, pl. 6.

[4] 'Provided also, that this act, nor anything therein contained, shall not extend to any city or town corporate, or to any sheriff, minister or ministers in the same, for the return of any inquest or panel to be made and returned of persons inhabiting in the said cities or towns corporate, but that they and every of them shall and may return such persons in every such inquest or panel as before this time they might and have been accustomed to do . . .'. The statute was perpetuated by 2 & 3 Edw. VI, c. 32.

per *Browne*[1] et *Stamford* al citie de Exceter, ils esteantes justices dassise la: quod nota.

[14]

A, fo. 26[f]; *L* 187[f].

Nota per *Portman* que si home soit seisie dun mannor en droit son feme et il et son feme font un leas de parcell les demeasnes de le dit mannor al estranger pur vie et puis le baron et son feme grant le mannor ouster al estranger en fee per fyne que ore le reversion des les terres yssint leases passa per cest fyne et cest case ne fuit deny per nully mes affirme. Quere si le lease fuit per baron tantum.

[15]

Nota que fuit agree en Comen Banke que si home fist leas pur ans de son mannor place ove les appurtenances que rien ore passa al lessee forsque le meason et lorchard, court, garden, stable et barne a ceo adjoynant ou appendant [*fol. 25v*] et nul terre ou pasture purtenant al un meason mes si home lesse son meason ove les appurtenances per cest paroll tenementum suum en Dale ove les appurtenaunces que ore tout le terre et pasture ove cest mese passa quar tout est tenementum auxibein le meason come le terre etc.

[16]

A, fo. 26 (foll. pl. 14); *L* 188–189 (sim.).

Nota per *Bromley* et deny per null que per lestatute 25 E. 3. de proditionibus ca. 15. que nontenure de parcell ne abata le breife forsque pur cest parte et coment que lestatute est issint generall uncore si precipe quod reddat soit port dun mannor le tenant plede non tenure de parcell de cest mannor tout abatera come al comen ley car le mannor est entier et ne poet estre yssint apportioned yssint lentent de lestatute ne fuit a remedier cest: quod nota per luy. Et il dit auxi que en precipe quod reddat joyntenancy de parcell nabatera le breife et ceo per lequiti de le dit estatute, come il semble, et uncore si severall tenancy soit plede en precipe quod reddat la le demaundant mainteynera son breife ou auterment il abate et ceo nest pas remedy per le dit estatute.

[1] Bromley *A, D, L*.

at nisi prius at the Guildhall, London, and also by Browne and Staunford at the city of Exeter when they were justices of assize there. Note that.

14. HUSBAND AND WIFE

Probably in the Common Pleas, Mich.1554.

Note, by Portman, that if someone is seised of a manor in right of his wife, and he and his wife make a lease of part of the demesnes of the said manor to a stranger for life, and then the husband and his wife grant the manor over to a stranger in fee, by fine, the reversion of the lands so leased now passes by this fine. This case was not denied by anyone, but affirmed. But what if the lease was by the husband only?

15. 'APPURTENANCES' OF A HOUSE

Common Pleas, Mich. 1554. Cf. p. 11, above, pl. 1; p. 99, below, pl. 10.

Note that it was agreed in the Common Bench that if someone makes a lease for years of his manor place, with the appurtenances, nothing passes to the lessee except the house and the orchard, court, garden, stable and barn thereto adjoining or appendant; and no land or pasture pertains to a house. If, however, someone leases his house with the appurtenances by the words 'his tenement in Dale with the appurtenances', now all the land and pasture pass with this house, for all are 'tenement', both the house and the land etc.

16. NON-TENURE AND JOINT TENANCY

Probably in the King's Bench in *Fulmerston* v. *Steward*: cf. Plowd., fo. 109.

Note, by Bromley and denied by no-one, that by the statute of treasons of 25 Edw. III, [stat. 5, c. 2], non-tenure of part does not abate a writ except for that part; and, although the statute is in general terms, if a *praecipe quod reddat* is brought for a manor, and the tenant pleads non-tenure of part of this manor, the whole writ shall abate, as at common law: for the manor is entire and cannot be apportioned, and it was not the intention of the statute to remedy that. Note that, according to him. He also said that, in a *praecipe quod reddat*, joint tenancy of part shall not abate the writ; and that is by the equity of the said statute, as he thought; and yet if several tenancy is pleaded in a *praecipe quod reddat*, the demandant there shall maintain his writ or else it will abate, and this is not remedied by the said statute.

[17]

A, fo. 26[f]; *L* 190[f].

Nota per *Bromeley* et affirme per toutes que si home tient de roy en soccage en cheife et devie, son heire al plein age, que ore son heire suera son livery et payera son primer season pur cest terre tantum issint tenus et nemy pur ses auters terres a luy descende de son pier tenus dauters seignors come si le terre fuit tenus per service de chivaler en cheife coment que les parolls de lestatute de Prerogativa Regis sont generall de eo qui tenet in capite per service de chivaler et nemi in socage.

[18]

A, fo. 26v (foll. pl. 19); *L* 192 (sim.).

Nota auxi per luy que si home plede un particuler act de parlament en ascun court le roy que per reason ceo doit estre plede sub pede sigilli per exemplification south le graund seale al enformer le court de lact ou auterment les justices ne preignont notice de lact mes il confes que lexperience est contrary a son opinion que fist la ley per reason de le contynuance et usage de cell.

[19]

A, fo. 26 (foll. pl. 17); *L* 191 (sim.).

[*fol. 26*] Nota en precipe quod reddat vers un enfant deins age <al graund cape il appiert et ne savera son default>[1] per reason de son enfancy en le graunde cape mes si le enfaunt appiert en court et est admitt per garden a pleder et puis fait default et petit cape est agard ore lenfant en cest petit cape savera son default ou il perdera le terre quod nota per <Bromeley, *Broke* Cheife Justice de le Comen Banke, *Portman* et *Stanford*>.[2]

[20]

A, fo. 26v (foll. pl. 18); *L* 193 (sim.); *D*, fo. 17, pl. 6 (1 & 2 Phil. & Mar.).

Nota per tout le court en Comen Banke que pur un reliefe due per le tenant al seignor que les executours le seignor avera action de debt [per le common ley][3] pur cest relief [et per le greinder oppinion le seignor mesme poet aver laction][4] quia non est annualis come auters rentes services sont.

[1] il ne besoigne de saver son default al graund cape *A, L.*
[2] Bromley, Brooke, Portman et Stamford *L.* Bromley *A.*
[3] *A, D.*
[4] *A, D.*

17. LIVERY AND PRIMER SEISIN

Probably in the King's Bench in *Fulmerston* v. *Steward*: see Plowd., fo. 109. Cf. above, p. 48, pl. 4 (under Trin. 1553), which is another version of the same report. See also *Davy's Case* (1555) Dyer, fo. 123b.

Note, by BROMLEY and affirmed by everyone, that if someone holds of the king in socage in chief, and dies, his heir being of full age, his heir shall now sue his livery and pay his primer seisin only for this land which is so held, and not for the other lands descended to him from his father which are held of other lords. Likewise if the land was held by knight-service in chief, even though the words of the statute Prerogativa Regis are general 'of him who holds in chief by knight-service' and not in socage.

18. PLEADING AN ACT OF PARLIAMENT

Perhaps contd from pl. 17.

Note also, by him, that if someone pleads a particular act of parliament[1] in any of the king's courts, this ought by reason to be pleaded under the half-seal (*sub pede sigilli*)[2] by exemplification under the great seal to inform the court of the act, or else the justices will not take notice of the act. But he confessed that the experience is contrary to his opinion, and experience makes law by reason of continuance and being put into practice.

19. DEFAULT BY AN INFANT

Probably in Serjeants' Inn, Mich. 1554. Cf. below, p. 81, pl. 24; *Ward* v. *Anderson*, below, p. 94, pl. 4.

Note that in a *praecipe quod reddat* against an infant under age, if he appears at the grand *cape* he shall not save a default in the grand *cape* by reason of his infancy; but if the infant appears in court and is admitted to plead through his guardian, and then makes default, and a petit *cape* is awarded, the infant shall save his default in this petit *cape* or else he would lose the land. Note that, by BROMLEY, BROOKE C.J. of the Common Bench, PORTMAN and STAUNFORD.

20. RELIEF CLAIMED BY EXECUTORS

Common Pleas, Mich. 1554.

Note, by the whole court in the Common Bench, that a lord's executors shall have an action of debt by the common law for a relief due from the tenant to the lord; and by the greater opinion[3] the lord himself shall have the action, because a relief is not annual as other rent-services are.

[1] I.e. as opposed to a general act.
[2] I.e. the great seal tipped onto a smaller blob of wax.
[3] Presumably meaning majority: cf. above, p. 60.

[21]

A, fo. 26v[f]; *L* 194[f].

Nota auxi que un port action de covenant en Comen Banke et declare sur un indenture portant date eisdem die et anno et ne declare devant ou lendenture fuit fait ne le jour et lan come lendenture fuit date et sur cest declaration et indenture charge le deffendant ove reparation des measons contrary al dit indenture a que le deffendant plede que il ad repaire accordant etc. et sur cest fueront al yssue et jurie al barre trie et jure et devant evidence cest matter monstre al court pur le declaration que fault le liew ou le indenture fuit fait et lan et jour del date de cel et pur ceo que poet estre que les reparations fueront faites devant laction commence et poet estre que ils fueront faites apres laction commence et yssint incertayne le court per bon advise discharge le jurye et que le pl. recovera rien per son breife. Mes fuit dit la per *Stanford* Justice que si en debt sur un obligation le pl. ne declare ou se fist ne lan et jour del date de cest et le defendant pleda releas ou payment de le playntiefe mesme et sur cest sont al yssue en cest case le jury serra prise, quar le declaration est admitt per cest plee et lissue et le tryall sur cest assettes certeine, mes en lauter case nappiert que le playntiefe ad ascun cause daction pur le non certentie de le declaration. Et cest case de *Stanford* ne fuit deny.

[22]

A, fo. 26v[f]; *L* 195[f]; *D*, fo. 17, pl. 7 (1 & 2 Phil. & Mar.).

Nota auxi per *Bromley* et *Portman*, *Broke* et *Stanford* que home avera action de son case vers auter que luy appell laron ou traytor generallment ou villein generalment sil fuit endammage per le parler coment [*fol. 26v*] que il ne declare coment il fuit laron, traytor ou villein quar il poet estre cye tant endammage per ceux parolls generallment parle come especiallment parle. Et uncore *Broke* dit que en auncient temps non fuit [issint][1] prise s. que ascun action sur le case gist pur ceux parolls sans declaration coment traytor, villein ou laron. Mes issint la ley nest tenus a cest jour et [ceo est][2] le melior [ley].[3]

[23]

A, fo. 26v[f]; *L* 196[f]; *D*, fo. 17, pl. 8 (1 & 2 Phil. & Mar.).

Nota si un yssue soit joyne sur point de le declaration que declaration en soy est male et le jury est jure[4] et prise a passer et pur le male declaration sont discharges

[1] *A, D, L.*
[2] *A, D, L..*
[3] *A, L.*
[4] trie *A, D, L.*

21. UNCERTAINTY IN A DECLARATION

Common Pleas, Mich. 1554.

Note also that someone brought an action of covenant in the Common Bench and declared on an indenture bearing date 'the same day and year' (*eisdem die et anno*), but did not before that declare where the indenture was made, nor the day and year in which the indenture was dated, and upon this declaration and indenture the defendant was charged with repairs of houses contrary to the said indenture;[1] to which the defendant pleaded that he had repaired in accordance etc., and thereupon they were at issue, and the jury were at the bar, tried and sworn. And before evidence was given, this matter was shown to the court; and since the declaration lacked the place where the indenture was made, and the year and day of the date thereof, and because it is possible that the repairs were done either before or after the action was commenced, and therefore it is uncertain, the court by good advice discharged the jury and awarded that the plaintiff should recover nothing by his writ. But it was said by STAUNFORD J. that if in debt on a bond the plaintiff does not declare where the bond was made, nor the year and day of its date, and the defendant pleads a payment or release from the plaintiff himself, and thereupon they are at issue, in that case the jury shall be taken, for the declaration is admitted by this plea, and the issue and trial thereon are sufficiently certain, whereas in the other case it does not appear that the plaintiff has any cause of action, because of the uncertainty of the declaration. This case put by STAUNFORD was not denied.

22. ACTION ON THE CASE FOR SLANDER

Common Pleas, perhaps contd from pl. 21. Cf. *OHLE*, vi. 793.

Note also, by BROMLEY and PORTMAN, BROOKE and STAUNFORD, that one shall have an action upon his case against someone else who calls him 'thief' or 'traitor' generally, or 'villein' generally, if he is damaged by the speaking, even though he did not specifically say in what way he was a thief, traitor or villein; for he may be just as much damaged by these words spoken generally as by words spoken specifically. And yet BROOKE said that in old times it was not so understood, namely that any action on the case lay for these words without specifying in what way he was a traitor, villein or thief. The law is not, however, so held at the present day; and this is better.

23. JEOFAILS

Probably in the Common Pleas, Mich. 1554; perhaps contd from pl. 21–22.

Note that if an issue is joined upon a point of the declaration, which declaration is bad in itself, and the jury is sworn and ready to pass, and they are discharged

[1] I.e. the failure to repair was a breach of the covenants in the indenture.

ore nul repleder serra mes lagard le court serra que le jury serra discharge et que le playntiefe preigna ryen per son breife entant que il est ore come[1] nul breife ne declaration [ussent estre fait].[2] Mes auterment serra si le barr soit male et yssue joyne sur cest ou replication et rejoynder males et yssue est joyne sur eux, ore repleder serra la ou le fault [commence],[3] [quar][4] le breife et le count et le declaration estoient bons que est le foundation de tout:[5] quod nota per le case jeofaile avantdit.

[24]

Nota per *Broke* Cheife Justice de Comen Banke que si un enfant en precipe quod reddat perde son terre per son default al graund cape per judgement que ore cest judgement est error et per breife il reversera le judgement pur son nonage: et ceo ne fuit deny per Bromeley nec *Portman.*

[25]

A, ff. 26v–27 (foll. pl. 23); *L* 197[f]; *D*, fo. 18, pl. 9 (1 & 2 Phil. & Mar.).

Nota per tout le court en le Comen Banck que si en debt sur un obligation le playntiefe declare lobligation estre fait en London[6] ou laction est port, le deffendant dit que il fuit nee al Dale en le countie de Lyncolne et fist lobligation la tiel jour et an et ceo enseala et deliver al playntiefe, a quel temps il fuit deins age, ore il navera cest especiall plee mes dira generalment que il fuit deins age al temps etc. car ceo estoit bein en le conusans des jurors s. le nonage et plein age auxibein en lun countie come en lauter en cest personall action. Mes si le defendant en tiell case voil avoider lobligation per dures demprisonment en auter countie que lou laction fuit port ore lissue serra trie en le countie ou le dures est alledge car ceo rest en conusans de cest countie tantum ou le dures fuit et nemy en lauter countie quar la lacte fuit fait: quod nota.

[26]

Abr. in *A*, fo. 27[f]; *L* 198–199[f].

Nota que si terres sont dones per le roy ou roygne al auter et a ses heires males et ne dit de son corps, per *Portman* le donee ad fee simple. Et yssint est si un devise

[1] come si *A.* si come *D.* come *L.*
[2] *A, D.* ust estre fait *L.*
[3] *A, D, L.* est *H.*
[4] car *A, D, L.* que *H.*
[5] daction *A, D, L.*
[6] Londres *A.* Hend: *L.*

on account of the bad declaration, there shall now be no repleader; but the court shall award that the jury be discharged and the plaintiff take nothing by his writ, inasmuch as it is now as if there was no writ or declaration. It would be otherwise, however, if the plea in bar was bad, and issue was joined upon it, or a replication or rejoinder were bad and issue was joined upon them; there a repleader shall begin where the fault is, for the writ and the count and the declaration stand good, and they are the foundation of everything. Note that: and the previous case of jeofail.[1]

24. DEFAULT BY AN INFANT

Common Pleas, Mich. 1554. Cf. above, p. 79, pl. 19; *Ward* v. *Anderson*, in the King's Bench, below, p. 94, pl. 4.

Note, by BROOKE C.J. of the Common Bench, that if an infant loses his land in a *praecipe quod reddat* through his default at the grand *cape*, by judgment, this judgment is error and he shall reverse the judgment by writ of error on account of his minority. This was not denied by BROMLEY or PORTMAN.

25. VENUE IN DEBT ON A BOND

Common Pleas, Mich. 1554.

Note by the whole court in the Common Bench that if the plaintiff in debt on a bond declares the bond to have been made in London, where the action is brought, and the defendant says that he was born in Dale in the county of Lincoln and made the bond there such a day and year, and sealed and delivered it to the plaintiff, at which time he was under age, he shall not have this special plea but must say generally that he was under age at the time etc. for this is fully within the knowledge of the jurors of either county, namely the minority and full age, in this personal action. If, however, the defendant in such a case wishes to avoid the bond by duress of imprisonment in a county other than that where the action was brought, the issue here shall be tried in the county where the duress is alleged, for that is solely in the knowledge of the county where the duress was, and not in the other county, for the act was done there. Note that.[2]

26. WORDS OF LIMITATION

Star Chamber, in or before Mich. 1554 (related by Portman J.).

Note that if lands are given by the king or queen to another and to his heirs male, without saying 'of his body', the donee has a fee simple: according to PORTMAN. So it is if someone devises land by his testament to another and to his

[1] See above, 80, pl. 21.
[2] Cf. above, p. 47, pl. 1.

terre per son testament al auter et a ses heires males le devisee avera fee simple et nemy estate en taile et cest case [*fol. 27*] de devise fuit adjudge yssint s. que le devisee avera fee simple ore tarde <in Camera Stellata>[1] per les justices et en le cas devant le done le roy fuit adjudge nad que estate al sufferance le roy. Mes *Portman* dit que sil fuit arguer arere pur son vie il s. le donee avera fee simple certeynment.[2]

[27]

A, fo. 27 (foll. pl. 29); *L* 201 (sim.).

Nota per toutes les justices assembles al Serjeantes Inne en Chauncerie Lane que si home soit endite de murder dun et auter est endite ove luy come accessory per procurement a faire le murder et sur cest indictment ils sont arraines et ambideux trove culpables et judgment et execution ewe sur le principall et laccessory pria son clergie que ore il avera son clergie per lestatute de repell anno 1° E. 6. Et sur le dit estatute auxi repeale les clergies adevant oustes per auter estatutes come felonies, quar le murder est un offence et accessory est auter, quar si home soit arrayne dun murder et trove rien culpable il poet bein estre arrayne come accessorie al dit murder s. auxibein come accessory devant come apres et ceo prove severall offences et si le roy pardon toutes offences ore murder nest pardon, uncore accessories a ceo sont.

[28]

A, fo. 27^{f}; *L* 202^{f}.

Nota auxi [agree per eux toutes][3] que si home comaunde auter a poysoner J. S. et il per cest comaundment tua luy ou si home commaund auter a tuer un ove dagger et il tua ove sword uncore cesty que yssint comaund est accessory al dit murder. Mes auterment est si home commaund auter a embleer <unam ovem>[4] de J. S. et il per cest comaundment emblea <un bove de J. S.>[5] ou ove[6] dun auter que cestui que issint commaund nest pas accessory quia en auter forme et auter felony mes le murder est tout un felony.

[1] en le Starchamber *A*. en Leschequer chamber *L*.
[2] clerement *A*.
[3] *A, L*.
[4] le barbites *A, L*.
[5] ses beofes *A, L*.
[6] les ovells *A*. les owells *L*.

heirs male: the devisee shall have a fee simple and not an estate in tail. This case of a devise was so adjudged recently in the Star Chamber, by the justices, namely that the devisee shall have a fee simple. And in the previous case of the king's gift it was adjudged that he only had an estate at the king's sufferance. PORTMAN, however, said that if it was argued again for his life the donee would certainly have a fee simple.

27. ACCESSORY TO FELONY

Serjeants' Inn, Chancery Lane, probably Trin. 1554 (cf. below, p. 84, pl. 34).

Note, by all the justices assembled at Serjeants' Inn in Chancery Lane, that if a man is indicted for murdering someone, and another is indicted with him as accessory for procuring him to do the murder, and upon this indictment they are arraigned and both are found guilty, and judgment and execution had upon the principal, and the accessory prays his clergy, he shall now have his clergy by the statute of repeal of 1 Edw. VI.[1] And the said statute also repealed the clergies before ousted by other statutes as felonies,[2] for the murder is one offence and accessory is another; for if someone is arraigned of a murder and found not guilty, he may well be arraigned as accessory to the said murder, namely either accessory before or after, and this proves that they are separate offences; and if the king pardons all offences, murder is not thereby pardoned, and yet accessory to the murder is.

28. ACCESSORY TO FELONY

Serjeants' Inn, contd.

Note also that if someone commands another to poison John Style, and by this command he slays him,[3] or if a man commands another to kill someone with his dagger and he kills him with his sword, the person who so commanded is nevertheless accessory to the said murder. It is otherwise, however, if someone commands another to steal a sheep of John Style's, and by this command he steals an ox of John Style's, or someone else's sheep, the person who gave such command is not an accessory, because it is in another form and is another felony, whereas the murder is all one felony.

[1] 1 Edw. VI, c. 12.

[2] I.e. the benefit of clergy was revived for accessories because it was available at common law before the legislation of Henry VIII and was not expressly taken away by the Edwardian statute. The statute restored benefit of clergy as it was in 1 Hen. VIII, with specific exceptions.

[3] I.e. by some means more immediate than poison.

[29]

A, fo. 27 (foll. pl. 26); *L* 200 (sim.).

Nota auxi per eux agree que si home [soit] committ al gaoll pur treason pur forger coyne le roy et le gaoler voluntariment luy suffer de escape que ceo est treason en le gaoler et hault treason. Et ne fuit mult deny que si le principall et accessory sont troves culpables et devant judgement le principall devie que ore nul judgement serra done vers lasccessorye.

[30]

A, ff. 27r–v (foll. pl. 28); *L* 203 (sim.); *D*, fo. 18, pl. 10 (1 & 2 Phil. & Mar.).

Nota fuit agree auxi que les justices dassise, oyer et terminer, justices de peace ou gaoll deliverie nont my power dassesser fynes sur les testes des jurors quex [fount][1] faux serement devant eux mes [solement][2] a doner eux jour devant eux mesmes ou le counsell le roigne.

[31]

A, fo. 27v[f]; *L* 204[f].

[*fol. 27v*] Nota auxi que si home ad un chamber en ascun Inne de Court ou aliours et il comitt le custodie de ceo a son servant que esteant dormant en le dit chamber un auter robbe le dit chamber ore cestui felon avera son clergie, quar lestatute anno 5º et 6º E. 6. parle toute de servantes en le plurall nomber: sicut accidit in casu Griffith de Lincolnes Inne, atturney le roygne.

[32]

Nota per *Portman* Cheif Justice de Bank le Roy que les justices doyer et terminer nont my power dacquiter suspectes per proclamation nient pluis que justices de peace ont power dacquiter et deliver eux per proclamation, quar il dit que le power de justices de oyer et terminer et de justices de peace est tantsolement pur

[1] *A, D.* denont *H.*
[2] totalment *H. Om. A.*

29. ESCAPE; ACCESSORY

Serjeants' Inn, contd. The first question arose again at Leicester assizes, Lent 1555: Dyer's circuit notebook, 110 Selden Soc. 406, pl. 18.

Note also that it was agreed by them that if someone is committed to gaol for treason in forging the king's coin, and the gaoler voluntarily suffers him to escape, this is treason in the gaoler – and high treason. And it was not much denied that if a principal and accessory are found guilty, and before judgement the principal dies, no judgment shall now be given against the accessory.

30. PUNISHMENT OF JURORS

Serjeants' Inn, contd.

Note also that it was agreed that justices of assize, of oyer and terminer, of the peace, or of gaol delivery, have no power to assess fines upon the heads of the jurors who make a false oath before them, but only to give them a day before themselves or the Queen's Council.

31. BURGLARY IN LINCOLN'S INN

Serjeants' Inn, contd.

Note also that if someone has a chamber in some inn of court, or elsewhere, and he commits the custody thereof to his servant, and while the servant is sleeping in the said chamber another robs the said chamber, this felon shall have his clergy: for the statute of 5 & 6 Edw. VI[1] speaks throughout of 'servants' in the plural number. This happened in the case of Griffith of Lincoln's Inn, the queen's attorney.[2]

32. DISCHARGE BY PROCLAMATION

Serjeants' Inn. contd. Cf. below, p. 98, pl. 5.

Note, by PORTMAN C.J. of the King's Bench, that the justices of oyer and terminer have no power to acquit suspects by proclamation, any more than justices of the peace have power to acquit and deliver them by proclamation: for he said that the power of justices of oyer and terminer and justices of the peace is solely

[1] 5 & 6 Edw. VI, c. 9. This removed clergy 'for robbing of any person or persons . . . in any part or parcel of their dwelling-houses or dwelling-places, the owner or dweller in the same house, or his wife, his children or servants, being then within the same house or place . . . or in any other place within the precinct of the same house or dwelling-place'.

[2] Edward Griffin or Griffith, bencher and one of the governors of Lincoln's Inn, Att.-Gen. 1552–58. His chambers were in the gatehouse of the inn: *Black Books of Lincoln's Inn*, i. 373.

arrayner et acquiter eux quex sont endites devant eux mesmes et eux a deliver et nul auters quex sont endites devant le coroner ou justice de peace al lour cesion. Mes il dit que acquiter per proclamation [appent][1] al justices de gaole deliverie tantum: causa patet. Mes Justice *Stanford*, Serjeant *Gawdy* et Serjeant *Rookeby* fueront toutes al contrary, et reason ceo voet ou auterment le comission doyer et terminer est a petit effect. Et ceo fuit lour opinion vers luy quant al acquiter et deliver suspectes devant eux per proclamation.

[33]

Nota auxi que il fuit agree per *Stanfort* et auters avantdites que si home ove felonious entent prise un chivall deins un closse et ad le chivall en son possession a carier hors de le closse et devant que il ad le chivall hors de le close il est prize ove le manner en le close que ore est felony coment que il ne fuit hors de close ove le chivall. Come si home emblera sheetes en son chamber en un inne et est prise ove le manner en le sale cest est felony adjudge en livers.

[34]

Abr. in *A*, fo. 31 (Mich. 2 & 3 Phil. & Mar.); *L* 234 (sim.); *D*, fo. 21, pl. 11 (sim.).

Nota per eux auxi clerment agree que si home emblea lanes hors de barbites en le campe per clippinge ou pullinge que amont al xii d. et ouster que ceo est felony et issint est si home occide mes barbites et prist eux ove luy secrement et feloniousment ou les felles de eux que cest est auxi felony.

[35]

A, fo. 29v (Mich. 2 & 3 Phil. & Mar.); *L* 223 (sim.).

[*fol. 28*] Nota que fuit agree per toutes les justices assembles al Serjeantes Inne in Chauncery Lane en le terme de Saint Trinitie lan avaundit que si home ymagine ou compasse le morte le roy ou roigne que cest compassa ou ymagyn tantum sans un acte overt provant son entent nest pas treason. Mes a preparer un dagger ou cuttel, harnes ou gonne afaire lacte cest overt acte sans pluis faire ove compasse et ymagination avauntdit est treason per lestatute anno 25° E. 3. et vyes lestatute.

[1] *Reads* appiert.

to arraign and acquit those who are indicted before themselves, and to deliver them, and not others who have been indicted before the coroner or justices of the peace at their sessions. But he said that acquittal by proclamation belonged solely to the justices of gaol delivery. The reason is apparent. But STAUNFORD J., Serjeant *Gawdy* and Serjeant *Rokeby* were absolutely to the contrary; and reason wills this, or else the commission of oyer and terminer is of little effect; and this was their opinion, against him, as to acquitting and delivering suspects before them by proclamation.

33. ASPORTATION IN LARCENY

Serjeants' Inn, contd.

Note also that it was agreed by STAUNFORD and the others aforesaid that if someone with felonious intent takes a horse within a close, and has the horse in his possession to carry out of the close, and before he has the horse out of the close he is taken red-handed ('with the mainour') in the close, this is felony even though he was not out of the close with the horse. Similarly if someone steals sheets in his chamber in an inn, and is taken with the mainour in the hall, this is adjudged in the books to be felony.[1]

34. STEALING WOOL FROM SHEEP

Serjeants' Inn, contd.

Note that it was also clearly agreed by them that if someone steals wool from sheep in the field by clipping or pulling, and it amounts to 12*d.* [in value] or more, this is felony. So it is if someone kills my sheep and takes them away with him secretly, and feloniously [?sells] the skins, this is also felony.

35. HIGH TREASON

Serjeants' Inn, Chancery Lane, Trin. 1554.

Note that it was agreed by all the justices assembled at Serjeants' Inn in Chancery Lane, in Trinity term in the year aforesaid, that if someone imagines[2] or compasses the king's or queen's death, this compassing or imagining is not treason without an overt act proving his intent. But preparing a dagger or knife, armour, or a gun, to do the act, is an overt act without doing any more, when coupled with the compassing and imagination aforesaid, by the statute of 25 Edw. III.[3] See the statute.

[1] Fitz. Abr., *Corone*, pl. 204 (YB 27 Edw. III, Lib. Ass., pl. 39).
[2] I.e. plots.
[3] Treason Act 1351, 25 Edw. III, st. 5, c. 2.

[36]

A, fo. 29v[f] (runs on from pl. 35); *L* 223 (sim.).

Et fuit agree auxi per eux que si un compasse ou ymagen le morte le royen ou roy et puis va al un auter home et fist luy privie de son entent et purpose et dit a luy que il semble que tiel home (et luy nosme) est un meete home pur le purpose a fair ceo cest discloser est un overt acte a faire le treason et coment que il ne dit al dit home que tiel person est un mete home pur le purpose mes va a luy et utter son entent a luy et fist luy privie a son entent coment it voet aver cest chose fist cest discloser est overt acte a faire le treason. Et si home conspire ou ymagyn le morte le roy ou royne et apres va al auter et fist luy privie a son entent et purpose, a que lauter assent et accepta de luy que yssint conspire ou ymagen un token destre privie enter eux quant le chose serra fait, come il frange un royall dore en 2 peces et dona a luy un moitie de cest et reserve lauter moitie, et dit quant un de eux monstra ou ostenda cest peece al auter que donques est temps a sturrer[1] en lour acte, cest treason en ambideux auxi en cestui que dona come en cestui que accepta lawre et cest done et acceptance sont overt actes en ambideux.

Termino Pasche annis regni Philippi et Marie 2° et 3°

[1]

A, ff. 29v–30[f] (still Mich. 2 & 3 Phil. & Mar.); *L* 224[f] (sim.); *D*, fo. 21, pl. 12 (sim.).

Jacques Granado chivaler port action de trespas pur ses [herbes][2] garbes prises al Newton en le com. de Devon versus Johannem Dyer que plede ryen culpable, et devant les justices de nisi prius en pays quant le jury [*fol. 28v*] fuit ent jure et charge sur evidence le case appiert destre tiel que un John Howe nuper prior nuper monasterii de Plimton[3] fuit seisie de le rectory de Newton en fee en droit son meason et per fait indent seale ove le covent seale ove lour assent lessa le dit rectorye ove les appurtenaunces al un Richard Drewe a primer jour doctober anno Regis H. 8. 30. et anno domini 1538 pur 25 ans rendant inde annuatim al dit prior et a ses successours xv li. ad festum Purificationis Beate

[1] styrrer *A*.
[2] *D only*.
[3] Plumpton *A, L*.

36. HIGH TREASON

Serjeants' Inn, contd. These points were ruled in *R.* v. *Duke of Buckingham* (1521) 102 Selden Soc. 124; 119 Selden Soc. 56. Note also *R.* v. *Throgmorton* (1554) Dyer, fo. 98b.

It was also agreed by them that if someone compasses or imagines the queen's or king's death, and then goes to another man and makes him privy to his intent and purpose, and says to him that he thinks a certain man (naming him) is a meet man for the purpose, to do the act, this disclosure is an overt act such as to constitute treason. Even if he does not say to the said man that such and such a person is a meet man for the purpose, but goes to him and utters his intent to him, and makes him privy to his intent how he will have this thing done, this disclosure is an overt act such as to constitute treason. And if someone conspires or imagines the king's or queen's death, and afterwards goes to another and makes him privy to his intent and purpose, to which the other assents, and he accepts from him (who so conspired or imagined) a token to be kept secret between them, [to be used] when the thing should be done, for instance, he breaks a gold ryal in two pieces and gives half of it to him and keeps the other half, and says that when one of them shows or holds out this piece to the other, then is the time to stir in their act, this is treason in both of them, as well in the one who gives as in the one who accepts the gold, and this gift and acceptance are overt acts in both.

Easter term in the second and third years of the reigns of Philip and Mary (1556)

1. GRANADO v. DYER

King's Bench, Pas. 1556. Record: KB 27/1169, m. 84d. (demurrer to the evidence; c.a.v. to Pas. 1556; no judgment); printed below. Also reported in Dyer, fo. 123 (noted Mich. 1555; argument, Pas. 1556). Probably the case referred to above, p. 56, at the end of pl. 2.

Jaques Granado, knight,[1] brought an action of trespass for his sheaves taken at Newton [St Cyres], in the county of Devon, against John Dyer,[2] who pleaded Not guilty; and before the justices of nisi prius in the country, when the jury was therein sworn and charged with evidence, the case appeared to be as follows: one John Howe, lately prior of the late monastery of Plympton, was seised of the rectory of Newton in fee, in right of his house, and by a deed indented, sealed with the convent seal, and with their assent, leased the said rectory with the appurtenances to one Richard Drewe from the first day of October in the thirtieth year of King Henry VIII (A.D. 1538) for 25 years, yielding £15 rent therefrom

[1] Knighted 1547.

[2] Elder brother of Dyer C.J.; clerk of the peace for Somerset; died 1558: 109 Selden Soc. xxxiii.

Marie et Inventionis Sancte Crucis [et][1] prima solutio erit et incipiet ad festum Purificationis Beate Marie anno domini 1539, et puis primo [die][2] Martis anno R. R. H. 8. 30 le dit monastery ove le dit rectory [per fait][3] enrolle [fuit][4] surrender et done al Roy H. 8. et a ses heires et successours et puis 28 Aprilis anno 31 le dit H. 8. lact pur avoider leases lou launcient rent ne fuit reserve fuit fait et cest rectorye fuit tout temps lease adevant, et cest fuit launcient rent et en leas a nullye al temps de cest leas, et puis le morte H. 8. le Roye E. 6. fuit seisie et lesse le dit rectory al dit playntiefe per ses lettres pattentes pur son vie et il port son dit action vers le dit defendant que fuit lassignee la feme de Drewe, executrix al dit Drew, longe temps devant le trespas et devant les lettres pattentes. Si le dit leas pur 25 ans soit void per lestatute, cest le matter que fuit demurr en judgement.

Et per toutes les justices de Bank le Roye fuit agree et argue per toutes eux que coment que cest rent ne soit annuallment reserve uncore entant que lestatute va en defeter leases bons al comen ley lestatute serra prise stricte juris come les parolls sont et nul parolls sont en lestatute dannualment durant le terme estre reserve et pur ceo lestatute observe en toute.

Et per *Porteman* Cheif Justice si cest paroll annualment ust estre en lacte uncore le lease serra bon car ceux parolls primo incipiente ad festum Purificationis nabate null rent mes tantsolement done joure et respect de payment a cest jour lymitt et a ces jour lymitt il paya tout lentier rent de le temps le leas arere al dit jour lymitt sur le dit leas yssint reserve.

Nota auxi que la fuit tenus diversitie perenter plees en action et plees sur evidence al jury quar les plees [*fol. 29*] en action doient estre certen sans doublenes ou auter choses uncertein ou contrariant mes si plees sur evidence sont uncertein contraryant ou comprehend en eux double matter uncore sills comprehend le veritie de le matter issint que le matter bein poet appere al court cest assettes bon et ne deface levidence per ascun voye per cest.

Record of the case

KB 27/1169, m. 84d.

Devon'. Memorandum quod die Martis proxime post octabas Sancti Hillarii isto eodem termino coram domina regina apud Westmonasterium venit Jacobus Granado miles per

[1] *A, L.*
[2] *A, D, L.*
[3] *A, D, L.* fuit *H.*
[4] *A, D, L.*

annually to the said prior and his successors at the feasts of the Purification of the Blessed Mary and of the Invention of the Holy Cross, the first payment to be and begin at the feast of the Purification of the Blessed Mary [25 March] A. D. 1539; and afterwards, on 1 March [1539], 30 Hen. VIII, the said monastery (with the said rectory) was surrendered and given to King Henry VIII and his heirs and successors by deed enrolled; and then, on 28 April [1539], 31 Hen. VIII, the act was passed for avoiding leases [of monastic land] where the old rent was not reserved;[1] and this rectory had always been leased before, and this was the old rent, but it was leased to no-one at the time of this lease; and after the death of Henry VIII, King Edward VI was seised and leased the said rectory to the said plaintiff for life, by his letters patent; and he brought his said action against the said defendant, who was the assignee of Drewe's wife, executrix of the said Drewe, long before the trespass and before the letters patent. And the matter which was demurred in judgment was whether this lease for 25 years was avoided by the statute.

And it was agreed by all the justices of the King's Bench, and argued by all of them,[2] that although this rent was not annually reserved, nevertheless since the statute operates to defeat leases which are good at common law it shall be taken strictly according to the words; and there are no words in the statute saying 'to be reserved annually during the term', and therefore the statute is observed in all respects.

According to Portman C.J., even if this word 'annually' had been in the act, the lease would still have been good, for these words 'first beginning at the feast of the Purification' do not abate any of the rent, but merely adjourn and respite payment until this appointed day, and at this appointed day he shall pay the whole of the rent so reserved, from the time of the lease, which is in arrear upon the said lease at the said appointed day.

Note also that there was held to be a distinction between pleas in an action and pleas upon evidence to the jury,[3] for pleas in an action ought to be certain, without doubleness or other things which are uncertain or contradictory, whereas if pleas upon evidence are uncertain or contradictory or contain double matter in them, nevertheless if they contain the truth of the matter, so that the matter can well appear to the court, this is good enough and in no way defeats the evidence.

Translation of the record

King's Bench, Hil. 1554.

Devonshire. Remember that on the Tuesday next after the octaves of St Hilary this same term Jaques Granado, knight, came before the lady queen at Westminster, by Richard Heywood his attorney. And he proffered here in the court of the lady queen, then being there, a

[1] 31 Hen. VIII, c. 13; below, pp. 89–90.

[2] I.e. they all delivered reasoned opinions. Dyer says the case was 'argued' by Portman C.J., Whiddon and Dalison JJ.

[3] I.e. demurrers to the evidence.

Ricardum Heywood attornatum suum. Et protulit hic in curia domine regine tunc ibidem quandam billam suam versus Johannem Dyer in custodia marescalli etc. de placito transgressionis. Et sunt plegii de prosequendo, scilicet Johannes Doo et Ricardus Roo. Quequidem billa sequitur in hec verba:

Devon'. Jacobus Granado miles queritur de Johanne Dyer in custodia marrescalli marescalcie domine regine coram ipsa regina existente de eo quod ipse vicesimo die Augusti anno regni[i] domini Edwardi nuper regis Anglie sexti sexto vi et armis etc. quadraginta carectatas tritici, quinquaginta carectatas ordei, viginti carectatas avenarum et quatuor carectatas feni ipsius Jacobi ad valenciam triginti librarum <apud Newton Sancti Ciricii in comitatu predicto>[i] adtunc et ibidem inventas cepit et abcariavit, cumque etiam predictus Johannes vicesimo primo die Augusti anno regni domine Marie nunc regine Anglie primo vi et armis etc. quadraginta alias carectatas tritici, quinquaginta alias carectatas ordei, viginti alias carectatas avenarum et quatuor alias carectatas feni ipsius Jacobi Granado ad valenciam triginti librarum <apud Newton Sancti Ciricii in comitatu predicto>[i] adtunc et ibidem inventas cepit et abcariavit, et alia enormia ei intulit, ad dampnum ipsius Jacobi centum librarum, et contra pacem tam dicti domini regis quam dicte domine regine nunc etc. Et inde producit sectam etc.

Et predictus Johannes, per Galfridum Tottyll attornatum suum, venit et defendit vim et injuriam quando etc. Et dicit quod ipse in nullo est inde culpabilis. Et de hoc ponit se super patriam. Et predictus Jacobus similiter. Ideo veniat inde jurata coram domina regina apud Westmonasterium die Jovis proxime post quindenam Pasche et qui nec etc. ad recognoscendum etc. quia tam etc. Idem dies datus est partibus predictis ibidem etc. Postea, continuato inde processu inter partes predictas per juratas positas inde inter eas in respectu coram domino rege et domina regina <apud Westmonasterium>[i] usque [diem] Martis proximum post octabas Sancti Michaelis extunc proxime sequentes nisi justiciarii [domini regis et domine regine][1] ad assisas in comitatu predicto capiendas assignati prius die Jovis proxime post festum Natalis [Beate Marie][2] Wirginis apud castrum Exonie in comitatu predicto per formam statuti etc. venissent pro defectu juratorum. Ad quem diem coram domino rege et domina regina apud Westmonasterium venerunt tam predictus Jacobus per attornatum suum predictum [*sic*]. Et prefati justiciarii coram quibus etc. miserunt hic recordum suum coram eis habitum in hec verba:

> Postea die et loco infracontentis coram Humfrido Broune milite et Willelmo Staunforde serviente domini regis et domine regine ad legem ac justiciariis eorundem domini regis et domine regine ad assisas in comitatu Devonie capiendas assignatis per formam statuti etc. ven[iunt] tam infranominatus Jacobus Granado per Johannem Hooper attornatum suum quam infrascriptus Johannes Dyer in propria persona sua. Et juratores jurate infraspecificate exacti similiter ven[iunt].
>
> Et super hoc Johannes Predyaux de Upton Pyne, generosus, de consilio predicti Jacobi in lege terre eruditus, juratoribus predictis in evidenc[iis][3] ostend[it] quod dominus Edwardus nuper rex Anglie sextus diu ante transgressionem interius specificatam fieri suppositam fuit seisitus de rectoria de Saynt Syres Newton cum pertinenciis in infrascripto comitatu Devonie in dominico suo ut de feodo in jure corone suo Anglie,

1 domine et regine. (*The king's reign began on 25 July 1554.*)

2 *Unclear words interlined.*

3 *The draftsman varies between singular and plural.*

certain bill of his against John Dyer, in the custody of the marshal etc., concerning a plea of trespass. And there are pledges for prosecuting, namely John Doo and Richard Roo. Which bill follows in these words:

Devonshire. Jaques Granado, knight, complains of John Dyer, being in the custody of the marshal of the lady queen's marshalsea before the queen herself, for this, that on 20 August [1552] in the sixth year of the reign of the lord Edward VI, late king of England, with force and arms etc. he took and carried away 40 cartloads of wheat, 50 cartloads of barley, 20 cartloads of oats, and four cartloads of hay, to the value of £30, belonging to the selfsame Jaques, at Newton St Cyres in the county aforesaid, being then and there found, and also[1] the aforesaid John on 21 August [1553] in the first year of the reign of the lady Mary, now queen of England, with force and arms etc. took and carried away another 40 cartloads of wheat, another 50 cartloads of barley, another 20 cartloads of oats, and another four cartloads of hay, to the value of £30, belonging to the selfsame Jaques, at Newton St Cyres in the county aforesaid, being then and there found, and inflicted other outrages upon him, to the damage of the selfsame Jaques of £100 and against the peace both of the said lord king and of the said present lady queen etc. And thereof he produces suit etc.

And the aforesaid John, by Geoffrey Tottyll his attorney, comes and denies the force and wrong when etc. And he says that he is in no wise guilty thereof. And of this he puts himself upon the country; and the aforesaid Jaques likewise. Therefore let a jury come before the lady queen at Westminster on the Thursday next after the quindene of Easter who neither etc. to make recognition etc. because both etc. The same day is given there to the parties aforesaid etc. Afterwards, the process therein having been continued between the parties aforesaid by the juries between them being put in respite before the lord king and lady queen at Westminster until the Tuesday next after the octaves of Michaelmas [1554] then next following, unless the justices of the lord king and lady queen assigned to take the assizes in the county aforesaid shall first, on the Thursday [13 Sept. 1554] next after the Nativity of the Blessed Mary the Virgin, have come to Exeter castle in the county aforesaid, by the form of the statute etc., for want of jurors. At which day both the aforesaid Jaques by his aforesaid attorney [and the aforesaid John by his aforesaid attorney][2] come before the lord king and lady queen at Westminster. And the said justices before whom etc. have sent here their record [made] before them, in these words:

> Afterwards, at the within-mentioned day and place, before Humphrey Browne, knight, and William Staunford, the lord king's and lady queen's serjeant at law, justices of the same lord king and lady queen assigned to take the assizes in the county of Devon by the form of the statute etc., come[3] both the within-named Jaques Granado, by John Hooper his attorney, and the within-written John Dyer in his own person. And the jurors of the jury specified within, being called, likewise come.
>
> And thereupon John Prideaux of Upton Pyne, gentleman,[4] of counsel learned in the law of the land with the aforesaid Jaques, shows in evidence to the aforesaid jurors that the lord Edward VI, late king of England, long before the within-specified trespass is supposed to have been done, was seised of the rectory of Newton St Cyres with the appurtenances in the within-mentioned county of Devon, in his demesne as of fee in right of his crown of England, and (being so seised therof) the same late king afterwards, and

[1] The draftsman here inserts an unnecessary *cum* (whereas).

[2] Words omitted, presumably by haplography.

[3] Tenses uncertain; the draftsman usually uses the present tense (paratus est, petit, dicit) but sometimes the perfect (demonstravit).

[4] Bencher of the Inner Temple; created serjeant at law 1555; died 1558. He is doubtless given the local addition 'of Upton Pyne' to distinguish him from John Prideaux (d. 1557) of Orcharton, Devon, who was not a lawyer.

et sic inde seisitus existens idem nuper rex postea et ante tempus transgressionis infrascripte, videlicet nono die Junii anno regni sui sexto per litteras suas patentes sub magno sigillo Anglie ac juratoribus predictis in evidenc[iis] ostensas, gerentes datam apud Westmonasterium eisdem die et anno, tradidit, dimisit et concessit predictam rectoriam cum pertinenciis eidem Jacobo habendum et tenendum sibi et assignatis suis pro termino vite sue, quarum quidem litterarum patentium pretextu [idem][1] Jacobus in rectoriam predictam cum pertinenciis ante infrascriptum tempus transgressionis predicte intravit et fuit inde seisitus in dominico suo ut de libero tenemento quousque infranominatus Johannes Dyer infraspecificato tempore transgressionis ille fieri [supposite][2] infrascripta triticum, ordeum, avenas [*sic*] in narratione predicta specificata existentia parcella decimarum garbarum rectorie predicte de novis partibus separatarum apud Seynt Cyres Newton infrascriptam inventa cepit et abcariavit prout [idem][3] Jacobus interius versus eum queritur. Et hoc paratus est verificare. Et petit quod juratores predicti veredictum suum pro eodem Jacobo in hac parte reddant etc.

Et Thomas Wylliams generosus in lege terre eruditus, adtunc de consilio prefati Johannis Dyer, ad probandum exitum interius junctum pro parte ejusdem Johannis Dyer juratoribus predictis pro eodem Johanne in evidenc[iis] [ostendit][4] quod diu antequam predictum nuper Rex Edwardus sextus aliquid habuit in predicta rectoria cum pertinenciis <quidam Johannes Howe nuper prior nuper dissoluti monasterii de Plympton in dicto comitatu Devonie fuit seisitus de predicta rectoria cum pertinenciis>[i] in dominico suo ut de feodo in jure nuper monasterii sui predicti, et sic inde seisitus existens idem nuper prior ex unanimi assensu et concensu tunc conventus ejusdem monasterii per eorum scriptum, sigilli suo communi sigillatum, juratoribus predictis similiter in evidenc[iis] ostensum ac gerentem datum apud Plympton predictam in domo sua capitulari ibidem primo die Octobris anno regni domini Henrici nuper regis Anglie octavi post conquestum tricesimo, quod fuit in anno Domini millesimo quingentismo tricesimo octavo, et infra annum proximum ante confectionem cujusdam actus in parliamento ejusdem domini Henrici nuper regis Anglie octavi apud Westmonasterium vicesimo octavo die Aprilis anno tricesimo primo regni sui, concernentis securitatem eidem nuper regi, heredibus et successoribus suis, de omnibus maneriis, terris, proficuis et hereditamentis alicujus monasterii seu aliarum domorum religiosarum disolutarum ad dissolvendarum ac quendam modum et formam quibus dimissiones et concessiones eorum seu eorum alicujus factas vel fiendas caperent effectum editi et provisi, dimisit et concessit cuidam Ricardo Drewe omnes decimas garbarum parochie de Seynt Cyres Newton predicta inter alia habendum et occupandum eidem Ricardo et assignatis suis ab eodem primo die Octobris pro et durante termino viginti et quinque annorum extunc proxime et immediate sequentium et plenarie complendorum, reddendo et solvendo inde annuatim prefato nuper priori et successoribus suis quindecim librarum legalis monete Anglie ad duos anni terminos, videlicet ad festa Purificationis Beate Marie et Inventionis Sancte Crucis aut infra sex septimanas proxime post utrumque dictorum festorum per equales portiones, prima solutione inde incipiente ad festum Purificationis Beate Marie quod extunc fuerit venturum in anno Domini quingentesimo tricesimo nono juxta computationem ecclesie Anglicane: prout in eodem scripto plenius liquet. Et idem Thomas Williams juratoribus predictis ulterius dicit et verificare pretendit quod predicte decime garbarum in predicto scripto dictorum nuper prioris et conventus continentes et specificate ante confectionem ejusdem dimissionis fuerunt communiter usitate locari et dimitti et non custod[iri] seu [reservari][5] in manurancia, cultura vel occupatione dicti

[1] eidem. [2] suppon'. [3] eidem.
[4] ostens'. [5] reservat'.

before the time of the aforesaid trespass, namely on 9 June [1552] in the sixth year of his reign, by his letters patent under the great seal of England, which were shown in evidence to the aforesaid jurors, bearing date at Westminster the same day and year, leased, demised and granted the aforesaid rectory with the appurtenances to the same Jaques, to have and to hold unto him and his assigns for term of his life, by reason of which letters patent the same Jaques entered into the aforesaid rectory with the appurtenances before the within-mentioned time of the aforesaid trespass and was thereof seised in his demesne as of freehold, until the within-named John Dyer, at the within-mentioned time when the trespass is supposed to have been done, took and carried away the within-mentioned wheat, barley [and] oats[1] specified in the aforesaid count, being part of the tithes of sheaves of the aforesaid rectory, severed from the nine parts, found at Newton St Cyres aforesaid, in the way that the same Jaques has within complained against him. And this he is ready to aver. And he prays that the aforesaid jurors should give their verdict for the same Jaques in that behalf etc.

And Thomas Williams,[2] gentleman, learned in the law of the land, then of counsel with the said John Dyer, in order to prove the within-joined issue on the side of the same John Dyer, shows in evidence to the aforesaid jurors that long before the aforesaid late King Edward VI had anything in the aforesaid rectory with the appurtenances a certain John Howe, late prior of the lately dissolved monastery of Plympton in the said county of Devon, was seised of the aforesaid rectory with the appurtenances in his demesne as of fee in right of his aforesaid late monastery, and (being so seised thereof) the same late prior, with the unanimous assent and consent of the then convent of the same monastery, by their writing sealed with their common seal, similarly shown in evidence to the aforesaid jurors and bearing date at Plympton aforesaid in their chapter house there on 1 October [1538] in the thirtieth year of the reign of the lord Henry VIII, late king of England, which was in the year of our Lord 1538, and within a year next before the making of a certain act in the parliament of the same lord Henry VIII, late king of England, published and enacted at Westminster on the twenty-eight day of April in the thirty-first year of his reign,[3] concerning an assurance to the same late king, his heirs and successors, in respect of all manors, lands, profits and hereditaments of any monastery or other religious house dissolved or to be dissolved, and the certain manner and form in which their leases and grants made or to be made by them or any of them should take effect, leased and granted to a certain Richard Drewe all the tithes of sheaves of the parish of Newton St Cyres aforesaid, amongst other things, to have and to occupy unto the same Richard and his assigns from the same first day of October for and during the term of twenty-five years then next and immediately following and fully to be completed, yielding and paying therefor annually unto the said late prior and his successors £15 of lawful money of England at two times of the year, namely at the feasts of the Purification of the Blessed Mary and the Invention of the Holy Cross, or within six weeks next after either of the said feasts, in equal instalments, the first payment thereof beginning at the feast of the Purification of the Blessed Mary which was then coming in the year of our Lord 1539 according to the computation of the English Church: as fully appears in the same writing. And the same Thomas Williams further says to the aforesaid jurors, and offers to verify, that the aforesaid tithes of sheaves mentioned and specified in the aforesaid writing of the said late prior and convent were commonly used to be set and

1 The hay is not mentioned here or subsequently.

2 Of Harford, Devon; son of Adam Williams, an attorney of Lyon's Inn; barrister of the Inner Temple (reader 1558); died 1566. There is a brass portrait of him, in armour, in Harford church.

3 31 Hen. VIII, c. 13. The translation here generally follows the wording of the statute.

nuper prioris pro manutentione hospitalitatis et bona domus custodia, et quod nullus status seu interesse de vel in dictis decimis garbarum pro termino vite, anni vel annorum tempore confectionis dimissionis et concessionis inde predictarum habuit suum esse vel continuationem, et etiam quod predictus redditus quindecim librarum est et fuit usualis et antiquus redditus et firmam reddi et reservari consuetum pro eisdem decimis garbarum per spacium viginti annorum proxime ante dictum vicesimum octavum diem Aprilis, pretextu cujus dimissionis prefatus Ricardus Drewe dictas decimas garbarum habuit et recepit et fuit inde inter alia modo quo prefertur possessionatus, et sic inde possessionatus existens idem Ricardus Drewe apud Seynt Cyres Newton predictam condidit testamentum et ultimam voluntatem suam et per eandem constituit et ordinavit quendam Matildam adtunc uxorem suam solam executricem suam testamenti illius ac postea ibidem obiit, post cujus quidem Ricardi mortem eadem Matilda fuit de predictis decimis garbarum inter alia possessionata, et sic inde possessionata existens eadem Matilda postea et ante predictum tempus transgressionis predicte, videlicet vicesimo die Marcii anno regni predicti nuper Regis Edwardi sexti secundo, apud Seynt Cyres Newton predictam per cartam suam indentatam, juratoribus predictis similiter in evidenc[iis] ostensam, concessit totum terminum et interesse sua que ipse habuit tunc ventura de et in predictis decimis garbarum cum pertinenciis eidem Johanni Dyer, virtute cujus concessionis idem Johannes fuit inde possessionatus, [et sic inde possessionatus][1] existens idem Johannes Dyer dicto tempore transgressionis infracontente frumentum, ordeum et avenas predicta existentia parcella decimarum garbarum dicte parochie de Seynt Cyres Newton a novis partibus [separatarum][2] apud Seynt Cyres Newton predictam inventa cepit et abcariavit prout ei bene licuit. Et hoc paratus est verificare. Unde petit quod juratores predicti veredictum suum pro eodem Johanne Dyer super has evidencias eis ostensas reddant.

Et predictus Johannes Prydyaux pro eodem Jacobo ulterius juratoribus predictis ad probandum et manutenendum exitum infrascriptum pro parte ejusdem Jacobi in evidenciis [ostendit][3] quod bene et verum est quod prefatus nuper prior de Plympton fuit de predicta rectoria cum pertinenciis seisitus in dominico suo ut de feodo in jure predicti nuper monasterii sui et sic inde seisitus idem nuper prior et ejusdem monasterii tunc conventus ex eorum unanimi assensu per predictam indenturam suam dimiserunt predictas decimas illas garbarum rectorie predicte cum pertinenciis inter alia prefato Ricardo Drewe pro predicto termino viginti et quinque annorum, reddendo et solvendo inde annuatim eidem nuper priori et successoribus suis quindecim libras legalis monete Anglie ad festa Purificationis Beate Marie et Inventionis Sancte Crucis per equales portiones, prima solutione inde incipiente ad festum Purificationis Beate Marie quod extunc proxime post confectionem ejusdem indenture fuerat venturum in anno Domini millesimo quingentesimo tricesimo nono, prout ex parte predicti Johannis Dyer juratoribus predictis superius in evidenciis ostensum fuit, et ulterius idem Johannes Predyaux pro parte predicti Jacobi juratoribus predictis in evidenciis demonstravit quod per quendam actum in parliamenti domini Henrici nuper regis Anglie octavi apud Westmonasterium in comitatu Midd' vicesimo octavo die Aprilis anno regni sui tricesimo primo incoato et ibidem tunc tenti et continuati usque ad vicesimum octavum diem Junii tunc proxime sequentem inter alia auctoritate ejusdem parliamenti inactitatum, ordinatum et stabilitum existit per ipsum nuper regem ac [dominos][4] spirituales et tem-

[1] *Conjectural haplography.*
[2] separatim.
[3] ostendend.
[4] duos.

leased before the making of the same grant and not kept or reserved in the manurance, tillage or occupation of the said late prior for the maintenance of hospitality and good housekeeping, and that no estate or interest of or in the said tithes of sheaves for term of life, year or years had its being or continuance at the time of the making of the aforesaid lease and grant thereof, and also that the aforesaid rent of £15 is and was the usual and old rent and farm accustomed to be yielded and reserved for the same tithes of sheaves by the space of twenty years next before the said 28 April,[1] by reason of which demise the said Richard Drewe had and received the said tithes of sheaves and was thereof possessed in manner aforesaid, amongst other things, and (being so possessed) the same Richard Drewe at Newton St Cyres aforesaid made his testament and last will and thereby appointed Maud, then his wife, his sole executrix of the testament, and afterwards died, and after Richard's death the same Maud was possessed of the aforesaid tithes, amongst other things, and (being so possessed) the same Maud afterwards, and before the aforesaid time of the aforesaid trespass, namely on 20 March [1548] in the second year of the reign of the aforesaid late King Edward VI, at Newton St Cyres aforesaid, by her indented charter, likewise shown in evidence to the aforesaid jurors, granted her whole term and interest which she had then to come of and in the aforesaid tithes of sheaves with the appurtenances to the same John Dyer, by virtue of which grant the same John was possessed thereof, and (being so possessed) the same John Dyer at the said time of the within-mentioned trespass took and carried away the aforesaid wheat, barley and oats, being part of the tithes of sheaves of the said parish of Newton St Cyres severed from the nine parts, found at Newton St Cyres aforesaid, as he was fully entitled to do. And this he is ready to aver. Wherefore he prays that upon this evidence the aforesaid jurors should give their verdict for the same John Dyer.

And the aforesaid John Prideaux, on behalf of the same Jaques, further shows in evidence to the aforesaid jurors, in order to prove and maintain the within-specified issue on the side of the same Jaques, that it is quite true that the said late prior of Plympton was seised of the aforesaid rectory with the appurtenances in his demesne in right of his aforesaid late monastery, and that (being so seised) the same late prior and the then convent of the same monastery, by their unanimous assent and consent, by their aforesaid indenture, leased the aforesaid tithes of sheaves of the aforesaid rectory with the appurtenances, amongst other things, to the said Richard Drewe for the aforesaid term of twenty-five years, yielding and paying therefor annually £15 of lawful money of England to the same late prior and his successors at the feasts of the Purification of the Blessed Mary and the Invention of the Holy Cross, in equal instalments, the first payment beginning at the feast of the Purification of the Blessed Mary which was then next coming after the making of the same indenture in the year of our Lord 1539, as has above been shown in evidence to the aforesaid jurors on behalf of the aforesaid John Dyer; and the same John Prideaux further shows in evidence to the aforesaid jurors, on behalf of the aforesaid Jaques, that by a certain act in the parliament of the lord Henry VIII, late king of England, at Westminster in the county of Middlesex, on 28 April [1539] in the beginning of the thirty-first year of his reign and there held and continued until 28 June then next following,[2] by authority of the same parliament, amongst other things it was enacted, ordained and established by the selfsame late king and the lords spiritual and temporal and commons in the same parliament then assembled, and by authority of the

1 These assertions relate to the statutory proviso which is more fully set out by Prideaux below.

2 31 Hen. VIII, c. 13. It seems irregular to give a public statute in 'evidence', the consequence of doing which is the following lengthy translation of the relevant part of the English text.

porales necnon communitat[em] in eodem parliamento tunc assemblatos ac auctoritate ejusdem quod non solum omnia nuper monasteria, abbathie, prioratus, domus monalium, collegia, hospitales, domus fratrum ac alia religiosa et ecclesiastica domus et loca, scitus, circuitus, procincta, maneria, dominia, grangia, mesuagia, terre, tenementa, prata, pasture, redditus, reverciones, servicia, bosca, decime, penciones, portiones, rectorie [appropriate],[1] vicarie, ecclesie, capelle, advocationes, nominationes, patronatus, annuitates, interesse, intrationes, conditiones, communia,[2] lete, curie,[3] libertates, privilegia, franchesia ac cetera quecumque hereditamenta deinceps immediate et tunc presencialiter sed etiam omnia alia monasteria, abbathie, prioratus, domus monialium, collegia, hospitales, domus fratrum ac alia religiosa et ecclesiastica domus et loca que extunc in posterum contingerent esse dissoluta, suppressa, renunciata, relicta, forisfacta, sursumreddita aut aliquibus aliis mediis deventa regie celcitudini necnon omnia scitus, circuitus, procincta, maneria, dominia, grangia, mesuagia, terre,[4] tenementa, prata, pasture, redditus, reverciones, servicia, bosca, decime, penciones, portiones, rectorie [appropriate],[5] vicaria, ecclesie, capelle, advocationes, nominationes, patronatus, annuitates, jura, interesse, conditiones, communia,[6] lete, curie, libertates, privilegia, franchesia ac alia hereditamenta quecumque spectantia sive pertinentia eisdem seu eorum alicui quandocumque et quam cito prout essent dissoluta, suppressata, renunciata, relicta, forisfacta, sursumreddita aut aliquibus aliis mediis [deventura][7] regie celcitudini essent vestita, arbitrata et adjudicata per auctoritatem ejusdem parliamenti in vera, actuali et reali seisina et possessionem predicti nuper regis, heredum et successorum suorum imperpetuum in statu et conditione prout ad confectionem ejusdem actus adtunc fuerunt ac sicuti omnia predicta nuper monasterii, abbathie, prioratus, domus monialium, collegia, hospitales, domus fratrum ac omnia religiosa et ecclesiastica domus et loca sic dissoluta, suppressata, renunciata, relicta, forisfacta, sursum data aut deventa regie celcitudini ut predictum est, quam etiam predicta monasteria,[8] abbathie, prioratus, domus monialium, collegia, hospitales, domus fratrum ac omnia religiosa et ecclesiastica domus et loca que imposterum contingerunt fore dissoluta, suppressata, renunciata, relicta, forisfacta, sursumreddita aut [deventura][9] regie celcitudini, scitus, circuitus, procincta, maneria, dominia, grangia, mesuagia, terre[10] et tenementa, ac cetera premissa quecumque forent et eorum quilibet foret in eodem acta specialiter et particulariter recitata, nominata et expressa <per expressa>[i] verba, nomina, titulos et facultates in suis generibus, naturis et qualitatibus, et ulterius inactitatum existebat in eodem parliamento, auctoritate predicta, quod si aliquis abbas, prior, priorissa, vel [alius][11] ecclesiasticus gubernator sive gubernatrix alicujus monasterii, abbathie, prioratus, domus monialium, collegii, hospitalis, domus fratrum seu [alii][12] religiosi domus vel [loci][13] que imposterum contingerent dissolvi, suppressi, renunciari, relinqui, forisfieri, sursum dari aut deveniri[14] regie celcitudini infra unum annum proxime ante [primum] diem ejusdem parliamenti fecissent aut deinceps imposterum facerent aliquam dimissionem sive concessionem sub suo conventuali aut communi sigillo seu aliter pro termino annorum seu vite vel vitarum de scitu, circuitu et procinctu predicti sui monasterii, abbathie, prioratus, domus monialium, collegii, hospitalis, domus fratrum seu [alii][15] religiosi[16] vel ecclesiastici domus sive loci vel alicujus partis eorundem vel aliquorum maneriorum, mesuagiorum, terrarum, tenementorum, rectoriorum [appropriatorum],[17] decimarum, pencionum, portionum sel aliorum hereditamentorum spectantium vel pertinentium predicto suo monasterio, abbathie, prioratus, domus monialium, collegio, hospitali, domus

[1] ac proprietat'. [2] co[m]munie. [3] Bur'. [4] terra. [5] approprietat'.
[6] co[m]munie. [7] devenir'. [8] monest'. [9] devenir'. [10] terra.
[11] alicujus. [12] alia. [13] loca. [14] devenire. [15] alterius. [16] relios.
[17] approprieatar'.

same, that not only all the late [dissolved][1] monasteries, abbeys, priories, nunneries, colleges, hospitals, houses of friars, and other religious and ecclesiastical houses and places, sites, circuits, precincts, manors, lordships, granges, messuages, lands, tenements, meadows, pastures, rents, reversions, services, woods, tithes, pensions, portions, appropriated rectories,[2] vicarages, churches, chapels, advowsons, nominations, patronages, annuities, [rights],[3] interests, entries, conditions, commons, leets, courts, liberties, privileges, franchises, and other hereditaments whatsoever, then forthwith, immediately and presently, but also all other monasteries, abbeys, priories, nunneries, colleges, hospitals, houses of friars, and other religious and ecclesiastical houses and places which thereafter in future should happen to be dissolved, suppressed, renounced, relinquished, forfeited, given up or by any other means come to the king's highness, and also all the sites, circuits, precincts, manors, lordships, granges, messuages, lands, tenements, meadows, pastures, rents, reversions, services, woods, tithes, pensions, portions, appropriated rectories, vicarages, churches, chapels, advowsons, nominations, patronages, annuities, rights, interests, entries, conditions, commons, leets, courts, liberties, privileges, franchises and other hereditaments whatsoever belonging or appertaining to the same, or to any of them, whensoever and as soon as they should be dissolved, suppressed, renounced, relinquished, forfeited, given up or in any other way come to the king's highness, should be vested, deemed and adjudged by authority of the same parliament in the very actual and real seisin and possession of the aforesaid late king, his heirs and successors for ever, in the like estate and condition as they were at the making of the same act, and as though all the aforesaid late monasteries, abbeys, priories, nunneries, colleges, hospitals, houses of friars and other religious and ecclesiastical houses and places thus dissolved, suppressed, renounced, relinquished, forfeited, surrendered or come to the king's highness, as is aforesaid, as also the aforesaid monasteries, abbeys, priories, nunneries, colleges, hospitals, houses of friars and other religious and ecclesiastical houses and places which thereafter should happen to be dissolved, suppressed, renounced, relinquished, forfeited, surrendered or come to the king's highness, the sites, circuits, precincts, manors, demesnes, granges, messuages, lands and tenements, and other premises whatsoever, and every of them, had been specially and particularly recited in the act and named and expressed by express words, names, titles and faculties in their kinds, natures and qualities; and moreover it was enacted in the same parliament, by the aforesaid authority, that if any abbot, prior, prioress, or other ecclesiastical governor or governess of any monastery, abbey, priory, nunnery, college, hospital, house of friars or other religious house or place which should in the future happen to be dissolved, suppressed, renounced, relinquished, forfeited, surrendered or come to the king's highness, had within one year next before the first day of the same parliament made, or should thereafter make, any lease or grant under his convent or common seal or otherwise for term of years or of life or lives of the site, circuit and precinct of his aforesaid monastery, abbey, priory, nunnery, college, hospital, house of friars or other religious or ecclesiastical house or place, or any part thereof, or of any manors, messuages, lands, tenements, appropriated rectories, tithes, pensions, portions or other hereditaments belonging or appertaining to his aforesaid monastery, abbey, priory, nunnery, college, hospital, house of

[1] The statute here refers to 'the said late monasteries . . .', referring to the previous section which is not here recited.

[2] The statute says 'parsonages appropriated'.

[3] Statute. Omitted here, but inserted later in the record.

fratrum sive religiosa vel ecclesiastica domus vel loci, que maneria, mesuagia, grangia, terre, tenementa, rectoria [appropriata],[1] decime, penciones, portiones ac cetera hereditamenta quecumque non fuissent ante eandem dimissionem communiter usitata tradi nec dimitti ad firmam sed custodita et reservata in manurancia, tillagio seu occupatione predicti gubernatoris sive gubernatricis pro manutenencia hospitalitatis et bona domus custodienda [aut][2] tunc fuerunt in manurancia, tillagio vel occupatione dicti gubernatoris vel gubernatricis pro manutenencia hospitalitatis et bona domus custodia[3] vel infra unum annum proxime ante primum diem ejusdem parliamenti fecissent seu imposterum facerent aliquam dimissionem sive concessionem pro termimo vite vel pro termino annorum de aliquibus maneriis, messuagiis, terris, tenementis, pratis, pasturis, boscis, rectoriis [appropriatis],[4] decimis, pencionibus, portionibus, ecclesiis, capellis seu aliis hereditamentis quibuscumque unde et in quibus aliquis status sive interesse pro termino vite, anni vel annorum ad tempus confectionis alicujus talis concessionis sive dimissionis tunc habuissent suum esse vel continuationem vel imposterum haberet suum esse seu continuationem et tunc non fuerunt determinata, finita seu exspirata vel ad tempus alicujus talis dimissionis fiende [non] esset determinata, finita vel exspirata aut infra unum annum proxime ante primum diem predicti parliamenti fecisset seu imposterum faceret aliquam dimissionem sive concessionem pro termino vite vel pro termino annorum de aliquibus maneriis, mesuagiis, terra, tenementis, pratis, pasturis, boscis, rectoriis [appropriatis],[5] decimis, pencionibus, portionibus, ecclesiis, capellis seu aliis hereditamentis quibuscumque super quas dimissiones et concessiones usuales et veteres redditus et firme consueta reddenda et reservata per spacium viginti annorum proxime ante predictum primum diem ejusdem parliamenti non extiterunt vel non fuerunt superinde reservata et reddita, vel si talis gubernator vel gubernatrix alicujus talis monasterii, abbathie, prioratus, domus monialium, collegii, hospitalis, domus fratrum vel [alii][6] religiosi vel ecclesiastici domus vel [loci][7] que imposterum contingerent dissolvi, supprimi, renunciari, relinqui, forisfieri, sursum dari vel deveniri regie celcitudini infra unum annum proxime ante predictum primum diem predicti parliamenti fecisset aut imposterum faceret aliquam barganiam seu venditionem suorum boscorum, qui bosci adtunc fuerunt crescentes et stantes, quod omnes et quilibet tales dimissio, concessio, bargania et [venditio][8] bosci seu boscorum essent penitus vacue et nullius effectus: prout in eodem actu inter alia plenius liquet. Et idem Johannes Prediaux ulterius pro prefato Jacobo juratoribus predictis in evidenciis dicit quod prefatus nuper prior de Plympton de predicta rectoria cum pertinentibus in forma predicta seisitus existens idem nuper prior et ejusdem nuper monasterii conventus postea et diu ante[9] dictum tempus infrascripte transgressionis, videlicet primo die Marcii anno regni predicti nuper Regis Henrici octavi tricesimo, apud monasterium suum predictum per quoddam scriptum suum sigillo suo communi sigillatum et in Curia Cancellarie ejusdem nuper Regis Henrici octavi apud Westmonasterium in comitatu Midd' de recordo irrotulatum, cujus data est in domo suo capitulari apud monasterium suum predictum ejusdem die et anno, ex eorum unanimi assensu et concensu dederunt et concesserunt ad per idem scriptum suum confirmaverunt et sursumreddiderunt prefato nuper Regi Henrici octavo totum dictum nuper monasterium suum de Plympton predicta cum pertinenciis necnon predicta rectoria de Seynt Cyres Newton cum pertinenciis ac revercionem et reverciones inde inter alia, habendum et tenendum et gaudendum prefato nuper regi, heredibus vel successo-

[1] approprietat'. [2] ante. [3] custodie. [4] approprietat' [5] appropriatat'
[6] alia. [7] loca. [8] venditiones. [9] antea.

friars or other religious or ecclesiastical house or place, which manors, messuages, granges, lands, tenements, appropriated rectories, tithes, pensions, portions or other hereditaments were not before the same lease commonly used to be set or let to farm but kept and reserved in the manurance, tillage or occupation of the aforesaid governor or governess for the maintenance of hospitality and good housekeeping, or were then in the manurance, tillage or occupation of the aforesaid governor or governess for the maintenance of hospitality and good housekeeping, or had within one year next before the first day of the same parliament made, or thereafter should make, any lease or grant for term of life or for term of years of any manors, messuages, lands, tenements, meadows, pastures, woods, appropriated rectories, tithes, pensions, portions, churches, chapels or other hereditaments, whatsoever they be, whereof and in which any estate or interest for term of life, year or years at the time of the making of any such grant or lease then had its being or continuance, or thereafter should have its being or continuance, and was not then determined, finished or expired, or at the time of any such lease to be made would not be determined, ended or expired, or within one year next before the first day of aforesaid parliament had made or thereafter should make any grant or lease for term of life or for term of years of any manors, messuages, lands, tenements, meadows, pastures, appropriated rectories, tithes, pensions, portions, churches, chapels or other hereditaments, whatsoever they be, upon which leases and grants the usual and old rents and farms accustomed to be yielded and reserved by the space of twenty years next before the aforesaid first day of the aforesaid parliament were not or would not be thereupon reserved and yielded, or if any such governor or governess of any such monastery, abbey, priory, nunnery, college, hospital, house of friars or other religious or ecclesiastical house or place which should thereafter happen to be dissolved, suppressed, renounced, relinquished, forfeited, given up or in any other way come to the king's highness within one year next before the aforesaid first day of the aforesaid parliament or thereafter should make any bargain or sale of his woods, which woods were then growing and standing, that all and every such lease, grant, bargain and sale of wood or woods should be utterly void and of none effect: as more fully appears in the same act, amongst other things. And the same John Prideaux further says in evidence to the aforesaid jurors on behalf of the said Jaques that, the said late prior of Plympton being seised of the aforesaid rectory with the appurtenances in form aforesaid, the same late prior and the convent of the same late monastery afterwards, and long before the said time of the within-mentioned trespass, namely on 1 March [1539] in the thirtieth year of the reign of the aforesaid late King Henry VIII, at their aforesaid monastery, by their certain writing sealed with their common seal and enrolled of record in the Court of Chancery of the same late King Henry VIII at Westminster in the county of Middlesex, dated in their chapter house at their aforesaid monastery the same day and year, by their unanimous assent and consent gave and granted and by the same writing confirmed and surrendered to the said late King Henry VIII all that their said late monastery of Plympton aforesaid with the appurtenances, and the aforesaid rectory of Newton St Cyres with the appurtenances, and the reversion and reversions thereof, amongst other things, to have, hold and enjoy unto the said late king, his heirs or successors for ever, to the sole proper ribus suis imperpetuum ad solum proprium usum et proficuum ipsius nuper regis, heredum et successorum suorum imperpetuum, prout per idem scriptum inter alia plenius liquet, quorum quidem doni et concessionis ac actus predicti pretextu idem nuper rex fuit seisitus de predicta rectoria cum pertinenciis in dominico suo ut de feodo in jure corone sue Anglie exonerata de predicta dimissione pro dicto termino dictorum viginti quinque annorum prefato Ricardo Drewe per prefatum nuper priorem inde in forma predicta facta, eo quod super eandem dimissionem de predictis decimis garbarum prefato Ricardo Drewe ut prefertur factam apparet juratoribus predictis quod nullus redditus, ut idem Johannes Prediaux asserit, fuit solubilis per eandem dimissionem a tempore confectionis ejusdem dimissionis usque festum Purificationis Beate Marie Virginis predicti anno Domini millesimo quingentesimo tricesimo nono, scilicet per spacium unius anni et septemdecim septimanarum, et idem nuper Rex Henricus octavus sic seisitus existens de et in eadem rectoria cum pertinenciis postea et ante predictum tempus transgressionis predicte de tali statu obiit inde seisitus, post cujus quidem dicti Henrici nuper regis mortem predicta rectoria cum pertinenciis descendebat prefato domino Edwardo nuper regi Anglie sexto ut filio et heredi ipsius nuper Regis Henrici octavi, per quod idem dominus Edwardus nuper rex Anglie fuit de predicta rectoria cum pertinenciis seisitus in dominico suo ut de feodo in jure corone sue Anglie, et sic inde seisitus existens idem nuper Rex Edwardus sextus postea per litteras suas patentes, juratoribus in evidenciis prius ostensis, tradidit et concessit predictam rectoriam cum pertinenciis eidem Jacobo pro termino vite sue, pretextu quarum litterarum patentium idem Jacobus fuit de predicta rectoria cum pertinenciis seisitus in dominico suo ut de libero tenemento quosque prefatus Johannes Dyer fecit transgressionem unde ipse interius se modo versus ipsum queritur. Et hoc paratus est verificare. Et petit quod juratores predicti veredictum suum pro ipso Jacobo in hac parte reddant.

Et predictus Thomas Williams pro predicto Johanne Dyer dicit quod evidencia predicta per prefatum Johannem Predyaux ex parte predicti Jacobi ostense minus sufficiens in lege existit ad exitum interius junctum ac narrationem et breve infrascripta ex parte ejusdem Jacobi probanda et manutenenda, quodque idem Johannes ad evidenciam illam in forma predicta ostensam necesse non habet nec per legem terre tenetur respondere. Et hoc paratus est verificare prout curia [consideraret][1] in hac parte. Unde petit quod juratores predicti ab aliquo veredicto inter partes predictas super exitum predictum reddendo exonerentur etc.

Et predictus Jacobus Granado dicit quod ipse sufficientes evidencias per consilium suum predictum juratoribus predictis ostendidit, quas quidem evidencias predictus Johannes Dyer non dedicit nec ad eas aliqualiter respondidit sed verificationem illam [admitti][2] necnon exitum interius junctum triari omnino recusavit, petit judicium et dampna sua occasione transgressionis predicte[3] sibi adjudicari etc.

Et quia curia dominorum regis et regine hic de judicio suo de et super premissis reddendo non dum [advisatur],[4] dies inde datus est partibus predictis in statu quo nunc coram domino rege et domina regina apud Westmonasterium usque diem Lune proxime post quindenam Sancti Hillarii de judicio suo inde audiendo eo quod curie dominorum regis et regine hic inde non dum etc. . . .

[*See opposite*]

1 consideravit.
2 admittit.
3 predicti.
4 advisar'.

use and profit of him the said late king, his heirs and successors for ever, as (amongst other things) more fully appears by the same writing; by reason of which gift and grant, and of the aforesaid act, the same late king was seised of the aforesaid rectory with the appurtenances in his demesne as of fee in right of his crown of England, discharged of the aforesaid lease for the said term of twenty-five years made to the said Richard Drewe by the said late prior in form aforesaid, inasmuch as upon the same lease of the aforesaid tithes of sheaves made to the said Richard Drewe as mentioned above it appears to the aforesaid jurors that no rent, as the same John Prideaux asserts, was payable under the same lease from the time of the making of the same lease until the aforesaid feast of the Purification of the Blessed Virgin Mary in the year of our Lord 1539, namely for a period of one year and seventeen weeks; and the same late King Henry VIII, being so seised of and in the same rectory with the appurtenances, afterwards and before the aforesaid time of the aforesaid trespass, died seised of the like estate, and after the death of the said late King Henry the aforesaid rectory with the appurtenances descended to the lord Edward VI, late king of England, as son and heir of him the said late King Henry VIII, whereby the same lord Edward, late king of England, was seised of the aforesaid rectory with the appurtenances in his demesne as of fee in right of his crown of England, and (being so seised) the same late King Edward VI afterwards by his letters patent, previously shown to the jurors in evidence, leased and granted the aforesaid rectory with the appurtenances to the same Jaques for term of his life, by reason of which letters patent the same Jaques was seised of the aforesaid rectory with the appurtenances in his demesne as of freehold until the said John Dyer did the trespass whereof he now complains against him within. And this he is ready to aver. And he prays that the aforesaid jurors should render their verdict for him the said Jaques.

And the aforesaid Thomas Williams, on behalf of the aforesaid John Dyer, says that the aforesaid evidence shown by the said John Prideaux on behalf of the aforesaid Jaques is insufficient in law to prove and maintain the within-joined issue and the within-written count and writ, on the side of the same Jaques, and that the same John has no need and is not bound by the law of the land to answer that evidence shown in form aforesaid. And this he is ready to aver in whatever way the court should award in that behalf. Wherefore he prays that the aforesaid jurors should be discharged from rendering any verdict between the aforesaid parties upon the aforesaid issue etc.

And the aforesaid Jaques Granado says that, [inasmuch as] he has shown sufficient evidence to the aforesaid jurors through his aforesaid counsel, which evidence the aforesaid John does not deny or in any way answer, but utterly refuses to admit the averment and to have the within-joined issue tried, he prays judgment and his damages by reason of the aforesaid trespass to be awarded to him etc.

And because the court of the lord king and lady queen here is not yet advised concerning the giving of its judgment upon and concerning the foregoing, a day is given therein to the aforesaid parties before the lord king and lady queen at Westminster in the same state as now until the Monday next after the quindene of St Hilary [1555] for hearing their judgment therein, forasmuch as the court of the lord king and lady queen here is not yet therein etc. . . .

[*Similar continuances to Pas. 1556; no judgment is entered*]

[2]

A, fo. 30^{f} (runs on from pl. 1); *L* 224^{f} (sim.); *D*, fo. 21, pl. 12 (2 & 3 Phil. & Mar.).

Et fuit la auxi agree que si ascun abbott ou covent ove le covent seale ont fait tiel lease sur que launcient rent et farme fuit reserve et use destre lesses adevant et nient en leas al temps de le dit leas, et puis le dit abbott et covent per lour fait releas le dit rent yssint reserve et puis surrender lour meason devant le dit acte et [deins le temps del][1] le proviso de le dit acte, que uncore le leas issint fait est bon quar est deins letter destatute que estatute[2] ne serra [prise][3] per ascun equitie.

[3]

A, fo. 30^{f}; *L* 225^{f}.

Nota labbott de Tewksbury per assent son covent per lour comen seale per fait demise al J. S. le reversion de certein terrs et tenementes ove les appurtenances en D. <a J. G. et a son feme et Jane lour file>[4] a tiendrer ore pur lour vies habendum et tenendum les dittes terres et tenementes al dit J. S. a fest de Saint Michell adonques prochein ensuant le morte ou surender le dit J. G. son feme et file tanque al fyne xxi ans adonques prochein ensuantes cest leas est bon coment que fuit nul atturnment quar le habendum declare lentent le lessor et les terres passont et nient le reversion, et le fait serra prise pluis fort envers lessor et pluis beneficiall pur lessee [si][5] poet estre per resonable construction. Et cest paroll reversion en le premisses de le fait serra prise pur les terres. Issint un paroll serra prise pur auter, come reverter pur le remainder, et le habendum declare lentent et meaninge le lessor que les terres passa et nemi le reversion. Et atturnment ne besoigne pas entant que lestate ne comense en J. S. tanque le primer estate soit determine per mort ou surrender etc. Et ceo fuit le clere opinion des justices de Comen Banke, *Brooke* Chefe Justice [solement][6] except, que fuit enconter: sicut accidit enter Throgmorton et Tracye.

[*fol. 29v*] Et sic nota si home a cest jour lessa per fait al auter le reversion de certein terre habendum et tenendum les terres pur ans a comenser al date le fait le leas est bon en possession et cest paroll reversion serra pur le terre quod nota.

[1] *A, D.*
[2] car auterment *A, D.*
[3] *A.*
[4] queux J. George {J. G. *L*} et sa feme et lour file tiendront per lour lease *A.*
[5] et *H.*
[6] *A, L.*

2. GRANADO v. DYER, contd

King's Bench, contd.

It was also agreed there that if any abbot or convent made such a lease under the convent seal, upon which the old rent and farm was reserved, and it used to be leased before but was not in lease at the time of the said lease, and then the said abbot and convent by their deed released the said rent so reserved, and then surrendered their house before the said act and the proviso of the said act, the lease so made is nevertheless good, for it is within the letter of the statute, which statute shall not be taken by any equity.

3. THROGMORTON v. TRACY

Common Pleas, Pas. 1556. Record: CP 40/1164, m. 436 (demurrer: c.a.v. to Pas. 1556; judgment for plaintiff); printed in Plowd. 145 and Rast. Ent. 572. Also reported in Plowd. 147; Dyer, fo. 124 (Mich. 1555).

Note that the abbot of Tewkesbury, by the assent of his convent, under their common seal, demised by deed to John Style the reversion of certain lands and tenements with the appurtenances in Dale [leased] to J. [George][1] and his wife, and Jane their daughter, to hold for their lives, to have and to hold the said lands and tenements unto the said John Style from the feast of Michaelmas next following the death or surrender of the said J. George, his wife and daughter, until the end of 21 years then next following. This lease is good, even if there was no attornment, for the habendum declares the lessor's intention, and the lands pass and not the reversion; and the deed shall be taken more strongly against the lessor and more beneficially for the lessee, if it may be, by reasonable construction. And this word 'reversion' in the premises of the deed shall be understood as the lands. Thus one word may be understood for another – as 'reverter' for 'remainder'. And the habendum declares the intention and meaning of the lessor that the lands should pass and not the reversion; and there is no need for attornment, inasmuch as the estate does not commence in John Style until the first estate is determined by death or surrender etc. And this was the clear opinion of the justices of the Common Bench, except for Brooke C.J., who was against it. This occurred between Throgmorton and Tracy.[2]

Thus note that if someone at the present day leases to another the reversion of certain land, by deed, to have and to hold the lands for years, to commence from the date of the deed, the lease is good in possession, and this word 'reversion' shall be [taken] for the land. Note that.

[1] *A* only.

[2] The plaintiff, John Throgmorton (d. 1580) of Feckenham, Worcs., recorder of Coventry and att.-gen. in the Marches 1552–54, was a bencher of the Middle Temple. The defendant, Richard Tracy (d. 1569) of Stanway, Glos., was a bencher of the Inner Temple.

[4]

Abr. in *A*, fo. 30v[f]; *L* 226[f].

Nota que fuit adjudge per bon advise isto eodem termino en Banke le Roy que si un enfant soit implede en breife de precipe quod reddat come formdon ou tiels semblables pur ses terres et lenfant perde per defaute que ore lenfant avera breife derror et pur ceo que il fuit deins age al temps de le judgement vers luy pronounce le judgement serra reverse et lenfant serra restore a tout ceo que il perde: sicut accidit in casu Johannis Ward petentis versus Isabell Anderson, Elen Ander[son] et Ann An[derson] tenentes pro terris Johannis Lockington in comitatu Eborum in brevi de dum fuit infra etatem, et les dittes 3 femes pur ceo que ils fueront deins age come appiert sur le breife derror apres que judgement et execution fuit ewe vers eux per default al graund cape en le dit breife de dum fuit infra etatem per John Haywood lour garden al eux admitt per le court assigne lour error pur ceo que ils al temps le dit judgement rendue vers eux et uncore sount deins age de xxi ans etc. Et sur ceo le court adjudge les dittes enfantes estre deins age tam per lour inspection quam per testimoignes des amyes des dittes enfantes et auters dignes et issint les dittes enfantes fueront adjudge deins age per le court. Et sur cet assignement derror en forme avantdit le dit Ward defendant en le breife derror et playntiefe en le primer breife demurre en ley et isto eodem termino per advise le judgement fuit reverse. Nota ycie lexamination le court et les proffes et le proffe del enfantes esteantes deins age. Et pur prover cest judgement un bon president fuit monstre en mesme le case et en mesme le matter.

Record of the case

KB 27/1172, m. 133, Rooper & Heywood

Domina regina mandavit dilecto et fideli suo Ricardo Morgan militi breve suum clausum in hec verba: Maria, Dei gracia Anglie, Francie et Hibernie Regina, fidei defensor et in terra ecclesie Anglicane et Hibernice supremum caput, dilecto et fideli suo Ricardo Morgan militi salutem. Quia in recordo et processu acetiam in redditione judicii loquele que fuit coram vobis et sociis vestris justiciariis nostris de Banco per breve inter Johannem Warde qui plene etatis est petentem et Isabellam Anderson, Elenam Anderson et Annam Anderson, filias et heredes Henrici Anderson, tenentes de duobus mesuagiis, duobus cotagiis, quatuor gardinis, quatuor bovatis terre, viginti acris prati, et quadraginta acris pasture cum pertinenciis in Lokyngton error intervenit manifestum ad grave dampnum ipsorum Isabelle, Elene et Anne sicut ex querela sua accepimus, nos, errorem si quis fuerit modo debito corrigi et eisdem Isabelle, Elene et Anne plenam et celerem justiciam fieri volentes in hac parte, vobis mandamus quod si judicium inde redditum sit tunc recordum et processum loquele predicte cum omnibus ea tangentibus nobis sub sigillo vestro distincte et aperte mittatis, et hoc breve, ita quod ea habeamus a die Sancte Trinitatis in tres septimanas ubicumque tunc fuerimus in Anglia ut, inspectis recordo et processu predictis, ulterius inde

4. WARDE v. ANDERSON

King's Bench, Pas. 1556. Record: KB 27/1172, m. 133; printed below. Also reported, sub nom. *Anderson* v. *Ward*, Dyer, fo. 104a (Pas. 1554 and Mich. 1555).

Note that it was adjudged by good advice this same term in the King's Bench that if an infant is impleaded in a writ of *praecipe quod reddat*, such as formedon or the like, for his lands, and the infant loses by default, the infant shall have a writ of error, and because he was under age at the time of the judgment pronounced against him the judgment shall be reversed and the infant restored to all he had lost: as happened in the case of John Ward, demandant, against Isabel Anderson, Ellen Anderson and Anne Anderson, tenants, for [lands in Lockington][1] in Yorkshire in a writ of *dum fuit infra aetatem*. The said three women, because they were under age (as appears upon the writ of error), after judgment and execution was had against them by default at the grand *cape* in the said writ of *dum fuit infra aetatem*, by [Richard] Haywood their guardian (admitted for them by the court), assigned their error because at the time of the said judgment given against them they were, and still are, under the age of twenty-one years, etc., and thereupon the court adjudged the said infants to be under age, both by inspecting them and by the evidence of friends of the said infants, and other worthy persons; and therefore the said infants were adjudged under age by the court; and upon this assignment of error, in form aforesaid, the said Warde (defendant in the writ of error and plaintiff in the first writ) demurred in law. And this same term, by advice, the judgment was reversed. Note here the examination of the court, and the proofs, and the proof of the infants' being under age. And to prove this judgment a good precedent was shown in the same case, and in the same matter.

Translation of the record

King's Bench, Michaelmas term 1554

The lady queen has sent her writ close to her beloved and faithful Richard Morgan, knight, in these words: Mary, by the grace of God of England, France and Ireland Queen, Defender of the Faith, and Supreme Head in earth of the Church of England and Ireland, to her beloved and faithful Richard Morgan, knight, greeting. Inasmuch as manifest error has intervened in the record and process, and also in the rendering of judgment, in the suit which was before you and your fellows, our justices of the Bench, by a writ between John Warde, who is of full age, demandant, and Isabel Anderson, Ellen Anderson and Anne Anderson, daughters and heirs of Henry Anderson, tenants, concerning two messuages, two cottages, four gardens, four bovates of land, twenty acres of meadow and forty acres of pasture with the appurtenances in Lockington, to the grave damage of them the said Isabel, Ellen and Anne, as we understand from their complaint, we, willing in this behalf to correct the error, if any there be, in due manner and to do full and speedy justice to the same Isabel, Ellen and Anne, command you that if judgment has been therein given then you shall send us the record and process of the suit with everything touching the same distinctly and openly under your seal, and this writ, so that we have may have them in three weeks from the day of the Holy Trinity, wheresoever we shall then be in England, and so that, after inspecting the

[1] Corrected from record. The text says 'the lands of John Lockington'.

fieri faciamus quod de jure et secundum legem et consuetudinem regni nostri Anglie fuerit faciendum. Teste me ipsa apud Westmonasterium xij° die Maii anno regni nostri primo.

Recordum et processus de quibus in breve predicto fit mentio sequuntur in hec verba:

PLACITA APUD WESTMONASTERII CORAM RICARDO MORGAN MILITE ET SOCIIS SUIS JUSTICIARIIS DOMINE REGINE DE BANCO DE TERMINO SANCTI MICHAELIS ANNO REGNI MARIE, DEI GRACIA ANGLIE, FRANCIE ET HIBERNIE REGINE, FIDEI DEFENSORIS ET IN TERRA ECCLESIE ANGLICANE ET HIBERNICE SUPREMUM CAPITIS, PRIMO rotulo ccccIxxxxj°

Ebor' Johannes Warde qui plene etatis est per Edwardum Kellet attornatum suum optulit se quarto die versus Isabellam Anderson, Elenam Anderson et Annam Anderson, filias et heredes Henrici Anderson, de placito duorum mesuagiorum, duorum cotagiorum, quatuor gardinorum, quatuor bovatarum terre, viginti acrarum prati, et quadraginta acraru, pasture cum pertinenciis in Lokyngton que idem Johannes in curia regine hic clamat ut jus suum versus prefatas Isabellam, Elenam et Annam per breve domine regine de dum fuit infra etatem. Et ipse non venerunt. Et summoneant etc. judicium tenementa predicta cum pertinenciis capiantur in manum domine regine et diem etc. Et predicte Isabella, Elena et Anna summonientur quod sint hic in crastino Purificationis Beate Marie etc.

PLACITA APUD WESTMONASTERIUM CORAM RICARDO MORGAN MILITE ET SOCIIS SUIS JUSTICIARIIS DOMINE REGINE DE BANCO DE TERMINO SANCTI HILLARII ANNO REGNI MARIE, DEI GRACIA ANGLIE, FRANCIE ET HIBERNIE REGINE, FIDEI DEFENSORIS ET IN TERRA ECCLESIE ANGLICANE ET HIBERNICE SUPREMUM CAPITIS, PRIMO rotulo ccxxxvj°

Ebor' Johannes Warde qui plene etatis est per Edwardum Kellett attornatum suum optulit se quarto die versus Isabellam Anderson, Elenam Anderson et Annam Anderson, filias et heredes Henrici Anderson, de placito duorum mesuagiorum, duorum cotagiorum, quatuor gardinorum, quatuor bovatarum terre, viginti acrarum prati, et quadraginta acraru, pasture cum pertinenciis in Lokyngton que idem Johannes in curia regine hic clamat ut jus suum versus prefatas Isabellam, Elenam et Annam per breve domini regine de dum fuit infra etatem. Et ipse non venerunt. Et alias fecerunt defaltam hic, scilicet a die Sancti Michaelis in tres septimanas proxime preteritas post summonitionem etc. per quod tunc preceptum fuit vicecomiti quod caperet mesuagia, terram et pratum predicta cum pertinenciis in manum domine regine et diem etc. et quod summoneat per bonos summonitores predictas Isabellam, Elenam et Annam quod essent hic in crastino Purificationis Beate Marie tunc proxime sequente ad respondendum predicto Johanne Warde tam de principali placito quam de predicta defalta etc. Et vicecomes modo testatur diem captionis etc. et quod summonivit etc. Ideo consideratum est quod predictus Johannes recuperet seisinam suam versus prefatas Isabellam, Elenam et Annam de mesuagiis, terra et prato predictis cum pertinenciis per defaltam etc. Et eedem Isabella, Elena et Anna in misericordia etc. Super quo venit predictus Johannes, per attornatum suum predictum et petit breve domine regine de habere faciendo seisinam ei de tenementis predictis cum pertinenciis vicecomiti comitatus predicti dirigendum. Et ei conceditur retornabile hic a die Sancte Trinitatis in xv dies etc.

Postea, scilicet die Veneris proximo post octabas Sancti Michaelis isto eodem termino coram domino rege et domina regina apud Westmonasterium veniunt predicte[1] Isabella Anderson, Elena Anderson et Anna Anderson per Ricardum Heywoode custodem suum per curiam dicti domini regis et dicte domine regine hic admissum et statim dicunt quod [in] recordo et processu predictis acetiam in redditione judicii predicti manifeste est erratum pro eo videlicet quod eedem Isabella, Elena et Anna dicto tempore redditionis judicii

[1] *Reads* pdci.

record and process aforesaid, we may further do therein what of right and according to the law and custom of our realm of England ought to be done. Witness my self at Westminster the twelfth day of May [1554] in the first year of our reign.

The record and process mentioned in the aforesaid writ follow in these words:

PLEAS AT WESTMINSTER BEFORE RICHARD MORGAN, KNIGHT, AND HIS FELLOWS, THE LADY QUEEN'S JUSTICES OF THE BENCH, FOR MICHAELMAS TERM [1553] IN THE FIRST YEAR OF THE REIGN OF MARY, BY THE GRACE OF GOD OF ENGLAND, FRANCE AND IRELAND QUEEN, DEFENDER OF THE FAITH, AND SUPREME HEAD IN EARTH OF THE CHURCH OF ENGLAND AND IRELAND roll 491

Yorkshire. John Warde, who is of full age, by Edward Kellett his attorney, proffers himself on the fourth day against Isabel Anderson, Ellen Anderson and Anne Anderson, daughters and heirs of Henry Anderson, in a plea concerning two messuages, two cottages, four gardens, four bovates of land, twenty acres of meadow and forty acres of pasture with the appurtenances in Lockington, which he same John claims here in the queen's court as his right against the said Isabel, Ellen and Anne by the lady queen's writ of *dum fuit infra aetatem.* And they did not come. And let them be summoned, and judgment that the tenements aforesaid be taken into the hand of the lady queen, and a day etc. Let the aforesaid Isabel, Ellen and Anne be summoned to be here on the morrow of the Purification of the Blessed Mary etc.

PLEAS AT WESTMINSTER BEFORE RICHARD MORGAN, KNIGHT, AND HIS FELLOWS, THE LADY QUEEN'S JUSTICES OF THE BENCH, FOR HILARY TERM [1554] IN THE FIRST YEAR OF THE REIGN OF MARY, BY THE GRACE OF GOD OF ENGLAND, FRANCE AND IRELAND QUEEN, DEFENDER OF THE FAITH, AND SUPREME HEAD IN EARTH OF THE CHURCH OF ENGLAND AND IRELAND roll 236

Yorkshire. John Warde, who is of full age, by Edward Kellett his attorney, proffers himself on the fourth day against Isabel Anderson, Ellen Anderson and Anne Anderson, daughters and heirs of Henry Anderson, in a plea concerning two messuages, two cottages, four gardens, four bovates of land, twenty acres of meadow and forty acres of pasture with the appurtenances in Lockington, which he same John claims here in the queen's court as his right against the said Isabel, Ellen and Anne by the lady queen's writ of *dum fuit infra aetatem.* And they did not come. And they have already made default, namely in three weeks from Michaelmas last past, after summons etc,. whereby the sheriff was commanded that he take the messuages, land and meadow aforesaid into the hand of the lady queen, and a day etc., and that by good summoners he summon the aforesaid Isabel, Ellen and Anne that they be here on the morrow of the Purification of the Blessed Mary then next following to answer to the aforesaid John Warde with respect both to the principal plea and to the aforesaid default etc. And the sheriff now testifies the day of the caption etc. and that he has summoned etc. Therefore it is awarded that the aforesaid John do recover his seisin against the said Isabel, Ellen and Anne of the aforesaid messuages, land and meadow, with the appurtenances, by default etc. And the same Isabel, Ellen and Anne are in mercy etc. Whereupon the aforesaid John, by his aforesaid attorney, comes and prays the lady queen's writ of *habere facias seisinam* to be directed on his behalf to the sheriff of the aforesaid county for the aforesaid tenements with the appurtenances. And it is granted him, returnable here in fifteen days from the day of the Holy Trinity etc.

Afterwards, namely on the Friday next after the octaves of Michaelmas this same term, the aforesaid Isabel Anderson, Ellen Anderson and Anne Anderson come before the lord king and lady queen at Westminster by Richard Heywoode, their guardian admitted by the court of the said lord and lady queen here, and at once say that manifest error has intervened in the aforesaid record and process, and also in the rendering of the aforesaid judgment, in that the same Isabel, Ellen and Anne at the said time of the rendering of the predicti, scilicet in predicto crastino Purificationis Beate Marie anno regni dicte[1] domine regine primo, fuerunt et quemlibet earundem Isabelle, Elene et Anne fuit et adhuc est infra etatem viginti unius annorum, vicelicet predicta Isabella etatis decem et novem annorum, predicta Elena etatis decem et septem annorum, et predicta Anna etatis quatuordecim annorum, et non amplius. Et hoc parate[2] sunt verificare etc. Et petunt breve domini regis et domine regine ad premuniendum prefatum Johannem Warde essendi coram eisdem domino rege et domina regina auditurum recordum et processum predictos. Et eis conceditur etc. per quod preceptum est vicecomiti quod per probos etc. scire faceret prefatum Johannem Warde quod sit coram domino rege et domina regina in octabis Sancti Hillarii ubicumque etc. auditurum recordum et processum predictos et ulterius etc. Idem dies datus est predictis Isabelle, Elene et Anne etc. Ad quem diem coram domino rege et domina regina apud Westmonasterium veniunt predicte[3] Isabella Anderson, Elena Anderson et Anna Anderson in propriis personis suis. Et vicecomes retornavit quod virtute brevis dictorum regis et regine sibi inde directi scire fecit prefatum Johannem Warde essendi coram dictis domino rege et domina regina ad diem et locum in eodem brevi contenta auditurum recordum et processus predicta, per Henricum Walter et Robertum Barton probos etc. prout idem breve in se exigit et requirit. Quiquidem Johannes Warde sic premunitus et quarto die placiti solempniter exactus in propria persona sua similiter venit. Super quo predicte Isabella, Elena et Anna ut prius dicunt quod in recordo et processu predictis acetiam in redditione judicii predicti manifeste est erratum, allegando errorem predictum per ipsas superius allegatum. Et petunt quod curia dominorum regis et regine hic procedat[4] ad examinationem tam recordi et processus predictorum quam erroris predicti quodque iidem Isabella, Elene et Anna ad omnia que occasione judicii predicti amiserunt restituantur etc. ac quod predictus Johannes Warde ad errorem predictum rejungat etc. Super quo, visis et inspectis per curiam dictorum dominorum regis et regine hic personis predictarum Isabelle, Elene et Anne et earum cujuslibet et super diligenti examinatione earundem Isabelle, Elene et Anne et diversorum amicorum suorum per eandem curiam circa premissa habitis, ac super relatione et testimonio diversarum honestarum personarum credencie dignarum <super sacrosancta Dei evangelia juratarum>[i] scienciam et noticiam etatis cujuslibet predictarum Isabelle, Elene et Anne habentium ac testimonium perhibentium quod predicte Isabella, Elena et Anna sunt infra etatem viginti unius annorum, videlicet Mathei Atkynson de Beverley in dicto comitatu Ebor', cordyner, etatis quinquaginta duorum annorum, Johannis Rede de Beverley predicta, taylour, etatis quadraginta annorum, Helene Alanson de Beverley predicta, vidue, etatis quadraginta et octo annorum, et Johanne Farer etatis xliiij annorum compatricis predicte Isabelle Anderson, consideratum est per dictam curiam dominorum regis et regine hic quod eedem[5] Isabella, Elena et Anna et earum quelibet ad presens infra etatem viginti unius annorum existunt et earum quelibet existit, et sic per eandem curiam eedem Isabella, Elena et Anna pro infra etatem viginti unius annorum ad presens adjudicantur etc. Et predictus Johannes Warde petit inde diem interloquendi. Et ei conceditur etc. Et super hoc dies inde datus est partibus predictis in statu quo nunc coram dominis rege et regine usque a die Pasche in xv dies ubicumque etc., videlicet prefato Johanni Warde ad errorem predictum interloquendum et tunc ad errorem[6] illum rejungendum etc.

Ad quem diem coram dominis rege et regine apud Westmonasterium veniunt tam predicte Isabella Anderson, Elena Anderson et Anna Anderson per custodem suum predictum quam predictus Johannes Warde per attornatum suum predictum. Et eedem[7] Isabella, Elena et Anna ut prius dicunt quod in recordo et processu predictis acetiam in redditione

[1] *Reads* dci. [2] *Reads* parati. [3] *Reads* pdca. [4] *Reads* procedant.
[5] *Reads* iidem. [6] *Reads* errores. [7] *Reads* iidem.

aforesaid judgment, namely on the aforesaid morrow of the Purification of the Blessed Mary in the first year of the reign of the said lady queen, were, and each of them the same Isabel, Ellen and Anne was and still is under the age of twenty-one years – namely the aforesaid Isabel is of the age of nineteen years, the aforesaid Ellen of the age of seventeen years, and the aforesaid Anne of the age of fourteen years – and no more. And this they are ready to aver etc. And they pray the writ of the lord king and lady queen to warn the said John Warde to be before the same lord king and lady queen to hear the aforesaid record and process. And it is granted them etc., whereby the sheriff is commanded that by reliable men etc. he cause the said John Warde to know that he should be before the lord king and lady queen in the octaves of St Hilary, wheresoever etc., to hear the record and process aforesaid and further etc. The same day is given to the said Isabel, Ellen and Anne etc. At which day the aforesaid Isabel Anderson, Ellen Anderson and Anne Anderson come in their own persons before the lord king and lady queen at Westminster. And the sheriff has returned that by virtue of the writ of the said lord king and lady queen therein directed to him he caused the said John Warde to know that he should be before the said lord king and lady queen at the day and place contained in the same writ to hear the record and process aforesaid, by Henry Walter and Robert Barton, reliable men etc., as the same writ in itself demands and requires. Which John Warde, having been so warned, and being solemnly demanded on the fourth day of the plea, likewise comes in his own person. Whereupon the aforesaid Isabel, Ellen and Anne, as before, say that there is manifest error in the record and process aforesaid, and also in the rendering of the judgment aforesaid, alleging the aforesaid error as alleged by them above. And they pray that the court of the lord king and queen here should proceed to the examination both of the record and process aforesaid and of the aforesaid error, and that the same Isabel, Ellen and Anne should be restored to all that they have lost by reason of the aforesaid judgment etc. and that the aforesaid John Warde should rejoin to the aforesaid error etc. Whereupon, the court of the lord king and lady queen here having seen and inspected the persons of the aforesaid Isabel, Ellen and Anne, and each of them, and upon diligent examination of the same Isabel, Ellen and Anne and various of their friends had by the same court concerning the foregoing, and upon the report and testimony of various honest persons worthy of credit, sworn upon the holy gospels of God, having knowledge and notice of the age of each of the aforesaid Isabel, Ellen and Anne and giving testimony that the aforesaid Isabel, Ellen and Anna are under the age of twenty-one years – namely Matthew Atkynson of Beverley in the said county of York, cordwainer, aged fifty-two years, John Rede of Beverley aforesaid, tailor, agred forty years, Helen Alanson de Beverley aforesaid, widow, aged forty-eight years, and John Farer, aged forty-four years, godfather of the aforesaid Isabel Anderson – it is considered by the said court of the lord king and lady queen here that the same Isabel, Ellen and Anne are and each of them at present is under the age of twenty-one years, and so the same Isabel, Ellen and Anne are adjudged by the same court to be at present under the age of twenty-one years etc. And the aforesaid John Warde prays leave to imparl herein. And it is granted him etc. Thereupon a day is given therein to the aforesaid parties, in the same state as now, before the lord king and lady queen until fifteen days from Easter day, wheresoever etc., namely to the said John Warde to imparl with respect to the aforesaid error and then to rejoin to that error etc.

At which day both the aforesaid Isabel Anderson, Ellen Anderson and Anne Anderson, by their aforesaid guardian, and the aforesaid John Warde, by his aforesaid attorney, come before the lord king and lady queen at Westminster. And the same Isabel, Ellen and Anne say (as before) that there is manifest error in the aforesaid record and process, and also in the rendering of the aforesaid judgment, alleging the aforesaid error as alleged by them above, and pray that the aforesaid John Warde should rejoin to the aforesaid error, and judicii predicti manifeste est erratum, allegando errorem predictum per ipsas superius allegatum, et petunt quod predictus Johannes Warde ad errorem predictum rejunget quodque curia dominorum rege et regine hic procedat ad examinationem tam recordi et processus predictorum quam erroris predicti etc.

Et predictus Johannes Warde dicit quod materia predicta superius per predictas Isabellam, Elenam et Annam in revocationem judicii predicti modo et forma predictis assignata minus sufficiens in lege existit ad revocandum judicium predictum aut ad coarctandum ipsum Johannem Warde ad materiam et allegationem illas respondendum. Unde pro defectu sufficientis materie ad revocandum judicium predictum idem Johannes Warde petit quod judicium predictum satis bonum adjudicetur et in omnibus affirmatur, dicta materia seu causa superius pro errore assignata non obstante etc.

Et predicte Isabella, Elena et Anna dicunt quod materia predicta superius pro errore predicto in forma predicta allegata sufficiens est in lege ad coarctandum ipsum Johannem Warde ad errorem illum rejungendum ac ad judicium predictum revocandum, quamquidem materiam idem Johannes Warde non dedicit nec ad eam aliqualiter respondit sed materiam illam admittere omnino recusat. Unde eedem Isabella, Elena[i] et Anna ut prius petunt quod judicium predictum ob errorem predictum et alios in recordo et processu predictis existentes revocetur, adnullatur et penitus pro nullo habeatur, ac quod eedem Isabella, Elena et Anna ad omnia que occasione judicii predicti amiserunt restituantur etc.

Et quia curia dominorum regis et regine hic de judicio suo de et super premissis reddendo non dum advisatur, dies inde datus est partibus predictis in statu quo nunc coram dominis rege et regine usque crastinum Sancte Trinitatis ubicumque etc. de judicio suo inde audiendo eo quod curia dominorum rege et regine hic inde non dum etc.
Ad quem diem coram dominis rege et regina apud Westmonasterium veniunt <tam predicte>[1] <Isabella, Elena et Anna per custodem suum predictum quam predictus Johannes Warde>[i] per attornatum suum predictum. Et quia curia dominorum regis et regine hic de judicio suo de et super premissis reddendo non dum advisatur dies inde datus est partibus predictis in statu quo nunc coram dominis rege et regina usque in octabis Sancti Michaelis ubicumque etc. de judicio suo inde audiendo eo quod curia dominorum regis et regine hic inde non dum etc. Ad quem diem coram dominis rege et regina apud Westmonasterium veniunt tam predicte Isabella, Elena et Anna per custodem suum predictum quam predictus Johannes Warde>[i] per attornatum suum predictum. Et quia curia dominorum regis et regine hic de judicio suo de et super premissis reddendo non dum advisatur dies inde datus est partibus predictis in statu quo nunc coram dominis rege et regina usque in octabis Sancti Hillarii ubicumque etc. de judicio suo inde audiendo eo quod curia dominorum regis et regine hic inde non dum etc. Ad quem diem coram dominis rege et regina apud Westmonasterium veniunt tam predicte Isabella, Elena et Anna per custodem suum predictum quam predictus Johannes Warde>[i] per attornatum suum predictum. Super quo, visis et per curiam dominorum regis et regine hic [inspectis] omnibus et singulis premissis, maturaque deliberatione inde habita, pro eo quod videtur curie dominorum regis et regine hic quod materia predicta superius pro errore in forma predicta assignata sufficiens est in lege ad coarctandum ipsum Johannem Warde ad errorem predictum rejungendum ac ad judicium predictum revocandum, ideo consideratum est quod judicium predictum ob errorem predictum et alios in recordo et processu predictis compertos revocatur, adnulletur et penitus pro nullo habeatur quodque predicte Isabella, Elena et Anna ad omnia que occasione judicii predicti amiserunt restituantur etc.

1 *Over an erasure, presumably:* partes predicte.

that the court of the lord king and lady queen here should proceed to the examination both of the record and process aforesaid and of the aforesaid error etc.

And the aforesaid John Warde says that the aforesaid matter assigned above in manner and form aforesaid by the aforesaid Isabel, Ellen and Anne in revocation of the aforesaid judgment is insufficient in law to revoke the aforesaid judgment or to compel him the said John Warde to answer that matter and allegation. Whereupon, for want of sufficient matter to revoke the aforesaid judgment, the same John Warde prays that the aforesaid judgment be adjudged perfectly good, and in every respect affirmed, notwithstanding the said matter or cause above assigned for error etc.[1]

And the aforesaid Isabel, Ellen and Anne say that the aforesaid matter alleged above in form aforesaid as the aforesaid error is sufficient in law to compel him the said John Warde to rejoin to the error and to revoke the aforesaid judgment, which matter the same John Warde does not deny, nor does he in any way answer the same, but utterly refuses to admit the matter. Whereupon the same Isabel, Ellen and Anne, as before, pray that the aforesaid judgment on account of the aforesaid error (and others existing in the aforesaid record and process) be revoked, annulled and utterly treated as naught, and that the same Isabel, Ellen and Anne be restored to all that they have lost by reason of the aforesaid judgment etc.

And because the court of the lord king and lady queen here is not yet advised of its judgment to be given upon and concerning the foregoing, a day is therein given to the aforesaid parties in the same state as now before the lord king and lady queen until the morrow of the Holy Trinity, wheresoever etc., for hearing their judgment therein, inasmuch as the court of the lord king and lady queen is not yet therein etc. At which day both the aforesaid Isabel, Ellen and Anne, by their aforesaid guardian, and the aforesaid John Warde, by his aforesaid attorney, come before the lord king and lady queen at Westminster. And because the court of the lord king and lady queen here is not yet advised of its judgment to be given upon and concerning the foregoing, a day is therein given to the aforesaid parties in the same state as now before the lord king and lady queen until the octaves of Michaelmas, wheresoever etc., for hearing their judgment therein, inasmuch as the court of the lord king and lady queen is not yet therein etc. At which day both the aforesaid Isabel, Ellen and Anne, by their aforesaid guardian, and the aforesaid John Warde, by his aforesaid attorney, come before the lord king and lady queen at Westminster. And because the court of the lord king and lady queen here is not yet advised of its judgment to be given upon and concerning the foregoing, a day is therein given to the aforesaid parties in the same state as now before the lord king and lady queen until the octaves of St Hilary, wheresoever etc., for hearing their judgment therein, inasmuch as the court of the lord king and lady queen is not yet therein etc. At which day both the aforesaid Isabel, Ellen and Anne, by their aforesaid guardian, and the aforesaid John Warde, by his aforesaid attorney, come before the lord king and lady queen at Westminster. Whereupon, all and singular the foregoing having been seen and inspected by the court of the lord king and lady queen, and mature deliberation thereupon had, forasmuch as it seems to the court of the lord king and lady queen here that the aforesaid matter above assigned for error in form aforesaid is sufficient in law to compel him the said John Warde to rejoin to the aforesaid error, and to revoke the aforesaid judgment, it is therefore awarded that the judgment aforesaid, on account of the aforesaid error, and others appearing in the record and process aforesaid, be revoked, annulled, and utterly treated as naught, and that the aforesaid Isabel, Ellen and Anne be restored to all that they have lost by reason of the aforesaid judgment etc.

[1] This is a demurrer to the assignment of error, instead of the more usual joinder in error, because the error assigned was an error in fact (infancy) which the defendant in error could not refute.

[5]

A, fo. 30[f]; *L* 227[f].

Nota que fuit agree termino Pasche annis regni Philippi et Marie 2° et 3° per les justices que les justices doyer et terminer nont pas power al acquiter suspectes devant eux per proclamation nient pluis que justices de peace ont quar our power nest semble al comissioners de gaole deliverie mes entend tantsolement a oyer et terminer choses devant eux mes ils s. les justices doyer et terminer nont pas power al arrayne homes devant eux mesmes mes justices de gaole deliverie ont per lestatutes queux nextend al justices de oyer et terminer.

[6]

Et nota que si commission doyer et terminer soit generall sans aver relation al jour certein si les justices al un foites seantes per le commission et ceo execute sans adjournment quant ils levient qu[ar] ore auterfoites ils ne poyent execute [*fol. 30*] le dit commission arrere ne serra sans novell comission. Mes si le commission soit al durer tanque al feast Omnium Sanctorum ore ils poyent executer lour commission sans adjournment al ascun temps quando ils voilont devant le dit feast: et ceo est le meliour voy, [quar][1] sils adjourne al jour certein ils ne poyent seer tanque le jour vient.

[7]

Nota per toutes les justices agree que un feme convict de felony navera unques son clergie coment que el bein poet lyer mes si soet pregnant ove un enfant el serra respect tanque lenfant soit nee sel soit trove issint per enquest des femes virtute brevis de ventre inspiciendo. Ils agreont auxi que si apres cest trover per les dittes femes apres al auter temps le feme issint convict ne pledera que el est preignant ou enseint quar per la ley el navera forsque un tryall en cest case pur cest matter: quod nota.

[8]

A, fo. 30v (foll. pl. 5); *L* 228 (sim.).

Nota que fuit agree per toutes les justices que si home compassa ou ymagen le mort le roygn en le comite de Midd. et en le comite de Lyncolne[2] fait lovert act, come pone sur luy un cote de mayle ou auter chose, ore il bein poet estre endite

[1] *Reads* que.

[2] Oxon. *A, L.*

5. DISCHARGE BY PROCLAMATION

King's Bench, Pas. 1556. Cf. above, p. 83, pl. 31.

Note that it was agreed in Easter term, 2 & 3 Phil. & Mar., by the justices, that the justices of oyer and terminer do not have power to acquit suspects before them by proclamation, any more than justices of the peace have, for their power is not like that of commissioners of gaol delivery but extends only to hearing and determining things before them; but the justices of oyer and terminer have no power to arraign men before themselves, whereas justices of gaol delivery have, by the statutes – which do not extend to justices of oyer and terminer.

6. ADJOURNMENT OF COMMISSIONS

Contd from pl. 5. Cf. below, p. 103, pl. 21 (Trin. 1557).

And note that if a commission of oyer and terminer is in general terms, without reference to a certain day, and the justices sit on one occasion by the commission and execute it without adjournment, once they rise they cannot execute the said commission again on another occasion, without a new commission. If, however, the commission is to last until the feast of All Saints, they may execute their commission without adjournment at any time when they wish before the said feast; and that is the better way, for if they adjourn to a certain day they cannot sit until the day comes.

7. PLEA OF PREGNANCY

Probably in Serjeants' Inn, Pas. 1556.

Note that it was agreed by all the justices that a woman convicted of felony shall never have her clergy, even if she can read well; but if she is pregnant with child she shall be respited until the child is born, provided she is found pregnant by an inquest of women by virtue of a writ *de ventre inspiciendo.* They also agreed that if, after this finding by the said women, the woman is later convicted again, she shall not [again] plead that she is pregnant or *enceinte,* for by the law she shall only have one trial in this case for this matter.[1] Note that.

8. R. v. WYATT; R. v. THROGMORTON

Cf. pl. 9, below. For *R.* v. *Wyatt,* see Dyer's report, 110 Selden Soc. 9.

Note that it was agreed by all the justices that if someone compasses or imagines the queen's death in the county of Middlesex, and commits the overt act in the county of Lincoln, as by putting on a coat of mail or something else, he may now well be indicted for the whole treason in the county of Lincoln, because

[1] Cf., to the same effect, Bro. Abr., *Corone,* pl. 97 (1536/37).

de tout le dit treason en le comite de Lin. quar limagination et le compassinge courge et va ove le overt fact mes via versa en cest case il ne poet estre endite en le comite ou le compassinge fuit tantum car ceo nest treason sans overt acte et loverte acte ne courge ove ceo etc.

[9]

A, fo. 30v[f]; *L* 229[f].

Nota auxi agree per eux toutes que si vi persons ymagyn et compasse a levyer gwerre versus le roygne et voylont et agreont enter eux que 2 de eux ferront tiel acte en tiel comite, et auters de eux auter acte en auter comite, et auters de eux auter chose en auter comite, pur assembler le people vers le royne, et puis 2 ou un de eux accordant a lour purpose font lacte et assemble le people et les auters ne font auter acte uncore cest acte issint fait per un our 2 de eux issint adevant enter eux agrees est treason en toutes les 6 persons et toutes sont traytours per cest acte. Mes auterment est en cest case si le compassinge ou ymagination fuit fait enter eux solement sans auter agreament et puis un ou deux de eux levia gwerre et assemble people les auters nient sachantes de cest ore ceo nest treason forsque en cestui ou en ceux que font lact et en lauters nemi: sicut accidit in casu Wyatt et Throgmorton.

Dyer's report of the case

Les Reports (1688 ed.), fo. 98b, pl. 56.

Nota que fuit declare al arraignement de Sir Nicholas Throgmorton, et auxy in le Starrechamber al Jury que luy acquite de la Treason et conspiracy ove Wyat in le lever de guerre, per lopinion des Justices, que si ij. ou plusors conspire de faire treason, come in lever de guerre, et ascun de eux apres ceo fait et execute, que ceo est treason in touts. Et hoc per communem legem, devant le declaration fait in 25 E. 3. cap. 2.

[10]

[*fol. 30v*] Nota per *Portman* Chefe Justice, *Broke* Cheif Justice de Comen Banke, *Stanfort* Justice, et auters serjeantes de Serjeantes Inne en Chauncery Lane que si home fist leas pur ans dun meason ove les appurtenaunces que ore ryen passa al lessee que le mese, orchard et gardein, que est et poet estre appurtenant al dit mease, quar nul terre poet estre dit appurtenant al mese forsque orchard et gardein. Mes si leas soit dun mease pur ans ove toutes les terres et tenementes al dit mese pertenant ore les terres que fueront use et ad estre occupye ove le dit mese passera per cest leas quar per usage ils poyent al dit mese apperteyner: et cest difference ils dyent fuit agree en Comen Banke en le cas sur Baldwyn jades the imagination and compassing run along and go with the overt act. Vice versa, however, he may not in this case be indicted in the county where the compassing alone was, for that is not treason without an overt act, and the overt act does not run with it etc.

9. R. v. WYATT; R. v. THROGMORTON

Contd from pl. 8. Also reported in Dyer, fo. 98b (Pas. 1554); printed below; 110 Selden Soc. 12.

Note that it was also agreed by all of them that if six persons imagine and compass to levy war against the queen, and appoint and agree among themselves that two of them shall do a certain act in a certain county, and others of them another act in another county, and others of them another thing in another county, to assemble the people against the queen, and then two (or one) of them do the act according to their purpose and assemble the people, and the others do no other act, nevertheless this act done by one or two of them, being so agreed between them beforehand, is treason in all six persons, and all are traitors by virtue of this act. It is otherwise in this case, however, if the compassing or imagination was done between them alone without other agreement, and then one or two of them levy war and assemble people, the others not knowing about it, this is not treason save in him (or those) who do the act, and not in the others. This happened in the case of Wyatt and Throgmorton.

Translation of Dyer's report

Easter term 1554.

Note that it was declared at the arraignment of Sir Nicholas Throgmorton and also in the Star Chamber to the jury who acquitted him of treason and conspiracy with Wyatt, in levying war, by the opinion of the justices, that if two or more conspire to commit treason, as by levying war, and any one of them afterwards does it, and puts it into execution, this is treason in all. And that was by the common law, before the declaration made in 25 Edw. III.

10. 'APPURTENANCES' OF A HOUSE

Serjeants' Inn, Chancery Lane. Cf. above p. 11, pl. 1; p. 78, pl. 15.

Note, by Portman C.J., Brooke C.J. of the Common Bench, Staunford J., and other serjeants of Serjeants' Inn, Chancery Lane, that if someone makes a lease for years of a house 'with the appurtenances', nothing passes to the lessee save the house, orchard and garden, which is and may be appurtenant to the said house, for no land may be said to be appurtenant to a house except an orchard and garden. But if a lease for years is made of a house with all the lands and tenements belonging to the said house, the lands which usually were and have been occupied with the said house shall pass by this lease, for they may belong to the said house by usage. They said that this distinction was agreed in the Common

Cheife Justice de Comen Banke, les dittes Portman et Bromeley esteant adonques in consilio ove luy.

[11]

Abr. in *A*, fo. 30v (foll. pl. 9); *L* 230 (sim.).

Nota per *Portman* Chefe Justice et per *Gawdy* clerement agree pur bon ley que si home soit arraine pur robberie ou manslaughter ou come un accessory al murder, ou ils doyent aver lour clergie per la ley, et ceo est per appell al suite del partie et sont troves culpables et ils ont lour lyvers devant judgement et sont deliveres al ordinarye, que en cest case nul purgation serra fait per lordinary mes le prisoner issint condempne remayna toutes dittes en prison sans purgation faire quia al sute del partie est condempne et en execution s. diliver al ordinarye a son sute. Mes auterment est quant ils sont troves culpables sur indictmentes al sute le roye et ont lour clergie devant judgement et sont deliveres al ordinary, ils poyent faire lour purgation quant ils sont condempnes non al suite le partie mes per la ley de corone.

[12]

Nota per toutes les justices que si un cause un patent de licence a carier ou vender laynes ou auters lettres patentes estre faites en nosme le roye et prist le graund seale dun auncient patent et cause le dit [seale] destre fixe a novell patent cye colourment come ne poet estre perceive et puis mitta en ure le pattent issint enseall que ceo est treason pur counterfayture le seale per lestatutue 25 E. 3.: sicut accidit in casu de Overton eodem termino. Et concordat 2 H. 4.

[13]

A, fo. 31 (foll. pl. 11); *L* 231 (sim.).

Nota que fuit agree per toutes les justices que si tenant en tail a cest jour soit attaint de haut treason que ore il forfeytera les dittes terres entayles al roy come terres en fee auxibein come si lattaynder fuissoit devant lestatute de repelles de treasons etc. fait 2° Marie, le dit statute nient obstant. [Mes Trin. primo Marie ils fueront de cest opinion.][1]

[1] *A*.

Bench in the case [of] Baldwyn,[1] late chief justice of the Common Bench, the said Portman and Bromley being then of counsel with him.

11. CLERKS CONVICT

Probably in Serjeants' Inn.

Note, by PORTMAN C.J., and clearly agreed by *Gawdy*, serjeant, as good law, that if someone is arraigned for robbery or manslaughter, or as an accessory to murder, where one ought to have clergy by the law, and this is by appeal at the suit of the party, and he is found guilty and has his book before judgment and is delivered to the ordinary, in this case no purgation shall be made [before] the ordinary, but the prisoner (being so condemned) shall remain always in prison without making purgation, because he is condemned at the suit of the party, and in execution (that is, delivery to the ordinary) at his suit. It is otherwise, however, when prisoners are found guilty at the king's suit and have their clergy before judgment and are delivered to the ordinary: they may make their purgation when they are condemned not at the suit of the party but by the law of the crown.

12. R. v. OVERTON

Probably in Serjeants' Inn, 1556. The judges here reversed a decision of 1545: *OHLE*, vi. 588. See also above, p. 66, pl. 21.

Note by all the justices that if someone causes a patent to be made out in the king's name for a licence to carry or sell wool, or other letters patent, and takes the great seal off an old patent and causes the seal to be fixed to a new patent so deceitfully that it cannot be perceived, and then puts in use the patent so sealed, this is treason for counterfeiting the seal, by the statute 25 Edw. III.[2] This happened in the case of Overton this term; and it agrees with 2 Hen. IV.[3]

13. FORFEITURE OF ENTAILS

Probably in Serjeants' Inn, 1556.

Note that it was agreed by all the justices that if a tenant in tail at the present day is attainted of high treason, he shall forfeit the said entailed lands to the king, in the same way as lands in fee, or just as if the attainder had been before the statute of repeals of treasons etc. made in 1 Mar.,[4] notwithstanding the said statute. (But in Trinity term 1 Mar. they were of [the other] opinion.[5])

[1] Sir John Baldwin, CJCP 1535–45.
[2] Treason Act 1351, 25 Edw. III, st. 5, c. 2.
[3] YB Trin. 2 Hen. IV, fo. 25, pl. 25.
[4] I Mar., sess.1, c. 1.
[5] *R.* v. *Lord Grey* (1554) above, at p. 72.

[14]

[*fol. 31*] Auxi fuit agree que si ascun home va ouster le mere sanz conge le roye ou per conge le roye que si le roy apres per son lettre commaund luy pur certein causes a reviender en le dit realme et a cest comaundment il ne revient mes contempna le dit commaundment que ore pur cest contempt le roy poet seisir ses beins et terres en ses maines et eux reteyner tanque le partie que issint contemna revient et voet estre justefie et mitta luy en grace le roy pur son contempt et sua les terres hors des mayns le roye per livery ou ouster le maine sine exitibus, come appiert per diverse presidentes in S[c]accario domini Regis et monstres as dittes justices: come en le case Seignor Wodstocke, comes Kantie, et ceo fuit sans ascun office de ceo trove adevant mes sur le contempte returne et appiert de record.

Dyer's report of the case

Les Reports (1688 ed.), fo. 128b, pl. 61.

Fuit move que si la Roigne mette un special commandment south l'privy seal, ou grand seal, a ascuns d'eux que sont ore in partibus transmarinis, et queux departont hors del Realme sans licence, s. que ils reviendrent deins le Realme a certen jour sur paine etc. et ils refuse a vener, lez terrez et chattels serront seisies al use le Roigne pur le contempt. Et un notable president fuit monstre de tiel semble matter in 19 E. 2. in Scaccario vers le Countee de Richmond appell William de Brittaine, le quel fuit mis in message per le Roy in Gascoigne qui recusavit declinare in Regnum per mandatum Regis, ob quod bona et catalla ac terra et tenementa sua fueront commaunde destre seisie in maines le Roy etc.

[15]

A, fo. 31 (foll. pl. 13); *L* 232 (sim.); *D*, fo. 20, pl. 10 (2 & 3 Phil. & Mar.).

Nota auxi agree per touttes que le roy poet fair un proclamation a lour subjectes quoad terrorem populi de mitter eux en feare de son displeasure et indignation mes nemi sur auter payne certein come a forfeyture terres ou beins ou de faire fyne ou de suffer imprisonment ou auters paynes quar nul proclamation en soy mesme poet faire un ley que ne fuit adevant mes proclamation serra a confirmer et ratefier un ley ou statute et nemy a chaunger un ley ou de faire un novel ley. Et uncore divers presidentes fueront troves et monstres hors del Exchequer a le contrary mes a cest les justices nient pas regard: quod nota bene.

Et per Justice *Stanfort* le roy poet faire proclamation a lyer subjectes de augmenter le coyne le realme a pluis haute que ceo est pur le benefitt ses subjectes mes de diminisher ou imbaser le dit coyne de meynder valewe per proclamation cest per luy ne estoit ove ley quia est al prejudice les subjectes, comẽt que aut-

14. CONTEMPT OF THE KING

Probably in Serjeants' Inn, 1556. Also reported in Dyer, fo. 128 (moved before all the judges, Hil. 1556); printed below.

It was also agreed that if anyone goes across the sea without the king's leave, or goes with the king's leave but the king afterwards by his letter commands him for certain causes to return to [this][1] realm, and he does not return upon this command, but is in contempt of the said command, the king may for this contempt seize his goods and lands into his hands and retain them until the party thus in contempt returns and [submits to justice],[2] and submits to the king's grace for his contempt, and sues the lands out of the king's hands by livery or ousterlemain without issues (*sine exitibus*): as appears by various precedents in the lord king's Exchequer, which were shown to the said justices, such as the case of Lord Woodstock, earl of Kent,[3] and that was without any office previously found thereof, but only upon the contempt returned and appearing of record.

Translation of Dyer's report

Hilary term 1556.

It was moved that, if the queen sends a special command under the privy seal, or great seal, to any of those who are now abroad and who left the realm without licence, that they should come back within the realm at a certain day, upon pain etc., and they refuse to come, their lands and chattels shall be seized to the queen's use for the contempt. And a notable precedent was shown of a similar matter in 19 Edw. II, in the Exchequer, against the earl of Richmond (called William of Brittany), who was sent a message by the king in Gascony and refused to return to the realm by the king's command, by reason whereof his goods and chattels and lands were commanded to be seized into the king's hands etc.

15. PROCLAMATIONS

Probably in Serjeant's Inn, 1556. See *OHLE*, vi. 64–65.

Note that it was also agreed by everyone that the king may make a proclamation to his subjects in terror of the people (*quoad terrorem populi*), to put them in fear of his displeasure and indignation, but not upon any certain penalty, such as forfeiture of lands or goods, or making fine, or suffering imprisonment, or other penalties, for no proclamation in itself may make a law which was not law before; for a proclamation is only to confirm and ratify a law or statute, not to change law or make new law. Although several precedents to the contrary were found and shown from the Exchequer, the justices paid no regard to them: which note well.

According to STAUNFORD J., the king may make a proclamation to bind his subjects by augmenting the coin of the realm to a higher value, for that is for his subjects' benefit; but to diminish or debase the said coin to a lower value by proclamation does not by itself stand with law, because it is to the prejudice of the

[1] Text reads: 'the said'.
[2] Text reads: 'will be justified'.
[3] Edmund Plantagenet, youngest son of King Edward I; attainted and beheaded 1330.

erment fuit mise en use per proclamation en le temps E. 6. per John, duke of Northumberland, le graund traytor: et malement ut credo.

[16]

Second part in *A*, fo. 31[f]; *L* 233[f] (sim.).

Nota que fuit adjudge en Banke le Roy si home sua appeall de mort dun home vers 2, un come principall et auter come accessorye, et apres declaration est nonsue en son appeall et le principall et accessorye sont novelment arraynes al sute le roy sur le declaration, le principall pleda son pardon que fuit allowe, et laccessory fuit per cest discharge auxi sans auter chose faire. Et in eodem termino home fuit endite de felony fait en[1] [*fol. 31v*] temps le roy E. 6. et pur ceo que lenditement fuit contra pacem domine regine nunc ou serra contra pacem dicti nuper regis et sans tiels perolls (contra pacem) en lenditement lenditement est void. Et le partie fuit discharge le lenditement per agard sans pluis faire.

[17]

A, fo. 34v (Trin. 4 & 5 Phil. & Mar.); *L* 256.

Nota que fuit la agree per toutes les justices que le combuster feloniousment dun barne, stable, oxhouse ou shepehouse, esteant parcell et adjoininge al dwelling meason, est felony coment que nul graine ou corne soit distroy per le combuster et coment que le barne ne soit parcell ne adjoinant al dwellinge house. Vide lestatute 23 H. 8. ca. 1. 23 H. 8. ca. 3, quex parle de combuster de dwellinge howses et barnes corne esteant en eux. Westm' 1. ca. 15, que parle de ceux que sont prises pur arson feloniosment. Et fuit agree per toutes [que] si le barne soit arse et nul corne esteant en cest ne nul parcell ne adjoinant al dwellinge howse ceo nest[2] felony mes trespas. M. 11 H. 7. fo. 1 agree que le combuster dun barne adjoinant al meason est felony per comen ley et pur cest le felon fuit pend.

[1] *Written again on fo. 31v.*
[2] *Altered from:* est.

subjects, even though it was otherwise used by proclamation in the time of King Edward VI by John, duke of Northumberland, the great traitor – and wrongly, as I believe.[1]

16. ACCESSORY; INDICTMENT

King's Bench, 1556. Cf. *R.* v. *Whalley* (1553) in Dyer, fo. 88.

Note that it was adjudged in the King's Bench that if someone sues an appeal for the death of a man against two, one of them as principal and the other as accessory, and after declaration he is nonsuited in his appeal, and the principal and accessory are newly arraigned at the king's suit, upon the declaration, and the principal pleads his pardon and it is allowed, the accessory is thereby discharged without more ado. And in the same term someone was indicted for a felony committed in the time of King Edward VI, and because the indictment said 'against the peace of our lady the present queen' whereas it should have been 'against the peace of the said late king', and without such words 'against the peace' in the indictment the indictment is void, the party was discharged of the indictment by award, without more ado.

[Trinity term, 1557][2]

17. ARSON

Serjeants' Inn, Fleet Street, Trin. 1557. Also reported in Dyer's circuit notebook, 110 Selden Soc. 411, no. 6. In *A*, these cases are under Trin. 1558.

Note that it was there[3] agreed by all the justices that the felonious burning of a barn, stable, ox-house or sheep-house, being part of and adjoining a dwelling house, is felony, even if no grain or corn is destroyed by the burning, and even if the barn is not part of or adjoining a dwelling house. See the statutes of 23 Hen. VIII, c. 1, and [25] Hen. VIII, c. 3, which speak of burning dwelling houses and barns, corn being in them; and Westminster I, c. 15, which speaks of those who are taken for arson committed feloniously. It was agreed by them all that if the barn is burned and there is no corn in it, and it is not part of or adjoining a dwelling house, this is not felony but trespass. Mich. 11 Hen. VII, fo. 1,[4] agrees that burning a barn adjoining a house is felony by common law, and the felon was hanged for it.

1 For this see *OHLE*, vi. 65; *Barrington* v. *Potter* (1553) Dyer, fo. 82.

2 The next seven entries are an interpolation, apparently continued from pp. 124–125, below: see 110 Selden Soc. 413.

3 This must refer to the case on p. 125 , below, pl. 5.

4 YB Mich. 11 Hen. VII, fo. 1, pl. 3; Spelman's report, 93 Selden Soc. 73.

[18]

A, fo. 34 (foll. pl. 19); *L* 258 (sim.); *D*, fo. 24, pl. 5 (4 & 5 Phil. & Mar.).

Et fuit agree per toutes que lextortion des ordinaries prise pur probate des testamentes, <committinge lettres dadministration>,[1] et pur prisel des mortuaries, poient estre dones en charge come ils fueront adevant lestatute de repelle pur le sea[2] <de Rome>[3] pur le restitution[4] de cest nient obstant lestatute.

[19]

A, fo. 34v (foll. pl. 17); *L* 257 (sim.); *D*, fo. 24, pl. 4 (4 & 5 Phil. & Mar.).

Et fuit agree que toutes offences en ascun estatute expresses poient estre enquires per les justices doyer et termyner coment que lestatute ne dona power a nully per expresse parolls denquirer de cest offence come lestatute de brawlinge et fightinge en esglis et cemitories et lestatute primo E. 6. ca. 5. pur conveyinge des chivals [and geldings][5] hors del realme.

[20]

Et fuit agree que cestui que est attaint de felony per judgement navera le benefitt de cemytory de sanctuary coment que il preigne cest et ceo clayme quar est home hors de monde et mort en ley.

[21]

A, ff. 34v–35 (foll. pl. 18); *L* 259 (sim.); *D*, ff. 24–25, pl. 6 (4 & 5 Phil. & Mar.).

[*fol. 32*] Et fuit agree [per touts les justices que][6] si le commission doyer et terminer soit al <enquirer al certein jour>[7] ou quamdiu nobis placuerit que cest commission ne besoigne ascun adjornment de session al session, mes en ceux cases si le commissioners adjourne cest commission al jour certein ore ils ne poient [seier][8] en le mesne temps tanque al jour de lour adjournement, et en cest case coment que un ou 2 commissioners adjornant le dit commission lou 4 doient ceo faire al jour certeine, uncore ceo ne discontinua lour commission

[1] commission de administration *A, L.* [2] *Written over:* fee.
[3] Apostolike *A, D, L.* [4] rest *A, L.* reason *D.* [5] *A, D, L.*
[6] *D.* per eux *A, L.* [7] endurer pur certen temps *A, L.* durer pur certein temps *D.*
[8] seiser. seer *A, D.*

18. EXTORTION BY ORDINARIES

Serjeant's Inn, Trin. 1557, contd.

And it was agreed by everyone that extortion by ordinaries, taken for probate of testaments, committing letters of administration, and in taking mortuaries, may be given in charge [to the grand jury] as before the statute of repeal for the see of Rome,[1] for the restoration thereof, notwithstanding the statute.

19. TRIAL OF STATUTORY OFFENCES

Serjeants' Inn, Trin. 1557, contd.

And it was agreed that any offence expressed in any statute may be enquired into by the justices of oyer and terminer, even if the statute gives no power to anyone by express words to enquire into this offence. For example, the statute of brawling and fighting in churches and churchyards;[2] and the statute of 1 Edw. VI, c. 5, for conveying horses and geldings out of the realm.

20. SANCTUARY

Probably in Serjeants' Inn, Trin. 1557, contd. Also reported in Dyer's circuit notebook, 110 Selden Soc. 411, no. 8, where a different explanation is given.

And it was agreed that someone who is attainted of felony by judgment shall not have the benefit of a churchyard for sanctuary, even though he takes to it and claims it, for he is a man out of this world and dead in law.[3]

21. ADJOURNMENT OF COMMISSIONS

Serjeants' Inn, Trin. 1557, contd. Also reported in Dyer's circuit notebook, 110 Selden Soc. 411, no. 7. Cf. p. 98, above, pl. 6.

And it was agreed by all the justices that if a commission of oyer and terminer is to last until a certain day,[4] or 'so long as it pleases us' (*quamdiu nobis placuerit*), this commission needs no adjournment from session to session; but if, in these cases, the commissioners adjourn this commission until a certain day, they may not sit in the mean time before the day of their adjournment: and in that case, if one or two commissioners adjourn the said commission to a certain day, where four ought to do it, this does not discontinue their commission, but upon a new

[1] For 'see of Rome' (*H*) the other texts read 'apostolic see'.

[2] 5 & 6 Edw. VI, c. 4, s. 1.

[3] For civil death of clerks attaint see *OHLE*, vi. 535, 574 n. 197.

[4] According to Dyer this was a 'new form': 110 Selden Soc. 411.

mes sur novell sommons ils poient seier sur cest commission quant ils voillont, et ladjornement per un ou per 2 lou 4 per le commission doient ceo faire cest void en ley. Mes si le dit comission ad nul jour en soy lymitt ne ad ceux parolls quamdiu nobis placuerit, mes le commission est generall sans jour, ou pro hac vice tantum, ore les comissioners accordant a lour commission doient adjorner cest commission de jour en jour et sils ne font issint a lour primer session lour commission est discontinue et determyne.

[22]

A, fo. 35 (foll. pl. 23); *L* 262 (sim.); *D*, fo. 25, pl. 9 (4 & 5 Phil. & Mar.).

Nota auxi agree per toutes [les justices][1] que si al nisi prius les jurors perenter partie et partie sont challenges pur cause de le hundreth yssint que ils remaynont que ore al prier le playntiefe ou defendant les justices causeront le viscount a faire[2] le pannell plein de circumstantibus per lestatute coment que ils remayne pur default des hundreders quar hundredors sont jurors et lentry est quant ils issint remayne que le jurie remaine pur default des jurors et nemi en default des hundredors. Come est en assise quant les recognitors remaine pur le challenge del viewe, quar la lentry est que les recognitors remaine pro defectu visus et nemi pro defectu recognitorum et la en cest assise en cest case ils ne serront prises de circumstantibus per lestatute. Vies lestatute de 35 H. 8. ca. 8.

[23]

A, fo. 35 (foll. pl. 24); *L* 261 (sim.); *D*, fo. 25, pl. 8 (4 & 5 Phil. & Mar.).

Nota auxi agree que les justices doyer et terminer ne poient enquirer de forcible entree accordant al statute 8 H. 6. ne ils ne poient agarder breife de restitution sur tiel enditement[3] eo que lestatute 8 H. 6. done cest power al justices de peace et cest power ne poet estre done as auters per auter commission. Mes uncore quant un tiel enditement est prise devant justices de peace et devant breife [*fol. 32v*] de restitution agard per eux ceo est remove en Banke le Roy que ore les justices le dit banke agardera breife de restitution sur cest enditement auxibein come les justices de peace puissoent, et ceo ils poient faire coment que lenditement [ne][4] fait mention que il est prie et ewe a request le partie. M. 7 E. 4. fo. 17. Vide residuum fo. 2. 1.3. apres.

[1] *A, D.*
[2] supplier *A, D.*
[3] judgment *A, D, L.*
[4] *A, D, L.*

summons they may sit upon this commission when they wish, for an adjournment by one or two, where four ought by the commission to do it, is void in law. If, however, the said commission has no day specified in it, nor the words *quamdiu nobis placuerit*, but is a general commission without day, or 'for this occasion only' (*pro hac vice tantum*), the commissioners ought according to their commission to adjourn this commission from day to day; and if they do not do so at their first session, their commission is discontinued and determined.

22. TALES DE CIRCUMSTANTIBUS

Serjeants' Inn, Trin. 1557, contd. Also reported in Dyer's circuit notebook, 110 Selden Soc. 412, no. 9.

Note that it was also agreed by all the justices that if at nisi prius the jurors between party and party are challenged because of the hundred, so that they remain, the justices shall (at the prayer of the plaintiff or demandant) cause the sheriff to fill up the panel with bystanders (*de circumstantibus*) by the statute, even though they remain for want of hundredors; for hundredors are jurors, and when they so remain the entry says that the jury remains for want of jurors (not for want of hundredors). [It is otherwise] in an assize when the recognitors remain on account of a challenge of the view, for there the entry is that the recognitors remain 'for want of the view' and not 'for want of recognitors'; and there, in the assize, they shall not in that case be taken from bystanders by the statute. See the statute of 35 Hen. VIII, c. [6].[1]

23. INDICTMENTS FOR FORCIBLE ENTRY

Serjeants' Inn, Trin. 1557, contd. Also reported in Dyer's circuit notebook, 110 Selden Soc. 412, no. 10, referring to a case of 1510 now printed in 116 Selden Soc. 605.

Note that it was also agreed that the justices of oyer and terminer may not enquire into forcible entry under the statute of 8 Hen. VI,[2] nor may they award a writ of restitution upon such an indictment, because the statute of 8 Hen. VI gives this power to the justices of the peace, and this power may not be given to others by another commission. When, however, such an indictment is taken before justices of the peace, and before a writ of restitution is awarded by them it is removed into the King's Bench, the justices of the said bench may now award a writ of restitution upon this indictment,[3] just as well as justices of the peace could; and they may do this even though the indictment [does not] mention that it is prayed and had at the request of the party. See 7 Edw. IV, fo. 17.[4] See the rest below, [p. 124].

[1] Cf. *OHLE*, vi. 360.
[2] 8 Hen. VI, c. 9.
[3] See also *Anon.* (1555) Dyer, fo. 122b.
[4] YB Mich. 7 Edw. IV, fo. 18, pl. 12; Fitz. Abr; *Justices de peas*, pl. 1.

[24]

A, fo. 36 (foll. pl. 21); *L* 260 (sim.); *D*, fo.25, pl. 7 (4 & 5 Phil. & Mar.).

Nota auxi per eux agree que si un commission de oyer et terminer soit direct al certein persons al enquirer a Farnham etc. que ore les commissioners ne poient seer al auter liewe que al F[arnham] ne ils ne poient adjourner lour commission ne doner judgement sur cest en auter liewe que F[arnham]. Et sils font auterment il est coram non judice et void mes lenditement poet estre remove devant les justices de Bancke le Roy ove les circumstances troves sur ceo devant mesmes les justices de oyer et terminer et la ils s. les justices de Banke le Roy procederont sur cest et doneront judgement auxi si verditt passa devant eux etc.

[25]

Nota agree per toutes que si un chivaler ou burges de parlament depart de le parlament sans conge devant le fyne ou prorogation de le dit parlament que ore al fyne del parlament enformation serra fait pur le roy per lour atturney en Banke le Roy vers ceux que departe et sur cest enformation proces serra agarde vers eux que yssint departe. Et si ils sur cest soient convictes ils serront fynes al roy pur lour contempt en mesme le Bancke come serra assesse per les justices de le dit Banke: sicut accidit as plusors quex departont al parlament annis 1 et 2 predictorum Regis et Regine Philippi et Marie et lour fynes assesse termino predicto. Mesme le ley et order serra vers seignors temporall et spirituall queux departont de le dit parlament sans conge devant le fyne de mesme le parlament et lour fynes serra assesse come devant est dit. Et vide accordant T. P. 3 E. 3. titulo Corone 161, en le case levesque de Winchester que departe le parlament sans conge.

[Easter term, 1556, and later][1]

24. ADJOURNMENT OF COMMISSIONS

Probably in the King's Bench, contd from pl. 16. It might be in Serjeants' Inn, contd from pl. 23; but it is not in Dyer's report.

Note also that it was agreed by them that if a commission of oyer and terminer is directed to certain persons to enquire at Farnham etc., the commissioners may not sit at any place other than Farnham, and they may not adjourn their commission or give judgment thereon in any place other than Farnham; and if they do otherwise it is *coram non judice* and void. But the indictment may be removed before the justices of the King's Bench, with the facts (*circumstances*) thereupon found before the same justices of oyer and terminer, and there they (namely the justices of the King's Bench) shall proceed upon it and give judgment as if the verdict had passed before them etc.

25. ATT.-GEN. v. FRECHEWELL, VERNON and MICHELL

King's Bench. Record: KB 27/1181, Rex m. 11 (Thomas Denton and 38 others prosecuted for leaving parliament on 12 Jan. 1555; only Peter Frechewell, Henry Vernon and Ralph Michell appear; most of the defendants' names are followed by blank spaces for their additions); this entry is in Hil. 1557.

Note that it was agreed by everyone that if a knight or burgess of parliament leaves the parliament without permission before the end or prorogation of the said parliament, information shall be laid for the king [and queen] by their attorney at the end of the parliament, in the King's Bench, against those who left; and upon this information process shall be awarded against them who so left, and if they are thereupon convicted they shall be fined with respect to the king for their contempt, in the same bench, at a sum which shall be assessed by the justices of the said bench. This happened to several of those who left the parliament in the years 1 & 2 Phil. & Mar., and their fines assessed in the term aforesaid. The same law and order shall be [observed] against lords temporal and spiritual who leave the said parliament without permission before the end of the same parliament, and their fines shall be assessed as is said above. See, in accord with this, Pas. 3 Edw. III, title 'Corone', 161,[2] in the case of the bishop of Winchester, who left the parliament without permission.

[1] It is not clear exactly where this term begins or resumes, but the next case does not seem to be part of the interpolation from Trin. 1557, and this is confirmed by the ending of pl. 23.

[2] Fitz. Abr., *Corone*, pl. 161 (YB Pas. 3 Edw. III, ff. 18–19, pl. 32).

[26]

Nota auxi agree per graund deliberation et bon advisement que coment que lestatute fait 1 et 2 Philippi et Marie ca. 10. est generall que toutes trialls pur treason serra tantsolement accordant al due course de le comen ley et nient auterment que uncore le dit statute ne repell lact fait 35 H. 8. ca. 2. pur triall des treasons ouster le mere mes que cest estatute estoit en son force et effect come fuit adevant le dit estatute fait en [*fol. 33*] les ans 1 et 2 Philippi et Marie pur 2 causes. Un pur ceo que al comen ley treasons faites oustre le mere ne fueront tries per lorder de comen ley ycy per la ley de le terre et donques ne poient estre auterment tryes que per le course le dit statute que fist le sole tryall en ceux treasons faites oustre le meere. Et lauter cause fuit pur ceo que le dit statute pur triall des toutes treasons parle tantum pur triall des treasons et ne parle des indictmentes et donques les indictmentes queux sont nul triall remayne come fueront devant et ceo est per forme de le dit statute 35 H. 8. en le countie ou le roy maunda son commission et donques per le comon ley le triall serra toutes foites en le dit countie lou lenditement fuit loialment prise et pur cest cause le dit statute 35 H. 8. remaina. Et auxi lentent des les fesors de le dit statute 1 et 2 Philippi et Marie ne fuit unques al auter entent que a repeller lactes faites pur 2 proves et accusors en treasons et nemi lauters actes faites pur triall des treasons ouster le mier mes fuit agree per eux toutes que les proves et accusors doient estre per fourme de lestatute fait 5 et 6 E. 6. et 1 E. 6. sur les indictmentes des treasons hault et petit (le dit statute 1 et 2 nient obstant) pur ceo que le dit statute parle tantum pur trialls des treasons et indictmentes nest pas triall: mes ascuns diont que les serjeantes le roy, latturney et sollicitor sont accusors sur levidence sur lendictment. Et auxi que les indictors sont accusors, et yssint fuit mise en ure: quere tamen, quar les indictors ne les counsellors ne sont accusours ne witnesses come semble per lestatute et ne fuit lentent les fesors de le dit estatute come semble.

[27]

A, fo. 31r–v (first case of Mich. 3 & 4 Phil. & Mar.); *L* 235 (sim.).

En cest terme le serjeantes case fuit bein argue et rule per les justices de le Comen Banke et les questions de le case fueront tiels come ensues:

26. TRIALS FOR TREASON

Serjeants' Inn, Pas. or Trin. 1556. Also reported in Dyer, fo. 131 (Trin. 1556).

Note that it was also agreed, by great deliberation and good advisement,[1] that although the statute made in 1 & 2 Phil. & Mar., c. 10, is in general terms, that all trials for treason shall be solely according to the due course of the common law and not otherwise, nevertheless the said statute does not repeal the act made in 35 Hen. VIII, c. 2, for trial of treasons beyond the sea, but that statute remains in force and effect as it was before the said statute made in the years 1 & 2 Phil. & Mar. This is for two reasons. First, because at common law treasons committed beyond the sea were not tried by the order of the common law here, by the law of the land, and therefore they cannot be tried otherwise than by the course of the said statute, which created the only trial for these treasons committed beyond the sea. The other reason was because the said statute for trial of all treasons speaks only of 'trial' for treasons, and does not speak of indictments, and therefore indictments (which are not trials) remain as they were before, and that is done under the said statute of 35 Hen. VIII in the county where the king sends his commission; and then, by the common law, the trial shall always be in the said county where the indictment was lawfully taken, and for that reason the said statute of 35 Hen. VIII remains. Moreover, the intent of the makers of the said statute of 1 & 2 Phil. & Mar. was never to do anything but repeal the acts made for two proofs and accusers in treason, and not the other acts made for trial of treasons beyond the sea. But it was agreed by all of them that the proof and accusers ought to follow the form of the statutes made in 5 & 6 Edw. VI, and in 1 Edw. VI,[2] upon indictments of high and petit treason, notwithstanding the statute of 1 & 2 [Phil. & Mar.], because the said statute speaks only of trials for treason, and an indictment is not a trial. Some say, however, that the king's serjeants, the attorney-general and solicitor-general are 'accusers' upon the evidence upon the indictment, and also that the indictors are 'accusers', and that is how it is put in practice. Query, however, for neither the indictors nor the counsel are accusers or witnesses by the statute, as it seems, and it was not the intention of the makers of the statute, as it seems.

27. THE SERJEANTS' CASE: HILL v. GRANGE

Common Pleas, Pas. 1556. (Dated Mich. 1556 in *A.*) Record: CP 40/1165, m. 412 (demurrer; judgment for defendant, Pas. 1556); printed in Plowd. 164 and Rast. Ent. 657. Also reported in Plowd. 167v; Dyer, fo. 130 (Pas. 1556); Bro. N.C. 125; BL MS. Harley 1691, fo. 97 (Mich. 1555). For the general call of serjeants in Mich. 1555, see Baker, *Order of Serjeants*, p. 170; 110 Selden Soc. 13.

This term the serjeants' case was well argued and ruled by the justices of the Common Bench. The questions in the case were as follows.

[1] Dyer says the case was moved before all the judges, Hare M.R., Sir John Baker, and the king's serjeants.

[2] 1 Edw. VI, c. 12; 5 & 6 Edw. VI, c. 11.

Home seisie dun mese a que C. acres de terre (temps hors de memorie) apperteine et ont use et per indenture lease le dit mease cum omnibus terris eidem messuagio pertinentibus et loppinion des toutes les justices la fuit que les dites C. acres de terre passont per le lease per ceux parolls mes fuit agree per eux que si leas ust estre de le mese ove les appurtenances que per cest rien passa forsque le mese le court, orchard et garden, le stable, barnes et auters measons a cest adjoynant deins le precinct le dit mese.

[*fol. 33v*] Le 2 question fuit que home fist leas des terres pur 20 ans per indenture date le 6. jour August 1° Marie a commencer de le date le leas rendant xl s. annulment al feast Dannunciation Beate Marie et Saint Michell per equall portions etc. Et fuit agree et adjudge per toutes les dittes justices forsque un que le lessor avera son demy an rent al feast de Saint Michell prochein ensuant le lease et le date deo ceo per cest paroll annualment quar auterment ne poet estre dit annualment.

Le 3 question fuit que home fist leas pur ans ou pur vie reservant rent al deux feastes ove condition que si le rent soit arere per le space de 10 jours prochein apres ascuns des dittes feastes que le lessor reentra et fuit adjudge per toutes les justices que le lessee ne besoigne al attender sur le terre tout lentier jour del darrein jour de les x jours de le rysinge le solle[1] tanque al <solle remissant>[2] mes tantsolement al darrein instant de le darrein jour des dittes x jours devant le <solle recesse>[3] pur tant de temps que largent poet estre tantsolement nombre nient pluis que le lessor est oblige a demander le dit rent [quar][4] auxi bon libertie ad lun come lauter.

Le 4 est que un comen person fist leas pur ans ou pur vie rendant rent ove un condition de reenter pur default de payment et puis le lessor graunt ouster son reversion en fee et fuit adjudge et agree per toutes les justices que le grauntee de le dit reversion poet assettes bein enter pur le condition enfreint per lestatute 32 H. 8. ca. 34. per les generall parolls en le corps de le dit acte coment que les terres fueront les terres dun abbe ou religious terres en les maines le Roy H. 8. ou nemi ou demises per luy ou per auters.

Le 5 question [est] que si un prior ou abbott ove lour covent fist leas per indenture pur ans rendant rent ove un condition de reeenter pur non payment de le dit rent et puis le reversion en fee devient al H. 8. que devie seisie de cest et le Roy E. 6. graunt cest reversion en fee al estranger et puis le condition est enfreint et le grauntee enter etc. Et loppinion des toutes les justices fuit que lentry le grauntee ou patentee le dit Roy E. 6. fuit congeable pur le condition issint enfreint, coment que lestatute 32 H. 8. ca. [3]4. parle de grauntes [*fol. 34*] de le dit roy H. 8. generallment les dittes grauntees entront, quar cest [parol][5] roy avera relation de toutes roys et le generall proviso auxi en le dit statute que fuit fait pur le benefitt les lessees prove bein lentent les fesours[6] estre issint quar

[1] soliel *A.* soiell *L.*
[2] recouchinge de ceo *A.* couchinge de ceo *L.*
[3] solis occasum *A.* occasum solis *L.*
[4] que *H.*
[5] *A, L.* general de *H.*
[6] *Written over:* feoffors. fesors *A, L.*

Someone seised of a house to which 100 acres of land belong, and have been used time out of mind, by indenture leases the said house 'with all the lands belonging to the same messuage'. And the opinion of all the justices there was that the said 100 acres of land pass by the lease, by virtue of those words. But it was agreed by them that if the lease had been of the house 'with the appurtenances', nothing would thereby pass except the house, the courtyard, orchard and garden, the stable, barns and other houses thereto adjoining, within the precinct of the house.[1]

The second question was: someone made a lease of lands for 20 years by indenture dated 6 August [1553], 1 Mar., to commence from the date of the lease, yielding 40*s.* annually at the feasts of the Annunciation of the Blessed Mary and Michaelmas in equal portions etc. And it was agreed and adjudged by all the said justices (except one) that the lessor should have his half-year's rent at Michaelmas next following the lease, and the date thereof, by virtue of the word 'annually'; for otherwise it could not be said to be 'annually'.[2]

The third question was: someone made a lease for years or for life, reserving rent at two feasts with a condition that it the rent should be in arrear for a period of ten days next after any of the said feasts the lessor should re-enter. And it was adjudged by all the justices that the lessee need not wait on the land throughout the whole of the last of the ten days, from sunrise to sunset ('solle remissant'), but only at the last instant of the last of the ten days before sundown ('solle recesse'), for a long enough time for the money to be counted out. No more is the lessor so bound to demand the said rent, for each should have as much freedom as the other.

The fourth question was: a common person makes a lease for years or for life, yielding rent, with a condition to re-enter for default of payment, and then the lessor grants over the reversion in fee. And it was adjudged and agreed by all the justices that the grantee of the said reversion may perfectly well enter for breach of the condition by virtue of the statute 32 Hen. VIII, c. 34, by the general words in the body of the said act, whether or not the lands were the lands of an abbot, or religious lands, in the hands of King Henry VIII, or demised by him or by others.

The fifth question: a prior or abbot, with his convent, makes a lease for years by indenture, yielding rent, with a condition to re-enter for non-payment of the said rent, and then the reversion in fee comes to Henry VIII, who dies seised thereof, and King Edward VI grants this reversion in fee to a stranger, and then the condition is broken, and the grantee enters etc. The opinion of all the justices was that the entry of the grantee or patentee of the said King Edward VI, for the condition thus broken, was permissible, even though the statute of 32 Hen. VIII, c. 34, speaks of grantees of the said King Henry VIII generally, that the said grantees shall enter: for this general word 'king' shall refer to all kings, and also the general proviso in the said statute (which was made for the benefit of lessees) proves well the intention of the makers to be thus, for that proviso

[1] Cf. above, p. 11, pl. 1; p. 78, pl. 15; p. 99, pl. 10. The occurrence of multiple vexed questions in serjeants' cases suggests that they were fictional.

[2] Cf. above, p. 56, pl. 2; p. 86, pl. 1

cest proviso done al lessees generall remedy vers les grauntees et per mesme le reason que les lessors averont semble remedy per reentry vers eux.

[28]

A, fo. 31v[f]; *L* 236[f].

Nota que en Banke le Roy en trespas de close debruse le deffendant plede Rien culpable et quant le jurie vient al barre le deffendant challenge un des dittes jurors devant que il fuit jure pur ceo que il auterfoites fuit un des inditeors de le dit defendant pur mesme le trespas et pria que il soit treit pur cest cause et monstre le record en courte ceo provant (come il doit et covient per la ley): et ceo fuit adjudge un principall challenge per le courte. Vide M. 8 H. 4, titulo Chalenge 79, et P. 7 E. 4, eodem [titulo][1] 53.

[29]

A, fo. 32v; *L* 244.

Nota que al Serjeantes Inne en Chauncery Lane cest question fuit debate: si un home emble avers ou beins et lowner des dittes beines issint emblees fait freshe sute apres le felon pur ses beins et luy apprehend issint que le felon waive les beins pur danger dapprehension et fua, et devant que lowner vient les officers pur le roy ou auters pur lour seignors seisont les beins issint wayves, et puis lowner vient et challenge ses beins, sil avera ses beins arere ou serront forfaites, ceo fuit le question. Et fuit tenus per *Porteman* Cheife Justice et per *Sir John Baker*, knight, que ils ne sont pas forfaites entant que lowner ad fait tout son endevor en fesant pursute de ville en ville. Et que nuls beins serra wayves mes lou le propertie ne poet estre conus a que ils sont issint que lowner fait son endevor per freshe sute. Et *Brooke* [Cheif Justice][2] et *Stanford* diont que beins wayves sont ceux queux sont emblees et le felon en pursute pur daunger dapprehension fua et wayva les beins issint per luy prise feloniousment: ore si les officers le roy ou auters seignors sei[sont] eux come beins issint wayves devant lowner vient le propertie est ore ale a toutes jours de lowner et serra adjudge en les seignors que seisant come waiffes coment que il fist freshe suite si le fresh suite ne soit deins le view toutes dittes de le felon. Mes ils toutes agreont que si le felon ne fua mes est apprehend [*fol. 34v*] ovesque les beins issint emblees que ore lowner avera

[1] *Reads* ter[m]i[n]o.

[2] *A only*.

gives the lessees a general remedy against the grantees, and for the same reason lessors should have a like remedy by re-entry against them.

28. CHALLENGE FOR CAUSE

King's Bench, 1556/57.

Note that in the King's Bench, in trespass for breaking a close, the defendant pleaded Not guilty, and when the jury came to the bar the defendant challenged one of the said jurors before he was sworn, because he was previously one of the indictors of the said defendant in respect of the same trespass; and he prayed that he be withdrawn for this cause, and showed in court the record proving this (as he ought, and is bound to do by the law). And this was adjudged by the court a principal challenge. See Mich. 8 Hen. IV, tit. 'Challenge', 79, and Pas. 7 Edw. IV, in the same [title], 53.[1]

29. WAIFS

Serjeants' Inn, Chancery Lane, 1556/57.

Note that this question was debated at Serjeants' Inn in Chancery Lane: if someone steals cattle, or goods, and the owner of the stolen goods makes fresh suit after the felon for his goods, and to apprehend him, and the felon thereupon abandons ('waives') the goods for fear of apprehension and runs away, and before the owner arrives the king's officers (or others on behalf of their lords[2]) seize the goods so waived, and then the owner arrives and claims his goods, shall he have his goods back or shall they be forfeit? That was the question.

It was held by PORTMAN C.J. and SIR JOHN BAKER, knight,[3] that they are not forfeit inasmuch as the owner had done all his endeavour in making pursuit from vill to vill; and that no goods shall be [treated as] waived except where the property cannot be known, i.e. to whom they belong, so long as the owner does his [best] endeavour by fresh suit.

BROOKE C.J. and STAUNFORD said that waived goods are those which are stolen, and the felon under pursuit runs away for fear of apprehension and abandons the goods thus taken by him feloniously. If the officers of the king or of other lords seize them as goods so waived, before the owner arrives, the property is now gone from the owner for ever, and shall be adjudged in the lords who seize them as waifs, even though the owner made fresh suit, if the fresh suit is not at all times within sight of the felon.

They all agreed, however, that if the felon did not run away but is apprehended with the goods thus stolen, the owner shall here have his goods without ques-

1 Fitz. Abr., *Challenge*, pl. 79 (YB Mich. 8 Hen. IV, fo. 2, pl. 4) and pl. 53 (YB Pas. 7 Edw. IV, fo. 4, pl. 11).

2 I.e. lords having the franchise of waif.

3 Bencher of the Inner Temple; chancellor of the Exchequer; privy councillor; died 1558.

ses beins sans question. Ou si le owner chalenge ses beins devant le seiser de eux apres le fuer de le felon. Et *Brooke* did que lestatute 21 H. 8. ca. 11 ne remedy nul chose pur restitution des beins emblees mes sur levidence le partie ou per auters per son procurement en mesme le manner come fuit en appell sur fresh suite al common ley. Et vide H. 21 E. 4, t[itulo] Estrey 2, que si beins emblees ne sont seises lowner poet seiser et prender coment que ils sont waiffes per le felon coment que soit 20 ans apres mes apres le seisir des dittes beins per ascun officer le partie que ad le propertie nad ascun remedy pur les beins mes a suer appell et issint lowner avera ses beins per restitution sil fait freshe suite. Et issint sur levidence done sur endictment per le partie ou per auters per son procurement il avera restitution des beins coment que adevant ils fueront waiffes et ceo per lestatute avandit.

[30]

A, ff. 32v–33f; *L* 245f; *D*, fo. 22, pl. 3 (3 & 4 Phil. & Mar.).

Nota que 2 homes fueront endites sur lestatute de <3 H. 4. ca. 2>[1] pur ceo que ils preignont un tiel feme contrary a son volunte feloniousment contra le forme le dit statute et le corone le [royne][2] et que deux auters homes (les dittes 2 homes) scientes lour factes eux <receptont et confortant>.[3] Et coment per le dit statute toutes, auxibein principalls factours come ceux que procure ou abette le felon destre fait ou recept le dit feme issint preigne sciant le matter, sont toutes come principalls: uncore fuit agree per toute le court en Banke le Roy que <cest receiptment>[4] apres des les dittes felons et eux issint confortantes sont[5] forsque accessories per le comen ley et nemy principalls per lestatute entant que ils ne procure ou abbett le felony destre fait ne receiptont le feme issint preigne apres mes les persons le felons et issint hors de le dit statute destre principa[l]s. Mes serront accessories per le commen ley, quar lestatute fait eux principalls felons come felons al comen ley a que accessories serront. Come en le cas dun rape dun feme, cest felony per lestatute et si home apres receipt le ravisher scient son facte il sera dit accessory come sur un felony per le comen ley: quod nota. Mes fuit ajudge per toutes les justices de le dit Banke, entant que lenditement ne [*fol. 35*] mention que les 2 principalls le dit feme marieront contra son gree ou luy defloweront, que le dit endictment ne vault ryen et pur cest cause auxibein les

[1] *Struck through.*
[2] *A, D.* roy *H, L.*
[3] receptaverunt et confortaverunt *A, L.*
[4] le recever de eux *A, L.*
[5] ne fait eux *A, D, L.*

tion. Or if the owner claims his goods before the seizure of them, after the felon ran away.

BROOKE said that the statute 21 Hen. VIII, c. 11, does not give any remedy for restitution of stolen goods except upon the evidence of the party, or others by his procurement, in the same manner as in an appeal upon fresh suit at common law. And see this in Hil 21 Edw. IV, title 'Estrey', 2,[1] that if stolen goods are not seized the owner may seize and take them back, even though they have been waived by the felon, and even if it is twenty years later; but after the seizure of the said goods by any officer, the party who has the property has no remedy for the goods except to sue an appeal, and thereby the owner shall have his goods by restitution if he makes fresh suit; and likewise upon evidence given upon indictment by the party, or by others at his procurement, he shall have restitution of the goods even though they were previously waived: and that is by the aforesaid statute.[2]

30. R. v. THOMPSON and YEWLEY

King's Bench, Hil. 1557. Record: KB 27/1181, Rex m. 10 (judgment of discharge, 21 Jan. 1557); printed below. Cited in 3 Co. Inst. 61, 72 ('3 & 4 Ph. & Mar. Justice Dalison's report'); Hob. 182 (from the record); cf. 12 Co. Rep. 20–21.

Note that two men were indicted upon the statute[3] for that they feloniously took a certain woman against her will, against the form of the said statute and against the king's crown, and that two other men received and comforted the said two men, knowing of their deeds. And although by the said statute both the principal doers and those who procure or abet the felony to be done, or receive the woman so taken, knowing the facts, are all [treated] as principals, it was nevertheless agreed by the whole court in the King's Bench that this receiving afterwards of the two felons and so comforting them makes them only accessories by the common law and not principals by the statute, since they did not procure or abet the felony to be done or receive the woman so taken afterwards, but only received the persons of the felons, and so they are outside the said statute with respect to being principals: but they shall be accessories by the common law, for the statute makes them principal felons like felons at common law, to whom there shall be accessories – as in the case of a rape of a woman, that is a felony by statute, and yet if someone afterwards receives the rapist, knowing what he has done, he shall be called an accessory as upon a felony by the common law.[4] Note that. But it was adjudged by all the justices of the said bench that, since the indictment did not mention that the two principals [caused] the said woman to marry against her will, or deflowered her, the indictment was invalid: and for

[1] Fitz. Abr., *Estrey*. pl. 2 (YB Hil. 21 Edw. IV, fo. 16, pl. 7).

[2] 21 Hen. VIII, c. 11.

[3] 3 Hen. VII, c. 2. For other prosecutions on the statute see *R.* v. *Polley and others* (1557) KB 29/109, m. 40d (acquitted); *Tichborne* v. *Eyre* (1558) 110 Selden Soc. 22 (in the Star Chamber); *OHLE*, vi. 621.

[4] Cf. above, p. 34, pl. 38.

principalls come les dittes accessories fueront acquites et discharges per curiam sans auter chose faire et le dit endictment adjudge male. Et coment que le preamble de le dit statute parle de mariage ou deflower, uncore lacte ne parle issint largement mes <que>[1] entant que le acte parle que tiel person ou persons que issint preigne ascun feme etc. serront dittes felons cest paroll (issint) avera relation et entendment accordant al prise en le preamble et ceo est a prender et marier ou deflower.

Record of the case

KB 27/1181, Rex m. 10.

Northr' comitatus Ebor' per indictamentum Mich. tercio et quarto Philippi et Marie. Alias scilicet die Lune videlicet vicesimo die Julii annis regnorum Philippi et Marie dei gracia regis et regine Anglie, Hispaniarum, Francie, utriusque Cicilie, Jerusalem et Hibernie, fidei defensorum, archiducum Austrie, ducum Burgundie, Mediolani et Brabantie, comitum Haspurgie, Flandrie et Tirollis, secundo et quarto, apud Northalverton in Northr' comitatus Ebor' predicti coram Roberto Maynell serviente ad legem, Jacobo Foxe, Roberto Tristram et Christofero Lepton, armigeris, custodibus pacis ac justiciariis domini regis et domine regine ad pacem ac ad diversa felonias, transgressiones et alia malefacta in Northr' comitatus predicti illata audienda et terminanda assignatis, per sacramentum xij juratorum extitit presentatum quod cum in statuto in parliamento domini Henrici septimi nuper regis Anglie progenitoris domine regine nunc anno regni sui tercio inter cetera ordinatum et statutum existit quod cum diverse femine tam virgines, vidue quam marite substanciam habentes in bonis et catallis, terris et tenementis, aut existentes heredes apparentes suis antecessoribus, sepe per malefactores contra voluntates suas capientur et abducentur et preteria marietentur eisdem malefactoribus vel aliis per eorum assensum vel rapientur in gravem offensionem majestatis divine et disparagationem earundem feminarum, ideo ordinatum est quod hujusmodi captiones imposterum judicentur pro[i] felonia et quod hujusmodi captores, malefactores, procuratores et receptores scientes offensionem predictam judicentur et reputentur felones principales, prout in eodem statuto plenius continetur, quidem tamen Rogerus Thomson de Allerston in Northr' comitatus predicti yoman et Petrus Yewley de eadem in eodem comitatu yoman, statutum predictum minime ponderantes, nec penam in eodem statuto contentam[i] verentes, vi et armis vicesimo die Marcii annis regnorum dictorum dominorum regis et regine nunc[i] secundo et tercio Margaretam Burton et Margeriam Burton, filias et heredes Rogeri Burton defuncti, contra voluntates suas felonice ceperunt, cariaverunt et abduxerunt contra formam statuti predicti et contra pacem dictorum domini regis et domine regine ac si[2] Stephanus Holforth de Allerston predicta in Northr' comitatus predicti generosus, sciens predictos Rogerus et Petrum feloniam predictam fecisse, apud Allerston predictam predictos Rogerum et Petrum die et anno supradictis felonice abbettavit et receptavit contra pacem dictorum dominorum regis et regine, coronam et dignitatem suas etc.

Quodquidem indictamentum dominus rex et domina regina nunc coram eis postea certis de causis venire fecerunt terminandum etc. — Per quod preceptum fuit vicecomiti quod non omitteret etc. quin caperet eos si etc. — Et modo, scilicet die Jovis proxime

[1] *Sic but otiose. Om. A.*

[2] *Sic, but seemingly otiose.*

that reason both the principals and the said accessories were acquitted and discharged by the court without more ado, and the said indictment was adjudged bad. Although the preamble to the said statute speaks of marriage or deflowering, nevertheless the act does not speak so broadly; but since the act says that a person or persons who 'so' take any woman etc. shall be called felons, and this word 'so' shall have reference and interpretation according to the terms of the preamble, and this must mean to take and marry or deflower.

Translation of the record

King's Bench, Hilary term 1557.

North Riding of Yorkshire, by indictment of Michaelmas 3 & 4 Phil. & Mar. Heretofore, namely on Monday 20 July [1556] in the second and fourth years of the reigns of Philip and Mary, by the grace of God king and queen of England, Spain, France, both Sicilies, Jerusalem and Ireland, defenders of the faith, archdukes of Austria, dukes of Burgundy, Milan and Brabant, counts of Hapsburg, Flanders and Tyrol, at Northallerton in the North Riding of Yorkshire aforesaid, before Robert Maynell, serjeant at law, James Foxe, Robert Tristram and Christopher Lepton, esquires, keepers of the peace and justices of the lord king and lady queen assigned to [keep] the peace and to hear and determine the various felonies, trespasses and other misdeeds committed in the North Riding of the county aforesaid, it was presented by the oath of twelve jurors that, whereas in the statute in the parliament of the lord Henry the Seventh, late king of England, forebear of the present lady queen, in the third year of his reign,[1] it was ordained and laid down amongst other things that, whereas various women, as well maidens, widows and wives, having substance in goods and chattels, lands and tenements, or being heirs apparent to their ancestors, are often taken and abducted by misdoers against their will and afterwards married to the same misdoers, or to others by their assent, or [defoiled],[2] to the grave displeasure of the divine majesty and in disparagement of the same women, it is therefore ordained that such takings shall hereafter be adjudged felony, and that such takers, misdoers, procurers and receivers, knowing of the offence aforesaid, shall be adjudged and reputed as principal felons, as is more fully contained in the same statute: nevertheless a certain Roger Thomson of Allerton in the North Riding of the aforesaid county, yeoman, and Peter Yewley of the same, in the same county, yeoman, little heeding the aforesaid statute, nor fearing the penalty contained in the same statute, with force and arms, on the twentieth day of March [1556] in the second and third years of the reigns of the said present lord king and queen, feloniously took, carried off and abducted Margaret Burton and Margery Burton, daughters and heirs of Roger Burton, deceased, against their wills, against the form of the aforesaid statute and against the peace of the said lord king and queen, and that Stephen Holforth gentlemann of Allerton aforesaid, in the North Riding of the aforesaid county, knowing the aforesaid Roger and Peter to have committed the aforesaid felony, at Allerton aforesaid feloniously abetted and received the aforesaid Roger and Peter on the day and year mentioned above, against the peace of the said lord king and queen, their crown and dignity etc.

This indictment the lord king and lady queen for certain reasons afterwards caused to come before them to be determined etc. — Therefore the sheriff was commanded to omit not etc. but take them if etc. — Now, namely on the Thursday [21 Jan. 1557] after the

[1] 3 Hen. VII, c. 2.

[2] So says the statute, meaning defouled or defiled (two different words which seem to have become confused); *rapire* (to snatch or ravish) is more ambiguous. The successful plea renders it as 'deflowered'. Cf. *NED*, defoul, v. 4.

post quindenam Sancti Hillarii isto eodem termino coram dominis rege et regina apud Westmonasterium venerunt predicti Rogerus Thomson, Petrus Yewley et Stephanus Holforth in propriis personis suis et reddiderunt se prisone marescalcie dominorum regis et regine coram ipsis rege et regina existente, qui committuntur marrescalli etc. Et statim de premissis eis et eorum cuilibet superius impositis allocuti qualiter se velint inde acquietari separatim[i] dicunt quod indictamentum predictum minus sufficiens in lege existit ad ponendum ipsos Rogerum, Petrum et Stephanum seu eorum aliquem eidem indictamento responsuros pro eo videlicet quod per indictamentum illud non fit mentio ubi, quo loco certo nec quo comitatu predicti Rogerus Thomson et Petrus Yewley ceperunt prefatam Margaretam Burton et Margeriam Burton seu earum alteram nec quod predicti Rogerus seu Petrus easdem Margaretam seu Margeriam aliquo tempore post hujusmodi captionem nuptierunt seu defloraverunt easdem Margaretam seu Margeriam aut earum alteram, prout per tenorem statuti predicti fore deberet: ideo pro insufficiencia ejusdem predicti Rogerus Thomson, Petrus Yewley et Stephanus Holforth petunt quod ipsi per curiam hic dimittantur et quod quilibet eorum de premissis per curiam hic dimittatur etc. Super quo, visis et per curiam hic intellectis omnibus et singulis premissis, consideratum est quod predicti Rogerus Thomson, Petrus Yewley at Stephanus Holforth eant inde sine die et eorum quilibet eat inde sine die etc.

[31]

A, fo. 33[f]; *L* 246[f].

Nota que home fuit trove armed en le Sale de Westm' en cest terme quant les justices le roy seiront[1] en lour liews fesant justice s. il fuit trove ove un [cote][2] de plate sur luy et covered ove un cloke et fuit prise et amesne maintenant devant le chauncellor et auters de le Counsell le Roy seiantes cest jour en le Starr Chamber, les chefe justices la esteantes presentes, et la sur le verities trove il fuit maintenant agard al Fleete pur son contempt et act avandit la a demurrer tanque son fyne fuit sur luy assesse. Et la fuit demaund de luy pur quel cause il fist issint en lopen sale esteant le liewe de justice et de peace et il respondera que il fist issint pur son savegard demesne quod nota.

[32]

A, fo. 33[f]; *L* 247[f]; *D*, fo. 23, pl. 6 (3 & 4 Phil. & Mar.).

Nota que un home fuit endite et arrayne pur ceo que il ferist un home en le Sale de Westm. et fuit trove culpable et fuit ajudge que ses beins et terres serront forfaites et que son mayn dexter serra decoupe: anno 41 E. 3, t[itulo] Coron 280. Quere que ley est [pur][3] forfayter ses terres mes poet estre que les proffittes des

[1] fueront seintes *A*. fueront seyants *L*.
[2] *A*. coate *L*. toge *H*.
[3] *A*, *D*.

quindene of Hilary this same term, before the lord king and lady queen at Westminster, the aforesaid Roger Thomson, Peter Yewley and Stephen Holforth came in their own persons and surrendered themselves to the prison of the Marshalsea of the lord king and lady queen being before them the said king and queen, and they were committed to the marshal etc. And, being forthwith asked concerning the foregoing matters above charged against them and each of them, how they would acquit themselves thereof, they say severally that the aforesaid indictment is insufficient in law to put them the said Roger, Peter and Stephen, or any of them, to answer to the same indictment, forasmuch as no mention is made in the indictment where, in what certain place or in what county, the aforesaid Roger Thomson and Peter Yewley took the said Margaret Burton and Margery Burton, or either of them, nor that the aforesaid Roger or Peter at any time after such taking married or deflowered the same Margaret or Margery or either of them, as by the tenor of the aforesaid statute there ought to have been: and therefore, for insufficiency of the same, the aforesaid Roger Thomson, Peter Yewley and Stephen Holforth pray that they may be dismissed by the court here, and that each of them may be dismissed by the court here concerning the foregoing etc. Whereupon, all and singular the foregoing having been looked into and understood by the court here, it is awarded that the aforesaid Roger Thomson, Peter Yewley and Stephen Holforth go therein without day, and that each of them go therein without day etc.

31. WEARING ARMOUR IN WESTMINSTER HALL

Star Chamber.

Note that a man was found armed in Westminster Hall this term, when the king's justices were sitting in their places doing justice, namely he was found with a [suit][1] of plate [armour] upon him, covered with a cloak; and he was taken and forthwith brought before the chancellor and others of the King's Council this day in the Star Chamber, the chief justices being there present, and there once the truth was found he was immediately awarded to the Fleet for his aforesaid contempt and act, there to remain until his fine was assessed upon him. And he was there asked why he did this in the open hall, being the place of justice and of peace, and he answered that he did so for his own safety.[2] Note that.

32. STRIKING IN WESTMINSTER HALL

Probably contd from pl. 31. Cf. Dyer, fo. 118; Staunford, *Plees del Coron* (1557), fo. 38; *OHLE*, vi. 590.

Note that someone was indicted and arraigned because he struck a man in Westminster Hall, and was found guilty, and it was adjudged that his goods and lands should be forfeited, and that his right hand should be cut off: 41 Edw. III, tit. 'Corone', 280.[3] Query by what law he should forfeit his lands: but it may be

[1] *A* says 'coat', but *H* says 'gown' (*toge*). It is not clear what is meant. Cf. 'coat of mail', above, p. 98.

[2] During Wyatt's rebellion in 1554 the judges and serjeants are said to have worn armour in court: J. Stow, *Annales* (1631), p. 619.

[3] Fitz. Abr., *Corone*, pl. 280 (41 Edw. III).

ses terres serront forfaites durant son vie. Vide lestatute 2 E. 3. ca. 3. que cestui que porte armor en presence des justices forfeitera larmor et serra imprison al volunt le roy.

[33]

[*fol. 35v*] Anthony Maii sua replegiare de ses avers vers John Melton et John Hamond et les dittes M[elton] et H[amond] come baylieffes al Jerome Maii, et John Maye font conusans per reason que un Innocente Maye fuit seisie des tenementes in queux le prisell est suppose etc. en son demesne come de fee et ent morust seisie et pur ceo que les tenementes sont et de temps dont etc. ont estre de la nature et tenure de gravelkind deins le countie de Kent les dittes tenementes discendont as dittes Jerom et John Maye come all fitz et heire le dit Innocent per consuetudinem predictam per force de quel les dittes Jerom et Johen enteront et fueront ent seisies en fee et pur damage fesant les dittes bailiefs font cognisaunce come en droit les dittes Jerome et John et hoc etc. Et le dit Antony en barre de le dit avowrie dit que long temps devant un John Maye le [senior][1] fuit seisie des tenementes en fee et ent fait feofment al John Scott et William Fynch en fee al use le dit John le senior en fee et puis le dit John senior en escript declare son volunte des tenementes avaundittes et voet que ses feoffees sufferont le dit John senior doccupier les dittes tenementes duront son vie et ouster voet que Robert son fitz et Elizabeth son feme averont les dittes tenementes duront lour vies remanere inde proximo heredi masculo de corporibus predictorum Roberti et Elizabethe legittime procreato imperpetuum. Et puis le dit John Maii leigne morust apres quel le dittes Robert Maii et Elizabeth aiant yssue male enter eux le dit Innocent leigne fitz et le dit Anthony et [Jasper][2] May enteront en les dittes tenementes et morust et le dit Innocent entra en toutes les dittes tenementes et fuit ent seisie de le 3 parte de eux en son demeasne come de fee tail

[1] *Reads* seisor.
[2] *Reads* Jeper.

that the profits of his lands shall be forfeited during his lifetime.[1] See the statute of 2 Edw. III, c. 3, that he who wears armour in the presence of the justices shall forfeit the armour and be imprisoned at the king's will.

[Michaelmas term, 1556][2]

33. MAYE v. MYLTON and HAMON

King's Bench, Mich. 1556. Also reported, sub nom. *May* v. *Milton and another*, in Dyer, fo. 133 (argued Trin. and Mich. 1556); printed below. Record: KB 27/1171, m. 119 (demurrer, Trin. 1554; c.a.v. to Pas. 1557); printed below.

Anthony May sued a replevin for his cattle against John Melton and John Hamond, and the said Melton and Hamond made acknowledgement as bailiffs of Jerome May and John May by reason that one Innocent May was seised of the tenements in which the taking is supposed etc. in his demesne as of fee, and died seised thereof, and because the tenements are and from time immemorial have been of the nature and tenure of gavelkind within the county of Kent, the said tenements descended to the said Jerome and John May as sons and heir of the said Innocent by the custom aforesaid, by virtue whereof the said Jerome and John entered and were thereof seised in fee, and the said plaintiffs made acknowledgment for damage feasant as in right of the said Jerome and John, and this [they are ready to aver] etc. The said Anthony, in bar of the said avowry, said that long before then one John May the elder was seised of the tenements in fee and made a feoffment thereof to John Scott and [Henry] Fynch in fee, to the use of the said John the elder, in fee, and then the said John the elder declared in writing his will of the aforementioned tenements, and willed that his feoffees should suffer the said John the elder to occupy the said tenement during his lifetime, and further willed that Robert his son and Elizabeth his [i.e. Robert's] wife should [thereafter] have the said tenements during their lives, remainder to the next heir male lawfully begotten on the bodies of the aforesaid Robert and Elizabeth, for ever; and then the said John May the elder died, after which the said Robert May and Elizabeth had issue male between them the

[1] Rowe, editor of the 1689 edition of *D*, comments on this (preface, sig. aa): 'I find here one *Quere* agreeing with the like in another Manuscript of great Antiquity and Authority, the question being, by what law a man should forfeit his lands for striking in the presence of the Justices, the Book of 19 E. 3. F. *Judgment* 174, is that the Law is so . . . But in a fair Volume which I have in Manuscript, of several years of Edw. 3. not printed, are Subjoyned in the end of the Report of that Case, these words . . . *Quere de Forfeiture de terres in hoc Casu, &c.* And in the Note taken from the Record by *Rolle*, it appears to have been no part of the Judgment, and that that is the very same Case appears by the Manuscript, where *N. de Cardoill, &c.* are said to be the parties Indicted.'

[2] It is not clear exactly where this term begins. The following case is dated Mich. 1556 in Dyer; but pl. 30 on p. 109 seems to belong to Hil. 1557.

per force de le dit volunt et des auters deux partes en son demeasne come de fee per intrusion et puis morust issint seisie apres quel morte les tenementes descendont al dit Jerome et John come fittz et heire le dit Innocent per le dit custome per que ils s. Jerome et John enteront et fueront ent seisies de le 3. parte en taile et de les 2 partes en fee per intrusion. Et le dit Anthony en son droit et en droit son frere Jasper May entra en 2 partes des tenementes in 3 partes destre devides et les dittes Anthony et Jasper fueront ent seisies en coparcinerie et pro indiviso ove les dittes Jerome et John. Et le dit Anthony mitta eins ses avers come bein luy list en les dittes John Melton et John Hamond a tort eux prist quel matter [*fol. 36*] etc. et pria ses damages et sur cest le partie demurre en jugement. Et divers questions fueront moves sur cest mattter.

Pri[m]erment si le playntiefe doit travers le morant seisie des toutes les dittes tenementes le dit Innocent en fee modo et forma. Si le barre al avowrie soit bon pur ceo que il dit que les dittes Jerome et John puis le morte Innocent May lour pier fueront seisies de 3 parte en taile et de 2 partes en fee per intrusion. Et fuit tenus per toutes les justices que ne besoigne ascun travers quar il est sufficient[ment] confes et avoid et le travers ne [ferra][1] fyne a toute le matter et oustre si le travers serra le matter en ley serra waiffe. Et quant al intrusion fuit tenus que il fuit bon auxi per toutes les justices de Bancke de Roy forsque *Dallison* entant que entrusion et abatement sont toute un en effecte et nul difference mes ex vi termini. Mes *Dallison* dit que entrusion est toutes temps apres le morte dun tenant pur vie quant un estranger de son torte entre, ceo est proprement instrustion quar il intruda sur le possession en fee de cestui en le reversion come [lheire][2] esteant en gard entruda sans gree ove le seignor pur son mariage ceo est proprement instrusion. Et abatement est toutes dittes lou un entra a tort en liew [lheire][3] apres le mort son auncester lou [lheire][4] nad actual possession adevante.

Si soit un estate taile joyne en Robert May et Elizabeth son feme et si le remainder issera a toutes les fittz s. al Innocent, Anthony et Jasper, ou al dit Innocent et ses heires tantum? Et fuit clerement agree per *Whiddon* et *Portman* Cheife Justice que toutes les trois fittz averont le terre. Et le reason de *Portman* fuit que entant que le volunt fuit que le remainder serra a lour prochein heire male etc. imperpetuum que per cest volunt ils toutes esteantes heires males per le costome averont le terre, quar un nest heire nient pluis que auter, et entant que il dit proximo heredi masculo en le singuler nomber ne poet faire estate en taile, mes entant que il dit apres imperpetuum cest per le volunte fist un fee simple per lentent le volunt: et donques est tout un come [si] il ad dit le remainder al droit heires le dit Robert et Elizabeth, quar il dit que proximo heredi per discent et nemy come purchasor en remainder, quar per cest generall paroll le remainder as ses droit heires il nad fee a graunter et a charger les terres et le heir le tenant pur vie en cest case paiera reliefe et serra en gard come heire a [*fol. 36v*] son pier. Mes en

1 *Reads* serra.
2 *Reads* leiher.
3 *Reads* liere.
4 *Reads* leiher.

said Innocent (the eldest son) and the said Anthony and Jasper May, [and they] entered in the said tenements, and died, and the said Innocent entered in all the said tenements and was seised thereof, of the third part in his demesne as of fee tail by virtue of this said will, and of the other two parts in his demesne as of fee by intrusion, and then died so seised, after whose death the tenements descended to the same Jerome and John as sons and heir of the said Innocent by the said custom, whereby they (namely Jerome and John) entered and were seised thereof, of the third part in tail and of the two thirds in fee by intrusion; and the said Anthony, in his own right and in right of his brother Jasper May, entered into two thirds of the tenements, and the said Anthony and Jasper were seised thereof in coparcenary and in undivided shares (*pro indiviso*) together with the said Jerome and John; and the said Anthony put in his cattle, as he was fully entitled to do, and the said John Melton and John Hamond wrongfully took them: which matter [he is ready to aver] etc.; and he prayed his damages. And upon this the parties demurred in judgment. Various questions were moved upon this matter.

Firstly, whether the plaintiff ought to traverse the said Innocent's dying seised of all the said tenements in the manner and form alleged, [and] whether the bar to the avowry is good, in that he says that the said Jerome and John after the death of their father Innocent May were seised of the third part in tail and of the two parts in fee by intrusion. And it was held by all the justices that there is no need for any traverse, for it is sufficiently confessed and avoided, and a traverse would not make an end of the whole matter, and moreover if there was a traverse the matter in law would be waived. As to the intrusion, it was held that that was good also, by all the justices of the King's Bench except DALISON, inasmuch as intrusion and abatement are all one in effect and there is no difference except in name. But DALISON said that intrusion is always after the death of a tenant for life, when a stranger of his wrong enters: this is properly intrusion, for he intrudes upon the possession in fee of the reversioner; for instance if the heir (being in ward) intrudes without settling with the lord for his marriage, this is properly intrusion. Abatement is always where someone enters wrongfully in place of the heir after his ancestor's death, where the heir had no actual possession previously.

[2.] Was there an estate tail jointly in Robert May and Elizabeth his wife, and should the remainder go to all the sons, namely to Innocent, Anthony and Jasper, or only to the said Innocent and his heirs? And it was clearly held by WHIDDON and PORTMAN C.J. that all three sons should have the land. PORTMAN's reason was that, since the will was that the remainder should be to the next heir male etc. for ever, by this will all of them (being heirs male by the custom) should have the land, for one is no more heir than another. Although he said 'to the next heir male', in the singular number, this cannot make an estate tail; but because he afterwards said 'for ever', this makes a fee simple, by the intention of the will, and therefore it is all one as if he had said, remainder to the right heirs of the said Robert and Elizabeth; for he said, 'to the next heir' by descent, and not as purchaser in remainder, for by these general words 'remainder to the right heirs' he has no fee to grant and to charge the lands, and the heir of the mesme le liver est agree que si le remainder ust estre specialment, come a John son fittz, que donques John le fittz avera le terre come purchasor per le remainder et ne ferra relief ne serra en gard, quia specialis limitatio. Yssint est en le cas al barre, per cest paroll proximo heredi masculo imperpetuum. Et auxi les voluntes et testamentes des homes serront toutes dittes prises beneficiall accordant a lour voluntes, et avera pluis beneficial construction a son entent que poet aver per la ley. Et pur ceo en le dit liver T. 9 H. [6],[1] fo. 23, en le case Farrington, il est agree que si home devisa terres a un muncke ou frier en religion pur son vie, le remainder ouster en fee ou en taile, que le remainder prist effect maintenant per voy de done. Auterment est dun done ou graunt. Et si terres sont devises al un home apres le morte son feme, en fee, le devisor avera la terre pur son vie per son volunte et devise per son entent. Auterment est dun done ou graunt. Si terre soit devise al un home et a ses assignes ou imperpetuum le devisee avera estate en fee per ceux parolls quia sont entent. 22 E. 3, t[itulo] Devise 20. Et issint si terre soit devise al un home et a ses heires males de son corps, le devisee ad issue fittz, cest fittz avera la terre per cest volunt per son entent de son volunt: et issint est loppinion des toutes les justices. T. 28 H. 6, t[itulo] Devise 18. Auterment est en les cases avauntdittes dun done ou graunt per feofment ou per auter assurance en la ley. Yssint ycie lentent le volunt fuit que son prochein heire male et ses heires avera la terre et leigne est prochein heire male. Et si toutes les fittz averont le terre ceo serra contrarie a son volunt et entent quar donques il voet aver dit a ses prochein heires males en le plurall nomber mes ycie il parle en le singuler nomber prochein heir male mes si le remainder ust estre a son prochein heire ou a son heire auterment serra quar cest paroll (heire) ymplia un generalitie s. heires. Et si le remainder ust estre a son prochein heire female semble que leigne file female avera la terre coment que il ad deux files quar el est prochein heire female. Et auxi en cest case al barre est pluis forte quar leigne fittz est heire al comen ley et les auters per le custome quar toutes [lheires][2] femalls enteront pur condition enfreint come heires ensemble. Mes toutes [*fol. 37*] lheires males per le costome de gavelkind ne enteront pas pur condition enfreint come heires a lour auncestor, mes leigne tantum, ne le puisne fittz come heire in borough-englishe ne entra pas pur un condition enfreint come heire, mes leigne fittz pur luy, coment que leheires males en gavelkind et le puisne fittz en borough englishe averont attaint ou breife derror dun judgement done vers lour auncestor quar ceo va ove terre daver restitution de ceo. 3 H. 4. agree pur le breife derror

[1] *Reads* 8.
[2] *Reads* leiheires.

tenant for life in this case shall pay relief and shall be in ward as heir to his father [. . .]

[To the contrary:][1] But in the same book it is agreed that if the remainder had been [limited] specially, as for instance to John his son, then John the son would have the land as purchaser by the remainder and would not pay relief or be in ward, because it is a special limitation (*quia specialis limitatio*). So it is in the case at bar, by reason of these words 'to the next heirs male for ever'. Moreover, men's wills and testaments shall always be understood by as beneficial a construction, according to their intention, as they can have by law. Therefore in the said[2] book Trin. 9 Hen. [VI], fo. 23, in *Farrington's Case*, it is agreed that if someone devises lands to a monk or friar in religion, for his life, remainder over in fee or in tail, the remainder takes effect immediately by way of gift. It is otherwise of a gift or grant. If lands are devised to someone after his wife's death, in fee, the devisor shall have the land for his life, by his will and devise according to its intention; but it is otherwise of a gift or grant. If land is devised to someone 'and his assigns', or 'for ever', the devisee shall have an estate in fee by these words, because they make [clear] the intention. 22 Edw. III, tit. 'Devise', 20.[3] Likewise if land is devised to someone and his heirs male of his body, and the devisee has issue a son, this son shall have the land by this will, by the intention of his will. That was the opinion of all the justices in Trin. 28 Hen. VI, tit. 'Devise', 18.[4] It is otherwise in the cases aforesaid of a gift or grant by feoffment or by other assurance in the law. Likewise here, the intention of the will was that his next heir male and his heirs should have the land, and the eldest is next heir male; and if all the sons should have the land it would be contrary to his will and intention, for then he would have said 'to his next heirs male', in the plural number, whereas here he speaks in the singular number, 'next heir male'. It would be otherwise, however, if the remainder had been to his next heir, or to his heir, for the word 'heir' implies a generality – namely, 'heirs'. And if the remainder had been to the next heir female, it seems that the eldest female heir should have had the land, even if there were two daughters, for she is next heir female. Moreover, in this case at the bar it is stronger, because the eldest son is heir at the common law, and the others by the custom, for all the heirs female would enter together as heir for breach of condition, whereas by the custom of gavelkind all the heirs male would not enter for breach of condition, as heirs to their ancestor, but only the eldest. Nor shall the youngest heir in borough English enter for breach of condition, as heir, but the eldest son for him, even though the heirs male in gavelkind and the youngest son in borough English shall have attaint or writ of error upon a judgment given against their ancestor, for it goes with the land to have restitution

1 Evidently something has been omitted, because the text here does not make perfect sense; and what follows seems to be a dissent from Portman C.J. and Whiddon J. The reference is presumably to *Farrington's Case*, mentioned below.

2 Again, this indicates that something has been omitted.

3 Fitz. Abr., *Devise*, pl. 20 (YB Mich. 22 Edw. III, fo. 16, pl. 59).

4 Fitz. Abr., *Devise*, pl. 18 (Trin. 28 Hen. VI).

ou atteint. Et auxi il appiert M. 11 E. 3, t[itulo] Debt 7, que un breife de debt port vers leigne fittz en gavelkind come heire a son auncestor sur obligation son auncestor lou fueront 3 fittz et teneont en coparceneryе fuit abate entant que toutes ne fueront en le breife, mes ceo fuit pur cause que le possession est chargeable al debt que charge eux toutes come heires. Mes semble per le liver que si les 2 fittz ent vendont le terre devant le breife purchase pur lour partes que leigne serra tout charge et nosme en le breife per son parte de le terre de tout le debt.

Dyer's report of the case

Les Reports (1688 ed.), fo. 133b, pl. 5 (omitting addition at end).

Home seisie de terre in Gavelkind in fee, per son darrein volunt in script, devise ceo al baron et sa feme pur terme de lour vies, le remainder inde proximo haeredi masculo de corporibus suis legitime procreato imperpetuum. Et puis le baron et feme ont issue iij fils et devyont, si leigne fits avera lentier remainder, ou en common ove ses freres fuit demurre in ley in Banco Regis. Et argue hoc termino et ultimo termino per divers.

Record of the case

KB 27/1171, m. 119.

Kantia. Johannes Mylton et Johannes Hamon summoniti fuerunt ad respondendum Anthonio Maye de placito quare ceperunt avera ipsius Anthonii contra vadium et plegios quousque etc. Et unde idem Anthonius per Johannem Webbe attornatum suum queritur quod predicti Johannes Mylton et Johannes Hamon vicesimo die Maii anno regni domini Edwardi sexti nuper Regis Anglie septimo apud Kennyngton in comitatu predicto in quodam loco vocato Bybroke ceperunt avera videlicet duos spadones ipsius Anthonii et ea injuste detinuerunt contra vadium et plegios quousque etc. Unde dicit quod deterioratus est et dampnum habet ad valenciam decem librarum. Et inde producit sectam etc.

Et predicti Johannes Mylton et Johannes Hamon per Johannem Barowe attornatum suum veniunt et defendunt vim et injuriam quando etc., omnem captionem et quicquid etc. et ut ballivi Jeronimi Maye et Johannis Maye bene cognoscunt captionem averiorum predictorum in predicto loco in quo etc. Et juste etc. quia dicunt quod locus in quo supponitur captionem averiorum predictorum fieri continet et predicto tempore captionis averiorum illorum fieri supposite continebat quatuor acras terre in Kennyngton predicta unde diu ante predictum tempus quo etc. quidam Innocentius Maye pater predictorum Jeronimi et Johannis Maye fuit seisitus in dominico suo ut de feodo, ipsoque Innocentio sic inde[i] seisito existente idem Innocentius obiit inde seisitus, post cujus quidem Innocentii mortem tenementa predicta cum pertinenciis, eo quod eadem tenementa cum pertinenciis sunt et a tempore cujus contrarii memoria hominum non existit fuerunt de natura <et tenura>[i] de gavelkind in predicto comitatu Kantie quodque omnia terre et tenementa in eodem comitatu earundem nature et tenure <sunt et>[i] <pro toto tempore predicto>[1] fuerunt partita et partitabilia inter heredes masculos, discendebant prefatis Jeronimo et Johanni ut filiis et hered' predicti Innocentii secundum consuetudinem predictam, per quod idem Jeronimus et Johannes in tenementa illa cum pertinenciis intraverunt et fuerunt inde seisiti in dominico suo ut de feodo, ipsisque Jeronimo et Johanne de tenementis il-

1 *Apparently altered from:* per totum tempus predictum.

thereof. (3 Hen. IV agrees,[1] as to the writ of error or attaint.) Also, it appears in Mich. 11 Edw. III, tit. 'Debt', 7,[2] that a writ of debt brought against the eldest son in gavelkind, as heir to his ancestor, upon his ancestor's bond, where there were three sons who held in coparcenary, should abate, inasmuch as they were not all in the writ. But that was because the possession is chargeable to the debt, which charges them all as heirs. It seems from the book, however, that if the two sons had sold their shares in the land before the writ obtained, the eldest would have been wholly charged (and named in the writ for his part of the land), with the whole debt.

Translation of Dyer's report

Michaelmas term 1556.

A man seised of gavelkind land in fee, by his last will in writing devised it to a husband and his wife for term of their lives, the remainder thereof 'to the next heir male of their bodies lawfully begotten, for ever'. Then the huband and wife had issue three sons and died. And it was demurred in the King's Bench whether the eldest son should have the entire remainder, or in common with his brothers. It was argued this term, and last term, by several.

Translation of the record

King's Bench roll, Trinity term 1554.

Kent. John Mylton and John Hamon were summoned to answer Anthony Maye concerning a plea why they took the beasts of the selfsame Anthony against gage and pledges until etc. And thereupon the same Anthony, by John Webbe his attorney, complains that the aforesaid John Mylton and John Hamon on the twentieth day of May [1553] in the seventh year of the reign of the lord Edward the sixth, late king of England, at Kennington in the county aforesaid in a certain place called Bybroke, took the beasts of the selfsame Anthony, namely two geldings, and unjustly withheld them against gage and pledges until etc., whereby he says he is the worse and has suffered damage to the extent of ten pounds. And thereof he brings suit etc.

And the aforesaid John Mylton and John Hamon, by John Barowe their attorney, come and deny the force and wrong when etc., the whole taking and whatever etc., and as bailiffs of Jerome Maye and John Maye fully acknowledge the taking of the aforesaid beasts in the aforesaid place in which etc. And justly etc., because they say that the place in which the taking of the aforesaid beasts is supposed to have been done contains, and at the aforesaid time when the taking of the beasts is supposed to have been done contained, four acres of land in Kennington aforesaid, whereof long before the said time when etc. a certain Innocent Maye (father of the aforesaid Jerome and John Maye) was seised in his demesne as of fee; and while he the said Innocent was thus seised thereof, the same Innocent died seised thereof; and after the death of the same Innocent, because the same tenements with the appurtenances are and from time whereof the memory of men is not to the contrary have been of the nature and tenure of gavelkind in the aforesaid county of Kent, and since lands and tenements in the same county of the same nature and tenure are and throughout the aforesaid time have been parted and partible among heirs male, the aforesaid tenements with the appurtenances descended to the said Jerome and John as sons and heirs of the aforesaid Innocent according to the custom aforesaid, as a result of which the same

1 YB Trin. 3 Hen. IV, fo. 19, pl. 4.
2 Fitz. Abr., *Debt*, pl. 7 (Mich. 11 Edw. III).

lis cum pertinenciis sic inde seisitis existentibus predicti Johannes Mylton et Johannes Hamon quia predicto tempore quo etc. invenerunt averia predicta in predicto loco in quo etc. herbam ipsorum Jeronimi et Johannis Maye tunc ibidem crescentem <depascentia et dampnum ibidem facientia iidem Johannes Mylton et Johannes Hamond ut ballivi ipsorum Jeronimi et Johannis Maye>[i] averia illa pro dampnis sic per ea ibidem factis ceperunt et illa imparcaverunt prout eis bene licuit. Et hoc parati sunt verificare. Unde petunt judicium et retornum averiorum predictorum una cum dampnis, misis et expensis suis per ipsos circa sectam suam in hac parte appositis juxta formam statuti in hujusmodi casu nuper[i] editi et provisi eis adjudicari etc.

Et predictus Anthonius Maye dicit quod predicti Johannes Mylton et Johannes Hamon per aliqua preallegata captionem averiorum predictorum in predicto loco in quo captio averiorum illorum facta fuit justam cognoscere non debent, quia dicit quod diu ante predictum tempus captionis averiorum predictorum facte et diu antequam predictus Innocentius Maye in cognitione predicta superius nominatus aliquid habuit in tenementis predictis cum pertinenciis quidam Johannes Maye senior[i] fuit seisitus de tenementis illis cum pertinenciis inter alia in dominico suo ut de feodo, ipsoque Johanne Maye sic inde seisito existente idem Johannes Maye diu ante predictum tempus captionis averiorum predictorum facte de tenementis illis cum pertinenciis inter alia feoffavit quosdam Edwardum Ponyng' militem, Willelmum Scott militem, Johannem Scott militem et Henricum Fynche armigerum habendum eis et heredibus suis imperpetuum ad usum predicti Johannis Maye senioris et heredum suorum[1] virtute cujus quidem feoffamenti iidem Edwardus Ponyng', Willelmus Scott, Johannes Scott[i] et Henricus Fynche fuerunt seisiti de tenementis predictis cum pertinenciis inter alia in dominico suo ut de feodo ad usum supradictum,[2] ipsisque Edwardo, Willelmo, Johanne Scott et Henrico de tenementis illis cum pertinenciis <ad usum illum>[i] sic seisitis existentibus[3] idem Johannes Maye senior[i] apud Kenyngton in comitatu predicto de tenementis illis cum pertinenciis unde etc. fecit et declaravit ultimam voluntatem suam in scriptis et per eandem voluit quod feoffati sui predicti paterent eundem Johannem Maye seniorem[i] habere, tenere et occupare tenementa predicta cum pertinenciis durante tota vita sua, et idem Johannes Maye senior[i] per eandem voluntatem suam ulterius voluit quod Robertus May filius <ejusdem Johannis May senioris per nomen Roberti May filii sui, qui quidem Robertus>[i] May fuit pater predicti Innocentii ac avus predictorum Jeronimi et Johannis Maye in recognitione predicta nominatorum,>[i] et Elizabeth uxor ejusdem Roberti Maye[i] tenerent, haberent, occuparent et gauderent tenementa predicta cum pertinenciis unde predictus locus in quo captio averiorum predictorum facta fuit est et predicto tempore factionis et declarationis predicte ultime voluntatis et predicto tempore captionis averiorum predictorum facte fuit parcella pro termino vitarum suarum remanere inde proximo heredi masculo de corporibus predictorum Roberti et Elizabeth legittime procreato imperpetuum, et postea <prefatis Edwardo Poynynges, Willelmo Scott, Johanne Scotte et Henrico Fynche ad usum predictum de tenementis predictis cum pertinenciis sic seisitis existentibus>[i] predictus Johannes Maye senior[i] apud Kennyngton predictam obiit, post cujus quidem Johannis Maye senioris[i] mortem predicti Edwardus Ponyng', Willelmus Scott, Johannes Scott et Henricus Fynche fuerunt seisiti de tenementis predictis cum pertinenciis unde etc. in dominico suo ut de feodo ad usum predictorum Roberti et Elizabeth et <prox' hered' mascul'>[4] de corporibus eorundem Roberti et Elizabeth legittime procreatorum[5] imperpetuum secundum voluntatem predictam, ipsisque Edwardo, Willelmo,

1 *Almost a whole line is here erased.*
2 *Several words following are erased.*
3 *Several words following are erased.*
4 *Apparently altered from:* proximi heredis masculi.
5 *Sic.*

Jerome and John entered into the tenements and were seised thereof in their demesne as of fee; and, while they the said Jerome and John were thus seised of the tenements with the appurtenances, the aforesaid John Mylton and John Hamon, as bailiffs of them the said Jerome and John Maye, forasmuch as at the said them when etc. they found the aforesaid beasts in the aforesaid place in which etc. depasturing the grass of them the said Jerome and John Maye and causing damage there, took and impounded the beasts for damage feasant by them there, as they were fully entitled to do. And this they are ready to aver. Therefore they pray judgment, and return of the aforesaid beasts to be awarded to them, together with their damages, outlay and expenses laid out by them about their suit in this behalf, in accordance with the statute[1] lately made and provided for such cases etc.

And the aforesaid Anthony Maye says that the aforesaid John Mylton and John Hamon ought not by reason of anything previously alleged to acknowledge as just the taking of the aforesaid beasts in the aforesaid place in which the taking of the beasts was made, because he says that long before the aforesaid time of the taking of the aforesaid beasts, and long before the aforesaid Innocent Maye (named in the aforesaid acknowledgment) had anything in the aforesaid tenements with the appurtenances, a certain John Maye the elder was seised amongst other things of the tenements with the appurtenances in his demesne as of fee; and while the selfsame John Maye was thus seised the same John Maye, long before the aforesaid time of the taking of the aforesaid beasts, enfeoffed a certain Edward Ponynges, knight, William Scott, knight, John Scott, knight, and Henry Fynche, esquire, of the selfsame tenements with the appurtenances, to have unto them and their heirs for ever to the use of the aforesaid John Maye the elder and his heirs, by virtue of which feoffment the same Edward Ponynges, William Scott, John Scott and Henry Fynche were seised amongst other things of the tenements aforesaid with the appurtenances in their demesne as of fee to the above-mentioned use; and while they the said Edward, William, John Scott and Henry were thus seised of those tenements to that use, the same John Maye the elder at Kennington in the county aforesaid made and declared his last will in writing concerning those tenements with the appurtenances whereof etc., and by the same willed that his aforesaid feoffees should suffer the same John Maye the elder to have, hold and occupy the aforesaid tenements with the appurtenances during his whole life; and the same John Maye the elder by his same will further willed that Robert Maye, son of the same John Maye the elder, by the name of Robert Maye his son (which Robert Maye was father of the aforesaid Innocent and grandfather of the aforesaid Jerome Maye and John Maye named in the aforesaid acknowledgment), and Elizabeth, wife of the same Robert Maye, should hold, have, occupy and enjoy the aforesaid tenements with the appurtenances, whereof the aforesaid place in which the taking of the aforesaid beasts was made is parcel, and was at the time of the making and declaring of the aforesaid last will and at the aforesaid time of the taking of the aforesaid beasts, for term of their lives, remainder thereof to the next heir male of the bodies of the aforesaid Robert and Elizabeth lawfully begotten, for ever; and afterwards, while the said Edward Ponynges, William Scott, John Scott and Henry Fynche were thus seised of the aforesaid tenements with the appurtenances to the aforesaid use, the aforesaid John Maye the elder died at Kennington aforesaid; and after the death of the said John Maye the elder the aforesaid Edward Ponynges, William Scott, John Scott and Henry Fynche were seised of the aforesaid tenements with the appurtenances whereof etc. in their demesne as of fee, to the use of the aforesaid Robert and Elizabeth and the next heir male[2] of the bodies of the same Robert and Elizabeth lawfully begotten for ever, in accordance with the aforesaid will; and while they the said Edward, William, John Scott and

[1] 21 Hen. VIII, c. 19; Dyer, fo. 141b; *OHLE*, vi. 377–378.

[2] The clerk seems to have been uncertain whether this should be plural, and removed the endings, but left the adjective in the plural.

Johanne Scott et Henrico de tenementis illis cum pertinenciis ad usum illum sic seisitis existentibus iidem Edwardus, Willelmus et Henricus Fynche apud Assheforde in comitatu Kantie[1] obierunt et predictus Johannes Scott eos supervixit et se tenuit intus in tenementis illis cum pertinenciis et fuit inde solus[i] seisitus in dominico suo ut de feodo per jus accrescendi ad usum supradictum, ipsoque Johanne Scott sic inde solo seisito existente idem Johannes Scott diu ante predictum tempus captionis averiorum predictorum facte de tenementis illis cum pertinenciis unde etc. obiit seisitus, post cujus quidem Johannis Scott mortem tenementa illa cum pertinenciis <eo quod eadem tenementa sunt et adtunc fuerunt de natura de gavelkynd predicta secundum consuetudinem de gavelkynd in predicto comitatu Kantie ab antiquo per totum tempus predictum usitatam>[i] discendebant quibusdam Willelmo Scott armigero, Reginaldo Scott et Ricardo Scott generosis ut filiis et hered' ipsius Johannis Scott secundum consuetudinem[2] predictam, virtute cujus predicti[3] Willelmus Scott, Reginaldus et Ricardus in tenementa predicta cum pertinenciis unde etc. <ante predictum tempus quo etc.>[i] intraverunt et fuerunt de eisdem seisiti in dominico suo ut de feodo ad usum supradictum usque ad et in quartum diem Februa[r]ii anno regni domini Henrici octavi nuper regis Anglie post conquestum vicesimo septimo, quo quidem quarto die Februarii virtute cujusdam actus parliamenti adtunc editi et provisi predicti Robertus et Elizabeth fuerunt seisiti de tenementis predictis in perpetuum[4] secundum voluntatem predictam remanere inde in forma predicta, ipsisque Roberto et Elizabeth sic inde seisitis existentibus iidem Robertus et Elizabeth apud Kennyngton predictam diu ante predictum tempus captionis averiorum predictorum facte obierunt, post quorum quidem Roberti et Elizabeth mortem tenementa predicta cum pertinenciis in quibus etc. eo quod eadem tenementa sunt et per totum supradictum tempus fuerunt de natura et tenura de gavelkynde ut predictum est <et per consuetudinem de gavelkynd predictam>[i] discendebant prefato Innocentio Maye <seniori filio predictorum Roberti et Elizabeth patris predictorum Jeronimi et Johannis Maye superius in cognitione predicta nominatorum>[5] ac prefato Anthonio Maye modo querenti et cuidam Jaspero Maye ut filiis et coheredibus masculis de corporibus predictorum Roberti et Elizbabeth legittime procreatorum, virtute cujus predictus Innocentius[6] in tenementa predicta cum pertinenciis unde etc. intravit et fuit[7] seisitus <de tercia parte tenementorum illorum cum pertinenciis>[i] virtute predicte ultime voluntatis predicti Johannis Maye[8] et de duabus partibus eorundem tenementorum cum pertinenciis residuum etc. in dominico suo ut de feodo per intrusionem,[9] ipsoque Innocentio sic inde seisito existente idem Innocentius de talibus statibus obiit de tenementis predictis seisitus, post cujus quidem Innocentii mortem tenementa illa cum pertinenciis unde etc. <per consuetudinem predictam>[i] discendebant prefatis Jeronimo et Johanni Maye in cognitione predicta superius nominatis ut filiis et coheredibus ejusdem Innocentii, virtute cujus iidem Jeronimus et Johannes Maye in tenementa predicta cum pertinenciis unde etc. intraverunt et de tercia parte eorundem tenementorum cum pertinenciis fuerunt seisiti in dominico suo ut de feodo talliato et de duabus partibus predictorum tenementorum cum pertinenciis residuo etc. in dominico suo ut de feodo per intrusionem, ipsisque Jeronimo et Johanne Maye de tenementis illis cum pertinenciis sic seisitis existentibus predictus Anthonius Maye modo querens in jure suo proprio ac in jure predicti Jasperi Maye fratris sui alterius[i] filiorum et coheredum predictorum Roberti May et Elizabeth <de corporibus eorum legittime procreatorum> secundum consuetudinem predictam in duas partes tenementorum predictorum cum pertinenciis unde etc. intraverunt, per quod ii-

[1] Kanco. [2] *Several words following are erased.* [3] pdcus.
[4] *Two following words are erased.* [5] *Written over an erasure.*
[6] *Several words following are erased.* [7] *One following word is erased, probably* inde.
[8] *Several words following are erased.* [9] *Written over an erasure.*

Henry were thus seised of the tenements with the appurtenances to that use the same Edward, William and Henry Fynche died at Ashford in the county of Kent, and the aforesaid John Scott survived them and held himself in in the tenements with the appurtenances and was thereof sole seised in his demesne as of fee by the *jus accrescendi* to the above-mentioned use; and while he the said John Scott was thus sole seised the same John Scott, long before the aforesaid time of the taking of the aforesaid beasts, died seised of those tenements with the appurtenances whereof etc.; and after the death of the said John Scott, forasmuch as the same tenements are and then were of the nature of gavelkind aforesaid according to the ancient custom of gavelkind used throughout the aforesaid time in the aforesaid county of Kent, the tenements descended to a certain William Scott esquire, Reynold Scott and Richard Scott, gentlemen,[1] as sons and heirs of him the said John Scott in accordance with the aforesaid custom, by virtue whereof the aforesaid William Scott, Reynold and Richard before the aforesaid time when etc. entered into the tenements aforesaid with the appurtenances whereof etc. and were seised of the same in their demesne as of fee to the above-mentioned use, until and on the fourth day of February [1536] in the twenty-seventh year of the reign of the lord Henry the eight after the conquest, late king of England, on which fourth day of February by virtue of a certain act of parliament then made and provided[2] the aforesaid Robert and Elizabeth were seised of the aforesaid tenements for ever[3] in accordance with the aforesaid will, remainder thereof in form aforesaid; and while they the said Robert and Elizabeth were thus seised the same Robert and Elizabeth died at Kennington aforesaid, long before the aforesaid time of the taking of the beasts aforesaid; and after the death of the said Robert and Elizabeth, since the same tenements are and throughout the above-mentioned time were of the nature and tenure of gavelkind as aforesaid, the aforesaid tenements with the appurtenances whereof etc. descended by the custom of gravelkind aforesaid to the said Innocent Maye, the elder son of the aforesaid Robert and Elizabeth, father of the aforesaid Jerome and John Maye named above in the aforesaid acknowledgment, and to the said Anthony Maye now plaintiff and to a certain Jasper Maye, as sons and coheirs male of the bodies of the aforesaid Robert and Elizbabeth lawfully begotten, by virtue of which the aforesaid Innocent entered into the aforesaid tenements with the appurtenances whereof etc. and was seised of the third part of those tenements with the appurtenances by virtue of the aforesaid last will of the aforesaid John Maye and of the remaining two parts of the same tenements with the appurtenances etc. in his demesne as of fee by intrusion; and while he said Innocent was thus seised the same Innocent died seised by such estates of the aforesaid tenements; and after the death of the said Innocent the tenements with the appurtenances whereof etc. by the aforesaid custom descended to the said Jerome and John Maye named in the aforesaid acknowledgment as sons and coheirs of the same Innocent, by virtue of which the same Jerome and John Maye entered into the aforesaid tenements with the appurtenances whereof etc. and were seised of the third part of the same tenements with the appurtenances in their demesne as of fee tail and of the remaining two parts of the aforesaid tenements with the appurtenances etc. in their demesne as of fee by intrusion; and while they the said Jerome and John Maye were thus seised of the selfsame tenements with the appurtenances the aforesaid Anthony Maye now plaintiff, in his own right and in right of the aforesaid Jasper Maye his other brother, as sons and coheirs of the aforesaid Robert Maye and Elizabeth lawfully begotten of their bodies according to the aforesaid custom, entered in two parts of

[1] According to an illuminated pedigree roll of the Scott family (*c.* 1605) in the editor's possession, Reynold was the son of Sir John [d. 1533], son of Sir William [d. 1524], son of Sir John [d. 1485]. Ponynges died in 1521.

[2] The Statute of Uses, 27 Hen. VIII, c. 10.

[3] This seems to be a mistake for 'for their lives', since the remainder is mentioned.

dem Anthonius et Jasperus Maye fuerunt seisiti de duabus partibus tenementorum illorum in tres partes dividendorum <in dominico suo ut de feodo talliato>[i] virtute ultime voluntatis predicte et tenementa predicta cum pertinenciis unde etc. tenuerunt in coparcineria et pro indeviso simul[i] cum predictis Jeronimo et Johanne Maye in cognitione predicta superius nominatis, ipsisque Anthonio Maye et Jaspero de predictis duabus partibus tenementorum predictorum cum pertinenciis unde etc. in forma predicta sic seisitis existentibus predictus Anthonius Maye ante predictum tempus captionis averiorum predictorum facte averia predicta in predictum locum in tenementis predictis[1] ad herbam ibidem crescentem depascenda posuit prout ei bene licuit, quequidem averia ipsius Anthonii Maye fuerunt in eodem loco in quo captio averiorum illorum superius facta fuit herbam ipsius Anthonii ibidem crescentem depascentia quousque predicti Johannes Mylton et Johannes Hamon predicto tempore captionis averiorum predictorum facte averia illa ceperunt et ea injuste detinuerunt contra vadium et plegios quousque etc. modo et forma prout idem Anthonius Maye superius versus eos se modo queritur. Et hoc paratus est verificare. Unde ex quo predicti Johannes Mylton et Johannes Hamon captionem averiorum predictorum in predicto loco in quo captio averiorum illorum facta fuit superius cognoverunt petit judicium et dampna sua predicta occasione captionis et injuste detentionis averiorum illorum sibi adjudicari etc.

Et predicti Johannes Mylton et Johannes Hamon dicunt quod placitum predictum per predictum Anthonium Maye in barram ad cognitionem predictum superius placitatum minus sufficiens in lege existit ad actionem ipsius Anthonii supradictam versus eosdem Johannem et Johannem manutenendam, ad quod quidem placitum iidem Johannes Mylton et Johannes Hamon necesse non habent nec per legem [terre] tenentur aliquo modo respondere. Unde pro defectu sufficientis placiti in hac parte iidem Johannes Mylton et Johannes Hamon ut prius petunt judicium et retornum averiorum predictorum una cum dampnis et expensis suis per ipsos circa sectam suam in hac parte appositis juxta formam statuti predicti eis adjudicari etc.

Et predictus Anthonius Maye dicit quod placitum predictum per ipsum Anthonium in barram ad cognitionem predictam superius placitatum bonum et sufficiens in lege existit ad actionem ipsius Anthonii supradictam versus predictos Johannem Mylton et Johannem Hamon habendam manutenendam quod quidem placitum materiamque in eodem superius contentam paratus est idem Anthonius probare, ad quod quidem placitum iidem Johannes Mylton et Johannes Hamon non respondunt nec illud aliqualiter dedicunt. Ideo ut prius petit judicium et dampna sua predicta occasione captionis et injuste detentionis averiorum predictorum sibi adjudicari etc.

Et quia curia domine regine hic de judicio suo de et super premissis reddendo nondum advisatur dies datus est partibus predictis coram domina regina usque in octabis Sancti Michaelis ubicumque etc. de judicio suo de et super premissis audiendo eo quod curia domine regine hic inde nondum etc. Ad quem diem coram domino Philippo nunc rege et domina Maria nunc regina apud Westmonasterium venerunt partes predicte per attornatos suos predictos. Et quia curia domini regis et domine regine hic de judicio suo de et super premissis reddendo nondum advisatur dies ulterius inde datus est partibus predictis coram dominis rege et regina usque in octabis Sancti Hillarii ubicumque etc. de judicio suo de et super premissis audiendo etc. eo quod curia domini regis et domine regine hic inde nondum etc. Ad quem diem coram domino rege et domina regina apud Westmonasterium venerunt partes predicte per attornatos suos predictos....

[*See opposite*]

1 *Several words following are erased.*

the aforesaid tenements with the appurtenances whereof etc., whereby the same Anthony and Jasper Maye were seised of two thirds of those tenements in their demesne as of fee tail by virtue of the aforesaid last will, and held the aforesaid tenements with the appurtenances whereof etc. in coparcenary and in undivided shares together with the selfsame Jerome and John Maye named in the aforesaid acknowledgment; and while they the said Anthony Maye and Jasper were thus seised of the aforesaid two parts of the aforesaid tenements with the appurtenances whereof etc. in form aforesaid, the aforesaid Anthony Maye before the aforesaid time of the taking of the aforesaid beasts put the aforesaid beasts in the aforesaid place in the tenements aforesaid in order to depasture the grass there growing, as he was fully entitled to do, which beasts of him the said Anthony Maye were in the same place in which the taking of the beasts was made, depasturing the grass of him the said Anthony growing there, until the aforesaid John Mylton and John Hamon at the aforesaid time of the taking of the beasts aforesaid took the beasts and unjustly withheld them against gage and pledges until etc., in the above manner and form in which the same Anthony Maye now complains against them. And this he is ready to aver. Therefore, since the aforesaid John Mylton and John Hamon have above acknowledged the taking of the aforesaid beasts in the aforesaid place in which the taking of the selfsame beasts was made, he prays judgment and that his aforesaid damages by reason of the taking and unjust withholding of the selfsame beasts may be awarded to him etc.

And the aforesaid John Mylton and John Hamon say that the aforesaid plea in bar as pleaded above to the aforesaid acknowledgment by the aforesaid Anthony Maye is insufficient in law to maintain the above-mentioned action of the selfsame Anthony against the same John and John, to which plea the same John Mylton and John Hamon have no need and are not bound by the law of the land in any way to answer. Therefore, for want of a sufficient plea in that behalf, the same John Mylton and John Hamon as before pray judgment and that return of the aforesaid beasts, together with their damages and expenses laid out by them about their suit in that behalf, in accordance with the form of the aforesaid statute, may be awarded to them etc.

And the aforesaid Anthony Maye says that the aforesaid plea in bar as pleaded above to the aforesaid acknowledgment by him the said Anthony is good and sufficient in law to maintain the above-mentioned action of the selfame Anthony against the aforesaid John Mylton and John Hamon, which plea, and the matter above contained in the same, the same Anthony is ready to prove, to which plea the same John Mylton and John Hamon do not answer, nor do they in any way deny it. Therefore, as before, he prays judgment and that his aforesaid damages by reason of the taking and unjust withholding of the aforesaid beasts may be awarded to him etc.

And because the lady queen's court here is not yet advised concerning its judgment to be given upon and concerning the foregoing, a day is given to the aforesaid parties before the lady queen until the octave of Michaelmas, wheresoever etc. for hearing their judgment upon and concerning the foregoing, inasmuch as the lady queen's court here is not yet therein etc. At which day the aforesaid parties came before the lord Philip, now king, and the lady Mary, now queen, at Westminster, by their aforesaid attorneys. And because the court of the lord king and lady queen here is not yet advised upon and concerning its judgment to be given upon and concerning the foregoing, a further day is given to the aforesaid parties before the lord king and lady queen until the octave of St Hilary [1555], wheresoever etc., for hearing their judgment upon and concerning the foregoing etc. inasmuch as the court of the lord king and lady queen here is not yet therein etc. At which day the aforesaid parties came before the lord king and lady queen at Westminster by their aforesaid attorneys....

[*Similar continuances to Easter term 1557, but no judgment*]

[34]

Nota que al Serjeantes Inne en Chauncerie Lane 25 October 1556 al assemblie des justices la fuit agree et resolve per eux toutes sur bon advisement que en toutes cases de hault treason et petit que 2 wittnesses ou accusors doient estre portes eins al temps del endictment al jurie pur proffe de ceo en lour dittes et accusations en escriptes signes ove lour nosmes in le testymony des auters que ceo fuit lour accusation que serra lie et declare al jurie de lendictment mes si les dittes witnesses ou accusors soient donques en vie ou present ou absent al temps de le ditt endictment nest matter issint que lour dittes sont recordes ut supra. Et que sur triall des toutes treasons graund ou petit sur lestatute 25 E. 3. sur larraynment de eux treasons ne besoigne ascun wittnesses ou accusors destre productes face to face vers le partie issint arraine mes sur lendictment come est avaundit pur ceo que ceo est ousta pur triall en toutes treasons per lestatute de 1° et 2° Phillippi et Marie ca. 10. Et mesme lorder serra observe en toutes auters treasons exceptes les treasons declares et [*fol. 37v*] faites per lestatute de 1° et 2° Phillippi et Marie ca. 10 queux treasons doient estre tries per witnesses ou accusors sur lendictment come est avaundit et sur larraynment doient estre facie ad faciem en presence sills sont en vies et deins le realme si le partie ceo require en forme come est conteigne en le dit statute 1 et 2 Philippi et Marie mes per le dit statute 1 et 2 forgeinge et counterfaytinge le coyne ou ascun coyne currant, signet, privey seale, graund seale ou signett manuell le trial serra come fuit al comen ley et nul auterment mes uncore les wittnesses ou accusors sur lenditement de ceux doient estre enforme adevant mes pur [le][1] coyne ympairer, counterfaiter ou forger, ceo serra order en triall et sur lenditement come fuit al comen ley per lestatute 1 et 2 Philippe et Marie. Mes pur misprision de treason la doient estre witnesses ou accusors sur lendictment de cest en forme adevant,[2] et sur larraynment les witnesses ou accusours doient estre face al face come devant est dit, quar le trial de misprision nest remedye per lestatute 1 et 2 Philippi et Marie car cest misprision nest treason.

[35]

Nota que witnesses ou accusors serront prises et ewes en petit treason sur lendictment come est avandit mes nemy sur larrainment mes serra order en mesme le manner order et forme come est avandit declare en hault et graund treason

[1] *Reads* ley.
[2] *Altered from:* avandit.

34. TRIALS FOR TREASON

Serjeants' Inn, Chancery Lane, 25 Oct. 1556. Also reported in Dyer, fo. 132; 110 Selden Soc. 16–18; Bro. Abr., *Corone*, pl. 219 (110 Selden Soc. 18); Saunders' reports, 110 Selden Soc. 19.

Note that at Serjeants' Inn in Chancery Lane, on 25 October 1556, at the assembly of the justices there, it was agreed and resolved by all of them upon good advisement that in all cases of high and petit treason two witnesses or accusers must be brought in to the [grand] jury at the time of the indictment, for proof thereof, or their sayings and accusations in writing signed with their names, with the attestation of others that this was their accusation, which shall be read and declared to the jury of indictment; but it does not matter whether the said witnesses or accusers are then alive, or present, or absent at the time of the said indictment, so long as their sayings are recorded as above.[1] And [it was agreed] that upon trial of all high or petit treasons upon the statute 25 Edw. III,[2] upon the arraignment for these treasons there is no need for any witnesses or accusers to be produced face to face against the party so arraigned, but only upon the indictment as aforesaid, because that is ousted for trial of all treasons by the statute of 1 & 2 Phil. & Mar., c. 10. And the same order shall be observed in all other treasons except the treasons declared and created by the statute of 1 & 2 Phil. & Mary., c. 10, which treasons ought to be tried by witnesses or accusers upon the indictment as aforesaid; and upon the arraignment they ought to be present, face to face, if they are alive and within the realm, and if the party so requests, in the manner provided by the said statute of 1 & 2 Phil. & Mar. By the said statute of 1 & 2, however, for forging and counterfeiting the coin [of the realm], or any current coin, the signet, privy seal, great seal, or sign manual, the trial shall be as it was at common law and not otherwise: nevertheless the witnesses or accusers upon an indictment for these offences ought to be informed beforehand. But for impairing, counterfeiting or forging coin, this shall be ordered as to the trial and indictment as it was at the common law, by the statute 1 & 2 Phil. & Mar. For misprision of treason, however, there ought to be witnesses or accusers upon the indictment, in form aforesaid, and upon the arraignment the witnesses or accusers ought to be face to face, as is said above; for the trial of misprision is not remedied by the statute of 1 & 2 Phil. and Mar., since this misprision is not treason.

35. TRIALS FOR PETIT TREASON

Serjeants' Inn, Mich. 1556, contd.

Note that witnesses or accusers shall be taken and had in petit treason upon the indictment, as aforesaid, but not upon the arraignment; but it shall be ordered

[1] As to whether the second accuser may be someone who merely repeats by hearsay what he has been told by the first accuser, see *R.* v. *Thomas* (1554) Dyer, fo. 99b.

[2] Treason Act 1351, 25 Edw. III, st. 5, c. 2.

pur ceo que lestatute parle generalment des toutes treasons et le generall pardone des toutes treasons pardon auxi pettie treason car ceo est treason: quod nota.

[36]

Vide lestatute 1 E. 6. ca. 12. et 5 E. 6. ca. 11. queux donent trialls en treason, petit treason et misprision de treason: et misprision de treason est un offence nosme en le dit statute 5 et 6 E. 6. coment nest merement expresse pur le triall.

[37]

Nota auxi per toutes les justices que misprision de treason est lou hault treason est reveled ou declare al auter person et cestui person a que il est issint reveale ou declare ne declare ceo al ascun de Counsaill ou al ascun des justices mes ceo custode secrement sans ascun reveler ou declaration ouster cest concelement de le treason sans auter acte faire est misprision. Et le payne de cest misprision <est>[1] si un soit trove culpable est perpetuall imprisonment et forfayture des ses beins et chattells et le profitt des ses terrs durant sa vie et ceo fuit et ore est misprision per le comen ley et le forfayture de cest coment que cest est declare misprision per lestatute 5 et 6. ca. 11. et per divers estatutes.

[38]

[*fol. 38*] Nota auxi per eux que coment que lestatute 1 Marie ca. 18. repell toutes treasons petit treasons et misprision de treason forsque tiels queux sont expresse et declare per lestatute 25 E. 3. et nuls misprisions de treasons sont la declares ou expresses en le dit statute 25 E. 3. uncore les misprisions remaynont come fueront al common ley adevaunt nient repells per le dit statute pur ceo que le dit statute de repealls repella toutes les dittes offences avauntdittes queux sont faites treason ou misprision per ascun estatute ou acte de parlament et cest misprision fuit al comen ley et nient per lestatute.

1 *Sic but otiose.*

in the same manner, order and form as is declared above for high and great treason, because the statute speaks generally of all treasons: and a general pardon of 'all treasons' pardons also petit treason, for it is treason. Note that.

36. TRIALS FOR MISPRISION OF TREASON

Serjeants' Inn, Mich. 1556, contd.

See the statutes of 1 Edw. VI, c. 12, and 5 [& 6] Edw. VI, c. 11, which give trials in treason, petit treason, and misprision of treason; and misprision of treason is an offence named in the said statute of 5 & 6 Edw. VI, even though it is not expressed clearly (*merement*) with respect to the trial.

37. MISPRISION OF TREASON

Serjeants' Inn, Mich. 1556, contd. Cf. Staunford, *Plees del Coron* (1557), fo. 37; *OHLE*, vi. 589.

Note also, by all the justices, that misprision of treason is where high treason is revealed or declared to another person, and the person to whom it is thus revealed or declared does not declare it to any of the Council, or to any of the justices, but keeps it secretly without any revealing or declaration over: this concealment of the treason, without performing any other act, is misprision; and the penalty for this misprision, if someone is found guilty, is perpetual imprisonment and forfeiture of his goods and chattels and the profits from his lands during his lifetime. This was, and still is, misprision by the common law, and so is the forfeiture for it, even though it is declared misprision by the statute of 5 & 6 [Edw. VI], c. 11, and by various [other] statutes.

38. MISPRISION OF TREASON

Serjeant's Inn, Mich. 1556, contd.

Note also, by them, that although the statute of 1 Mar., c. [1],[1] repeals all treasons, petit treasons, and misprisions of treason, except for those which were expressed and declared by the statute of 25 Edw. III,[2] and there are no misprisions of treason declared or expressed in the said statute of 25 Edw. III, nevertheless misprisions remain as they were at common law before then, unrepealed by the said statute, because the said statute of repeals repeals all the aforesaid offences which are made treason or misprision by any statute or act of parliament, whereas this misprision was at common law and not by statute.

[1] 1 Mar., sess. 1, c. 1.

[2] Treason Act 1351, 25 Edw. III, st. 5, c. 2.

[39]

Nota auxi per eux si un seignor de parlament soit endite de misprision de treason que il serra trie de cest et arraine per ses peres come en case de hault treason, felony ou murder ou de petit treason. Mes des toutes auters comen offences, come sur endictment de forcible entre, riott ou rowt, ils serront tries per xii loyall homes come auters serront et nemy per lour peres.

[40]

Nota que si home port appele de mort vers auter que plede Rien culpable et de hoc ponit se de bono et malo super patriam, sur quel ple le playntiefe demurre et le ple le deffendant est adjuge bon, le judgement serra que le defendant ala al diew vers le playntiefe mes quant al roy le defendant soit arraine a sone sute de novell. Et ceo fuit ajuge 14 H. 7. en [Banke][1] le Roy, et precedent monstre de ceo. Et en cest terme de Saint Michell en appell vers un que gaga battaill ove lappellant et lappellant demurre en ley et le ple ajudge bon il fuit acquite vers lappellant et arraine de novell al sute le roy: sicut in casu Swymburne. Vide T. 47 E. 3. fo. 5, et t[itulo] Coron 103. Et per *Stanford* Justice de Comen Banke si lappellee en appell gage battaill et etc. et quant ils sont en le campe lappellant relinquishe le battelle ore lappelle serra discharge sans novell arrainment al sute le roy mes si lappellant ad issint relinquishe en courte et nient en campe ou ad demurre en ley sur le gager de battaill la lapellee serra novellment arraine al suite le roy T. 47 E. 3. fo. 5, t[itulo] Coron 103.

[41]

A, ff. 31v–32 (foll. pl. 28); *L* 237 (sim.); *D*, fo. 22, pl. 4 (3 & 4 Phil. & Mar.).

Un [Bassett][2] suit al roy et roien un petition pur terre en lour maines esteantes ratione attincture Edwardi ducis Somersett en nature dun formedone en le remainder, [quel remainder][3] en droit discende a luy s. le petitioner en taill dun de ses auncestors, le dit petitioner adonques et uncore esteant deins age. Et en

[1] *Reads* blanke.
[2] *A, D, L.* Bussent *H.*
[3] *A, D, L.*

39. TRIAL BY PEERS

Serjeants' Inn, Mich. 1556, contd. This may be the source for Staunford, *Plees del Coron*, fo. 152A. Cf. what seems to be a mistaken report of this case by John Whiddon in 110 Selden Soc. 250.

Note also, by them, that if a lord of the parliament is indicted of misprision of treason he shall be tried for it and arraigned by his peers, as in the case of high treason, felony, murder, or petit treason. But for all other offences, as for instance upon an indictment for forcible entry, riot, or rout, they shall be tried by twelve lawful men, as others shall be, and not by their peers.

40. ARRAIGNMENT AT THE KING'S SUIT

King' Bench, Mich. 1556.

Note that if someone brings an appeal of death against another, who pleads Not guilty, and thereof puts himself for good and ill upon the country, and upon this plea the plaintiff demurs, and the defendant's plea is adjudged good, the judgment shall be that the defendant go quit (*ala al diew*) as against the plaintiff. As against the king, however, the defendant shall be arraigned again at his suit. This was adjudged in 14 Hen. VII in the King's Bench, and a precedent shown of it.[1] And in this Michaelmas term, in an appeal against someone who waged battle with the appellant, and the appellant demurred in law, and the plea was adjudged good, he was acquitted as against the appellant but arraigned again at the king's suit, as in the case of Swynburne:[2] see Trin. 47 Edw. III, fo. 5, and tit. 'Corone', 103.[3]

And, according to Staunford J. of the Common Bench, if the appellee in an appeal wages battle etc., and when they are in the field the appellant relinquishes the battle, the appellee is now discharged without a new arraignment at the king's suit; but if the appellant had thus relinquished [battle] in court, and not in the field, or demurred in law upon the wager of battle, the appellee would be freshly arraigned at the king's suit. Trin. 47 Edw. III, fo. 5, tit. 'Corone', 103.

41. ARTHUR BASSET v. REGEM ET REGINAM

Exchequer Chamber, upon a petition of right. Also reported in Dyer, fo. 133 (Mich. 1556) and ff. 136–138 (Hil. 1557); 110 Selden Soc. 19.

One [Basset] sued to the king and queen for land which was in their hands by reason of the attainder of Edward, duke of Somerset, by way of a petition in the nature of a formedon in the remainder, which remainder in right descended to him (that is, the petitioner) in tail from one of his ancestors, the said petitioner then (and still) being under age. And in the Exchequer Chamber, before all

1 Probably a record. Cf. YB Mich. 14 Hen. VII, fo. 2, pl. 8, which is not exactly in point.

2 *Reade* v. *Rotherforth and Swynburne* (1555), below, pp. 138–145.

3 Fitz. Abr., *Corone*, pl. 103 (YB Hil. 47 Edw. III, fo. 5, pl. 10).

Lexchequor [*fol. 38v*] Chamber devant toutes les justices, latturney le roy pria que le paroll demurre durant le nonage le petitioner.

Et puis que le matter fuit debate auxibein al barre come al banke devant le chauncellor Dengliterre et toutes les justices de <les 2 Bankes>[1] il fuit agree et ajudge que le paroll demurre durant le mynoritie le petitioner auxibein come [si ceo fuisset][2] en breife de formedone en le remainder ou en le reverter en queux cases le paroll demurrer durant le nonage le demandant: quod nota. Mes *Saunders* et le chefe baron fueront al contrarie.

Termino Pasche 3 et 4 Philippi et Marie

[1]

A, fo. 31[f] (still Mich. 3 & 4 Phil. & Mar.); *L* 238[f] (sim.); *D*, ff. 22–23, pl. 5 (sim.).

Nota que il fuit adjuge en Banke le Roy isto eodem termino que si un alien come Frencheman[3] ou auters aliens font ou comittont ascun manner de treason en cest realme que ore ils serront tries totes per les gentes Anglois et ne[my] per le moitie des aliens de son condition per le forme de les statutes en cest case proviewe. Vide lestatute 27 E. 3. ca. 8. E. 3. ca. 13. et 8 H. 6. ca. 8. quar ceux estatutes sont oustes en treason per lestatute 1 et 2 Philippi et Marie ca. 10. quar per cest estatute treasons serront tries come fuit al comen ley et nemi auterment: et sic accidit in casu dun Sheires esteant Frenchman que vient a Depe en Fraunce ove un Stafford et auters Anglois traitors al castell de Scarboroughe in comitatu Eborum et la preignent le dit castell et ceo tient enconter le roy et la le dit Staff[ord] fist un proclamation de rebellion et en slaunder de roien, le roy, et ses Spaniardes, et portant armor come enemies le roy et royen vers le dit roy et royen, et realme, et le Frenchmen auxi avoit mesme le judgement.

[1] lun bancke et lauter *A, L.*
[2] *A, L.* si esset *D.* il fuit *H.*
[3] Francois *L only.*

the justices, the king's attorney prayed that the parol might demur during the petitioner's minority.

After the matter was well debated, both at the bar and the bench, before the chancellor of England, and all the justices of the benches,[1] it was agreed and adjudged that the parol should demur during the petitioner's minority, just as it would in a writ of formedon in the remainder or in the reverter, in which cases the parol shall demur during the demandant's minority. Note that. SAUNDERS and the CHIEF BARON,[2] however, were to the contrary.

Easter term, 3 & 4 Phil. & Mar. (1557)

1. R. v. SHERLLES

King's Bench, 25 May 1557. Record: KB 8/37 (Baga de secretis); calendared in *4th Report of the Deputy Keeper of Public Records*, app. II, pp. 258–259. Also reported in Dyer, fo. 144 (sub nom. Sherleys); 109 Selden Soc. 176; Catlyn's notes, Alnwick Castle MS. 475, fo. 178v (sub nom. Sheres); Bro. Abr., *Treason*, pl. 32; and see *OHLE*, vi. 616.

Note that it was adjudged in the King's Bench this same term that if an alien, such as a Frenchman, or some other alien, does or commits any kind of treason in this realm, they shall be tried wholly by Englishmen and not by a jury half of aliens of his condition under the terms of the statute provided for such cases: see the statutes [28] Edw. III, c. [13]; 8 Hen. VI, c. [29].[3] For those statutes are ousted in treason by the statute 1 & 2 Phil. & Mar., c. 10, for by that statute treasons are to be tried as they were at common law and not otherwise. This happened in the case of Sheires,[4] being a Frenchman, who came from Dieppe in France with one Stafford and other English traitors to Scarborough Castle in Yorkshire, and there seized the said castle and held it against the king and queen; and there the said Stafford made a proclamation of rebellion and in slander of the queen, the king, and his Spaniards, and they wore armour[5] as enemies of the king and queen, against the said king and queen and realm; [and he was sentenced for high treason]; and the Frenchman also had the same judgment.

[1] Also Hare M.R. and Sir John Baker: Dyer, fo. 133.

[2] Sir David Broke.

[3] See *OHLE*, vi. 612–614; Dyer, fo. 144.

[4] Described in the record as Jean Sherlles of Rouen, *alias* Jean Grasset of Rouen. He was indicted with Thomas Stafford and others (who pleaded Guilty), but pleaded Not guilty and was tried by special commission before Saunders C.J. in Westminster Hall. The other commissioners were Sir Francis Englefield, Sir John Baker, Sir Nicholas Hare M.R., Brooke C.J.C.P., Whiddon and Dalison JJ.

[5] Perhaps: 'bore arms'.

[2]

Contd in *A, D* and *L* from pl. 1.

Nota auxi la agreed per toutes les justices que si ascun alien estre[anger] vient en cest realme ove ascun traitor ou les enemies le roy ou roien esteant Anglois et auxi aidant ou asistant en cest realme vers le roy et royen ou auterment ils esteant en cest realme ou vient hors de auter realme al eux s. les enemies et traitors esteant en cest realme et eux aidant et assistant coment que la fuit guere ou peas enter cest realme hors de que etc. et cest realme uncore cest est treason en les dittes aliens estrangers et ils suffront pur ceo come traitors sicome ilz fueront Anglois traitors. Mes si guer soit [*fol. 39*] enter cest realme et un auter, come en Fraunce, et en cest temps le Frenchmen vient en battell array en cest realme per terr ou per ewe et preignont un forte ou castell en cest realme et ceo teignont come enemies vers le roy et royen cest nest treason mes serront subdues per la <ley martiall>[1] et per gladium. Mes auterment est (ut supra) quant ils vient eins en power et en company des enemies le roy et roien esteant traitors come adevant est dit. Et semble que si Frenchmen vient en cest realm ove power vers le roy et royen et icy levie guer vers eux coment que Fraunce fuit en amitie adevante que uncore que cest nest pas treason en le Frenchmen esteant en le alliance de le roy et royen et auxi cest est cause de <le rumpier de le truse>[2] et cause de guer enter les dittes realmes quod nota.

[3]

Abr. in *A*, fo. 32^{f}; *L* 239^{f}.

Nota auxi agree en le Comen Banke que si home soit attainte de treason, felony ou de murder que ore le feme cestui que est issint attaint serra dishable en le ley a demander ou challenge son dower vers le feoffee son baron coment que le feoffment fuit fait devant le felony, treason ou murder: et cest per le comen ley. Mes per le estatute 1 [E.][3] 6. ca. 12. la feme serra endowable nient obstant le attainder son barron en treason, felony ou murder, mes per lestatute 3 et 5 E. 6. ca. 11 apres le attainder en treason de le baron la feme ne sera endow, mes apres le attainder le baron en felony et murder la feme sera endowable per le dit primer estatute quod nota.

1 marshall ley *A*.
2 breach de peace et league *A*.
3 *Reads* R.

2. R. v. SHERLLES, contd

King's Bench, contd from pl. 1.

Note also that it was there agreed by all the justices that if any alien stranger comes into this realm with any traitor, or with the king's or queen's enemies, being English, and is also aiding and assisting in this realm against the king and queen; or else, being in this realm, or coming from another realm to them (that is, to the enemies and traitors being in this realm), aids and assists them, then, whether or not there was war or peace between the realm from which they came etc. and this realm, it is treason in the said alien strangers, and they shall suffer for it as traitors just as if they were English traitors. If, however, there is a war between this realm and another, as with France, and in time of war the Frenchmen come in battle array into this realm, by land or water, and seize a fort or castle in this realm, and hold it as enemies against the king and queen, this is not treason but they shall be subdued by the martial law and by the sword. But it is otherwise in the case above, when they come in with power and in company with the king's and queen's enemies, being traitors, as aforesaid. And it seems that if Frenchmen come into this realm with power against the king and queen, and levy war here against them, even though France was previously in amity, this is nevertheless not treason in the Frenchmen, being in the allegiance (*alliaunce*) of the king and queen. Moreover, this is a cause of a breach of the truce and a cause of war between the said realms. Note that.

3. GATE v. WISEMAN

Common Pleas, Hil. 1557. Record: CP 40/1168, m. 760 (demurrer; c.a.v. to Hil. 1557); printed in Bendl. 55, pl. 91. Also reported in Dyer, fo. 140 (Hil. 1557). The case arose from the attainder of Sir John Gate of Pleshey, Essex.

Note that it was also agreed in the Common Bench[1] that if someone is attainted of treason, felony or murder, the wife of him who is so attainted shall be disabled in law to demand or claim her dower against her husband's feoffee, even if the feoffment was made before the felony, treason or murder; and that is by the common law. By the statute of 1 Edw. VI, c. 12, however, the wife shall be endowable notwithstanding her husband's attainder of treason, felony or murder. But by the statute of [5 & 6] Edw. VI, c. 11, after the husband's attainder for treason the wife shall not be endowed; but after the husband's attainder for felony and murder the wife shall be endowable by the said first statute. Note that.

1 According to Dyer, it was decided by the judges in Brooke C.J.'s chambers, without argument by counsel: at which Serjeant (Anthony) Browne was very angry. The record has a continuance to Hil. 1557 but no judgment.

Termino Trinitatis 3 et 4 Philippi et Marie al Serjeantes Inne in Fleetstreete 1557[1]

[1]

A, fo. 32[f] (first case of Trin. 3 & 4 Phil. & Mar.); *L* 240[f] (sim.); *D*, fo. 21, pl. 1 (sim.).

Fuit agree per toutes les justices la, *Brooke* Chefe Justice de le Comen Place et *Stanfort* except, que cest person que est bygamus avera son clergie a cest jour per lestatute primo E. 6. ca. 12. que repell lacte De [Bigamis][2] ca. 5. que devant ousta bygamus de lour clergie. *Dyer* agrea al *Brooke* et *Standford.*

[2]

Abr. in *A*, fo. 32[f]; *L* 241[f].

Et fuit auxi agrea la per toutes les justices que si le principall pria son liver apres verditt et devant judgement et ad son liver a luy allowe que le accessorie sera per cest dismisse et oustrement dischardge mes si il praya son liver apres [*fol. 39v*] judgement et ad ceo que ore ceo nient obstant le accessorie respoignera et ne sera dischardge. Vide 10 H. 4, titulo Corone. T. 2 E. 3. que le accessorie respoignera coment le principall ad son pardon allowe, placito 151, et eodem termino H. 3 H. 7. 53 E. 3. H. 7. fo. 58.

[3]

A, fo. 32[f]; *L* 241 (contd).

Et fuit la auxi agree per toutes que si home ad son clergie apres judgement et ne fuit demande adevant que il ne ferra son purgation [mes serra clerke sans purgation].[3] Vide lestatute et un proviso 23 H. 8. ca. primo, et titulo Corone, M. 40 E. 3. 91. M. 12 R. 2. 109. que cest que est [convict][4] en appell per verditt et ad son clergie devant judgement ne ferra son purgation mes sera adjuge come clerke attainte.

1 De termino Trinitatis 3[tio] et 4[to] Phillippi et Marie *A (before the next case).* Trin. iii[o] et iiii[o] Phil. et Mar. *L.*
2 *A, L.* Bygamus *H.*
3 *A.*
4 *A, L.* attaint *H.*

Trinity term, 3 & 4 Phil. & Mar. (1557) at Serjeants' Inn in Fleet Street

1. DE BIGAMIS

Serjeants' Inn, Fleet Street, Trin. 1557. Also reported in Dyer's circuit notebook, 110 Selden Soc. 411, no. 1. The report of this meeting is contd in pl. 2–5, below, and then above, pp. 102–104, pl. 17–23.

It was agreed by all the justices there, except BROOKE C.J. of the Common Pleas and STAUNFORD, that a person who is *bigamus* shall have his clergy at the present day by the statute of 1 Edw. VI, c. 12, which repeals the statute De Bigamis, c. 5,[1] which had previously ousted *bigami* from their clergy. DYER agreed with BROOKE and STAUNFORD.

2. PRINCIPAL AND ACCESSORY

Serjeant's Inn, Fleet Street, Trin. 1557, contd. Also reported in Dyer's circuit notebook, 110 Selden Soc. 411, no. 2.

And it was also agreed there by all the justices that if a principal [felon] prays his book after verdict but before judgment, and has his book allowed to him, the accessory shall be thereby dismissed and utterly discharged. But if he prays his book after judgment, and has it, the accessory shall nevertheless answer and shall not be discharged. 10 Hen. IV, tit. 'Corone'; Trin. 2 Edw. III, and same title, pl. 151,[2] say that the accessory shall answer even if the principal has his pardon allowed; and Hil. 3 Hen. VII, [in the same title], pl. 53; Pas. 3 Hen. VII, [pl,] 58.[3]

3. PURGATION

Serjeant's Inn, Fleet Street, Trin. 1557, contd. Also reported in Dyer's circuit notebook, 110 Selden Soc. 411, no. 3.

And it was also agreed there by everyone that if someone has his clergy after judgment, and it was not demanded earlier, he shall not make his purgation but shall be a clerk without purgation. See the statute and proviso, 23 Hen. VIII, c. 1; and Mich. 40 Edw. III, tit. 'Corone', 91, and Mich. 12 Ric. II, 109,[4] that he who is convicted in an appeal by verdict, and has his clergy before judgment, shall not make purgation but shall be adjudged as a clerk attaint.

1 *SR*, i. 43.

2 Fitz. Abr., *Corone*, pl. 466 (Mich. 10 Hen. IV) and pl. 151 (YB Trin. 2 Edw. III, fo. 27, pl. 17).

3 Fitz. Abr., *Corone*, pl. 53 (YB Mich. 3 Hen. VII, fo. 12, pl. 10) and pl. 58 (YB Hil. 3 Hen. VII, fo. 1, pl. 3).

4 Fitz. Abr., *Corone*, pl. 91 (YB Mich. 40 Edw. III, fo. 42, pl. 23) and pl. 109 (Mich. 12 Ric. II).

[4]

A, fo. 32[f]; *L* 242[f]; *D*, fo. 22, pl. 2 (3 & 4 Phil. & Mar.).

Et fuit agree auxi per toutes que si home soit endite quod felonice fregit domum mansionalem in nocte et null mention est fait de ascon chose asporte ou de ascon entree fait en le meason mes sur le evidence lentent appiert a committer un felony en le meason et sur ceo le jury trove luy culpable uncore cest nest nul felony sinon que lenditement fuit ea intentione ad feloniam sive murdrum [ibidem][1] faciendum ou burgulariter fregit et intravit. Vide lestatute 27 H. 8. ca. 3. et 5 et 6 E. 6. ca. 10.

[5]

A, fo. 32v[f]; *L* 243[f].

Nota que fuit agree per toutes si un estraunger sojorne[2] en auter meason et le meason est enfreinte en le nuite et lestranger robbe en le meason sans ascun feare mys en luy que uncore cestui que robbe en le mannor avera son clergie cest burgulory nient obstant quia hors de lestatute 5 et 6 E. 6. ca. 9. Vide residuum en le 3 et 4 fol. adevante.

[De termino Trinitatis 4to et 5to Phillippi et Marie][3]

[1]

A, fo. 33v (first case of Trin. 4 & 5 Phil. & Mar.); *L* 248 (sim.).

Home purchase en fee 3 tenementes en Londres que sont tenus de le royen per service de chivaler et il per son volunt en escriptes devisa[4] les dites tenementes

[1] *A, L.*
[2] sudjourne *A.*
[3] *A (immediately before the next case).* T. Annis Philippi et Marie 1558 *H.* Trinit. iiii° et iii° Phil. et Mariæ *inserted in L.*
[4] *Written over:* demisa.

4. BURGLARY

Serjeants' Inn, Fleet Street, Trin. 1557, contd. Also reported in Dyer's circuit notebook, 110 Selden Soc. 411, no. 4.

And it was also agreed by everyone that if someone is indicted that he feloniously broke a mansion house in the night, and no mention is made of anything taken away or of any entry made in the house, but upon the evidence it appears that his intention was to commit a felony in the house, and thereupon the jury find him guilty, nevertheless this is no felony unless the indictment says 'with the intention of committing a felony (or murder) there', or 'burglariously broke and entered'. See the statutes 27 Hen. VIII, c. 3, and 5 & 6 Edw. VI, [cc. 9, 10].

5. BURGLARY AND CLERGY

Serjeants' Inn, Fleet Street, Trin. 1557, contd. Also reported in Dyer's circuit notebook, 110 Selden Soc. 411, no. 5.

Note that it was agreed by everyone that if a stranger stays in someone else's house, and the house is broken into in the night, and the stranger is robbed in the house without any fear being put in him, he who robs in this way shall have his clergy, despite the burglary, because it is outside the statute of 5 & 6 Edw. VI, c. 9.[1] (See the rest in the third and fourth leaf above.[2])

Said to be Trinity term 4 & 5 Phil. & Mar. (1558) [3] but partly 1557

1. CLARVAUX'S CASE

Serjeants' Inn, Fleet Street, perhaps Trin. or Mich. 1557. Also reported in Dyer, fo. 155, who says the question was put to the board of Serjeants' Inn in Trin. 1557 (but reports it under Mich. 1557).

Someone purchased in fee three tenements in London which are held of the queen by knight-service,[4] and by his will in writing he devised the said tenements

[1] Cf. 5 & 6 Edw. VI, c. 10, which allows clergy for all felonies not specified in the act.

[2] This refers to the interpolation above, pp. 102 – 104.

[3] Heading in *A. H* says 1558, but omits the term.

[4] The tenements were in the parish of St Benet, Gracechurch Street, including the Saracen's Head, and had come to King Henry VIII through the dissolution of Merton Priory, Surrey. They were granted to Ralph 'Clarvys' on 18 March 1541 to hold in chief by knight-service: *Letters and Papers of the Reign of Henry VIII*, ed. J. Gairdner and R. H. Brodie, xvi (1898), p. 330, no. 678(50); and cf. p. 460, no. 947(37) (licence to alienate the same). The will of 'Radulphe' Clarvaux, alias Clarves, grocer, of Gracechurch Street, was proved in the Commissary Court of London in 1557.

a son executors pur xxi yeres ou tant de eux come le ley voet a payer ses debtes etc. et puis devie. Si ore cest devise soit bon pur tout per custome de Londres que fuit devant lestatutes de voluntes ou si el soit restraine per les dittes estatutes de voluntes a faire son volunt de tiels tenementes forsque de les 2 partes de eux eo quod per lestatute le 3 parte est reserve al royen ou un tenure est en capite per service de chivaler ou per service de chivaler?

Et fuit loppinion de toutes les justices assemble al Serjeantes Inne en Fletestrete que le volunte est bon en cest case pur toute accordant al custome de London eo que custome de London est que chescun home poet deviser ses tenementes esteantes en fee a quicumque que il voet. Et ceo fuit devant les dittes estatutes faites et per [*fol. 40*] les dittes estatutes cest custome nest tolle ne lentent les dittes estatutes ne fuit a abrogater le dit custome et devises que fueront bones devant les dittes estatutes mes a faire voluntes bones queux ne fueront bones ne poet estre faites per le ley devant les dittes estatutes. Come en case de lestatute de mortmaine que est en le negative que nul home donera ou devisera les terres en mortmaine sans ascun savinge en le acte et uncore home poet deviser et doner per son volunte ou auterment ses terres en London en mortmaine, lestatute de mortmaine nient obstant, pur ceo que le dit estatute nad enfringe le dit custome. A fortiore en cest case, entant que lestatute est en le affirmative et nient en le negative. Mes per lestatute de enrollmentes de bargaynes[1] et sales de terre cest restreigne le custome de London et auters cities tanque il fuit save per lestatute eo que cest estatute de enrollmentes fuit et est en le negative et fuit fait pur cest purpose et lentent lestatute fuit yssint mes issint ne fuit lentent de lestatutes de voluntes.

[2]

A, fo. 33v^f; *L* 249^f.

Nota que fuit dit[2] per eux toutes la que coment que le custome [de][3] burgage terr [est en socage][4] uncore si apres les terrs vient per done ou auterment al tenure en cheiff ou service de chivaler que cest ne chaunge le custome que va toutes dittes[5] ove le terre et ne ove le tenure. Come [de][6] terre en gavelkind, le custome fuit des terr[es] en socage, quar gavelkind terr[es] fueront toutes en socage, et uncore si les terres fueront chaunges per dones ou auterment en service de chivaler cest nest alter le custome de gavelkind pur toutes males a enheriter quia va ove le terre.

1 *Altered from:* bygames.
2 *Altered from:* demaund. agree *A, D, L.*
3 *Altered to:* va al. de *A, D, L.*
4 *A, D, L.* que est en fee *H.*
5 *Altered unnecessarily to:* foits.
6 *Reads* le.

to his executors for 21 years (or as many as the law permits) to pay his debts etc., and then died. Is this devise, which was before the Statutes of Wills,[1] good for the whole by the custom of London, or is he restrained by the said Statutes of Wills to make his will only for two-thirds of the tenements, inasmuch as the third part is reserved to the queen where the tenure is in chief by knight-service, or by knight-service?

And it was the opinion of all the justices assembled in Serjeants' Inn in Fleet Street that the will is good in this case for the whole, according to the custom of London, inasmuch as the custom of London is that everyone may devise his tenements (being in fee) to whomever he wills. That was before the said statutes were made; and the custom is not taken away by the said statutes, nor was it the intention of the said statutes to abrogate the said custom, [or to annul] devises which were good before the said statutes, but only to make good wills which could not by law be made before the said statutes. Likewise in the case of the Statute of Mortmain,[2] which is in the negative, that no one should give or devise his lands in mortmain, without any saving in the act: one may nevertheless devise and give his lands in London in mortmain, by will or otherwise, despite the Statute of Mortmain, because the said statute does not break the said custom.[3] A fortiori in this case, since the statute is in the affirmative and not in the negative. On the other hand, the Statute of Enrolments of Bargains and Sales of Land[4] does restrain the custom of London and other cities, unless saved by statute, since this Statute of Enrolments was and is in the negative and was made for that purpose, and that was the intention, whereas it was not the intention of the Statutes of Wills.[5]

2. CLARVAUX'S CASE, contd

Serjeants' Inn, Fleet Street, contd.

Note that it was said by all of them there that although the custom of burgage land is in socage, nevertheless if the land comes by gift or otherwise to be held in chief or by knight-service this does not change the custom, which always runs with the land and not with the tenure. Likewise of land in gavelkind: the custom was for lands in socage, for gavelkind lands were all held in socage, and yet if the lands are changed by gift or otherwise into knight-service, that does not alter the custom of gavelkind for all males to inherit, because it runs with the land.[6]

[1] 32 Hen. VIII, c. 1, explained by 34 & 35 Hen. VIII, c. 5.
[2] De Viris Religiosis (*SR*, i. 51).
[3] For the doctrine that the customs of London were not repealed by general statutes see *OHLE*, vi. 81 n. 192.
[4] 27 Hen. VIII, c. 16.
[5] Dyer says the case was raised again in the Court of Wards in Pas. 1563, with the same result.
[6] Cf. above, p. 6, pl. 15.

[3]

A, fo. 33v[f]; *L* 250[f]; *D*, fo. 23, pl. 2 (4 & 5 Phil. & Mar.).

Nota que il fuit agree per eux toutes la esteantes que si home soit en execution pur le debt de auter home en le Fleete que le royen ne poet luy prender en sa protection en ses guerres[1] hors de le prison tanque le debt soit pay et satisfie entant que il est en execution pur le debt dun estraunger et per cest aler le execution est discharge que ne poet estre per la ley en tiel manner. Mes si il fuit en execution pur le debt le royen en le Flete ou en auter prison la le royen poit luy dischardge et preigne en son protection ou en ses guers a son pleasure quia il est son debt demesne que bein el poet dischardge: quod nota.

[4]

Abr. in *A*, fo. 35v; *L* 266.

Et quant a le case de murder enter Herbert et Maunsefild si il sera adjuge homicide ou murder ils ne fueront concludes adhuc mes restant pur melior prove si la feme que fuit issint occise fuit la en parte takinge ove Mansefild et de son parte ou el vient come un estranger ou come amy de ambideux partes. Et issint le descisement de cest case resta.

Mes *Saunders* Cheife Justice[2] et auters la fueront clere en opinion que si deux pugnant ensemble al entent un a occiser auter ou auterment un de bater et murder auter et un estranger veigne enter eux a eux partera et un de eux luy occise que ore cest occision de lestranger en tiel maner est murder coment que la ne fuit malice adevant enter le estranger et cestui que luy occise entant que il s. lestranger fuit tua en le malice que fuit porte en le auter.

[1] *Altered from:* gyves.
[2] Baron *A.* [Saunders became CB Exch. in 1559.]

3. THURLAND'S CASE

Serjeants' Inn, Fleet Street, contd. Also reported in Dyer, fo. 162 (before all the judges of both benches, Trin. 1557).

Note that it was agreed by all of them who were there that if someone is in execution in the Fleet for the debt of another man, the queen may not take him into her protection [for service] in her wars outside the prison,[1] until the debt has been paid and satisfied, since he is in execution for the debt of a stranger and by letting him go the execution would be discharged, which cannot be done in that way by the law.[2] If, however, he was in execution in the Fleet or some other prison for the queen's debt, the queen could discharge him and take him into her protection or [to serve] in her wars at her pleasure, because it is her own debt, which she may well discharge. Note that.

4. HERBERT and MANSELL'S CASE

Probably in Serjeants' Inn. Also reported in Dyer, fo. 128 (Hil. 1556); printed below, p. 129; see *OHLE*, vi. 556. Contd in pl. 5, where the facts are set out. It seems from the opening words, and from the word 'thus' in line 3, that there must have been a previous report of this case, or else pl. 5 should come before this.

As to the case of murder between Herbert and [Mansell], whether it should be adjudged homicide or murder, they have not yet come to a conclusion but have postponed it for better proof as to whether the woman who was thus killed[3] was there taking part with [Mansell], and on his side, or whether she came along as a stranger, or as a friend of both parties. And so the decision of this case was put off (*resta*).[4]

But SAUNDERS C.J.[5] and others were of the clear opinion that if two people are fighting together with the intention of killing each other, or of beating or [wounding][6] each other, and a stranger intervenes to separate them, and one of them kills him, this killing of the stranger in this way is murder, even though there was no previous malice between the stranger and the one who killed him, inasmuch as he (namely, the stranger) was slain in the malice which the other bore.

[1] *H* originally said 'en ses gyves' (in his shackles). According to Dyer, the prisoner was licensed to go to Berwick on royal service, accompanied by a keeper.

[2] Cf. *OHLE*, vi. 95.

[3] Mansell's sister.

[4] The outcome is not known.

[5] *A* says Chief Baron, but Saunders was not appointed to that office until 1559.

[6] Conjectural emendation; the text says 'murdering'.

Annis Regni Regis Philippe et Marie 4° et 5°. 1558

[5]

Un Sir George Herbert chivaler sur un displeasure que il avoit a un Sir Rice Mansfild chivaler et son fittes assemble luy mesme ove xl persons et plusors en nomber ove luy injuste et riotouslye al meason le dit Sir Rice al purpose de [aver][1] affray et poigne ove le dit Sir Rice et son fittes et ove nul entent a tuer ascun person et la esteant al dit meason ove le dit nomber il quarela ove le dit Sir Rice ove parols unsemely et en cest temps vient hors un feme que fuit cousin al ambideux parties que adevant travala pur quietter le matter perenter eux a pacifier le dit debate a que feme le dit Herbert nad nul kinde de malice ou querrell et un des servantes le dit Herbert jetta un sax ou un pier de hors un mure que cade sur le dit feme et luy wound sur le teste sur que el morust. Et si cest soit wilfull murder en Herbert et en ses complices (come fuit agree que il fuit homicide en luy et en ses complices) cest fuit le question enter les justices al Serjeantes Inne en Chauncery Lane.

Et per *Sanders*[2] Cheif Justice, *Whiddon, Browne, Heigham* Cheif Baron, et *Dalison,* fueront agrees estre wilfull murder pur ceo que il comense sur un unloyall acte estre fait al person dun home en quel acte ils ont malice a faire un male chose enconter la ley et en cest malice le morte de le feme devient et pur ceo murder. Come si home commaund auter a carier al J. S. poyson a luy distroier et le home carier cest al J. S. et luy poison ore cest est murder quar J. S. est poison en cest malice que J. S. serroit si le poison fuit done a luy. Yssint si un hier un auter a tuer J. S. et puis [*fol. 41*] cestui que est issint hier tua J. S. cest est wilfull murder en cestui que tua et est accessori en cestui que commanda et hier et en lauter case de poisoninge ambideux wilful murders ore per lestatute 1 E. 6. ca. 12. Et auxi quant home fist un torte il sera adjuge per la ley en le pluis extreme torte et icy Herbert fist un tort en le assemblie le people et sur ceo sera adjuge murder quant un est morte en cest et ne[my] homicide que est le pluis sans offence.

Serjeant *Browne* et *Catlin,* latturney le royen *Griffith,* et le Solicitor, fueront de mesme loppinion. *Broke* Cheife Justice de Comen Place, *Stanford, Dyer* et *Morgan*

[1] *Reads* avera.
[2] *Written over:* Stanford

4 & 5 Phil & Mar. (1558)

5. HERBERT and MANSELL'S CASE

Serjeants' Inn, Chancery Lane. Contd from pl. 4.

One Sir George Herbert, knight,[1] for displeasure which he had against Sir Rhys [Mansell], knight,[2] and his son, assembled himself with forty or more persons in number, unlawfully and riotously, at the house of the said Sir Rhys for the purpose of having an affray and fight with the said Sir Rhys and his son, but with no intention of slaying any person; and, while there at the said house with the said number, he quarrelled with the said Sir Rhys with unseemly words, and at that time a woman came out, who was a kinswoman of both parties and had previously worked to quiet the matter between them and to pacify the said dispute, to which woman the said Herbert had no kind of malice or quarrel, and one of the said Herbert's servants threw a rock (*sax*) or stone out of a wall which fell upon the said woman and wounded her on the head, whereof she died. Whether this was wilful murder in Herbert and his accomplices – it being agreed that it was homicide[3] in him and his accomplices – was the question among the justices at Serjeants' Inn, Chancery Lane.

And it was agreed by SAUNDERS C.J., WHIDDON, BROWNE, HEIGHAM C.B.,[4] and DALISON, to be wilful murder, because it began upon an unlawful act to be done to a man's person, in which act they had malice to do an evil thing against the law, and in that malice the woman's death happened, and therefore it is murder. Similarly if someone commands another to carry poison to John Style to destroy him, and the man carries it to John [Dale] and poisons him, this is murder, for John [Dale] is poisoned in this malice that John Style would have been in, had the poison been given to him. Likewise if someone hires another to slay John Style, and then he who is so hired slays John Style, this is wilful murder in him who slew, and accessory in him who commanded and hired: but in the other case of poisoning they are both wilful murderers now by the statute of 1 Edw. VI, c. 12. Moreover, when someone does a wrong he shall be adjudged by the law in the most extreme wrong; and here Herbert did a wrong in assembling the people, and thereupon it shall be adjudged murder when someone is dead as a result, and not homicide, which is the [lesser] offence.

Serjeants *Browne*[5] and *Catlyn*, the queen's attorney-[general] *Griffith*, and the solicitor-[general], were of the same opinion. But BROOKE C.J. of the Common

[1] Of Plas Newydd, Swansea, Glam., and Lincoln's Inn; J.P. and sometime sheriff of Glam.; vice-admiral in South Wales; elder brother of William, 1st earl of Pembroke. The feud with Mansell went back to the 1530s. See *HPHC 1509–58*, ii. 338; *OHLE*, vi. 556. The present dispute concerned his right as vice-admiral to the cargo of a French vessel wrecked near Oxwich.

[2] Of Margam, Glam.; died 1559: *HPHC 1509–58*, ii. 565.

[3] I.e. at least manslaughter.

[4] Appointed on 2 March 1558.

[5] Anthony Browne, who succeeded Brooke C.J. in Sept. 1558.

Justices et *Prideaux*, serjeant le royen, fueront al contrary que il ne fuit murder mes manslaughter: quar murder est occisio hominis ex malicia precogitata et a cest feme ils nont ascun malice. Mes ils disont que si Mansefild ou ascons de ses servantes en son company ust este issint morte que cest ust este murder clerement mes cest feme ne vient pas en aide de Mansefild ou de Herbert mes fuit un pacifier perenter eux a que ambideux parties portent bon volunte pur que etc. [quar][1] ils diont que libertie de home et dower dun feme sont favor en ley.

Dyer's report of the case

Les Reports (1688 ed.), fo. 128, pl. 60.

Un home seisist certain biens des french homes in temps de guerre sur le ewe, et eux porta a sa meason: et un estranger pretend destre deputy Admiral, ove graund multitude de homes, veigne al meason lou les biens sont ove force, et fist assault sur eux que sont in le meason al gate del meason, hors de quel meason issuist un feme generosa sans weapon, et est tue per un des servants que veigne de prender lez biens, per le jetter de un piece[2] a un auter in le gate. Et le party que veigne de prender les biens, reporta et dit (devant son veignant) que il voille faire luy un Cokes que serva lez biens, et dit ouster que il voille causer luy de scier le basest in sa meason. Si ceo soit murder pur le mort del feme quaere, et cest case fuit move inter omnes Justiciarios et divers teignont s. *Saunders, Highman* chief Baron, *Whiddon, Brown* et *Dalison* Justices, et *Brown* et *Catlyn* Serjeants, Latturney et Solliciter, que sil appiert que la feme vient in defence ou part de Maunsel, que adonques ceo fuit murder in Herbert et touts ses companions. Sed *Brook, Stamford, Morgan, Dyer,* et *Pridyaux* al contrary: car nul malice fuit prepence devers la feme, et murder ne poit estre extend pluis ouster que il fuit intend etc. Et lez primers teignont que si 2. combate per appointment devant fait de ceo faire, et un estranger indifferent intervenient de eux parter, et il est tue per un de eux, est murder in luy, et ascun diont in ambideux, sed lauter parte noluerunt ad hoc concordare.

[6]

Nota que la fuit auxi rehers le case le Seignor Dacres de Sowth ou il ove ses companions et complices fueront accordes al enter en auter parke et la hunt et tua dames et si ascun eux resist que il eux occider et accordant ils entront en le parke et un home vient a un de eux et demanda que il ad a faire la et lauter luy

[1] que, *altered from:* Et.
[2] Probably misreading 'piere' (stone).

Place, STAUNFORD, DYER[1] and MORGAN[2] JJ., and *Prideaux*,[3] queen's serjeant, to the contrary, that it was not murder but manslaughter: for murder is the killing of a man with malice aforethought (*occisio hominis ex malicia praecogitata*), and they had no malice towards this woman. They said, however, that if Mansell or any of his servants in his company had been so killed, that would clearly have been murder. But this woman did not come in aid of Mansell or Herbert, but was a peacemaker between them, to whom both parties bore good will; wherefore etc. And they said that a man's liberty and a woman's dower are favoured in law.[4]

Translation of Dyer's report

Hilary term 1556.

A man seized certain goods from Frenchmen upon the sea in time of war, and brought them to his house; and a stranger, pretending to be deputy admiral, came with force to the house where the goods were, with a great multitude of men, and assaulted those who were in the house, at the gate of the house; and a gentlewoman came out of the house, without any weapon, and was slain by one of the servants who came to take the goods, as a result of throwing a [stone] at another in the gate. The party who came to take the goods had announced and said (before his coming) that he would make him a cox who saved the goods, and further said that he would cause him to know the basest in his house. The question was, whether this is murder in respect of the woman's death? And this case was moved among all the justices. Some of them, namely SAUNDERS, HEIGHAM C.B., WHIDDON, BROWNE and DALISON, Justices, *Browne* and *Catlyn*, serjeants, the attorney [general], and the solicitor [general], held that if it appeared that the woman came in defence of or on behalf of Maunsel, then this was murder in Herbert and all his companions. But BROOKE, STAUNFORD, MORGAN, DYER, and *Prideaux* to the contrary: for there was no malice aforethought towards the woman, and murder cannot be extended further than was intended etc. The first group held that if two people fight by previous appointment to do so, and an indifferent stranger intervenes to separate them and is killed by one of them, it is murder in him; and some say it is murder in both; but the other group would not agree that.

6. R. v. LORD DACRE (1541/2)

Mich. 1541 or later, cited in pl. 5. Also reported in 109 Selden Soc. 2; Bro. Abr., *Corone*, pl. 171; printed below; and on another point (trial by peers), ibid., *Jurours*, pl. 48; *Trialls*, pl. 142; Moo. K.B. 86; E. Hall, *Chronicle*, 842; *Letters & Papers of Hen. VIII*, xvi. 931 etc.; see *OHLE*, vi. 576.

Note that there was also rehearsed the case of the Lord Dacre of the South, where he with his companions and accomplices agreed to enter another's park, to hunt there and kill deer, and agreed that if anyone should resist [they] would kill him, and they entered the park accordingly, and someone came up to one of them and asked what he was doing there, and the other killed him, his lordship

[1] Appointed J. K. B. on 23 April 1558.
[2] Died 19 Aug. 1558.
[3] Died 29 Sept. 1558.
[4] Relevance unclear.

occide, le seignor esteant en le parke un quarter [de un league distant][1] et nul rien cognoscer de cest fact et uncore cest fuit adjuge murder en le dit seignor et toutes ses complices. Et le seignor et auters pur cest fueront pendus en temps H. 8. circa annum 33 de son reigne.

Brooke's report of the case

Bro. Abr., *Corone*, pl. 171.

34 H. 8. Nota que si xij. vient pur faire robery, affray, riot, vel hujusmodi, queux sont illoyalx actz, un deux enter in le meason et tua home, ou fait auter illoyal act, toutz lauters que veignont ove luy pur faire illoyal act sont principals. Et eadem lex in le case de Fines Seignior Dacres que un de son company tua home in huntinge in un forest, et le Seignior Dacres et lauters hunters come Mantell et alii fueront principalx, et fueront touts pendes.

[7]

Auxi fuit monstre la un president que un de son tort demeasne enter en un orchard et la spoile un pere tree et un vient a luy et rebuker luy de cest et il fuit per luy occise: et cest fuit murder auxi, agree, et il fuit arraine et endita sur cest.

[8]

Nota per les justices auxi 2 homes entendont a pugner ensemble ils appoint un liew a cest afaire, et quant ils sont ensemble lun tua lauter, cest est clerement wilfull murder en cestui que tua coment que son entent fuit mes a luy abater et wounda quar cest va a son person et est tua en cest malice. Issint est si home gist en agate de un auter a luy bater ou luy spoiler de ses biens, en semble manner home fist assault sur [*fol. 41v*] un auter a cest entent a luy spoiler de ses beins ou luy bater, et en cest agate et assault le home vers que lassault est tue ceo est clerement murder per toutes les justices entant que un kind de malice vient al person dun home [et ceo per toutes les justices].[2] Et vide lestatute 12 R. 2. ca. 1 ou statute 2 pur cest agayt, assault ou malice pretense.

[1] *Altered from:* di lege a costome.

[2] *Written twice, the second time substituting* cest *for* ceo.

being in the park a quarter of a league distant and in no way whatever aware of this fact: and yet this was adjudged murder in the said lord and all his accomplices. And his lordship and the others were hanged for this in the time of Henry VIII, around the thirty-third year of his reign.[1]

Translation of Brooke's report

1542/3.

34 Hen. VIII. Note that if twelve people come to commit a robbery, affray, riot, or such like, which are unlawful acts, and one of them enters the house and kills someone, or does some other unlawful act, all the others who came with him to do the unlawful act are principals. The same law was applied in the case of Fiennes, Lord Dacre, where one of his company killed a man while hunting in a forest, and the Lord Dacre and other hunters, such as Mantell and others, were principals; and they were all hanged.

7. HERBERT and MANSELL'S CASE, contd

Precedent of uncertain date, cited in Serjeants' Inn.

There was also shown there a precedent where someone of his own wrong entered an orchard and there stole from (*spoile*)[2] a pear tree, and someone came up to him and rebuked him, and was killed by him; and this was also agreed to be murder, and he was indicted and arraigned upon it.

8. HERBERT and MANSELL'S CASE, contd

Serjeants' Inn, contd.

Note also, by the justices, that where two men intend to fight together and appoint a place to do it, and when they are together one of them kills the other, this is clearly wilful murder in the one who killed, even though his intention was only to beat or wound him, for that goes to the person and he is slain in that malice. So it is if someone lies in wait to beat another, or to rob him (*luy spoiler*) of his goods, and in like manner if someone assaults another with the intention of robbing him of his goods or beating him, and in this ambush and assault the man against whom the assault is made is slain, this is clearly murder, according to all the justices, since a kind of malice came to a man's person. That [was agreed] by all the justices. And see the statute of 12 Ric. II, stat. 2, c. 1, for this 'ambush, assault or malice prepensed'.

1 According to Dyer, he pleaded guilty: 109 Selden Soc. 2 ('atteynt per confession et pendu apud Tyborn').

2 Cf. the next case.

[9]

A, fo. 35v (the last case from Dalison in *A*); *L* 267 (sim.).

Nota que *Browne*, serjeant le roien, report et dit que il fuit de opinion des justices que si un feme servant al auter feme conspire ove auter que fuit son lover[1] et il robba son mistres que el s. le maiden vient luy aider a cest et en le <night temps>[2] le maide occulte le dit home privement en le meason et quant le mistres fuit en slepe[3] le dit home vient hors de son liew et tua le mistres [et] luy robba de ses beins et cest fuit petit treason en le <dit maiden>[4] et murder en le dit home et uncore lentent de le maiden[5] ne fuit mes que daver son mistres robbe et nemi estre murder mes entant que le mistres fuit murder per tiell malicious practise le feme cest fuit le cause que il serra adjuge murder et petie treason en le maiden et murder en le dit home pur son privey entent de malice.

[10]

Et *Brooke* Cheiffe Justice de Common Place dit que en toutes cases ou home ove luy mesme ou multitude ove luy vient a faire un unloyall chose come abater un home ou a disseiser un home ou luy ousta de son meason que ore si cestui home en cest entry ou en cest batre soit occise per luy ou per ses companions ou per ascun de eux que cest est murder. Auterment est si un estranger est occise en cest entre ou batrie, cest nest que homicide quar cest vient per chaunce medly mes en le primer case le malice et occise vient al partie mesme: quod nota.

[11]

Et en Leschequor Chamber devant le chauncelor Dengleter et toutes les justices et barons la esteantes un case fuit move et debate pur le roy et royen s. que en temps E. 6. le Counsaill le dit roy direct lour lettres al Seignor Edward North adonques chauncellor de Augmentations de le Coron en le nome le roy avandit comaundant le dit chauncellor per les dittes lettres a deliver al J. S. three hundreth fooders of leadd pur le price et rate de chescun fooder al iiii li. le fooder et que le dit Seignor Edward, chauncellor, preigne de le dit J. S. et de suertie

[1] paramour *A, L.*
[2] nuicte *A, L.*
[3] sa lecte *A, L.*
[4] feme servant *A, L.*
[5] maide *A, L.*

9. HERBERT and MANSELLS' CASE, contd

This seems to be a recollection of the case reported in Dyer, fo. 128a (Hil. 1556), who says that Portman C.J., Brooke C.J.C.P., and Hare M.R. held the maid guilty of petit treason; but (David) Broke C.B., Dalison and Staunford JJ. were contrary.

Note that *Browne*, queen's serjeant,[1] reported and said that he was of opinion with the justices that where a woman, being another woman's servant, conspired with someone else who was her lover [that he should rob] her mistress, and she (the maid) would come to assist him in this, and in the night-time the maid hid the man secretly in the house, and when the mistress was asleep the said man came out of his hiding place and slew the mistress and robbed her of her goods, this was petit treason in the maid and murder in the man. Nevertheless the maid's intention was only to have her mistress robbed, and not murdered; but since the mistress was murdered by this woman's malicious scheming, that was the reason why it was adjudged petit treason in the maid and murder in the said man, on account of her secret malicious intent.

10. HERBERT and MANSELL'S CASE, contd

Serjeants' Inn, contd.

BROOKE C.J. of the Common Place said that in all cases where someone comes accompanied with a multitude of people to do an unlawful act, such as beating someone or disseising someone, or putting him out of his house, if this man is killed during this entry or battery, by him or his companions (or any of them), this is murder. It is otherwise if a stranger is killed in this entry or battery: that is but homicide,[2] for it comes by chance medley. In the first case, however, the malice and killing come to the party himself.

11. R. v. LORD NORTH

Exchequer Chamber, on an information in the Exchequer, Trin. 1558. Also reported in Dyer, fo. 161 (Trin. 1558).

In the Exchequer Chamber before the chancellor of England, and all the justices and barons who were there, a case was moved and debated on behalf of the king and queen: in the time of Edward VI, the said king's Council directed their letters to [Sir] Edward North, then chancellor of the Augmentations of the Crown, in the name of the aforesaid king, commanding the said chancellor by the said letters to deliver to John Style[3] three hundred fothers of lead at the price and rate of £4 for each fother, and the said [Sir] Edward (the chancellor) took

[1] Anthony Browne, who became C.J.C.P. in Sept. 1558.
[2] I.e. manslaughter.
[3] Dyer gives the name as 'Renagre', perhaps the Robert Renyger, comptroller of the customs in Southampton, who occurs as plaintiff in the first case reported by Plowden.

ove luy obligation pur le payment de cest per le rate avandit et Seignor Edward mitta un Benger son servant a preigne le dit obligation de J. S. et ses suerties que fist accordant al use de le dit roy et en son nosme. Et puis le dit Benger port le dit obligation a le dit chauncellor et le dit chauncellor ceo receiva de luy et [ensuite][1] redeliver cest obligation a Benger a custodier savement et puis le dit Benger per covin perenter luy et le dit J. S. et ses suerties devant ewe embesela le dit obligation et ceo perde et cancell que obligation fuit de la [sum de 2000 li.][2] Si ore [*fol. 42*] sur cest matter le Seignor North sera chardge de le dit debt a responder a roy et royen ceo fuit le question. Et fuit le clere opinion et judgement des toutes les dittes justices et barons que le dit seignor serra charge de le debt et obligation entant que il fist ceo nient come judge de record mes il fist ceo per vertue de son warant et letter et pur ceo il respondera pur le negligence de son servant et multo magis entant que il receiva le dit obligation de son servant et ne deliver ceo al officers s. al treasurer, que ad le custody de ceux bandes, puis son receite de ceo. Et fuit agree auxi que coment que il ad receive ceo de son authoritie demesne per luy ou per son servant sans tiel warrant que uncore il serra charge per perde ou negligence de son servant de cest bande eo que checun que preigne tiel bande pur le roy est chargeable et quant son servant preigne cest obligation per son comaundment cest prender fuit le prender de son maister ovesque il s. le maister respondera coment lobligation ne unques vient al mains son maister. Mes si le dit seignor come chauncellor ad preigne un obligation ou recognisance dal un al use le roy et en son nosme come judge de record en son proper person come besoigne et fist nul auter chose et puis obligation ou recognisance est embesell et perde per ses clerkes ou auters officers la il ne serra charge. Mes ycie il ne preigne nest obligation come judge quar cest doit estre en proper person mes mitta son servant pur cest prender. Et auxi entant que le seignor fist ceo per garrant il ne fist ceo come judge virtute officii mes virtute waranti mes fuit la per le mult parte agree que si le dit seignor ad preigne cest obligation ou recognisance come judge et ad ceo en son custodie et deliver ceo a son servant a custodier que est apres perde et embesell per luy ou per son servant que ore il respondera pur le debt entant que le reteignment puis fuit un torte quar il doit aver deliver ceo a lofficer que serra charge ove ceo maintenant apres son prisell et nemi a reteigner ceo ou deliver al auter. Mes Justice *Stanford* dit que cest torte et acte fynable mes nemi a responder al debt entant que il fist ceo come judge de recorde.

1 *Reads* enfact.

2 *Written over:* bien of viii li.

from the said John Style and his sureties[1] a bond for payment thereof, according to the rate aforesaid, and [Sir] Edward sent one Benger[2] his servant to take the said bond from John Style and his sureties, who did so accordingly to the use of the said king and in his name; and then the said Benger brought the said bond to the said chancellor, and the said chancellor received it from him, and forthwith redelivered this bond to Benger to keep safely; and then the said Benger, by covin previously had between him and the said John Style and his sureties, embezzled the said bond and lost it, and cancelled the bond, which was for the sum of £2,000. Shall the Lord North now be charged to answer the king and queen for the said debt? That was the question.

And it was the clear opinion and judgment of all the said justices and barons that the said lord shall be charged with the debt and bond, since he did this not as a judge of record but by virtue of his warrant and letter, and therefore he shall answer for the negligence of his servant. And this is especially so inasmuch as he received the said bond from his servant and did not deliver it to the officer, namely the treasurer, who had the keeping of these bonds, after his receipt of it. It was also agreed that, even if he had received it on his own authority, by himself or his servant, without such a warrant, he would still be charged for the loss or negligence of his servant, with respect to this bond, because everyone who takes such a bond for the king is chargeable; and when his servant takes this bond by his command, this was his master's taking, for which the master shall answer even though the bond never came to his master's hands. If, however, the said lord, as chancellor, had taken a bond or recognizance from someone to the use of the king, and in his name, as a judge of record, in his own person (as it behoves), and done nothing else, and then the bond or recognizance was embezzled and lost by his clerks or other officers, he would not be charged. But here he did not take this bond as a judge, for that ought to be in his own person, but sent his servant to take it. Moreover, since the lord did this by warrant, he did not do it as a judge *virtute officii*, but *virtute waranti.*

It was, however, agreed there by the majority that if the said lord had taken this bond or recognizance as a judge, and had it in his keeping, and delivered it to his servant to keep, and it was afterwards lost and embezzled by him or by his servant, he should here answer for the debt inasmuch as retaining it afterwards was a wrong: for he ought to have delivered it at once, after taking it, to the officer who is to be charged with it, and not to have retained it or delivered it to another.

STAUNFORD said that this was a finable wrong and act, but he should not answer for the debt, since he did it as a judge of record.

[1] Two persons called Winchcome: Dyer.

[2] Identified by Dyer as Thomas Benger. One of this name was of Strand Inn and Great Milton, Oxon; knighted 1553; served in Princess Elizabeth's household; subsequently M.P. (1559) and feodary for the duchy; died 1572: *HPHC 1559–1603*, i. 427. See also p. 35, above.

[12]

A, fo. 35; *L* 263; *D*, fo. 25, pl. 10 (4 & 5 Phil. & Mar.).

[*fol. 42v*] Nota per toutes les justices <auxi bien de le Banke le Roy come de Comen Place>[1] que si un pannell dun jurie soit panel pur apparaunce al un jour et adjorne ouster al auter jo[u]r, a que jour un deux que primes appert et est nosme primer en le panel adeprimes fist default et le residue apperte, et les defendants challendge 3 des les jurors et puis toutes paravailes.[2] Et donques vient cestui que [primes][3] appert [et primes fait default et pria que son apparance soit primes recorde][4] pur saver son fine pur le contempt, et le co[u]rt recorde apparaunce[5] et apres cest le deffendant pria que il serra jure et que il ne challenge toutes paravailes et il est paramount et non paravaile. Et le playntiefe dit que il ne poit estre jure tanque lour challenges fuit adeprimes tries quar coment que il <est nosme en le primer de>[6] le panell uncore en ley quant il vient apres le challenge il vient eins paravail quar ore per les justices il ne serra jure tanque le challenges sont peruses et tries come fuit dit et alleage per le playntiefe: quod nota.

[13]

Abr. in *A*, fo. 35v[f]; *L* 264[f].

Nota que un Holdnall un de le gard le roy et royen fuit indicta en Banke le Roy cest terme pur parler sedicious et slaunderous parols vers le roien et le roy contra pacem etc. ac contra formam diversorum statutorum in eodem casu editorum et provisorum et sur cest indictament fuit arraine et plede Non culpable et trove fuit culpable et puis le recorde de le indictament fuit viewe et appiert que les 3 moys fueront pas apres le jour suppose en le dit indicatment de son offence et cest fuit pas devant le jour de son indictament et son arraynement et pur ceo il ne poet [aver][7] le punishment sur le estatute ent fait 1° et 2° Philippi et Marie ne il ne poet aver son punishment per lestatute 2 R. 2. ca. 5. ne per le estatute 12 R. ca. 11. quar ceux estatutes [parlont][8] tantum vers seignors, earles et barons et auters officers graundes. Mes fuit agree per toutes les justices que il est punnishable per lestatute W. 1. ca. 34, que toucha auxibein les nobles come le roy, et per cest estatute il avera perpetuall imprisonment et ferra un fyne al roy. Et la fuit agre que les justices de Banke le Roy poent committer luy al pillorie

1 de ambideux bankes *A, L.*
2 le panell *A, L.*
3 *A, D, L.* puis *H.*
4 *A, D, L.* fuit receve *written over:* fist reward *H*
5 son lingringe *A, D, L.*
6 est primer nosme en *A.* est le primer nosme en *L.* soit le primer nosme in *D.*
7 *Reads* avera.
8 *Reads* per lestat'.

12. CHALLENGES

Serjeants' Inn or Exchequer Chamber, 1558. Perhaps the same as *Drew* v. *Marrow*, reported in Dyer, fo. 158 (Hil. 1558).

Note, by all the justices both of the King's Bench and the Common Place, that if a panel of a jury is impanelled for appearance at a day, and adjourned over to another day, at which day one of those who first appeared and was named first in the panel at the outset made default, and the rest appeared, and the defendant challenged three of these jurors and then all those below,[1] and then the one who appeared first, and made default first, came along and prayed that his appearance might be recorded to save his fine for the contempt, the court [would] record his appearance. And after this the defendant prayed that he should be sworn, and said that he did not challenge all below, and he is above and not below. And the plaintiff said that he could not be sworn until their challenges were first tried; for although he is named in the first panel, nevertheless when he comes after the challenge he comes in below: for now (according to the justices) he shall not be sworn until the challenges are gone through and tried, as was said and alleged by the plaintiff. Note that.

13. R. v. OLDNOLL

King's Bench, 8 Nov. 1557. Also reported in Dyer, fo. 155 (Mich. 1557; sub nom. Oldnoll, yeoman of the guard). Record: KB 27/1184, Rex m. 12d (judgment of perpetual imprisonment); printed below.

Note that one Holdnall, one of the king's and queen's guard, was indicted in the King's Bench this term for speaking seditious and slanderous words against the queen and the king, 'against the peace etc. and against the form of various statutes made and provided in that case'; and upon this indictment he was arraigned and pleaded Not guilty, and was found guilty. Then the record of the indictment was inspected, and it appeared that three months had passed after the day supposed in the said indictment as the day of his offence, and this time had passed before the day of his indictment and his arraignment, and therefore he cannot have the punishment under the statute made for this in 1 & 2 Phil. & Mar., c. [3]; nor can he have his punishment by the statute of [1] Ric. II, c. 5, or by the statute of 12 Ric. [II], c. [2]: for these statutes speak only of lords, earls and barons, and other great officers. It was, however, agreed by all the justices that he is punishable by the Statute of Westminster I, c. 34, which touches not only nobles but also the king; and by this statute he shall have perpetual imprisonment and shall make a fine to the king. And it was there agreed that the justices of the King's Bench may commit him to the pillory and then imprison him,

[1] Or 'the whole panel'.

et puis luy imprison auxibein come le Counsaill poent et come les justices dassise poient en lour circute mes il diont que cest est le sure voy come est avandit.

Record of the case

KB 27/1184, Rex m. 12d.

Midd' per indictamentum istius termini. Alias scilicet die Lune proxime post tres septimanas Sancti Michaelis isto eodem termino coram domino rege et domina regina apud Westmonasterium per sacramentum xii juratorum extitit presentatum quod cum iidem dominus rex et domina regina nunc Philippus et Maria, dei gracia rex et regina Anglie, Hispaniarum, Francie, utriusque Cicilie, Jerusalem et Hibernie, fidei defensores, archiduces Austrie, duces Burgundie, Mediolani et Brabantie, comites Haspurgi, Flandrie et Tirolis, ut piissimi et christianissimi principes hoc regnum suum Anglie quampluribus heresibus atque erroniis opinionibus jam diu fedum, maculatum et dampnabiliter infectum ab hujusmodi heresibus [et] erroribus diligentissime purgare et mundare totis viribus suis conati fuerunt ad maximam omnipotentis dei gloriam et honorem omniumque fidelium subditorum suorum tam corporis quam anime salutem et sanitatem, quidam tamen Willelmus Oldnoll, unus valectorum garde domine regine impie et erronie religionis et opinionis erga deum a diu jam existens ac cum diversis heresibus male infectus deum preoculis non habens nec debitum legiansie sue considerans sed instigatione diabolica seductus, machinans et intendens cordialem dilectionem et obedienciam quam veri et fideles legii et subditi dictorum dominorum regis et regine erga ipsos regem et reginam gerunt et de jure gerere tenentur delere et extinguere, vicesimo die Julii annis regnorum predictorum dominorum regis et regine tercio et quinto, apud civitatem Westmonasterii in predicto comitatu Midd', falso, nequiter, scandalose ac maliciose ex sua propria imaginatione contra dictos dominos regem et reginam hec falsa, sediciosa et scandalosa dicta et verba Anglicana dixit, asseruit et propalavit prout sequitur, videlicet, That the quenes majestye was base borne and that in Paules chercheyard a two peny boke myght be had whyche shulde prove hys sayinge to be trew, and that she dyd nothynge wythe all that she had but for traytors and for suche as be enymyes to her mother and to her self and tha[t] he trusted to se the lady Elyzabethes grace to restore godes honour and to put away this poperye that now ys browght into this realme. Et ulterius idem Willelmus Oldnoll, die, anno et loco predictis falso, scandalose ac maliciose ex sua propria imaginatione contra predictos dominos regem et reginam hec falsa, sediciosa et scandalosa dicta et verba Anglicana dixit, asseruit et propalavit prout sequitur, videlicet, That the quenes majestie entendyth to have a kynge to be crownyd here in this realme whyche thynge he sayd she shuld never bryng to passe more then in other realmes wyche he rehersyd, videlicet Naples, Jerusalem and Spayne, where he sayde the kynge was never crownyd, nether shuld be wythe us, for he sayd ytt wold coste many a man hys lyff before he shuld be crownyd, and that he the sayd Wylliam wold be one of them that shuld spend hys lyff in that cause, and therunto he sayde that[i] he was sworne and so was also al the persons of this land wyche were of any laufull age, contra legeancie sue debitum ac contra formam diversorum statutorum in hujusmodi casu editorum et provisorum necnon contra pacem dictorum domini regis et domine regine, coronam et dignitatem suas etc.

Per quod preceptum fuit vicecomiti quod non omitteret etc. quin caperet eum si etc. — Et modo, scilicet die Lune proxime post crastinum Animarum isto eodem termino, coram domino rege et domina regina apud Westmonasterium venit predictus Willelmus Oldnoll sub custodia Thome Harvey, marrescalli Marescalcie hospicii domini regis et domine regine, in cujus custodia preantea ex causis predictis commissus fuit virtute brevis domini regis et domine regine de habeas corpus ad subjiciendum ei inde directi, ad barram hic ductus in propria persona sua, qui committitur marescalli etc. Et statim idem Willelmus just as the Council may, and as the justices of assize may in their circuits. But they said that the sure way is as stated above.

Translation of the record

King's Bench, Michaelmas term 1557.

Middlesex, by indictment of this term. Heretofore, namely on the Monday next after three weeks from Michaelmas this same term, it was presented before the lord king and lady queen at Westminster by the oath of twelve jurors that, whereas the same present lord king and lady queen Philip and Mary, by the grace of God king and queen of England, Spain, France, both Sicilies, Jerusalem and Ireland, defenders of the faith, archdukes of Austria, dukes of Burgundy, Milan and Brabant, [and] counts of Hapsburg, Flanders and Tyrol, have endeavoured with all their power, as the most pious and Christian princes, diligently to purge and clean this realm of England, which has long been defiled, stained and damnably infected with many heresies and erroneous opinions, from such heresies and errors, to the greatest glory and honour of almighty God, and for the health and soundness of all their faithful subjects, both in body and in soul, nevertheless a certain William Oldnoll, one of the yeomen of the queen's guard, having long been of an impious and erroneous religion and opinion with respect to God, and ill infected with various heresies, not having God before his eyes, nor considering the duty of his allegiance, but being seduced by the instigation of the Devil, scheming and intending to erase and extinguish the cordial love and obedience which true and faithful lieges and subjects of the said lord king and queen bear and rightfully ought to bear, against them the said king and queen, on the twentieth day of July [1557] in the third and fifth years of the reigns of the aforesaid lord king and queen, at the city of Westminster in the aforesaid county of Middlesex, falsely, wickedly, slanderously and maliciously of his own imagination spoke, asserted and published against the said lord king and queen these following false, seditious and slanderous English sayings and words, namely, 'That the queen's majesty was base born, and that in Paul's churchyard a twopenny book might be had which should prove his saying to be true, and that she did nothing with all that she had but for traitors and for such as be enemies to her mother and to her self, and that he trusted to see the lady Elizabeth's grace to restore God's honour and to put away this popery that now is brought into this realm'. And the same William Oldnoll further, on the day and in the year and place aforesaid falsely, slanderously and maliciously of his own imagination spoke, asserted and published against the said lord king and queen these following false, seditious and slanderous English sayings and words, namely, 'That the queen's majesty intendeth to have a king to be crowned here in this realm, which thing he said she should never bring to pass more than in other realms (which he rehearsed, namely Naples, Jerusalem and Spain) where he said the king was never crowned, neither should [he] be with us, for he said it would cost many a man his life before he should be crowned, and that he the said William would be one of them that should spend his life in that cause, and thereunto he said that he was sworn, and so was also all the persons of this land which were of any lawful age', against the duty of his allegiance and against the form of various statutes enacted and provided for such cases, and also against the peace of the said lord king and queen, their crown and dignity etc.

Therefore the sheriff was commanded that he omit not etc. but take him if etc. — And now, namely on the Monday [8 Nov. 1557] next after the morrow of All Souls this same term, the aforesaid William Oldnoll came before the lord king and lady queen at Westminster in the custody of Thomas Harvey, marshal of the Marshalsea of the Household of the lord king and lady queen, into whose custody he had previously been committed for the causes aforesaid by virtue of the lord king and lady queen's writ of *habeas corpus ad subjiciendum* therein directed to him, being brought to the bar in his own person; and he was commit-

Oldnoll habito auditu indictamenti predicti dicit quod ipse in nullo est inde culpabilis. Et de hoc ponit se super patriam. Et Thomas Whyte miles qui pro domino rege et domina regina in hac parte sequitur similiter etc. Ideo fiat inde jurata coram domino rege et domina regina apud Westmonasterium hac instante die Lune etc. Et juratores per vicecomitem comitatus predicti impanellati exacti similiter veniunt, qui ad veritatem de premissis [dicendam][1] electi, triati et jurati dicunt super sacramentum suum quod predictus Willelmus Oldnoll est culpabilis de toto transgressione et contemptu predictis ac de locutione et propalatione falsorum, sediciosorum et scandalosorum dictorum et verborum predictorum in indictamento predicto superius specificatorum modo et forma prout per indictamentum illud versus eum superius supponitur. Super quo, visis premissis, consideratum est quod predictus Willelmus Oldnoll ducetur per prefatum marescallum usque ad prisonam Marescalcie dominorum regis et regine coram ipsis rege et regina et ibidem seu alibi ubi domino regi et domine regine placuerit decetero in prisona imperpetuum remaneat etc. ac quod finem et redemptionem eisdem dominis rege et regine faceret prout curie consideraverit etc.

[14]

A, fo. 35v[f] (ending 'en Thimbleby et Grayes case'); *L* 265[f] ('Nimbleby et Grayes case'); *D*, ff. 25–26, pl. 11 (sim.).

Nota que un Dennis et un John May fueront indites en le comite de Lincolne pur robbery John Oker de cc li. resceiver le royen en cest comite et cest cc li. fuit parcell de son resceipt et le indictment fuit prise devant les justices dassise en cest comite et remova en Banke le Roy et les dittes Dennys et John fueront arraines sur cest queux plede Non culpable severalment et joint venire facias issist al vicount de Lincolne, que retorna la pannell queux appieront, et Dennis et John Maii auxi. Den[nis] challenge iii or des jurors peremtorie et le court perceiva que il voil aver ses challenges peremptorie al jurie, toute come il poit per la ley, le court al prier latturney le roy sever Dennis de le dit John sans ascun [*fol. 43*] entre de allower de ses challenges ou de treit deux hors de le pannell. Et donques fuit demande de le dit John Maii si il voet challenge ascun de les jurors et il dit que il voet refuse nul home de les jurors et issint relinquishe son challenge et sur cest les 4 devant challenges peremptorie per Dennis ove auters en[2] le pannell al nomber de xii fueront tries et juries a trier le dit John. Et donques vient le dit Dennis al barre arrere[3] per mandatum curie et challenge ouster auters peremptorie issint que le jurie remayna vers luy et ceux xii queux fueront jure a trier le dit John trove le dit John culpable per que le dit John ad son judgement estre pendus. Et si cest jugement soit erronious[4] ou ne entant que ceux queux fueront primes challenge peremptorie fueront jures a trier le dit John.

Et fuit agree per les justices que ne fuit error mes que le judgement fuit bien done quar nest semble [al] appell assise ou action de trespas vers 2 queux plede

[1] *Reads* dicendi. [2] *Altered from:* cest. [3] *Altered from:* arraine.
[4] *Altered from:* arrain que.

ted to the marshal etc. And at once the same William Oldnoll, having heard the aforesaid indictment, says that he is in no wise guilty thereof; and thereof he puts himself upon the country; and Thomas Whyte, knight,[1] who sues for the lord king and lady queen in this behalf, likewise etc. Therefore let a jury be made up before the lord king and lady queen at Westminster this instant Monday etc. And the jurors impanelled by the sheriff of the aforesaid county, having been called, likewise come; and they, having been chosen, tried and sworn to say the truth concerning the foregoing, say upon their oath that the aforesaid William Oldnoll is guilty of the whole trespass and contempt aforesaid, and of the speaking and publication of the aforesaid false, seditious and slanderous sayings and words specified above in the aforesaid indictment, in manner and form as is above supposed against him by the indictment. Whereupon, the foregoing having been looked into, it is awarded that the aforesaid William Oldnoll be led by the said marshal to the prison of the Marshalsea of the lord king and queen before them the said king and queen, and remain there, or elsewhere at the pleasure of the lord king and queen, perpetually from henceforth in prison etc., and that he make fine and ransom with the same lord king and queen as the court shall consider etc.

14. R. v. THYMBLEBY and GRAY

King's Bench, probably Mich. 1557. Also reported, sub nom. *Thymolby and Gray's Case*, in Dyer, fo. 152 (Mich. 1557). Record: KB 27/1182, m. 20 (bailed); KB 27/1183, m. 8 (judgment), printed below; KB 29/190, m. 54 (outlawry at Lincoln), m. 64d (*habeas corpus* for Thymbleby, Pas. 1557; committed to marshal).

Note that one Dennis [Thymbleby] and one John [Gray] were indicted in Lincolnshire for robbing John Oker of £200, he being the queen's receiver in that county, and this £200 was part of his receipts; and the indictment was taken before the justices of assize in that county and removed into the King's Bench. And the said Dennis and John were arraigned thereupon and pleaded Not guilty separately; and a joint *venire facias* issued to the sheriff of Lincoln, who returned the panel which appeared, and Dennis and John [Gray] also appeared. Dennis challenged three of the jurors peremptorily, and the court perceived that he wanted to have his peremptory challenges to the whole jury, as he was entitled by the law, and at the prayer of the king's attorney the court severed Dennis from the said John, without any entry of allowing his challenges or of withdrawing two out of the panel. Then the said John [Gray] was asked whether he wished to challenge any of the jurors, and he said that he would refuse no man [i.e. of the jurors], and thus waived his challenge. Thereupon the four (before the peremptory challenge by Dennis), with others in the panel to the number of twelve, were tried and sworn to try the said John. Then the said Dennis came to the bar again by command of the court and further challenged others peremptorily, so that the jury remained against them. These twelve who were sworn to try the said John found the said John guilty, as a result of which the said John had his judgment to be hanged. Is this judgment erroneous or not, inasmuch as those who were first challenged peremptorily were sworn to try the said John?

It was agreed by the justices that it was not error, but the judgment was well given; for it is not like an appeal, assize or action of trespass against two, who

[1] Clerk of the crown in the King's Bench: 94 Selden Soc. *362.*

al yssue et un joynt venire facias issuist[1] la le challenge dun deffendant dun juror ou plusours si ils sont treites vers lun sera treit vers lauter quia ad sectam partis, mes cest est al suite le roy et serra several. Et auxi per lauter cause nul judgement fuit done sur cest challenge que ils serront treites mes le court respect ceo tanque le dit John fuit tries et le jurie charge sur luy issint ils remaynont jurors al auter s. al John May. Et auxi le dit John reles et relinquishe ses challenges al toutes per que il fuit apres pendu.

Vide pur le appell vers 2 ove un: titulo Challenge, T. 9 E. 4, pl.[2] 56, et libro en le case de Beawchampe en appell et vide titulo Challenge, M. 1 H. 5, pl.[3] 70 al contrarie [de] cest liver de 9 E. 4. come semble: mes la un des deffendantes en appell challenge un pur cause et cest tria vers luy et auter deffendant donques voet luy challenger et non potuit pur ceo que il ne pria cest al commencement.

Record of the case

KB 27/1183, Rex m. 8.

Lincoln' <per indictamentum termino Pasche tercio et quarto Philippi et Marie.>[i] Alias scilicet xxiiij^{o} die Marcii annis regnorum Philippi et Marie regis et regine nunc tercio et quarto apud castrum Lincolnie in comitatu Lincolnie coram Willelmo Stamford milite et Jacobo Dyer milite justiciariis ipsorum dominorum regis et regine ad assisas in comitatu <predicto capiendas ac ad gaolam in comitatu predicto de prisonibus in eadem gaola existentibus deliberandam et ad pacem in comitatu predicto conservandam necnon ad diversa felonias, transgressiones et alia malefacta in eodem comitatu perpetrata audienda et terminanda assignatis per sacramentum>[4] juratorum extitit presentatum quod Dionisius Thymbleby nuper de Grantham in partibus de Kesteven in comitatu predicto generosus, Stephanus Corlyck nuper de Grantham predicta in partibus et comitatu predictis yoman, Nicholaus Burded nuper de Grantham predicta in partibus et comitatu predictis yoman, et Johannes Gray nuper de Grantham predicta in partibus et comitatu predictis yoman, duodecimo die Novembris anno regnorum Philippi et Marie regis et regine nunc secundo et tercio vi et armis etc. in Johannem Oker generosum unum ballivorum et receptorum dictorum dominorum regis et regine in comitatu Lincolnie predicto assignatorum et Thomam Wylson servientem ipsius Johannis Oker apud Gonnerbye in comitatu predicto in regia via adtunc et ibidem existentes insultum fecerunt et ipsos Johannem Oker et Thomam Wylson verberaverunt, vulneraverunt et maletractaverunt ita quod de vitis eorum desperabantur et manus eorum ac etiam pedes suos cum diversis cordis ligaverunt ac manibus et pedibus suis sic ut premittitur ligatis ducentas libras in pecuniis numeratis de bonis et catallis dictorum dominorum regis et regine in custodia et manibus dicti Johannis Oker adtunc et ibidem existentibus a persona predicti Johannis Oker apud Gonnerbye predictam adtunc et ibidem inventis felonice ceperunt et asportaverunt contra pacem dictorum dominorum regis et regine nunc etc. In cujus rei testimonium Willelmus Cicell, miles, unus justiciariorum dictorum dominorum regis et regine in partibus et comitatu predictis huic inquisitioni

[1] *Altered from:* yssint.
[2] *Altered from:* fo.
[3] *Altered from:* fo.
[4] *Written over an erasure.*

plead to issue, and a joint *venire facias* issues, and there is a challenge by one of the defendants to one or more of the jurors, if they are withdrawn against one they shall be withdrawn against the other, because it as at the party's suit; this, however, is at the king's suit and they shall be separate. Moreover there is another reason: no judgment was given upon the challenge, that they should be withdrawn, but the court respited it until the said John was tried and the jury charged upon him, so that they remained jurors as to the other (namely, John [Gray]). Furthermore, the said John released and waived his challenge to all of them. And so he was afterwards hanged.

See for the appeal against two, with [challenge by] one, in the title 'Challenge', Trin. 9 Edw. IV, pl. 56, and in the [year] book in Beauchamp's case, in an appeal;[1] and see tit. 'Triall', Mich. 1 Hen. [VI], pl. 70,[2] to the contrary of the book of 9 Edw. IV, as it seems; but there one of the defendants in an appeal challenged one juror for cause, and it was tried against him, and another defendant then wanted to challenge him, and he could not, because he did not pray it at the outset.

Translation of the record

King's Bench, Trin. 1557.

Lincolnshire. (By an indictment of Easter term, 3 & 4 Phil. and Mary.) Heretofore, namely on 24 March in the third and fourth years of the reigns of Philip and Mary, the present king and queen, at Lincoln castle in the county of Lincoln, before William Stamford, knight, and James Dyer, knight, justices of them the said king and queen assigned to take the assizes in the county aforesaid, and to deliver the gaol in the county aforesaid of the prisoners in the same gaol, and to keep the peace in the county aforesaid, and to hear and determine the various felonies, trespasses and other misdemeanours perpetrated in the same county, it was presented by the oath of the jurors that Dennis Thymbleby late of Grantham in the parts of Kesteven in the aforesaid county, gentleman, Stephen Corlyck late of Grantham aforesaid in the aforesaid parts and county, yeoman, Nicholas Burded late of Grantham aforesaid in the aforesaid parts and county, yeoman, and John Gray late of Grantham aforesaid in the aforesaid parts and county, yeoman, on the twelfth day of November [1555] in the second and third year of the reigns of Philip and Mary, the present king and queen, with force and arms etc. made assault upon John Oker, gentleman, one of the bailiffs and receivers of the said lord king and queen assigned in the aforesaid county of Lincoln, and Thomas Wylson, the said John Oker's servant, at Gonerby in the aforesaid county, then and there being in the highway, and beat, wounded and ill treated them the said John Oker and Thomas Wylson so that they despaired of their lives, and tied their hands and feet with various cords, and (their hands and feet being so tied as aforesaid) feloniously took and carried away £200 in coin then and there found, of the goods and chattels of the said lord king and queen, then and there being in the keeping and hands of the said John Oker, from the person of the aforesaid John Oker, at Gonerby aforesaid, against the peace of the said present lord king and queen etc. In witness whereof William Cicell, knight, one of the justices of the said lord king and lady queen in the parts and county aforesaid, applied his seal to this inquisition. – Which indictment the lord king and lady queen, for certain reasons, afterwards caused to come before themselves to be determined etc. – Therefore

[1] Fitz. Abr., *Challenge*, pl. 56 (*Beauchamp's Case*, YB Trin. 9 Edw. IV, fo. 27, pl. 40).

[2] Unidentified; not in Fitz. Abr., *Triall*. Cf. YB Mich. 10 Hen. VI, fo. 16, pl. 51 (Fitz. Abr., *Challenge*, pl. 31), which distinguishes real and personal actions.

sigillum suum apposuit. – Quodquidem indictamentum dominus rex et domina regina nunc postea certis de causis coram eis venire fecerunt terminandum etc. – Per quod preceptum fuit vicecomiti quod non omitteret etc. quin capiat eos si etc. – Et modo, scilicet die Mercurii proximo post octabas Sancte Trinitatis isto eodem termino coram domino rege et domina regina apud Westmonasterium veniunt predicti Dionisius Thymblebye et Johannes Gray in propriis personis suis et redderunt se prisone marescalli marescalcie dominorum regis et regine coram ipsis rege et regina existentis <occasione predicta>[i] qui committuntur marescallo etc. Et statim de premissis eis superius impositis separatim[i] allocuti qualiter se vellent inde acquietari separatim dicunt quod ipsi in nullo sunt inde culpabiles. Et inde de bono et malo separatim ponunt se super patriam. Ideo veniat separatim inde jurata coram domino rege et domina regina a die Sancti Michaelis in tres septimanas <ubicumque etc.>[i] et qui etc. ad recognoscendum etc. quia etc. Idem dies datus est prefato Dionisio Thymblebye et Johanni Gray sub custodia prefati marescalli etc.

Ad quasquidem tres septimanas Sancti Michaelis coram domino rege et domina regina apud Westmonasterium venerunt predicti Dionisius Thymblebye et Johannes Graye sub custodia prefati marescalli ad barram hic ducti in propriis personis suis. Et juratores inter dictos dominos regem et reginam ac prefatum Johannem Graye impanellati exacti similiter venerunt qui ad veritatem de premissis dicendam electi, triati et jurati dicunt super sacramentum suum quod predictus Johannes Graye de felonia et roberia predictis ei superius impositis est culpabilis et quod ipse nulla habet terras, tenementa, bona nec catalla. Ideo consideratum est quod predictus Johannes Graye suspendatur etc. Et juratores inter dictos dominum regem et dominam reginam ac prefatum Dionisium Thymblebye similiter exacti, quidem eorum venerunt et electi, triati et jurati fuerunt, et quidam eorum calumpniati fuerunt peremptorie per prefatum Dionisium Thymblebye et quidam eorundem juratorum pro eo quod ipsi inter predictos dominum regem et dominam reginam et prefatum Dionisium Thymblebye pro parte ipsius Dionisii suspecti inveniuntur a panello penitus extrahuntur, et residuum juratorum predictorum non venerunt, prout patet per panellum etc. Ideo eadem jurata inter dictos dominum regem et dominam reginam et prefatum Dionisium Thymblebye de premissis ponitur in respectum coram domino rege et domina regina usque a die Sancti Hillarii in xv dies ubicumque etc. et quod vicecomes appon' viginti tales cum amot' etc. Idem dies datus est prefato Dionisio Thymblebye in custodia prefati marescalli ibidem etc. Ad quamquidem quindenam Sancti Hillarii coram domino rege et domina regina apud Westmonasterium venit predictus Dionisius Thymblebye sub custodia prefati marescalli in propria persona sua. Et juratores exacti, quidem eorum venerunt et quidem eorum non venerunt, prout patet per panellum etc. Ideo jurata illa ad diem illam remanet capienda pro defectu juratorum etc. Et ut prius jurata predicta ulterius ponitur in respectum coram domino rege et domina regina usque a die Pasche in xv dies ubicumque etc. Et quod decem tales etc. apponat. Idem dies datus est prefato Dionisio Thymblebye in custodia prefati marescalli etc. Ad quasquidem tres septimanas [*sic*] Pasche coram domino rege et domina regina apud Westmonasterium venit predictus Dionisius Thymblebye sub custodia prefati marescalli in propria persona sua. Et juratores jurate exacti similiter venerunt qui ad veritatem de premissis [dicendam][1] electi, triati et jurati dicunt super sacramentum suum quod predictus Dionisius Thymblebye est culpabilis de feloniis et roberiis ei superius impositis et quod ipse nulla habet terras, tenementa, bona neque catalla. Super quo, visis omnibus et singulis premissis, consideratum est quod predictus Dionisius Thymblebye suspendatur. <cul[pabilis] ca[talla] nul[la] s[uspendatur]>[2]

1 *Reads* dicendi.
2 *Marginal note.*

the sheriff was commanded that he omit not etc. but take them if etc. – And now, namely on the Wednesday [23 June 1557] next after the octave of the Holy Trinity this same term, before the lord king and lady queen at Westminster, come the aforesaid Dennis Thymbleby and John Gray in their own persons, and surrender themselves to the prison of the marshal of the marshalsea of the lord king and lady queen, being before them the said king and queen, by reason of the foregoing; and they are committed to the marshal etc. And, being forthwith asked, concerning the foregoing matters above charged against them, how they would acquit themselves thereof, they severally say that they are in no wise guilty thereof; and of this they put themselves, for good and ill, upon the country. Therefore let a jury severally come therein before the lord king and lady queen in three weeks from Michaelmas wheresoever etc. and who etc. to make recognition etc. because etc. The same day is given to the said Dennis Thymbleby and John Gray, under the custody of the said marshal etc.

At which three weeks from Michaelmas, before the lord king and lady queen at Westminster, the aforesaid Dennis Thymbleby and John Gray came, being led the bar here in their own persons under the custody of the said marshal. And the jurors impanelled between the said lord king and queen and the said John Gray, having been called, likewise came; and, having been chosen, tried and sworn to say the truth concerning the foregoing, they say upon their oath that the aforesaid John Gray is guilty of the aforesaid felony and robbery above charged against him, and that he has no lands, tenements, goods or chattels. Therefore it is adjudged that the aforesaid John Gray be hanged etc. And the jurors between the said lord king and lady queen and the said Dennis Thymbleby having been likewise called, some of them came and were chosen, tried and sworn; and some of them were challenged peremptorily by the said Dennis Thymbleby; and some of the said jurors were completely withdrawn from the panel because they were suspected, as between the aforesaid lord king and lady queen and the said Dennis Thymbleby, of being on the side of the selfsame Dennis; and the rest of the aforesaid jurors did not come, as appears by the panel etc. Therefore the same jury between the said lord king and lady queen and the said Dennis concerning the foregoing is put in respite before the lord king and lady queen until fifteen days from Saint Hilary wheresoever etc. and that the sheriff put in twenty *tales* 'cum amot.' etc. The same day is given to the said Dennis Thymbleby in the custody of the said marshal there etc. At which quindene of St Hilary, before the lord king and lady queen at Westminster, the aforesaid Dennis Thymbleby came in his own person under the custody of the said marshal. And, the jurors having been called, some of them came and some of them did not come, as appears by the panel etc. Therefore the jury remains to be taken at that day for want of jurors etc. And, as before, the aforesaid jury is further put in respite before the lord king and lady queen until fifteen days from Easter day wheresover etc. and that [the sheriff] put in ten *tales.* The same day is given to the said Dennis Thymbleby in the custody of the said marshal etc. At which [quindene] of Easter, before the lord king and lady queen at Westminster, the aforesaid Dennis Thymbleby came in his own person under the custody of the said marshal. And the jurors, having been called, likewise came; and, having been chosen, tried and sworn to say the truth concerning the foregoing, they say upon their oath that the aforesaid Dennis Thymbleby is guilty of the felonies and robberies above charged against him, and that he has no lands, tenements, goods or chattels. Whereupon, all and singular the foregoing having been looked into, it is adjudged that the said Dennis Thymbleby be hanged. (Guilty. No chattels. To be hanged.)

Michaelis Philippi et Marie 4° et 5° 1557

[1]

Abr. in *A*, fo. 33v (Trin. 4 & 5 Phil. & Mar.); *L* 251 (sim.).

Nota que loppinion des justices assembles al Serjeantes Inne en Fleestreete que si le roy grant al un lycence de aliener[1] en mortmain[2] que cest lycence est bon et endura coment que le roy morust que fist le lycence yssint en mortmaine mes si le roy lycence son tenant al aliener al auter en fee ore si cest lycence ne soit execute en le vie cest roy que issuit lycence que ore cest licence est void per le mort cestui roy quar il est ore tenant al auter [*fol. 43v*] roy mes en le case de mortmaine auterment est. Yssint le melior oppinion fuit que le Roy E. le 6. graunta lycence al auter a carier graine ou laynes ouster le myer ou beer coment que le graunt nest a lycence pur le roy et ses successors que le dit lycence est bon et liera le royen que ore est apres le morte de dit Roy E. le 6: quod nota.

[2]

Un appeall de morte dun home fuit porte per Richard Reede vers Rotherfourtes, Wilkinson, Slater, Nixson et Dod come principalls pur le mort Jerratt Reede, frater al dit Richard Reede, et vers John Swinburne come accessories mesme le morte. Nyxon fuit utlage. Slater tender battaill, le playntiefe demurre en ley sur le ple, et le ple fuit adjudge bon et Slater dimisse a son libertie. Ratherfourtes, Wilkinson et Swynburne eux mittant sur le pais et le jurie al nisi prius en le pais esteant prist a passer le playntiefe fuit nonsuite en paies et cest recorde. Et puis les dittes Rotherfurth, Wilkinson et Swyneburne fueront arrere arraine a suite le roy, et devant tryall Wilkinson fist default, et per nisi prius en pais Rotherfurth fuit acquite per verdit et auxi Swynburne come accessorie a Nyxon, et lour damage[s] severalment assesses per le jurie et divers troves abbettors en deffault le sufficiency le playntiefe a render damages assesses. Et puis apres Wilkinson vient et fuit eodem modo acquite per verditt, et sur cest Swynburne pria son judgement dacquitall et proces vers abbettours. Et puis fuit advise per le corte que Slater adevant dismissa sur son plea de battaill veigne eins en courte arere

[1] emer *L*.
[2] *Repeated as:* ou al alin[er] en mortmaine.

Mich. 4 & 5 [Phil. & Mar.], 1557

1. DEMISE OF THE CROWN: PREROGATIVE LICENCES

Serjeants' Inn, Fleet Street, Mich. 1557.

Note, by the opinion of the justices assembled at Serjeants' Inn in Fleet Street, that if the king grants someone a licence to alienate in mortmain[1] this licence is good (in the case of mortmain) and will last even though the king who gave the licence dies. If, however, the king licenses his tenant to alienate to another in fee, and this licence is not executed in the king's lifetime, the licence becomes void by that king's death, for the licensee is now another king's tenant, whereas in the case of mortmain it is otherwise. Thus the better opinion was that, where King Edward VI granted someone a licence to carry grain or wool across the sea, or beer, even though the grant is not a licence by the king 'and his successors', the said licence is good and shall bind the present queen after the death of the said King Edward VI.[2] Note that.

2. READE v. ROTHERFORTH and others

King's Bench, Mich. 1557. Record: KB 27/1164, m. 159 (proceedings at the queen's suit 1555–56, noted below; KB 27/1181, m. 120 (Swynburne's *scire facias*; tried before Dalison and Rastell JJ. at Newcastle assizes, 12 Aug. 1557), printed below; KB 27/1183, m. 103 (jur. resp.). Earlier stages also reported in Dyer, fo. 120 (Mich. 1555) and fo. 131 (Pas. 1556; and see above, p. 121).

An appeal of a man's death was brought by Richard Reede against [Rotherforth], Wilkinson, Slater, Nixon and Dod, as principals, for the death of Jerratt[3] Reede, brother of the said Richard Reede, and against John Swynburne as accessory to the same death. Nixon was outlawed. Slater tendered battle, the plaintiff demurred in law upon the plea, the plea was held good, and Slater was dismissed at his liberty. Rotherforth, Wilkinson and Swynburne put themselves upon the country, and when the jury at nisi prius in the country was ready to pass, the plaintiff was nonsuited in the country, and this was recorded. Then the said Rotherforth, Wilkinson and Swynburne were arraigned again at the king's suit, and before trial Wilkinson made default; and by nisi prius in the country Rotherforth was acquitted by verdict, and also Swynburne as accessory to Nixon, and their damages were separately assessed by the jury; and various people were found abettors [of the appeal] in default of the plaintiff's sufficiency to render the damages assessed. Then, afterwards, Wilkinson came and was acquitted in the same way by verdict. Thereupon Swynburne prayed his judgment of acquittal, and prayed process against the abettors. Then it was advised by the court that Slater, previously dismissed upon his plea of battle, should come back into court and be

[1] Perhaps 'to buy or to alienate in mortmain'.

[2] This seems to be a reference to the case of 1553 in Dyer, fo. 92a.

[3] I.e. Gerard. In the English warrant, set out in the record below, it is 'Garrat'.

et arraine al sute le roy et issint fuit et il fuit discharge sur son arrainment per le [conusance][1] latturney le roy per warrant le roy et royen. Et sur cest Swinburne ad son judgement dacquitall et scire facias vers les abbettors, queux abbettors appere et un justifie per reason de le commen voice et fame etc. et les auters pled[ont] que ils ne abettont, et sur cest ples fueront al issue. Et al nisi prius fuit trove que ilz abettont et que cestui que justefie fuit abettor de son torte demesne sanz tiel cause et sur cest Swinburne ad son judgement vers les dittes abbettors et execution. Et tout cest matter fuit in comitatu Northumberland. Nota ycie que nient obstant que Wilkingson un des principalls fait deffault apres issue joyne, Swyneburne come accessorie al Rotherfurth et a Nyxon fuit acquite eo que il est per le ley accessorie a chescun de eux et issint accessorye ne targe son tryall per [default] dun principall.

Note from the record

KB 27/1164, m. 159.

Richard Reade, gentleman, brother and heir of Gerard (or Garret) Reade, brings an appeal against Ralph Rotherforthe of Ovingham, Northumberland, gentleman, James Slayter[2] of Ovingham, yeoman, John Wylkynson of Bellingham, yeoman, and John Swynborne of Ryton, co. Durham, gentleman, together with Archibald Dodd and Patrick Nyxson of Bellingham, yeomen, who do not appear, for the death of his brother at Ovingham on 30 August [1551], 5 Edw. VI, around 7 a.m., from a wound to the head with a 'lanstaf' held by Dodd and a club held by Rotherforthe, the others (except Swynborne) being present aiding and abetting, and Swynborne having been accessory before the fact on 27–29 August. Rotherforthe, Wylkynson and Swynborne plead Not guilty and put themselves upon the country, but the process with respect to Swynborne is stayed until the other principals have been convicted. All three are mainprised. Slayter pleads Not guilty and wages battle, to which Reade demurs; and in Easter term judgment is given on the demurrer in favour of Slayter, who is thereupon discharged. On 8 August 1553 at Newcastle assizes, before

[*Continued opposite*]

Et super hoc predictus Johannes Swynborne petit judicium de et super premissis per curiam dominorum regis et regine coram ipsis rege et regina sibi reddi ac quod idem Johannes per eandem curiam dominorum regis et regine hic super premissis exonerari et pro eo quod super diligenti inspectione recordi et processus predictorum per eandem curiam dominorum regis et regine videtur eidem curie quod predictus Jacobus Sclayter qui superius de principali facto mortis predicti [appellatur], cui quidam Jacobo predictus Johannes Swynborne ut accessarius in forma predicta similiter appellatur, de murdro predicto juxta jura[3] hujus regni Anglie adhuc non triatur <nec legittimo modo inde adhuc acquietatus

[1] *Reads* commission *or* conussion.
[2] In this record variously spelt Sclayther, Slather, Slayther and Slayter.
[3] juria.

arraigned at the king's suit. That was done, and he was discharged upon his arraignment by the commission of the king's attorney, by the king's and queen's warrant. Thereupon Swynburne had his judgment of acquittal, and a *scire facias* against the abettors, which abettors appeared. One of the abettors justified by reason of the common voice and fame etc., and the others pleaded that they did not abet, and upon these pleas they were at issue, and at nisi prius it was found that they did abet and that the one who justified was abettor 'of his own wrong, without such cause'; and thereupon Swynburne had his judgment against the said abettors, and execution. All this matter was in the county of Northumberland. Note here that although Wilkinson, one of the principals, made default after issue joined, nevertheless Swynburne was acquitted as accessory to Rotherforth and Nixon, inasmuch as by the law he is accessory to each of them. Thus the accessory shall not be delayed of his trial for want of a principal.

Note from the record

King's Bench, Michaelmas term 1552.

[*Continued from opposite page*]

Edward Saunders and William Dallyson, justices of assize, Reade is nonsuited after the retirement of the jury, and the jury are charged to enquire into the damages and the abettors. Rotherforthe, Wylkynson and Swynborne are thereupon discharged from Reade's appeal, but are instantly arraigned at the queen's suit, plead Not guilty, and are bailed. Nyxson is returned outlawed in Nov. [1553], 1 Mar., and Dodd is reported dead in Michaelmas term [1554], 1 & 2 Phil. & Mar. On 14 Aug. 1555, Rotherforthe and Swynborne are acquitted at Newcastle assizes before Saunders and Dalyson, justices of assize, information being given for the king and queen by Christopher Wraye; judgment is given for them to be discharged, and for damages to be recovered against the abettors (as appears in the later record on pp. 141–144, below). The following year Wylkynson, who defaulted earlier, is likewise acquitted at Newcastle assizes, George Salven appearing for the king and queen,[1] and there is a similar enquiry. The record continues:

And thereupon the aforesaid John Swynborne prays judgment upon and concerning the foregoing to be given for him by the court of the lord king and lady queen before them the said king and queen, and that the same John may be discharged of the foregoing by the same court of the lord king and lady queen here; and forasmuch as upon diligent inspection of the aforesaid record and process by the same court of the lord king and lady queen it seems to the same court that the aforesaid James Slayter, who is above likewise appealed of the principal fact of the aforesaid death, to which James the aforesaid John Swynborne is likewise appealed as accessory in form aforesaid, has not yet been tried for the aforesaid murder in accordance with the laws of this realm of England or in lawful manner acquitted thereof, since the same James has not yet been arraigned at the suit of the lord king

[1] Wray and Salven were barristers of Lincoln's Inn, probably here acting as clerks of the crown on the Northern circuit.

exsitit pro eo>[i] quod idem Jacobus ad sectam dominorum regis et regine de premissis adhuc non arectatur, ad quorum sectam idem Jacobus legittime modo adjudicari debet antequam predictus Johannes Swynborne de premissis exonerari debet, ideo preceptum est vicecomiti comitatus Northumbrie quod capiat predictum Jacobum si etc. et salvo etc. ita quod habeat corpus ejus coram predictis dominis rege et regine in crastino Animarum ubicumque etc. ad respondendum dominis regi et regine de principali facto mortis predicti Gerardi Reade etc. Idem dies datus est predicto Johanni Swynborne per breve de nisi prius etc. Ad quodquidem crastinum Animarum coram domino rege et domina regina apud Westmonasterium veniunt tam predictus Jacobus Slayter sub custodia Georgii Heron armigeri vicecomitis dicti comitatus Northumbrie virtute dicti brevis sibi inde directi ad barram hic ductus in propria persona sua quam prefatus Johannes Swynbourne similiter in propria persona sua. Quiquidem Jacobus Slayter committitur marescalli etc. Et statim quoad sectam dominorum regis et regine in hac parte idem Jacobus Sclayter de felonia et murdro predictis allocutus qualiter se vellet inde acquietari dicit quod ipse in nullo est inde culpabilis. Et inde de bono et malo ponit se super patriam. Et Edwardus Gryffyn armiger attornatus dominorum regis et regine, qui pro ipsis rege et regina sequitur, virtute cujusdam warranti dominorum regis et regine cum privato sigillo ipsorum regis et regine sigillati eidem Edwardo directi pro eisdem domino rege et domina regina dicit et cognovit placitum predictum per prefatum Jacobum Slayter in forma predicta superius placitatum fore verum prout idem Jacobus superius placitando allegavit. Cujusquidem warranti tenore sequitur in hec verba:

> Philip and Mary by the grace of God Kynge and Quene of Englond, Spayne, Fraunce, both Cicelles, Jerusalem and Irelond, Defenders of the Faithe, Archedukes of Austrige, Dukes of Burgundie, Myllan and Brabant, Counties of Haspurge, Flaundres and Tiroll, to our trustie and welbeloved Edward Gryffyn our attorney generall, gretyng. Wheare as we be enformed that there hathe been of late one appeale of murdre dependyng before our moost deare brother Edward the sixte late kynge of Englond in his benche agaynst James Slather, late of Ovyngeham in the countie of Northumberlond yeoman and other at the sute of one Richard Reade, brother and heyre of Garrat Reade, gent', in the whyche appeale[i] the said James Slayther pleaded not gyltie and for tryall offred battaill unto the playntiffe, upon the whyche plee the said Richard Reade dyd demurre in the lawe, and by judgement of the said courte the said plee and answere was allowed for a good and sufficient barre unto the said appeale, whereupon the said James as agaynst the said playntief was discharged of the said matter and appeale, and yet not so as agaynst us, but ought for his further tryall theryn by our lawes to be arrayned at our sute in that behalf, we [will] that if the said James upon his arraynement at our sute plede non gyltie or any other plee or plees for his discharge of the same that ye for us and in our name in that behalfe confesse and knowledge all suche plee or plees as soe pleaded by the said James Slather to be true, so that the said James Slather maie be clerely discharged and dismissed, and theise our letters shalbe your sufficient warraunt and discharge in this behalf. Yeoven under our privie seale at our manour of Saynt James the xijth of Novembre the thyrde and fourthe yeres of our reignes.

Super quo, visis et per curiam intellectis tam placito predicti Jacobi Slather quam dicta cognitione predicti Edwardi Gryffyn regis et regine [attornati] ejusdem placiti in forma predicta facta, consideratum est quod predictus Jacobus Slather eat inde sine die etc. Et quoad prefatum Johannem Swynbourne, accessarium in hac parte, visis et per curiam hic intellectis omnibus et singulis premissis, consideratum est quod idem Johannes Swynbourne similiter eat inde sine die etc.

and lady queen,[1] at whose suit the same James ought lawfully to be adjudged before the aforesaid John Swynburne ought to be discharged from the foregoing, therefore the sheriff of the county of Northumberland is ordered to take the aforesaid James if etc. and safely etc. so that he have his body before the aforesaid lord king and lady queen on the morrow of All Souls, wheresoever etc., to answer the lord king and lady queen with respect to the principal fact of the death of the aforesaid Gerard Reade etc. The same day is given to the aforesaid John Swynburne by writ of nisi prius etc. At which morrow of All Souls before the lord king and lady queen at Westminster come both the aforesaid James Slayter, in the custody of George Heron, esquire, sheriff of the said county of Northumberland, by virtue of the writ directed to him therein, brought to the bar here in his own person, and the said John Swynburne likewise, in his own person; which James Slayter is committed to the marshal etc. And with respect to the suit of the lord king and lady queen in that behalf, the same James Slayter, being forthwith asked how he would acquit himself of the murder and felony aforesaid, says that he is in no wise guilty thereof; and thereof for good and ill he puts himself upon the country. And Edward Gryffyn, esquire, attorney-[general] of the lord king and lady queen, who sues for the selfsame king and queen, by virtue of a certain warrant of the lord king and lady queen, sealed with the privy seal of them the said king and queen, directed to the same Edward, says on behalf of the same lord king and lady queen and confesses the aforesaid plea as pleaded above by the said James Slayter in form aforesaid to be true, as the same James has above alleged in pleading. The tenor of which warrant follows in these words:

> Philip and Mary, by the grace of God King and Queen of England, Spain, France, both Sicilies, Jerusalem and Ireland, Defenders of the Faith, Archdukes of Austria, Dukes of Burgundy, Milan and Brabant, Counts of Hapsburg, Flanders and Tyrol, to our trusty and well beloved Edward Gryffyn, our attorney-general, greeting. Whereas we be informed that there hath been of late an appeal of murder depending before our most dear brother Edward the sixth, late king of England, in his Bench, against James Slayter, late of Ovingham in the county of Northumberland, yeoman, and others, at the suit of one Richard Reade, brother and heir of Garret Reade, gentleman, in the which appeal the said James Slayter pleaded not guilty and for trial offered battle unto the plaintiff, upon the which plea the said Richard Reade did demur in the law, and by judgment of the said court the said plea and answer was allowed for a good and sufficient bar unto the said appeal, whereupon the said James as against the said plaintiff was discharged of the said matter and appeal, and yet not so as against us, but ought for his further trial therein by our laws to be arraigned at our suit in that behalf, we will that if the said James upon his arraignment at our suit plead not guilty or any other plea or pleas for his discharge of the same that you, for us and in our name in that behalf, confess and acknowledge all such plea or pleas as so pleaded by the said James Slayter to be true, so that the said James Slayter may be clearly discharged and dismissed, and these our letters shall be your sufficient warrant and discharge in this behalf. Given under our privy seal at our manor of St James, the twelfth of November [in] the third and fourth years of our reigns.

Whereupon, both the plea of the aforesaid James Slayter and the said confession of the same plea by aforesaid Edward Gryffyn, the king and queen's attorney, made in form aforesaid, having been seen and fully understood by the court here, it is awarded that the aforesaid James Slayter go thereof without day etc. And with respect to the said John Swynburne, the accessory in that behalf, all and singular the foregoing having been seen and understood by the court here, it is awarded that the same John Swynburne likewise go thereof without day etc.

[1] Slayter having been discharged by the judgment on demurrer to his plea of battle in the appeal.

Record of Swynburne's *scrie facias*

KB 27/1181, m. 120.

Dominus rex et domina regina mandaverunt vicecomiti Northumbrie <breve suum>[i] clausum in hec verba:

Philippus et Maria Dei gracia Rex et Regina Anglie, Hispaniarum, Francie, utriusque Cicilie, Jerusalem et Hibernie, Fidei Defensores, Archiduces Austrie, Duces Burgundie, Mediolani et Brabantie, Comites Haspurgi, Flandrie et Tirolis, vicecomiti Northumbrie salutem. Cum per quandam juratam patrie nuper in curia nostra coram Edwardo Saunders milite et Willelmo Dallyson nuper servienti ad legem, justiciariis nostris ad assisas in comitatu tuo capiendas assignatis apud castrum ville Novi Castri super Tinam in comitatu tuo per breve nostrum de nisi prius die Mercurii proximo ante festum Assumptionis Beate Marie annis regnorum nostrorum secundo et tercio inter nos et Johannem Swynborne nuper de Ryton in comitatu episcopatus Dunolmensis generosum super non prosecutione cujusdam brevis domini Edwardi nuper regis Anglie sexti, fratris nostri dicte regine, de appello per Ricardum Rede generosum, fratrem et heredem Gerardi Rede, versus Radulphum Rotherforth nuper de Ovingeham in comitatu tuo generosum, Jacobum Slayther nuper de Ovingeham in comitatu tuo yoman, Archeboldum Dodde nuper de Bellyngeham in comitatu tuo yoman, Johannem Wylkynson nuper de Bellingeham predicta in comitatu tuo yoman, et Patricium Nixson nuper de Bellyngeham predicta in comitatu tuo yoman de principali facto mortis predicti Gerardi Rede quondam fratris sui et versus predictum Johannem Swynborne per nomen Johannis Swynburne nuper de Ryton in comitatu episcopatus Dunolmensis generosum de accessario mortis predicti Gerardi Rede captam compertum existit quod predictus Johannes Swynborne in nullo fuit culpabillis de felonia et murdro predicti Gerardi Rede nec ea occasione aliqualiter se retraxit, super quo ad petitionem predicti Johannis Swynburne tunc et ibidem quesitum fuit per justiciarios predictos a juratoribus[1] predictis que dampna predictus Johannes Swynburne occasione premissorum sustinuit, quiquidem juratores adtunc et ibidem dixerunt quod predictus Johannes Swynborne sustinuit dampna tam occasione falsi appelli predicti necnon infamie imprisonamenti et arestationis corporis sui quam pro misis et custagiis suis per ipsum circa sectam suam in ea parte appositis ad ducentas et viginti libras, et iidem juratores similiter ad requisitionem predicti Johannis Swynborne onerati ad inquirendum utrum predictus Ricardus Rede sufficiens fuit ad satisfaciendum prefato Johanni Swynborne de predictis ducentis et viginti libris necne ac si idem Ricardus Reade adhoc non fuit[2] sufficiens tunc ad inquirendum qui fuerunt abbettatores predicti Ricardi Rede ad prosequendum appellum predictum, quiquidem juratores dixerunt super sacramentum suum quod predictus Ricardus Rede non fuit sufficiens ad satisfaciendum dampna predicta ac quod Thomas Carye, constabularius, nuper de Proude in comitatu tuo armiger, Gilbertus Erington de Wyssenton in comitatu predicto gent', Thomas Rede de Close in comitato tuo gent', Gawinus Rede de Costenside in comitatu tuo, yoman, Willelmus Ogle de Horseley in comitatu tuo gent' et Gilbertus Heron de Haulbarnes in comitatu tuo gent' ex sua malicia instigaverunt, abbettaverunt et procuraverunt predictum Ricardum Rede ad capiendum et prosequendum appellum suum predictum versus predictum Johannem Swynborne in forma predicta prout in curia nostra coram nobis liquet de recordo, de quibusquidem felonio et murdro idem Johannes Swynborne postea per judicium curie nostre coram nobis apud Westmonasterium fuit acquietatus, prout in eadem curia liquet etiam de recordo, jamque ex parte predicti Johannis Swynborne in curia nostra coram

[1] juritor'.
[2] *Sic.*

Translation of the record of Swynburne's *scire facias*

King's Bench, Hilary term 1557.

The lord king and lady queen have sent their writ close to the sheriff of Northumberland in these words:

Philip and Mary, by the grace of God King and Queen of England, Spain, France, both Sicilies, Jerusalem and Ireland, Defenders of the Faith, Archdukes of Austria, Dukes of Burgundy, Milan and Brabant, Counts of Hapsburg, Flanders and Tyrol, to the sheriff of Northumberland greeting. Whereas it appears by a certain jury of the country lately taken in our court before Edward Saunders, knight, and William Dallyson, lately serjeant at law, our justices assigned to take the assizes in your county, at the castle of Newcastle upon Tyne in your county, by our writ of nisi prius, on the Wednesday next before the feast of the Assumption of the Blessed Mary [14 Aug. 1555] in the second and third years of our reigns, between us and John Swynburne[1] late of Ryton in the county of the bishopric of Durham, gentleman, upon the non-prosecution of a certain writ of the lord Edward the sixth, late king of England, brother of ourself the said queen, upon an appeal by Richard Rede, gentleman, brother and heir of Gerard Rede, against Ralph Rotherforth late of Ovingham in your county, gentleman, James Slayther late of Ovingham in your county, yeoman, Archibald Dodde late of Bellingham in your county, yeoman, John Wylkynson late of Bellingham aforesaid in your county, yeoman, and Patrick Nixson late of Bellingham aforesaid in your county, yeoman, for the principal fact of the death of the aforesaid Gerard Rede, formerly his brother, and against the aforesaid John Swynburne, by the name of John Swynburne late of Ryton in the county of the bishopric of Durham, gentleman, as accessory to the death of the aforesaid Gerard Rede, that the aforesaid John Swynburne was in no wise guilty of the felony and murder of the aforesaid Gerard Rede and in no way withdrew himself for that reason; whereupon at the beseeching of the aforesaid John Swynburne the aforesaid jurors were then and there asked by the aforesaid justices what damages the aforesaid John Swynburne had sustained by reason of the foregoing, which jurors then and there said that the aforesaid John Swynburne had sustained damages of £220, both by reason of the aforesaid false appeal and the infamy of imprisonment and bodily arrest and also for his outlay and costs laid out by him about his suit in that behalf; and the same jurors being likewise charged at the request of the aforesaid John Swynburne to enquire whether the aforesaid Richard Rede was sufficient to satisfy the said John Swynburne in respect of the aforesaid £220, or not, and if the same Richard was not sufficient then to enquire who were the abettors of the aforesaid Richard Rede in prosecuting his aforesaid appeal, the jurors said upon their oath that the aforesaid Richard Rede was not sufficient to satisfy the aforesaid damages and that Thomas Cary, late constable of 'Proude' in your county, esquire, Gilbert Eryngton of 'Wyssenton' in the aforesaid county, gentleman, Thomas Rede of Close in your county, gentleman, Gawain Rede of 'Costenside' in your county, yeoman, William Ogle of Horsley in your county, gentleman, and Gilbert Heron of 'Haulbarnes' in your county, gentleman, of their malice instigated, abetted and procured the aforesaid Richard Rede in taking and prosecuting his aforesaid appeal against the aforesaid John Swynburne in the form aforesaid, as appears of record in our court before our self, of which felony and murder the same John Swynburne was afterwards acquitted by judgment of our court before ourself at Westminster, as also appears of record in the same court; and now on behalf of the aforesaid John Swynburne in our court before ourself we understand that execution of the aforesaid damages for

[1] The record varies between the spellings Swynburne and Swynborne.

> nobis accepimus quod executio <de dampnis>[i] predictis prefato Johanni Swynborne adhuc restat facienda, unde nobis supplicavit idem Johannes sibi de remedio congruo versus abbettatores in hac parte provideri: et nos in hac parte fieri volentes quod est justum, tibi precipimus quod per probos et legales homines de balliva tua scire facias prefatis Thome Cary, Gilberto Eryngton, Thome Rede, Gawino Rede, Willelmo Ogle et Gilberto Heron quod <sint coram nobis in octabis Sancti Hillarii ubicumque tunc fuerimus in Anglia ostensuris>[i] si quid pro se habeant aut dicere sciant quare predictus Johannes Swynburne executionem versus eos de predictis dampnis ducentarum et viginti librarum habere non debeat si sibi viderit expediri et ulterius facturis et recepturis quod curia nostra consideraverit in hac parte. Et habeas ibi nomina eorum per quod eis scire feceris et hoc breve. Teste W. Portman apud Westmonasterium xvj° die Octobris annis regno nostri tercio et quarto.

Ad quem diem coram domino rege et domina regina apud Westmonasterium venit predictus Johannes Swynborne in propria persona sua. Et vicecomes retornavit quod virtute dicti brevis sibi inde directi scire fecit prefatis Thome Carye, Gilberto Erington, Thome Rede, Gawino Rede, Willelmo Ogle et Gilberto Heron per Willelmum Sherhedd, Jacobum Newton et Gilbertum Browne probos etc. essendi coram dictis domino rege et domina regina juxta formam brevis illius. Et predicti Thomas Carie, Gilbertus Erington, Thomas Rede, Gawinus Rede, Willelmus Ogle et Gilbertus Heron sic premuniti et quarto die placiti solempniter exacti per Johannem Barowe attornatum suum veniunt. Et super hoc predictus Johannes Swynborne dicit quod predicti Thomas Cary, Gilbertus Eryngton, Thomas Rede, Gawinus Rede, Willelmus Ogle et Gilbertus Heron quartodecimo die Aprilis anno regni domini Edwardi nuper regis Anglie sexti sexto apud Close in parochia de Heddon super Murum in comitatu predicto ac diversis aliis diebus et locis antea et postea in eodem comitato falso et malicio abbettaverunt et procuraverunt predictum Ricardum Rede ad capiendum et prosequendum predictum appellum versus predictum Johannem Swynborne in forma predicta contra formam statuti inde editi et provisi ad dampnum ipsius Johannis Swynborne ducentarum et viginti librarum et amplius, unde petit executionem de predictis ducentis et viginti libris sibi adjudicari etc.

Et predicti Thomas Cary, Gilbertus Erington, Gawinus Rede, Willelmus Ogle et Gilbertus Heron per attornatum suum predictum veniunt et defendunt vim et injuriam quando etc. Et dicunt quod predictus Johannes Swynborne executionem versus eos de predictis ducentis et viginti libris habere non debet quia predicti Thomas Carye, Gilbertus Eryngton, Gawinus Rede, Willelmus Ogle et Gilbertus Heron dicunt quod non instigaverunt, abbettaverunt nec procuraverunt predictum Ricardum Rede ad capiendum et prosequendum appellum predictum versus predictum Johannem Swynborne modo et forma prout predictus Johannes Swynborne superius versus eos narravit. Et de hoc ponunt se super patriam. Et predictus Johannes Swynborne similiter etc.

Et predictus Thomas Rede dicit quod post murdrum predicti Gerardi Rede communis vox et fama fuit in comitatu predicto quod predictus Johannes Swynborne procuravit predictos Radulphum Rotherforde, Jacobum Slayther, Archiboldum Dodde, Johannem Wylkynson et Patricium Nyxson ad murdrandum predictum Gerardum Rede, virtute cujus idem Thomas Rede dictis die et anno apud Close predictam instigavit, procuravit et abbettavit predictum Ricardum Rede ad capiendum et prosequendum appellum suum predictum versus prefatum Johannem Swynborne modo et forma prout ei bene licuit. Et hoc paratus est verificare etc.

Et predictus Johannes Swynburne dicit quod ipse per aliqua per predictum Thomam preallegata ab executione dampnorum predictorum versus eundem Thomam Rede habenda precludi non debet, quia dicit quod predictus Thomas simul cum predictis Thoma Cary, Gilberto Erington, Gawino Rede, Willelmo Ogle et Gilberto Heron die et anno et the aforesaid John Swynburne still remains to be carried out, whereupon the same John has besought us to provide him a suitable remedy against the abettors in that behalf: and we, wishing to do what is just in that behalf, command you that by reliable and lawful men of your bailiwick you cause the said Thomas Cary, Gilbert Eryngton, Thomas Rede, Gawain Rede, William Ogle and Gilbert Heron to be aware that they must be before ourselves in the octave of St Hilary [1557], wherever we shall then be in England, to show whether they have or know anything to say why the aforesaid John Swynburne ought not to have execution against them for the aforesaid damages of £220, should it seem to him expedient, and further to do and receive what our court shall award in that behalf. And have there the names of those by whom you have caused them to be aware, and this writ. Witness W[illiam] Portman[1] at Westminster on the sixteenth day of October [1556] in the third and fourth years of our reign.

At which day the aforesaid John Swynburne comes before the lord king and lady queen at Westminster in his own person. And the sheriff has returned that by virtue of the said writ therein to him directed he caused the said Thomas Cary, Gilbert Eryngton, Thomas Rede, Gawain Rede, William Ogle and Gilbert Heron, by William Sherhedd, James Newton and Gilbert Browne, reliable men etc., to be before the said lord king and lady queen in accordance with the terms of the writ. And the aforesaid Thomas Cary, Gilbert Eryngton, Thomas Rede, Gawain Rede, William Ogle and Gilbert Heron, having been so warned, and being on the fourth day of the plea solemnly called, come by John Barowe their attorney. And thereupon the aforesaid John Swynburne says that the aforesaid Thomas Cary, Gilbert Eryngton, Thomas Rede, Gawain Rede, William Ogle and Gilbert Heron on the fourteenth day of April [1552] in the sixth year of the reign of the lord Edward the sixth, late king of England, at Close in the parish of Heddon on the Wall in the county aforesaid, and at various other days and places in the same county, both before and afterwards, falsely and maliciously abetted and procured the aforesaid Richard Rede in taking and prosecuting the aforesaid appeal against the aforesaid John Swynburne in form aforesaid, against the terms of the statute therein made and provided, to the damage of him the said John Swynburne of £220 and more, whereupon he prays execution of the aforesaid £220 to be awarded to him etc.

And the aforesaid Thomas Cary, Gilbert Eryngton, Gawain Rede, William Ogle and Gilbert Heron, by their aforesaid attorney, come and deny the force and wrong when etc. And they say that the aforesaid John Swynburne ought not to have execution against them in respect of the aforesaid £220, because the aforesaid Thomas Cary, Gilbert Eryngton, Gawain Rede, William Ogle and Gilbert Heron say that they did not instigate, abet or procure the aforesaid Richard Rede in taking and prosecuting the aforesaid appeal against the aforesaid John Swynburne in manner and form as the aforesaid John Swynburne has above counted against them. And of this they put themselves upon the country; and the aforesaid John Swynburne likewise etc.

And the aforesaid Thomas Rede says that after the murder of the aforesaid Gerard Rede it was commonly reported and reputed in the aforesaid county that the aforesaid John Swynburne procured the aforesaid Ralph Rotherforde, James Slayther, Archibald Dodde, John Wylkynson and Patrick Nyxson to murder the aforesaid Gerard Rede, by virtue whereof the same Thomas Rede on the said day and year, at Close aforesaid, instigated, procured and abetted the aforesaid Richard Rede in taking and prosecuting his aforesaid appeal against the said John Swynburne in manner and form as was lawful for him. And this he is ready to aver etc.

And the aforesaid John Swynburne says that he ought not to be barred by anything previously alleged by the aforesaid Thomas from having execution of the aforesaid dam-

[1] Chief Justice.

loco in narratione predicta specificatis ex malicia sua propria absque causa per predictum Thomam superius placitando allegatam prefatum Ricardum Rede ad capiendum et prosequendum falsum appellum suum predictum versus ipsum Johannem et alios in appello illo nominatos abbettavit et procuravit modo et forma prout superius supponitur. Et hoc petit quod inquiratur per patriam. Et predictus Thomas Rede similiter. Ideo tam quoad triandum exitum illum quam predictum alium exitum superius inter predictum Johannem Swynborne et predictos Thomam Cary, Gilbertum Eryngton, Gawinum Rede, Willelmum Ogle et Gilbertum Heron junctum veniat inde jurata coram dominis rege et regina a die Pasche in xv dies ubicumque etc. et qui nec etc. ad recognoscendum etc. quia tam etc. Idem dies datus est partibus predictis etc.

Postea continuato inde processu[1] inter partes predictas de placito predicto per juratas positas inde inter eas in respectum coram domino rege et domina regina usque in octabis Sancti Michaelis <extunc proximo sequentibus>[i] ubicumque etc. nisi justiciarii domini regis et domine regine ad assisas in comitatu predicto capiendas assignati prius die Jovis proximo post festum Sancti Laurencii Martiris apud castrum Novi Castri super Tinam in comitatu predicto per formam statuti etc. venerunt pro defectu juratorum etc. Ad quem diem coram domino rege et domina regina apud Westmonasterium veniunt partes predicti per attornatos suos predictos. Et prefati justiciarii coram quibus etc. misunt hic recordum coram eis habitum in hec verba:

> Postea, die et loco infracontentis, coram Willelmo Dalyson uno justiciariorum domini regis et domine regine ad placita coram dictis domino rege et domina regina tenenda assignatorum et Willelmo Rastell serviente ad legem, justiciariis domini regis et domine regine ad assisas in comitatu Northumbrie capiendas assignatis apud castrum Novi Castri super Tinam in comitatu predicto per formam statuti[i] etc. venerunt tam infranominatus Johannes Swynburne in propria persona suam quam infranominati Thomas Cary, Gilbertus, Thomas Rede, Gawinus, Willelmus Ogle et Gilbertus Heron per attornatos suos infraspecificatos. <Et juratores jurate infraspecificate>[i] exacti, quidem eorum videlicet Johannes Wytherington de Mytforth gent', Anthonius Fenwyk de Lanshawes gent', Lancelotus Ogle gent', Lancelotus Lesley gent', Johannes Chester gent', Robertus Hoyseley gent', Cristoferus Redshawe gent' et Thomas Rotherforthe gent' venerunt, qui ad veritatem de infracontentis dicendam electi, triati et jurati existunt, et quia residuum juratorum jurate predicte non comparuerunt prout patet in panello, ideo alii de circumstantibus per vicecomitem electi ad requisitionem predicti Johannis Swynborne ac per mandatum justiciariorum de novo apponuntur secundum formam statuti in hujusmodi casu editi et provisi, quorum nomina patent in quodam panello predicto panello annexo, ac quidam juratores sic de novo appositi, videlicet Thomas Bradforthe gent', Thomas Ilderton gent', Anthonius Mytforthe armiger et Georgius Carre de Lesbury similiter venerunt, qui ad veritatem de infracontentis simulcum aliis juratoribus predictis prius impanellatis et juratis dicendam electi, triati et jurati dicunt super sacramentum suum quod infranominati Thomas Carye, Gilbertus Erington, Gawinus Rede, Willelmus Ogle et Gilbertus Heron instigaverunt, abbettaverunt et procuraverunt infranominatum Ricardum Rede generosum, fratrem et heredem Gererdi Rede, ad capiendum et prosequendum falsum appellum versum predictum Johannem Swynborne de morte predicti Gererdi quondam fratris predicti Ricardi Rede modo et forma prout in recordo infrascripto allegatur. Et ulterius juratores predicti dicunt super sacramentum suum quod predictus Thomas Rede simulcum predictis Thoma Carye, Gilberto Eryngton, Gawino Rede, Willelmo Ogle et Gilberto Heron ex malicia sua propria absque causa per ipsum Thomam Rede interius placitando allegata procuravit et abbettavit predictum Ricardum Rede ad capiendum et prosequendum appellum suum predictum versus predictum Johannem Swynborne modo et forma prout in recordo infrascripto allegatur. Et assident

[1] processus.

ages against the same Thomas Rede, because he says that the aforesaid Thomas, together with the aforesaid Thomas Cary, Gilbert Eryngton, Gawain Rede, William Ogle and Gilbert Heron, at the day, year and place specified in the aforesaid count, of his own malice, without the cause alleged above in pleading by the aforesaid Thomas, abetted and procured the said Richard Rede in taking and prosecuting his aforesaid false appeal against him the said John and others named in the appeal, in manner and form as is supposed above. And he prays that this may be enquired into by the country; and the aforesaid Thomas Rede likewise. Therefore, both to try that issue and also to try the aforesaid other issue joined above between the aforesaid John Swynburne and the aforesaid Thomas Cary, Gilbert Eryngton, Gawain Rede, William Ogle and Gilbert Heron, let a jury come before the lord king and lady queen in fifteen days from Easter day [1557], wheresoever etc., and who neither etc. to make recognition etc. because both etc. The same day is given to the parties aforesaid etc.

Afterwards the process was continued therein between the parties aforesaid in respect of the aforesaid plea by the juries being put in respite between them before the lord king and lady queen until the octave of Michaelmas then next following, wheresoever etc., unless the justices of the lord king and lady queen assigned to take the assizes in the county aforesaid should first have come to the castle of Newcastle upon Tyne in the county aforesaid on the Thursday [12 August 1557] next after the feast of St Lawrence the Martyr, by the form of the statute etc., for default of the jurors etc. At which day the aforesaid parties come before the lord king and lady queen at Westminster by their aforesaid attorneys. And the said justices before whom etc. have sent here their record, [made] before them, in these words:

Afterwards, at the day and place contained within, before William Dalyson, one of the justices of the lord king and lady queen assigned to hold the pleas before the said lord king and lady queen, and William Rastell, serjeant at law, justices of the lord king and lady queen assigned to take the assizes in the county of Northumberland, at the castle of Newcastle upon Tyne in the aforesaid county, by the form of the statute etc., there came both the within-named John Swynburne in his own person and the within-named Thomas Cary, Gilbert, Thomas Rede, Gawain, William Ogle and Gilbert Heron by their within-specified attorneys. And the jurors of the jury specified within having been called, some of them, namely John Wytherington of Mitford, gentleman, Anthony Fenwyk of 'Lanshawes', gentleman, Lancelot Ogle, gentleman, Lancelot Lesley, gentleman, John Chester, gentleman, Robert Hoyseley, gentleman, Christopher Redshawe, gentleman, and Thomas Rotherforthe, gentleman, came and were chosen, tried and sworn to say the truth concerning the matters contained within; and because the rest of the jurors of the aforesaid jury did not appear, as is evident from the panel, therefore others were chosen by the sheriff from the bystanders at the request of the aforesaid John Swynburne, and by command of the justices they were newly put in, according to the terms of the statute made and provided for such cases, the names of whom appear in a certain panel annexed to the aforesaid panel; and some of the jurors thus newly put in, namely Thomas Bradforthe, gentleman, Thomas Ilderton, gentleman, Anthony Mytforthe, esquire, and George Carre of Lesbury, likewise came and were chosen tried and sworn to say the truth concerning the matters contained within; and together with the aforesaid other jurors formerly impanelled they say upon their oath that the within-named Thomas Cary, Gilbert Eryngton, Gawain Rede, William Ogle and Gilbert Heron did instigate, abet and procure the within-named Richard Rede, gentleman, brother and heir of Gerard Rede, in taking and prosecuting a false appeal against the aforesaid John Swynburne for the death of the aforesaid Gerard, formerly brother of the aforesaid Richard Rede, in manner and form as is alleged in the within-written record. And the aforesaid jurors further say upon their oath that the aforesaid Thomas Rede, together with the aforesaid Thomas Cary, Gilbert Eryngton, Gawain Rede, William Ogle and Gilbert Heron, of his own malice, without the cause alleged within in pleading by the selfsame Thomas Rede, did procure and abet the aforesaid Richard Rede in taking and prosecuting his aforesaid dampna ipsius Johannis Swynborne occasione premissa ultra misas et custagia sua per ipsum circa sectam suam in hac parte apposita ad ducentas et viginti libras, et pro misis et custagiis illis ad tresdecim solidos et quatuor denarios.

Ideo consideratum est quod predictus Johannes Swynborne recuperet versus predictos Thomam Carye, Gilbertus Eryngton, Thomam Rede, Gawinum Rede, Willelmum Ogle et Gilbertum Heron dampna sua predicta per juratores predictos in forma predicta assessa, et iidem Thomas Carye, Gilbertus Eryngton, Thomas Rede, Gawinus Rede, Willelmus Ogle et Gilbertus Heron in misericordia etc. Et super hoc predictus Johannes Swynborne gratis hic in curia remittit prefatis Thome, Gilberto, Thome, Gawino, Willelmo et Gilberto quadraginta libras tresdecim solidos et quatuor denarios de dampnis predictis parcellam. Ideo iidem Thomas, Gilbertus, Thomas, Gawinus, Willelmus et Gilbertus de predictis xl li. xiijs. iiij d. parcella etc. sint quieti etc.

Dampna — clxxx li. unde clericis clxxx s. quos solvuntur secundario

[3]

Nota auxi que coment que le ple en barre de Slater fuit adjudge [pur][1] luy et issint dischardge vers le playntiefe en appell, uncore il fuit arraine al suite le roy per judgement le courte et fait a vener einz.

[*Fol. 44*] Nota auxi que coment il fuit dismisse per le corte al un temps ceo fuit mes vers le partie playntiefe et nemi vers le roy, mez vers le roy fuit eins arrere estre arraine sur le declaration en appell [a son][2] suite. Et issint si le corte dischardge un felon sur son arrainment de lenditement pur ceo que ils pensont que lenditement nest bon payant son fees et puis ils perceiva lenditement bon ils poient charger le gaylor que il soit [arrayne][3] arrere devant eux et estoit a son deliveraunce et responder sur lenditement nient obstant lour primes judgement si issint soit que lour judgement ne soit enter: quod vide en le liver appell les Plees del Coron en enditementes fo. 97. Mes coment en lauter case en appell le judgement fuit enter cest ne fuit materiall entant que ne fuit [unques][4] dischardge vers le roy mes vers le partie.

[4]

Nota auxi ycie que scire facias fuit agard vers les abettours et ne[mi] venire facias ne distringas come lestatute parle et le scire facias ne fait pas mention de tout le record mes generalment coment que fuit acquite et le declaration fuit come le breife de scire facias fuit non de plees des abettors.

1 *Reads* per.
2 *Reads* as.
3 *Written over:* arrere, *as it to replace it.*
4 *Reads* usq[ue].

appeal against the aforesaid John Swynburne in manner and form as is alleged in the within-written record. And they assess the damages of the selfsame John Swynburne by reason of the foregoing, beyond his outlay and costs laid out by him about his suit in that behalf, as £220, and for the outlay and costs 13*s.* 4*d.*

Therefore it is awarded that the aforesaid John Swynburne do recover against the aforesaid Thomas Cary, Gilbert Eryngton, Thomas Rede, Gawain Rede, William Ogle and Gilbert Heron his aforesaid damages as assessed by the aforesaid jurors in form aforesaid; and the same Thomas Cary, Gilbert Eryngton, Thomas Rede, Gawain Rede, William Ogle and Gilbert Heron in mercy etc. And thereupon the aforesaid John Swynburne freely here in court remitted to the said Thomas, Gilbert, Thomas, Gawain, William and Gilbert £40. 13s. 4d., part of the aforesaid damages. Therefore let the same Thomas, Gilbert, Thomas, Gawain, William and Gilbert be quit of the aforesaid £40. 13*s.* 4*d.* etc.

Damages — £180, whereof 180s. to the clerks, which are paid to the Secondary

3. READE v. SLAYTER

King's Bench, contd from pl. 2. Record of Slayter's judgment: KB 27/1164, m. 159; noted above, pp. 139–140.

Note also that although Slater's plea in bar was adjudged for him, so that he was discharged as against the plaintiff in the appeal, he was nevertheless arraigned at the king's suit by judgment of the court and made to come in. Note also that although he had already been dismissed by the court, that was only as against the party plaintiff and not against the king; but as against the king he was in again, to be arraigned upon the declaration in the appeal at his suit. Likewise, if the court discharges a felon upon his arraignment upon indictment, paying his fees, because they think the indictment not good, and later they perceive the indictment to be good, they may charge the gaoler that he should be brought before them to stand to his judgment and answer upon the indictment, despite their former judgment, provided their judgment was not entered. See this in the book of *Plees del Coron*, in 'Indictment', fo. 97.[1] But in the other case of an appeal, even if the judgment was entered it would be immaterial, for he was never discharged as against the king, but only against the party.

4. SWYNBURNE v. READE

King's Bench, contd.

Note also here that a *scire facias* was awarded against the abettors and not a *venire facias* or *distringas* as the statute says; and the *scire facias* did not mention the whole record but said in general terms that he was acquitted; and the declaration was as the writ of *scire facias* was, not as the abettors' pleas.

[1] Staunford, *Plees del Coron*, fo. 97A, citing Fitz. Abr., *Corone*, pl. 27.

[5]

A, fo. 33v (Trin. 4 & 5 Phil. & Mar., foll. pl. 1); *L* 252 (sim.).

Nota que les justices de nisi prius per cest ont auctoritie al enquirer per le jurie que acquitant les parties en appell des abettors et des damages auxibein come les justices de Banke le Roy ont, quar lestatute 14 H. 6. ca. 1. nest enconter cest mes que ils puissont estre enquire al comen ley devant lestatute. Mes per les parolls de lestatute les justices de nisi prius ne poient done judgement des damages come poient doner jugement sur lacqital et attainder en felony et treason come est agree M. 10 E. 4. fo. 16. que liver ne parle ne est enconter lenquirer des abettors en apell al nisi prius: quod nota. Et vide contra per Justice *Stanford* en son liver appell Plees de Coron, en title de Nisi Prius, fo. 156. Sed vide come est adjuge icie et cest fuit en temps *Bromley* Chefe Justice, *Porteman* Chefe Justice, et *Saunders* Chefe Justice, ove les auters justices en Banke le Roy.

Michaelis Philippi et Marie 4 et 5. 1557[1]

[6]

Abr. in *A*, fo. 34r–v; *L* 255.

Nota que un home done al auter un mortall wounde le primer jour de Maii et 3 auters persons sciantes le dit wounde receive, compfort et harber cestui que issint done 2 jors et nient plus, le 10 jor de Maii le home morust de le [*fol. 44v*] dit wound: et fuit tenus et agree per toutes les justices en Banke le Roy que lez 3 homes ne fueront accessories quar a cest temps de lour recept fuit nul fellony ne murder tanque il fuit morte et si cestui home que dona le wound fuit arrest pur le felony et murder et devant le morte mise aler alardge cest nest escape apres le morte clerement. Mes si en cest case les 3 homes onte aide et compfort cestui que done le stroke contynualment al jour de le morte ou apres donques il fuit clerement accessorie, ou si les 3 ont procures ou comaundes le dit felony ou murder estre fait en forme avaundit, per cest ils ont estre accessories clerement. Mes en le primer case entant que il appiert per le declaration en appell port vers le principall et eux come accessories que le receipt et aide fueront apres le stroke et devant le morte le dit home les dittes 3 accessories fueront discharge. Et uncore nota que en enditement de murder lenditement serra que il done le stroke tiel jour et il [languisha tanque][2] a tiel jour apres, a quel jour il morust,

[1] *Otiose heading in H (cf. p. 148).*

[2] *A, L.* languissant *H.*

5. SWYNBURNE v. READE, contd

King's Bench, contd.

Note that the justices of nisi prius have authority thereby to enquire by the jury who acquitted the parties in an appeal as to the abettors and the damages, just as the justices of the King's Bench have; for the statute of 14 Hen. VI, c. [2], is not against this, but they may enquire as at common law before the statute. By the words of the statute, however, the justices of nisi prius may not give judgment for damages, as they may give a judgment upon the acquittal and attainder in felony and treason, as is agreed in Mich. 10 Edw. IV, fo. 16,[1] which book does not say anything against enquiring into the abettors in an appeal at nisi prius. Note that. But see, to the contrary, Staunford J. in his book called *Plees del Coron*, in the title of 'Nisi Prius', fo. 156.[2] Observe nevertheless how it is adjudged here; and this was in the time of Bromley C.J., Portman C.J., and Saunders C.J.,[3] with the other justices in the King's Bench.

6. ACCESSORIES TO MURDER

King's Bench, Mich. 1557.

Note that someone gave another a mortal wound on 1 May, and three other persons, knowing of the said wound, received, comforted and harboured him for two days and no more; on 10 May the man died from the said wound; and it was held and agreed by all the justices in the King's Bench that the three men were not accessories, for at the time of their receiving there was no felony or murder until he was dead; and if the person who gave the wound was arrested for felony and murder, and set at large before the death, that would clearly not have been an escape after the death. In this case, however, if the three men had aided and comforted the person who gave the stroke continuously until the day of the death, or thereafter, then they would clearly have been accessories. Or if the three had procured or commanded the said felony or murder to be done in the aforesaid way, they would thereby clearly have been accessories. But in the first case, since it appears by the declaration in an appeal brought against the principal and against them as accessories that the receiving and aiding were after the stroke but before the said man's death, the said three accessories were discharged. Note, nevertheless, that in an indictment for murder the indictment shall say that he gave the stroke on such and such a day and that he languished

1 YB Mich. 39 Hen. VI, fo. 14, pl. 12.

2 Staunford, *Plees del Coron*, fo. 156v, which in fact cites YB 10 Edw. IV.

3 Sir Thomas Bromley died on 15 May 1555 and was replaced as C.J.K.B. by Sir William Portman. Portman died on 5 Feb. 1557 and was replaced by Sir Edward Saunders.

et sic ipse le primer jour s. le jour de le stroke felonice murderavit etc. et ne suppose le murder al 2 jour de son morte que il ne murder luy cest jour mes le murder va ove le stroke. Mes nota que lusage en Banke le Roy est en cest case en appell vers un que en son declaration il declare que il feloniousment luy tua[1] le primer jour de May tiel primer jour tanque al ultimum jour de Maii et sic ille modo et forma predictis feloniousment luy murder: et ceo est le melior forme, car ceux modo et forma avera relation al toutes les factes. Issint est le course en appell vers plusors supposant que un luy dona le stroke et les auters fueront aidantes presentes et auxiliantes etc. et issint ils toutes modo et forma predictis luy tua et murder feloniusment etc.: et cest est bon order.

Michaelis Philippi et Marie 4 et 5. 1557[1]

[7]

A, fo. 34 (runs on from pl. 1 on p. 148, below); *L* 253 (sim.); abr. in *D*, fo. 24, pl. 3 (4 & 5 Phil. & Mar.).

Un Raffe port action sur le case en Banke le Roye vers Anthony Auger militem et ils fueront al yssue et le jurye vient al barre et le deffendant challenge larray le pannell eo que le dit pannell et larray de cest fuit favourablement fait per le viscount et monstre son nosme et per ses mynisters al denomination le playntiefe et pria quod panellum et array predicta quassetur et le playntiefe dit bene et duement fait et deux triors fueront appointes per le court et jures a trier cest matter, et fuit done en evidence per le deffendant que le pannell fuit favorablement fait et array per le subvicount et nosme son nosme et ne parle rien de le viscount: et uncore le courte adjuge que levidence fuit bein en cest matter et prove son yssue, quar si favour soit en le subvicount il est auxi en ley en le vicount, quar le vicount respondera pur luy. Et toutes returnes serra en le nosme le vicount, et il serra amercy pur toutes males returnes. Et fuit dit que cest fuit lentry de challenge de larray per le vicount et ses ministers. Et puis larray fuit affirme et per le courte le deffendant en apres [*fol. 45*] ne challenge les polles sans monstre le cause al comencement pur ceo que il adeprimes challenge larray de toutes que

1 *Sic but evidently a slip: see opposite.*
2 *Otiose heading in H (cf. p. 148).*

until such and such a day afterwards, on which day he died, 'and thus he on (the first day, that is, the day of the stroke) murdered etc.', without alleging the murder to have been on the second day (the day of his death), for he did not murder him on that day, but the murder goes with the stroke. Note, however, that the usage in the King's Bench in this case, in an appeal against someone, is that in his declaration he declares that he feloniously [struck][1] him on the first day of May (this being the first day) [and he languished] until the last day of May, and so he feloniously murdered him 'in manner and form foresaid' (*modo et forma praedictis*); and that is the better way, for these words *modo et forma* refer to all the facts. That is also the course in an appeal against several persons, supposing that one gave him the stroke and the others were present aiding and assisting etc., 'and thus they all, *modo et forma praedictis*, feloniously slew and murdered him etc.'; and that is good order.

7. ROLF v. AUCHER

King's Bench, Mich. 1557. Four different assumpsit actions were brought by Rolf against Aucher this term; the first three entries end with a *venire facias* (KB 27/1182, mm. 40, 156, 169) and the fourth with a verdict for £2,803 damages (ibid., m. 186). No challenge is entered on the record. Cf. three earlier actions by Aucher against Rolf: KB 27/1174, m. 40 (case); KB 27/1177, m. 115 (case); KB 27/1178, m. 123 (detinue).

One [Rolf] brought an action on the case in the King's Bench against Sir Anthony [Aucher], knight, and they were at issue. The jury came to the bar, and the defendant challenged the array of the panel because the said panel and the array thereof was made favourably by the sheriff (setting out his name) and by his ministers at the plaintiff's nomination; and prayed that the panel and array aforesaid be quashed. The plaintiff said it was well and duly made, and two triers were appointed by the court and sworn to try this matter. And it was given in evidence by the defendant that the panel was favourably made and arrayed by the under-sheriff (naming his name), and nothing was said of the sheriff. But the court nevertheless adjudged that the evidence was good in this matter and proved his issue; for if there is favour in the under-sheriff, it is also in law favour in the sheriff, for the sheriff shall answer for him, and all returns shall be in the sheriff's name and he shall be amerced for all bad returns. And it was said that the entry of a challenge to the array was 'by the sheriff and his ministers'. Then the array was affirmed; and according to the court the defendant could not afterwards challenge the polls[2] without showing the cause at the outset, because he had already challenged the array of them all, and it had been found against him;

1 The text says 'slew' (*tua*), which must be a slip.

2 I.e. individual jurors.

fuit trye vers luy mes le playntiefe poet challenger les polles apres sans monstre cause al comencement.

Et en mesme le ple fuit tenus et agree per toutes si ascun un deux ou trois fueront mise en le pannell al denomination dun des parties que adonques le pannell est male en toute et serra quashe en toute quod nota bene coment que le ple de le challenge soit que larray le pannell fuit array et fait per le viscount et ses ministers al denomination le playntiefe ou deffendant.

Nota auxi agree per le court la que si le playntiefe nominate vi persons a le viscount our subvicount a mitter en le pannell et deliver les nosmes a luy s. al viscount ou subvicount et puis apres longe temps devant le returne de le pannell il s. le playntiefe countermaund cest per ces lettres al dit viscount et voet que il s. le viscount ne mitta ceux sur le pannell en nul condition ore si le vicount accept cest countermaund et returne auters en le pannell tout est bene et duement fait mes si le vicount returne en le pannell ascuns des vi persons devant monstres a luy donques le pannell nest duement fait mes est male et serra quashe.

Pasche Philippi et Marie 4° et 5°.

[1]

A, ff. 33v–34 (Trin. 4 & 5 Phil. & Mar.); *L* 253 (sim.); *D*, ff. 23–24, pl. 3 (sim.).

En action sur le case les parties fueront al yssue sur lassumption et quant le jury fueront prist al barre le deffendant challenge larray del pannell s. quod arraiamentum pannelli predicti factum fuit per J. S. armigerum, vicecomitem comitatus Lincolnie, ad nominationem querentis et en favorem querentis. Le playntiefe dit que bien et duement fait, 2 triors fueront esliewe per le courte et jures etc., et fuit done en evidence pur le deffendant que le playntiefe nominate at vicounte toute le pannell. Et le subvicount et son garson fueront jures [et examine][1] sur cest, queux diont que le vicount dit il ne poet cognoscer que il doit returne sur le pannell et le playntiefe dit que la fuit un pannell que darrein passe enter Rauffe et auters, queux sont bons freehoulders, et le vicount dyt, Portes a moy cest pannell que jeo eux viewer, et le playntiefe issint fait, et le vicount empannel cest pannel et ceo returne <mes il dit que le playntiefe[2] voet luy a mytter>[3] eins ascons de eux pur luy quicunque il voile, et il dit que il retorne le pannel come indifferent [come il poet][4] sans ascun regard de nomination le

[1] *A, D, L.*

[2] ne *inserted here, probably in error.*

[3] et ils disont que le pl. ne voet que ils mitteront *A, L.* et ils disoient pur le playntif que il mitteroit *D*

[4] *A, D, L.*

but the plaintiff could challenge the polls afterwards without showing cause at the outset.

And in the same plea it was held and agreed by them all that if any one, two or three [jurors] were put into the panel at the nomination of one of the parties, the whole panel is bad and shall be quashed in its entirety – note that well – even though the challenge is that the array of the panel was arrayed and made by the sheriff and his ministers at the nomination of the plaintiff or defendant.

Note also that it was agreed by the court there that if the plaintiff nominates six persons to the sheriff or under-sheriff to be put into the panel, and delivers the names to him (that is, to the sheriff or under-sheriff), and then long afterwards, but before the return of the panel, he (the plaintiff) countermands it by his letters to the said sheriff, and wills that he (the sheriff) should not put them[1] upon the panel in any condition, and the sheriff accepts this countermand and returns others in the panel, all is now well and duly done. But if the sheriff returns in the panel any of the six persons before indicated to him, the panel is not duly made, but is bad and shall be quashed.

Easter term, 4 & 5 Phil. & Mar. (1558)

1. CHALLENGE TO THE ARRAY

King's Bench, Pas. 1558. Perhaps the same case as the last.

In an action on the case the parties were at issue upon the undertaking, and when the jury were ready at the bar the defendant challenged the array of the panel: 'that the array of the aforesaid panel was made by John Style, esquire, sheriff of Lincolnshire, at the nomination of the plaintiff and in favour of the plaintiff'. The plaintiff said that it was well and duly made, and two triers were chosen by the court and sworn etc. And it was given in evidence for the defendant that the plaintiff nominated the whole panel to the sheriff, and the under-sheriff and his lad (*garson*) were sworn and examined thereupon and stated that the sheriff said he did not know whom he ought to return on the panel, and the plaintiff said there was a panel which recently passed between one Rauffe and others,[2] and they were good freeholders; and the sheriff said, 'Bring me that panel, so that I may see it', and the plaintiff did so, and the sheriff impanelled that panel and returned it; but they said that the plaintiff did not will him to put anyone in for him, but only those whom he (the sheriff) wished; and he said that he returned the panel as indifferently as he could, without any regard to the plaintiff's nomination or any other reward.[3] Notwithstanding this, the court held clearly that the

[1] I.e. the six he had previously nominated.

[2] Perhaps *Rolf* v. *Aucher*, above, p. 146, pl. 7.

[3] *A* and *D* add 'respect or fee'.

playntiefe ou dauter regard[1] ew: et cest nient obstant le court tient clerement que le pannel ne fuit duement fait, entant que ceux fueront empannell queux le playntiefe, nosma quar le nomination le playntiefe est le substance et nemi [favor][2] en le playntiefe, quar cest favour ne poet estre [proprement][3] trye sans denomination ou auter tiel [choses ceo devant][4] provant. Mes uncore les tryours affirme larray bon et les 2 triors [*fol. 45v*] ove auters viii de cest pannel fueront tries et jures de le principall et donques le defendant apres que le primer pannel fueront peruses et tries come il doit et nient adevant challenge le [array del][5] dit tales pur mesme le cause adevant: et fuit tenus per tout le court que il poit bein prender le dit challenge a cest temps, et ne poit auterment faire, quar poit estre que sufficient en le primer pannell [voile aver appeire et destre jures en quel case serroit en vaine de challendge et trye][6] larray de tales, incipient a tiel home et nosmer son nosme et fyniant a tiel home et nosmant son nosme etc. Et yssint il fist, mes lauter array sur cest fuit auxi affirme destre duement fait come lauter pannel fuit adevant. Et nota que ceux x persons de le primer pannel adevant jures et tries en cest trier larray le tales et nul auter de le tales entant que le primer pannel fuit affirme. Mes auterment serra si le primer pannel ust estre quashe quar les 2 auters de le tales trieront larray les tales. Et cest per tout le courte en Banke le Roye.

[Finis secundum Dalison Justice del Bancke le Roy][7]

Hucusque ex libro manu Willelmi Dallison conscriptum
Willelmus Lambert examinavit
1569

H. T.

[1] respecte ou fee *A, D, L.*
[2] *A, D, L. Blank in H.*
[3] *A, D, L.*
[4] matter precedent *D.* ceo *A, L.*
[5] *A, D, L.*
[6] *A, D, L.* soit tries et peruses et donques le challenge de *H.*
[7] *A, L (following p. 146, above, pl. 7).*

panel was not duly made, since those impanelled were those whom the plaintiff named. For it is the plaintiff's nomination which is the substance, not favour in the plaintiff; for that favour cannot be properly tried without a nomination or some other previous matter proving it. The triers nevertheless affirmed the array to be good, and the two triers with another eight of this panel were tried and sworn of the principal [panel]. Then the defendant, after the first panel was gone through and tried – as he ought, and not before then – challenged the array of the said *tales* for the same cause as before. And it was held by the whole court that he may well take the challenge at this time, and cannot do otherwise: for it may be that sufficient jurors in the first panel will appear and be sworn, in which case it would be in vain to challenge and try the array of the *tales* beginning at such and such a man, naming his name, and ending at such and such a man, naming his name. And so he did; but the other array was also affirmed to have been duly made, as the other panel was before. Note that the ten persons of the first panel who were earlier tried and sworn therein shall try the array of the *tales*, and not others from the *tales*, inasmuch as the first panel had been affirmed. It would be otherwise, however, if the first panel had been quashed, for then two others from the *tales* would try the array of the *tales*. This was [held] by the whole court in the King's Bench.

[The end, according to Dalison, Justice of the King's Bench[1]]

Thus far from a book written
in the hand of William Dallison,
checked by William Lambert
1569

H.T.

[1] Explicit in *A*.

INDEXES

INDEX OF NAMES

INDEX OF SUBJECTS